korea

Directed by Hans Johannes Hoefer
Produced, Edited and Designed by Leonard Lueras and Nedra Chung
Updated by Jennifer Kang

APA PRODUCTIONS

THE INSIGHT GUIDES SERIES RECEIVED SPECIAL AWARDS FOR EXCELLENCE FROM THE PACIFIC AREA TRAVEL ASSOCIATION.

REPUBLIC OF KOREA

Fifth Edition (Reprint)
© APA PRODUCTIONS (HK) LTD.
Published by APA Productions (HK) Ltd.
Printed by APA Press Pte. Ltd.
Colour Separation in Singapore by Colourscan Pte Ltd

APA PRODUCTIONS

Publisher and Chairman: Hans Johannes Hoefer
Marketing Director: Yinglock Chan
General Manager: Henry Lee
Administration Manager: Alice Ng
Editorial Manager: Vivien Kim
Executive Editor: Adam Liptak

Project Editors

Helen Abbott, Diana Ackland, Mohamed Amin, Ravindralal Anthonis, Roy Bailet, Louisa Cambell, Jon Carroll, Hillary Cunningham, John Eames, Janie Freeburg, Bikram Grewal, Virginia Hopkins, Samuel Israel, Jay Itzkowitz, Phil Jaratt, Tracy Johnson, Ben Kalb, Wilhelm Klein, Saul Lockhart, Sylvia Mayuga, Gordon MaLauchlan, Kal Müller, Eric Oey, Daniel P. Reid, Kim Robinson, Ronn Ronck, Robert Seidenberg, Rolf Steinberg, Sriyani Tidball, Lisa Van Gruisen, Merin Wexler.

Contributing Writers

A.D. Aird, Ruth Armstrong, T. Terence Barrow, F. Lisa Beebe, Bruce Berger, Dor Bahadur Bista, Clinton V. Black, Star Black, Frena Bloomfield, John Borthwick, Roger Boschman, Tom Brosnahan, Jerry Carroll, Tom Chaffin, Nedra Chung, Tom Cole, Orman Day, Kunda Dixit, Richard Erdoes, Guillermo Garcia-Oropeza, Ted Giannoulas, Barbara Gloudon, Harka Gurung, Sharifah Hamzah, Willard A. Hanna, Elizabeth Hawley, Sir Edmund Hillary, Tony Hillerman, Jerry Hopkins, Peter Hutton, Neil Jameson, Michael King, Michele Kort, Thomas Lucey, Leonard Lueras, Michael E. Macmillan, Derek Maitland, Buddy Mays, Craig McGregor, Reinhold Messner, Julie Michaels, M. R. Priya Rangsit, Al Read, Elizabeth V. Reyes, Victor Stafford Reid, Harry Rolnick, E.R. Sarachchandra, Uli Schmetzer, Ilsa Sharp, Norman Sibley, Peter Spiro, Harold Stephens, Keith Stevens, Michael Stone, Desmond Tate, Colin Taylor, Deanna L. Thompson, Randy Udall, James Wade, Mallika Wanigasundara, William Warren, Cynthia Wee, Tony Wheeler, Linda White, H. Taft Wireback, Alfred A. Yuson, Paul Zach.

Contributing Photographers

Carole Allen, Ping Amarand, Tony Arruza, Marcello Bertinetti, Alberto Cassio, Pat Canova, Alain Compost, Ray Cranbourne, Alain Evrard, Ricardo Ferro, Lee Foster, Manfred Gottschalk, Werner Hahn, Dallas and John Heaton, Brent Hesselyn, Hans Hoefer, Luca Invernizzi, Ingo Jezierski, Wilhelm Klein, Dennis Lane, Max Lawrence, Lyle Lawson, Philip Little, Guy Marche, Antonio Martinelli, David Messent, Ben Nakayama, Vautier de Nanxe, Kal Müller, Günter Pfannmuller, Van Philips, Ronni Pinsler, Fitz Prenzel, G.P. Reichelt, Dan Rocovits, David Ryan, Frank Salmoiraghi, Thomas Schollhammer, Blair Seitz, David Stahl, Bill Wassman, Rendo Yap, Hisham Youssef.

While contributions to Insight Guides are very welcome, the publisher cannot assume responsibility for the care and return of unsolicited manuscripts or photographs. Return postage and/or a self-addressed envelope must accompany unsolicited material if it is to be returned. Please address all editorial contributions to Apa Productions, P. O. Box 219, Orchard Point Post Office, Singapore 9123.

Distributors:

Australia and New Zealand: Prentice Hall of Australia, 7 Grosvenor Place, Brookvale, NSW 2100, Australia. **Benelux:** Uitgeverij Cambium, Naarderstraat 11, 1251 Aw Laren, The Netherlands. **Central and South America; Mexico; Portugal and Spain:** Cedibra Editora Brasileira Ltda, Rua Leonidia, 2-Rio de Janeiro, Brazil. **Denmark:** Copenhagen Book Centre Aps, Roskildeveji 338, DK-2630 Tastrup, Denmark. **Europe (others):** European Book Service, Flevolaan 36-38, P. O. Box 124, 1380 AC Weesp, Holland. **Hawaii:** Pacific Trade Group Inc., P. O. Box 1227, Kailua, Oahu, Hawaii 96734, U.S.A. **Hong Kong:** Far East Media Ltd., Vita Tower, 7th Floor, Block B, 29 Wong Chuk Hang Road, Hong Kong. **India and Nepal:** India Book Distributors, 107/108 Arcadia Building, 195 Narima Point, Bombay-400-021, India. **Indonesia:** Java Books, Box 55 J.K.C.P, Jakarta, Indonesia.

Israel: Steimatzky Ltd., P.O. Box 628, Tel Aviv 61006, Israel (Israel title only). **Italy:** Zanfi Editori SRL. Via Ganaceto 121, 41100 Modena, Italy. **Caribbean:** Kingston Publishers, 1-A Norwood Avenue, Kingston 5, Jamaica. **Kenya:** Camerapix Publishers International Ltd., P. O. Box 45048, Nairobi, Kenya. **Korea:** Kyobo Book Centre Co., Ltd., P.O. Box Kwang Hwa Moon 1 658, Seoul, Korea. **Philippines:** National Book Store, 701 Rizal Avenue, Manila, Philippines. **Singapore and Malaysia:** MPH Distributors (S) Pte. Ltd., 601 Sims Drive #03-21 Pan-I Warehouse and Office Complex, S'pore 1438, Singapore. **Switzerland:** M.P.A. Agencies-Import SA, CH. du Croset 9, CH-1024 Ecublens, Switzerland. **Taiwan:** Caves Books Ltd., 103 Chungshan N.Road, Sec. 2, Taipei, Taiwan, Republic of China. **Thailand:** Far East Publications Ltd., 117/3 Soi Samahan, Sukhumvit 4 (South Nana), Bangkok, Thailand. **United Kingdom and Ireland:** Harrap Ltd., 19-23 Ludgate Hill, London EC4M 7PD, England, United Kingdom. **Mainland United States and Canada:** Graphic Arts Center Publishing, 3019 N.W. Yeon, P.O. Box 10306, Portland OR 97210, U.S.A. (The Pacific Northwest title only); Prentice Hall Press, Gulf & Western Building, One Gulf & Western Plaza, New York, NY 10023, U.S.A. (all other titles).

French editions: Editions Gallimard, 5 rue Sébastien-Bottin, F-75007 Paris, France. **German editions:** Nelles Verlag GmbH, Schleissheimer Str. 371b, 8000 Munich 45, West Germany. **Italian editions:** Zanfi Editori SLR, Via Ganaceto 121 41100 Modena, Italy. **Portuguese and Spanish editions:** Cedibra Editora Brasileira Ltda, Rua Leonidia, 2-Rio de Janerio, Brazil.

APA PHOTO AGENCY PTE. LTD.

The Apa Photo Agency is S.E. Asia's leading stock photo archive, representing the work of professional photographers from all over the world. More than 150,000 original color transparencies are available for advertising, editorial and educational uses. We are also linked with Tony Stone Worldwide, one of Europe's leading stock agencies, and their associate offices around the world:
Singapore: Apa Photo Agency Pte. Ltd., P.O. Box 219, Orchard Point Post Office, Singapore 9123, Singapore. **London:** Tony Stone Worldwide, 28 Finchley Rd., St. John's Wood, London NW8 6ES, England. **North America & Canada:** Masterfile Inc., 415 Yonge St., Suite 200, Toronto M5B 2E7, Canada. **Paris:** Fotogram-Stone Agence Photographique, 45 rue de Richelieu, 75001 Paris, France. **Barcelona:** Fototec Torre Dels Pardais, 7 Barcelona 08026, Spain. **Johannesburg:** Color Library (Pty.) Ltd., P. O. Box 1659, Johannesburg, South Africa 2000. **Sydney:** The Photographic Library of Australia Pty. Ltd., 7 Ridge Street, North Sydney, New South Wales 2050, Australia. **Tokyo:** Orion Press, 55-1 Kanda Jimbocho, Chiyoda-ku, Tokyo 101, Japan.

"The Hermit Kingdom". "The Land of Morning Calm"."The Kingdom of White Clad People". Chosŏn. Korea.

The Republic of Korea is also one of the last countries in Asia to open its doors to the outside world, and—in both ancient and contemporary journals—one of the world's most misunderstood countries.

Hoefer

When freelance editors Leonard Lueras and Nedra Chung first visited Korea in January, 1976, they were aware of the sobriquets and stereotypes associated with Korea, and they hoped the place would surprise them, but they had no notion that it would entrance them the way it did.

For Lueras, a roving Honolulu-based journalist, Korea was one of those countries all conscientious American newspapermen should visit. It was the strategic Asian place where thousands of Koreans, Americans and their allies had died in a tough war, and from a "story" point-of-view was a region any reporter worth his typewriter should get to know personally in order to put contemporary world history into perspective.

Chung

Chung, meanwhile, had more personal reasons for visiting Korea. As the granddaughter of Koreans who immigrated to Hawaii at the beginning of this century to work on plantations and seek American fortunes, she had always been interested in her ancestors' homeland. In her Honolulu home Korean food was eaten, and her parents still spoke Korean, but the country, Korea, was a mystery. Three generations is nearly a century of genetic-cultural absence, and the psychological and social realities of "being Korean" had long ago been muted in the process called Americanization.

Both Lueras and Chung—like most Americans—had stark, almost black and white, visions of the country. It was a "place" somewhere between Japan and China, and if you believed the cold ink news dispatches datelined Seoul and P'anmunjŏm, it was a bleak country, constantly at war or on the verge of war—a rugged vision of M-48 assault tanks and olive drab soldiers grinding through frozen mountain passes.

That vision was quickly transformed. The two travelers arrived in Seoul on a snowy day, checked into a traditional Korean inn near the Secret Garden, and proceeded to discover a people, culture and place of vivid colors, charm and sophistication. Not only were the Koreans one of the most hospitable, fiery and matter-of-fact people they had ever encountered in Asia,

Lueras

but the physical setting they lived in was more varied and inspirational than anything they'd optimistically expected. In subsequent visits, which became more frequent and lengthy during the next four years, they found themselves marveling at the beauty of white sand resorts, the spectre of zen monks chanting ancient sutras in granite niches, and the sounds of spirited grandmothers, each a flowing, pastel apparition, singing and dancing in fields of pink summer blossoms. And beyond such romance, there was the economic boom of a country on the move. There was a defiant, positive feeling of accomplishment, well-being and success in the crisp Korean air.

These encounters with unknown Korea became *Korea,* this book and the eighth title in Apa Productions' award-winning series of Insight Guides about worldwide destinations. Lueras and Chung didn't plan it that way, but the idea of producing a book about Korea became a reality in 1978. At that time, Apa's chief executives—publisher Hans Hoefer and managing director Leo Haks—had commissioned Lueras and Chung to create a book about their "home country"—Hawaii. The two set to work on that publication (which became a best-seller in Hawaii within a few weeks after its release in April, 1980), but they also convinced Hoefer and Haks that a Korea book would be a daring, but potentially successful, addition to Apa's travel book series.

Korea, like all Apa Insight Guides, was a long time in the making, but worth the wait. Indeed, this book by more than 20 creative people represents more than a century of first-hand human experience in that country.

Lueras was a relative newcomer to Korea,

but for those four years spent more than half of his traveling and editorial time in-country. As a journalist, Lueras has worked for nearly 10 years as a reporter for *The Honolulu Advertiser,* has written and edited a half dozen books on Asia-Pacific subjects, and has contributed articles and photographs to numerous publications in the United States and Asia. He is also an editor-at-large for *Pacific Magazine,* the prestigious, travel and culture magazine published by Emphasis Inc. of Tokyo.

Editor Chung, meanwhile, has worked on Apa books about Hawaii and the Philippines, and has written on Korea-related subjects for prominent Korean literary publications. Chung co-wrote with Lueras most of the travel section of this book, compiled and wrote nearly all the Guide In Brief section, and coordinated the preparation of preliminary and final textual and cartographic materials throughout the book.

The new edition of *Insight Guide: Korea* was prepared under the careful direction of freelance travel writer **Jennifer Robinson** alias Jennifer Kang, whose marriage to a local brought her all the way from Oregon, USA.

Probably the first person to join Chung and Lueras in the creation of this book was Tokyo-based photographer Greg Davis. Davis and Lueras have worked together on various Asia-related projects over the years, and Davis, who has been regularly visiting and photographing Korea during the past decade, was a logical contributor to this book. You'll find numerous sensitive photos by Davis throughout *Korea.* Also watch for his fine Asian photo studies in publications such as *Life, Geo, Pacific* and other international magazines.

James Wade, the columnist-composer-author and "senior Korea hand" who contributed the first section essay on Korean life cycles, has for many years contributed articles to Asian magazines and professional journals. He also has written and edited several anthologies of Korea-related books, including titles such as *One Man's Korea* and *West Meets East.*

Barbara Mintz, who takes you on a proper and serendipitous stroll through old and new Seoul, was born in Honolulu but has lived since 1962 in Korea with her husband Grafton, a copy editor for *The Korea Times.* Leaving teaching positions at Ohio State University, they came to Korea as Fullbright lecturers in English.

Norman Thorpe, our expert on "toasting spirits", has been in Korea since 1968—first with the U.S. Army, second as a student and freelance writer, and since mid-1978 as Seoul staff correspondent for *The Asian Wall Street Journal.* Thorpe has a masters degree in Korean studies from the University of Washington at Seattle.

Jon Carter Covell, meanwhile, takes us by the hand on a cultural tour of this artistically exciting country. Covell, who has authored 10 books on Japanese art and is now writing several titles about Korean art, is often referred to as the first Westerner to obtain a doctorate in Japanese art history, which she studied at Columbia University after graduation from Oberlin College. She has lived

Davis

Wade

Mintz

Sibley

Sibley

Kendall

Ferrar

much of her life in the Far East, where she specializes in Buddhism and its artistic expressions. In 1978 Covell received a Fulbright grant for research in Korea.

Gary Clay Rector, a former guitar-maker for the Gibson guitar firm at Kalamazoo, Michigan, came to Korea in December, 1967 as a Peace Corps volunteer. While working in public health centers in rural areas of North Kyŏngsang Province, he became very interested in Korean folk music. After studying Korean music for several years under Kim Byung Sup, Korea's eminent sŏlchanggo (hourglass folk drum) player, Rector has become one of the foreign community's most-respected authorities on the subject. Appropriately, Rector wrote this book's story about Korean music and dance.

Laurel Kendall, our resident expert on Korean shamans and housewives, is now a research fellow in the Psychiatry Department of the University of Hawaii. After conducting extensive field work in the shamanist spheres of a Korean village, she received a doctors degree in anthropology from Columbia University in 1980. Kendall first went to Korea in 1970 as a Peace Corps volunteer.

Norman Sibley is a native of New Hampshire who first came to Korea at age four with his Christian missionary parents. He grew up in Korea—at Taegu, Koje-do and Seoul—and later, after graduating from the College of the Atlantic, returned to Korea to co-edit with his wife, Greta, and other friends, *Korea Quarterly*, an English language culture and arts publication devoted

horpe

Rector

Covell

acmillan

Sohn

aliher

to promoting a greater understanding of Korea. Sibley, a multi-talented author-architect-graphic designer and photographer, penned our travel section essay on Korea's south crescent, contributed numerous photographs, an architectural rendering of Kyŏngju's Pulguk Temple, and gave much appreciated guidance to *Korea's* editors.

Greta Diemente Sibley, co-editor and design director of *Korea Quarterly,* is a "Specialist" on Korean Buddhism and its complicated iconography. Hence her contribution, a "Who's Who" look at Korea's Buddhist pantheon.

Gertrude Ferrar, who orients us to Korea's creation, geology, geography and flora and fauna in a sympathetic opening essay, is a native New Yorker who first came to Korea in 1963 "where I've resided ever since." In her own words, "I run a language school, write (both over my own name and as a ghost writer), study Korean flora and fauna, and take people on long walks about which some complain mightily."

Korea's historian, meanwhile, is Michael E. Macmillan, a resident of Honolulu who has variously worked as a radio broadcaster,

newspaper reporter (for *The State* of Columbia, South Carolina, and for *The Honolulu Advertiser*), and as a "perpetual student". Macmillan recently was also publications editor at the University of Hawaii's Center for Korean Studies (America's major center for Korean studies) where he edited several books on Korean subjects.

Ho-min Sohn, coordinator of the University of Hawaii's Department of East Asian Languages, is one of the world's foremost experts on the Korean language. His essay on Korea's *han'gul* alphabet is representative of numerous articles, lectures and papers he has presented at international lingtics symposiums in Korea and abroad. Sohn holds a doctors degree in linguistics from the University of Hawaii and has been Ph.D. qualified by Indiana University. He is also a former editor of *Korean Linguistics,* the journal of the International Circle of Korean Linguistics (ICKL).

Korea's diverse religious spectrum was reviewed by Tom Coyner, a former Korean Peace Corps program developer and Seoul-based executive with the Chase Manhattan Bank. Coyner, who now resides in Los Angeles with his Korean wife, Yeri, and son, Ben, also contributed photographs to *Korea.*

Another longtime Koreaphile who contributed to the delicate "cultural balance" of this book is Korea hand Ken Kaliher, a journalist who has lived in Korea on and off since 1969, the year the U.S. Army assigned him to its advisory group in Seoul. After Army days, Kaliher returned to Korea with the Peace Corps in 1972. Between 1976 and 1981 he edited English copy and wrote for Orient Press, at that time one of Korea's two general news agencies, and reported for ABC Radio in the United States. He is now a member of the advisory staff to the U.S. military in Korea. For *Korea,* Kaliher authored the lively essay on "Other Pleasures," which you'll find to your delight in the Guide in Brief section.

Yeoman graphics support came from several fine sources. Prominent among individual photographers were the contributions of Emil Alfter, who was stationed in Korea for several years as a deputy attaché with the German Embassy in Seoul; Mi Seitelman, a former chief command photograher with the U.S. Eighth Army's headquarters staff; and Lee Nam Soo, one of the Korea's finest native photographs. Other key shots were clicked by Norman Thorpe, Barbara Mintz, Tom Coyner, Sanford Zalburg and the late Ray Jerome Baker of Honolulu.

TABLE OF CONTENTS

TABLE OF CONTENTS

OTHER INSIGHT GUIDES TITLES

COUNTRY/REGION

ASIA
Bali
Burma
Hong Kong
India
Indonesia
Korea
Malaysia
Nepal
Philippines
Rajasthan
Singapore
Sri Lanka
Taiwan
Thailand

PACIFIC
Hawaii
New Zealand

NORTH AMERICA
Alaska
American Southwest
Northern California
Southern California
Florida
Mexico
New England
New York State
The Pacific Northwest
The Rockies
Texas

CARIBBEAN
Bahamas
Barbados
Jamaica
Puerto Rico
Trinidad and Tobago

EUROPE
Great Britain
France
Germany
Greece
Ireland
Italy
Spain

MIDDLE EAST
Egypt
Israel

GRAND TOURS
Australia
East Asia
California
Canada
Continental Europe

GREAT ADVENTURE
Indian Wildlife

THE WIND OF THE FUTURE

A light breeze blew through the eastern seas for decades, centuries, thousands of years making no noise, causing no commotion, and passing unnoticed throughout the world. A Korean breeze, as cool and gentle as the spring air, as steady and pure as the autumn hues. Storms arose and passed, quakes shook and died, but the breeze always returned. Then, all of a sudden, five thousand years of light wailing swirled into one great gust of wind, set the seas in motion and sent tremors throughout the world. Like a hurricane which sweeps through at dawn, the calm kingdom that said nary a word has brought its strength to the fore. Now Korea welcomes; Korea beckons the world.

Koreans cherish their long history, and are proceeding with caution into the frontiers of the new world despite the speed at which they are moving. Following invasions from their neighbors and from the west, thirty years of brutal occupation by the Japanese, and a fratricidal war spurred on by powers greater than themselves and their northern brethren, it took only two decades for Korea to burst into the international scene. Korea today is the fourteenth largest exporter by value in the world, and the standard of living is bounding ahead. Nonetheless, the people retain their traditional values and abide by the faiths of their forefathers. They are proud, they are fierce, and they are as strong a people as the world has ever known.

The country is tiny and so mountainous that even farming requires the acumen of an engineer. Minerals are so scarce that nearly every product manufactured must be made from imported materials. The division of the country makes it necessary to spend enormous amounts of manpower on security, a fact of life which tries not only the strength of the economy but also the will of every one of Korea's 40 million people.

None of these difficulties, however, have hindered Korea from rushing ahead; the Koreans are simply unwilling to give in. They have suffered troubles in the past and they have never expected smooth sailing. This is a homogenous group raised by the strictures of Confucianism and the tolerance of Buddhism, two philosophies which give the people the strength to keep on, and the patience to wait for results.

Seoul today, which houses one quarter of Korea's population, looks much like any other international city with skyscrapers reaching toward the heavens and traffic jams stalling the human race below. Neons light the city at night and workers pile into vehicles early in the morning, seven days a week. Business suits are as common here as in New York city and the pace of life is quickly approaching that of the frantic Western bustle.

Yet in the neighborhoods of Seoul and throughout the countryside, women still hang peppers to announce the birth of a baby boy, children bow to their grandparents, fortune-tellers warn of future trouble and offer portents of luck. Buddhist monks wander the streets for alms; and families take to the mountains to worship the natural beauty of their land.

Korea is an anomaly in so many ways that it never ceases to surprise. It is a country that dares to tempt fate, to go against the grain of its quiet, trodden past, that dares to enter the rush of nations without donating, in the process, its dignity. This is Korea; the wind of the future.

Alone, cup in hand,
I view the distant peaks.
Even if my love came to me,
Would I be any happier?
The peaks neither speak nor smile;
But what happiness, O what joy!
—*from* New Songs in the
Mountain *by Yun Sŏn-do*
(1587-1671)

". . . the distant peaks." The mountains. The hills. Korea. Wherever one walks, drives or flies in this country, one sees distant peaks.

Whether in the joyous lyricism of the great *sijo* poet Yun, or in the many paintings of Korea's amazing Diamond Mountains, those peaks rise figuratively and literally in any reference to this country. Even Korea's great creation epic, the *Wei-shu*, notes that the founding of legendary Chosŏn, took place atop T'aebaek Mountain in north Korea.

From Manchuria south to Cheju Island in the East China Sea, the entire country is ribbed by low-rising, sharp and often bare mountain ridges. Because these "mountains" never rise more than 2,800 meters in elevation, armchair geologists jump to the conclusion that Korea is a young land. But Korea is in fact one of the world's oldest known land areas, dating back to the pre-Cambrian period (1,600 to 2,700 million years ago) in Earth's evolution.

Korea's basic foundation of granite and limestone is old and tough, like her people. And were it not for strenuous reforestation programs conducted during the past two decades, she might look even older.

The Korean peninsula is relatively small—about the size of Rumania or New Zealand—but it becomes even smaller when you consider that only about 20 per cent of its total land area is flatland. The peninsula's overall size (including north and south) is about 1,000 kilometers long and 216 kilometers wide at its narrowest points. Seoul, Korea's major city, is, as the magpie flies, about 1,100 kilometers from Peking and about 1,400 kilometers from Tokyo.

Preceding pages: A would be Korean princess peers through a Yi dynasty palanquin screen; traditional mask dancers; entrance of Sunamsa (temple), Chollanam-do; early morning walk; Admiral Lee's statue on Kwanghwa Moon. Left, pine covered ridges of mountain between Yanggu and Inje.

As you cruise up and down this peninsula, take note that you are traveling on an ancient land bridge that is tilted toward the west and into the Yellow Sea.

This tipping, caused by volcanic pressure on the peninsula in ancient geologic times, has left the offshore area of Korea's West Coast dotted with hundreds of islands. Also, in concert with the Yellow Sea's tremendously wide tide changes, this west side sinking produced far reaching, shallow inlets which look like huge, placid, sky blue lakes at high tide.

The East Coast fronting the Japan Sea features mountains marching right down to a coast line marked by tiny coves. These eastern waters produce great tasty coldwater catches of cuttle fish and salmon, while the West Coast supplies clams, oysters, large and small shrimp, sea snails and abalone.

Migratory Pit Stop

Where the water is shallow enough, there are great expanses of sedge to play host to a variety of water birds. The most glorious of them is the Manchurian crane. This bird was presumed to be nearly extinct but in 1977 Dr. George Archibald, head of the International Crane Foundation, found a large colony in Korea's Demilitarized Zone.

The shallow waters and inlets of the western side of the country are home to the white-naped crane and many different kinds of ducks, geese, and swans. Korea also acts as part-time home for birds which follow Asian migration routes which cut through the country.

The total bird population has been rising in recent years in concert with government regulations prohibiting the shooting of feathered friends. Where only a few years ago, the pheasant seemed on its way to extermination, it is now common. The sparrow population has increased so enormously as a result of this bird-killing ban that sparrow netting is now permitted for a limited period every autumn.

There are several seriously endangered bird species in Korea. The aforementioned Manchurian crane has been greatly reduced in numbers and the Tristram's woodpeaker population is way down, but its numbers are increasing. Birdwatchers report that more than 20 birds are now living in the protected area of the Kwangnŭng Forestry Research Institute Branch.

Bears and Wildcats, But No DMZ Tigers

Wild mammals have not fared so well as birds. The Korean tiger is still celebrated in art, but he is virtually extinct. So is the local leopard, though some outdoorsmen speculate that leopards may still be roaming forests in the remote north of Korea.

One of life's great ironies is that the demilitarized zone (DMZ) between north and south Korea has provided a place of peace and quiet where wildlife can proliferate.

One creature carrying on in this DMZ refuge is a small wildcat who has all but completely disappeared in mountains south of the 38th parallel. There also are some of the small native Korean bears. These bears are

now protected, but they almost disappeared for good because the eating of bear meat has long been considered to be very good for one's health. An entire community of otters—about a hundred of them—was found along the Naktong River at about the same time bears were found on Mount Chiri.

Snake Consommé

Korea has a large snake population, but none of these serpents are aggressive and only one is truly deadly. Quick treatment for any snake bite, however, can prevent tragedy. If you see a snake, stand still and give him time to get away.

Cheju Island off Korea's south coast is famous for its horses. Because of this island's sub-tropical climate, there is forage for horses year round and Cheju horses are permitted to run free.

Korea also has a unique breed of dog, Chindo, which is a medium-sized, short-haired canine with a moderately pointed snout, heavy shoulders, and a coloring that varies from light cream beige to almost brown. The breed seemed in danger of extinction a few years ago, but the government now forbids, as a preservation measure, the taking of Chindo dogs from their native island.

"Too Many Azaleas"

Korea's forest flora is closely related to that of neighboring China and Japan. The nation's indigenous plants are most likely to be preserved in temple gardens where for centuries Buddhist monks have tended Korea's living things with loving care. It is here that the finest specimens of gingko trees, a variety of maple, and herbaceous plants thrive.

Korea has such a large population of azaleas that it is often impossible to walk across a forest clearing without trampling on them. Indeed, wild weigelia, spirea, viburnums, hydrangeas, boxwood, holly, daphne, and a host of other plants are all considered "weeds." It is now against the law to dig up such plants in the wild or cut down a tree without government permission, however. The woody plants have become common in Korea as a result of successful reforestation programs.

Korean roadsides in autumn are iced with a floral froth of lavender, pink, white and deep red cosmos. City streets are often edged with gingkos, aialanthus, London plane trees, sumac and pawlonia and just about every village has an ancient zelkova or persimmon tree.

Oddly enough, the azalea which covers almost every mountainside and fills every untilled field is not the national flower. That official honor was bestowed on the rose of Sharon. During the Japanese occupation, Japanese officials in some areas tried to stamp it out, but that only made the Korean population even more determined to cultivate it.

Left, a pair of dacing Manchurian cranes in the demilitarized zone north of Seoul. Right; wild cosmos blossoms.

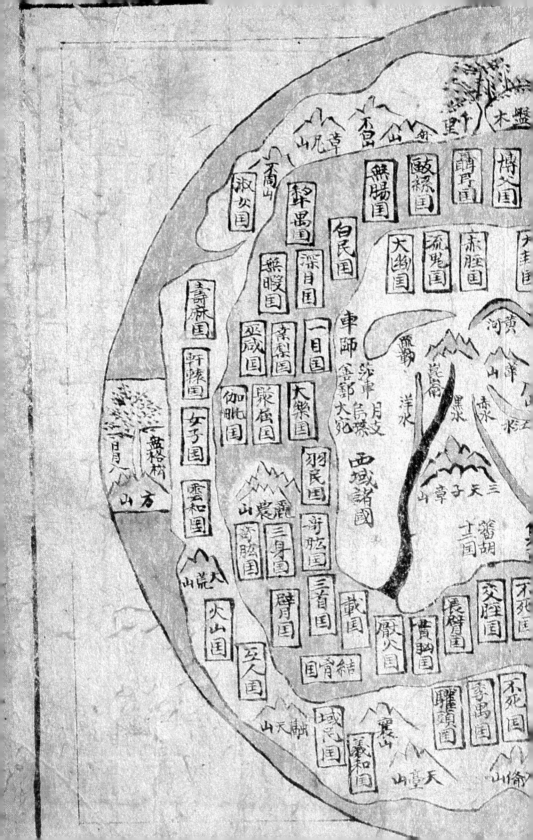

大澤

深目国　封䨂

無腸国　比肩国　始州国　大人国

玄股国　勞民国　山天虛

廣野

国纓拘　三野

姑射山　毛民国　俀人国　人長三丈尺

国慎甫　朝鮮　明狙邑　暘国　少昊国　中榮国

龜山　太山　日本国　褎　龍伯国

中國　扶桑　甘山　柜格山　日月山

衡山　天台　真朦　方丈　其肅　可邱国　夏州国　波流

暹邏　蓬萊　來　瀛洲　君子国　鰲明山

琉球国　山叢桑　中容国

安南国　足明国　扶桑国　鳩踽国　天人国　女人国

岐舌国　食水国　金二国　長沙国　石建　壤民国

盈民国　鼠姓国　僑天山　門山　燕　待

白洲

20

KOREA: 5,000 YEARS OF TURBULENT 'CALM'

Centuries of existence in the shadow of stronger neighbors has given Korea a history filled with turbulence that belies the familiar nickname, "Land of the Morning Calm." At a strategic crossroads of northeast Asia, the Korean peninsula has been trampled on by armies of Chinese and Japanese, Mongols and Manchus, Russians and Americans. Despite these onslaughts Koreans have maintained a distinct political and cultural identity.

Koreans, of course, have borrowed many attributes of Chinese civilization and have, in turn, transmitted elements of that civilization to Japan. Still, Korea is neither a China in miniature nor an offshoot of Japan, and the ability of Koreans to preserve their identity while enduring the depredations of intruders is one of the most striking themes in modern history. The Koreans have not merely endured, but have produced artistic, scientific, and literary achievements of great distinction.

Tan'gun, the Bear-Woman's Son

The retelling of Korean history begins with the mythical founder of the nation, Tan'gun. According to myth, Hwanung, the son of the Divine Creator, had descended to earth and proclaimed himself king when he heard the prayers of a bear and tiger who wished to become human beings. He gave each of them 20 pieces of garlic and a piece of artemisia and told them they would be transformed if they would eat the plants and withdraw from the sun's light for one hundred days. The animals ate the offering and retired to their caves, but the tiger's restlessness drove him out. The bear remained for a hundred days and emerged as a woman.

The first wish of the bear-woman was to have a son. So she prayed beneath a sandalwood tree, became pregnant and bore a son, Tan'gun, whose reign is said to have begun in 2333 B.C. He ruled, the story goes, until 1122 B.C., when Kija, supposedly a descendant of the Shang royal line of China, arrived in Korea and established himself as ruler. Thereafter, Tan'gun resumed his spirit form and disappeared.

Although we may give little credence to the

myth, archaeological studies demonstrate that human life on the peninsula is very old. Paleolithic sites were discovered in the 1960s, and yielded stone tools estimated to be about thirty thousand years old. The oldest evidence of a Neolithic society has been assigned a date of 4270 B.C.

At Lolang, near modern P'yŏngyang, the Chinese built a great outpost of Han culture. At its peak, the colony was populated by some four hundred thousand people but the Han commanderies were not able to integrate the Korean peoples into the Chinese political

realm. The Chinese were opposed from the outset, and local resistance forced the abandonment of all the Korean colonies, except Lolang, within a few decades.

After the collapse of the Later Han dynasty, one of the Korean tribal states, Koguryŏ, had begun to emerge as a tribal alliance of nomadic people in southeastern Manchuria in the 1st Century A.D. By the 4th Century, Koguryŏ had grown into a kingdom with a centralized government built around a hereditary military aristocracy. Frequently at war with the Chinese, the Koguryŏ people came by the 5th Century to dominate the northern half of the Korean peninsula, and all of Manchuria to the regions of the Amur, Sunggari, and Liao rivers.

Preceding pages: an old Chinese-Korean map identifies China as the "Middle Kingdom" and other countries as outside, peripheral states. Right, the now extinct Korean tiger, once worshiped as a messenger of mountain spirits.

The Three Kingdoms Period

The southern part of the peninsula was peopled by a number of distinctive but related tribes that had, by the 3rd Century A.D., formed three weak tribal confederations: Mahan, Chinhan, and Pyŏnhan. It was in this area—during the 3rd and 4th Centuries—that the Paekche and Silla tribes arose, who, with Koguryŏ, dominated the so-called Three Kingdoms period in Korea.

Paekche emerged among the Mahan tribes of the southwest. Led by a royal clan, Paekche occupied the area south of the Han River and initially placed its capital in the vicinity of modern Kwangju. In subsequent years Paekche expanded its territory, organized a bureaucratic government along Chinese lines,

and established relations with the Eastern Chin state of south China.

Last to develop as a major kingdom was Silla, whose origins consisted of a loose federation of tribes in the southeastern corner of Korea. Silla's transition from tribal league to kingdom took place in the late 4th and early 5th Centuries.

Another tribal federation, the Kaya league, occupied the southern coast of the peninsula in the lower reaches of the Naktong River. Until its annexation by Silla in 562, the Kaya territory was an important point of contact between the Korean states and the inhabitants of Japan.

The centuries during which these three kingdoms were emerging were full of strife.

Between 396 and 404, Koguryŏ King Kwang-gaet'o forced Paekche to withdraw from the Han River valley and move its capital further south. In 433 Silla joined forces with Paekche to fight Koguryŏ; then a few years later Silla turned and attacked Paekche.

China, then under the Sui dynasty, launched unsuccessful attacks against Koguryŏ in 598 and 612. These military failures contributed to the collapse of Sui in 618 and the rise of the T'ang dynasty. T'ang sent expeditions against Koguryŏ in 645 and 647. They, too, failed. T'ang then allied with Silla and attacked Paekche as a preliminary to striking Koguryŏ from the south. By 660, T'ang had destroyed Paekche, and the two allies turned on Koguryŏ, which fell in 668.

After the defeat of Paekche and Koguryŏ, the Chinese tried to establish an administration to govern the peninsula, including Silla. Silla's response was to help the Koguryŏ resistance movement in the north, and also move against the T'ang troops in the south. By 671, Silla had taken the old Paekche capital; by 676 Silla had expanded to the Taedong River. The Chinese had to withdraw into Manchuria. Finally, in 735, China was forced to recognize Silla's dominion over all the areas south of the Taedong.

North of the Taedong River a coalition of tribes founded the state of Parhae, whose rulers were mostly Koguryŏ people. Parhae remained dominant in Manchuria and northern Korea until it was conquered by the Khitan in 926.

The Sillan conquest of the peninsula often is taken as the beginning of a unified Korean state that continued to exist until the division of north and south Korea in 1945. However, Silla's unification was, at best, tenuous.

Luxurious Buddhism

Chinese civilization had flowed into Korea throughout the Three Kingdoms period. Buddhism and Confucianism, art and architecture, the written language of China, and bureaucratic organizational principles were all introduced.

Of all the importations from China, none flourished more luxuriantly under unified Silla than Buddhism. Believing that Buddhism would protect the state and bring good fortune, Silla's rulers lavished state funds on temples and Buddhist images, and dispatched monks to China and India to study the religion. The epitome of the Buddhistic art of the period may still be seen in the Sŏkkuram stone grotto near the Sillan capital of Kyŏngju. It and Korea's most famous temple,

Pulguk-sa, were begun in 751 when Silla was at its height.

The early influence of Chinese civilization was profound, but it did not supplant the native culture. In fact, Silla's success in unifying the peninsula stemmed in part from the strength of such native institutions as the *hwarang* and the *kolp'um* or "bone-rank" system. The *hwarang*, or "flower knights," was a paramilitary youth organization for the training and education of the sons of the Silla elite. Some of Silla's most able leaders were shaped by the precepts of the *hwarang*..The *kolp'um* system was a highly stratified hierarchy of rank based on birth with royalty and the aristocracy monopolizing the high offices.

The T'ang administrative system became the model for the state structure of unified Silla, but Chinese forms were altered to meet Korean needs. Nowhere is the difference between the Chinese model and the Sillan adaptation clearer than in the recruitment of officials for government. In T'ang China, officials were selected on the basis of examinations. In Silla, positions were filled according to birth, not talent.

While the T'ang dynasty did not impose direct rule on Korea, it did dominate Silla and later Korean kingdoms through the tributary system. As long as the ceremonial obligations of the tributary system were met, the Koreans were free to conduct their affairs as they saw fit.

Koreans In Japan

The Three Kingdoms and united Silla periods constituted centuries of profound Korean influence on Japan. There were frequent migrations of Koreans to Japan from the 4th through the 7th Centuries, especially during times of turmoil in the Korean kingdoms. With the emigrants went Korean and Chinese technological, intellectual, and cultural influences. Monks from Paekche and Koguryŏ staffed the first Buddhist monastery in Japan, built in the 6th Century. Architects and builders from Paekche were largely responsible for the great burst of temple construction that occurred during that century.

Men from the peninsula became the tutors of Japan's famed Prince Shōtoku, and others brought expertise in calendrics and Chinese medicine. The oldest extant Japanese embroidery has been attributed to women

from Koguryŏ who became prominent at the Japanese court. Nearly one third of the nobles in the register of families compiled in 815 were of Korean descent.

Silla reached its zenith in the middle of the 8th Century, then entered upon a century and a half of civil strife and disintegration. The growth of the royal clan led to intense internal rivalries over the crown. Moreover, the heart of the social and political order, the *kolp'um* system, came under attack from lower echelons who felt excluded from power. Another discontented element was the merchants who were amassing great wealth. At the same time, the greed of large provincial landowners contributed to the weakening of government. By the late 9th Century many

farmers were abandoning their fields to survive by banditry.

The 9th and early 10th Centuries were years of upheaval. As early as 768, major revolts broke out among the aristocracy and in 780, King Hyegong was assassinated. Uprisings also raged in the countryside.

Out of this chaos arose rebel chieftains who struggled for centuries until the appearance of Wang Kŏn. Supported by the landlord and merchant class from which he sprang, Wang Kŏn grew in power over the next two decades. In 935 King Kyŏngsun handed over the government to Wang Kŏn, who reunited the peninsula, named his new state Koryŏ, and began a dynasty that lasted more than four hundred and fifty years.

Left, an early portrait of the 8th Century Sŏkkuram Buddha at Kyŏngju; right, serene Buddhas of Silla.

The founding of Koryŏ represented more than a mere change of dynastic names. Wang Kŏn's power was based on a non-aristocratic élite. He also was helped by some Silla aristocrats whose power derived from their landholdings and by some discontented Sillan intellectuals.

Although the *kolp'um* system had been destroyed, Koryŏ was still a society founded on status-consciousness and sharp class distinctions. Ancestry continued to be of great importance in determining one's position in the social hierarchy. Whereas the old ruling

class had consisted of warrior-aristocrats, the élite of Koryŏ came to be the literati who occupied the civil offices in the government.

For the first time in Korea, Wang Kŏn invoked the Chinese notion of the "mandate of Heaven" as his rationale for assuming the throne. He justified his rule by claiming moral superiority.

Wang Kŏn and his successors in the 10th and 11th centuries built a centralized government, but subordinated it to the wishes of an oligarchy. A competitive civil examination system was created in 958 to fill the highest offices with those members of the ruling class most highly schooled in Chinese literature and the Confucian Classics. Advancement depended greatly on social status.

Although the government apparatus outwardly resembled the Confucianized government of China, the influence of Confucianism as a way of life was limited in Koryŏ times. Buddhism remained the most pervasive spiritual force throughout the dynasty. Wang Kŏn himself was a Buddhist and patronized the religion, and monasteries wielded considerable secular power and influence by accumulating land and wealth through money-lending and commercial activities.

An abrupt change came about in August, 1170. A military escort conveying the king and royal party on an outing revolted and killed every man in the party, except the king himself. The king was banished to Kŏje island, where he was murdered. He was replaced on the throne by a younger brother.

Historians have interpreted the coup as a military revolt against discrimination suffered at the hands of civilian officials and against the debauchery of the royal court under King Uijong (r.1146–1170). It introduced a period in which most important positions in government went to military men. More reliance was placed on native political and economic institutions and a period of general breakdown ensued. There were countercoups, wide-spread slave and peasant uprisings, and violent infighting among the developing private armies of the new military masters. The dominant figure to emerge was Ch'oe Chŭng-hŏn, who built an independent base of power while suppressing the provincial uprisings. He then turned against rival military leaders, who he eliminated by 1196.

The military rulers found that they lacked the administrative expertise to run the country so they began luring civilian scholar-officials into service. An unprecedented fusion of the two groups through intermarriage followed. In time the civil aristocracy began to revive, building strength toward an eventual challenge of the military supremacy. In the middle 13th Century, the Mongol invasions took place.

The Mongols Take Over

The Mongols were the most formidable of a number of peoples with whom the Koreans clashed during the Koryŏ period. As early as 916, in the wake of the collapse of the T'ang dynasty in China, the Khitan had begun to dominate Manchuria and Mongolia and sought formal relations with Koryŏ. As with the Jurchen and the Mongols who followed, the Koreans regarded the Khitan as culturally inferior and resisted their approaches.

By the 980s, the Khitan had established a Chinese-style state called Liao, had overrun Parhae, and had begun attacking the Jurchen tribes along the middle reaches of the Yalu River. A new bid for diplomatic relations with Koryŏ was repulsed, and in 993 the Khitan invaded. The peace settlement suspended contacts with China's Sung government.

ments were indecisive; the Jurchen turned against the Liao state, which they eliminated. Then they proclaimed the Chin dynasty in 1115 and took all of north China from the Sung dynasty. Koryŏ was compelled to declare fealty to Chin and cut its ties with the southern Sung court.

A century after the Chin conquest, there were more clashes as the Mongols swept into China and Manchuria from central Asia, pressing the Khitan down into the peninsula.

In 1010, the Khitan invaded again; then again in 1018 when the Koreans rejected Khitan demands that Koryŏ cede strategic border areas and become a vassal of Liao. This incursion led to stalemate, but the wary Koreans began building a defensive stone wall reminiscent of the Great Wall of China. Completed in 1044, it stretched from the mouth of the Yalu on the west coast to Kwangp'o on the east.

More trouble came as the 12th Century opened. The Jurchen invaded northern Koryŏ in 1104 and remained until a large army was sent against them in 1107. Repeated engage-

Left, Koreans call Confucius *Kongja*; right, Unjn Miruk "Buddha of the Future" at Kwanchok Temple near Nonsan.

The Koryŏ government agreed to ally with the Mongols to end the Khitan threat, but they had no taste for a lasting alliance with the new intruders. The Mongol armies were not easily appeased, however, and Koryŏ reluctantly began meeting demands for exorbitant tribute payments in return for the help the Mongols had given. These payments began in 1219 and continued until 1224, when relations were broken off after the murder of a Mongol envoy to Korea. Only the Mongols' preoccupation with other campaigns and their own internal politics spared Koryŏ from immediate retaliation.

The reckoning came in 1231. The Mongols quickly overran most of northern Korea, laid siege to Kaesŏng, the capital, and forced the government to surrender. But when the Mongols relaxed their grip the following year, the Koryŏ government fled from Kaesŏng, with most of the city's population, and took refuge on Kanghwa island at the mouth of the Han River on the west coast.

Thereupon the Mongols invaded Korea in force, but could not cross the narrow channel separating Kanghwa from the mainland. Thus the government remained inviolate, though isolated and helpless, during further Mongol incursions. In the next twenty-five years all the major cities were sacked and widespread destruction was inflicted on the countryside.

The question was: Should they continue resistance or capitulate? In 1258, Ch'oe Ŭi was overthrown by another military official, Kim Chun. The hapless Ch'oe was too fat to

force and restored his father to the throne. Wŏnjong himself went to the Mongol court and offered complete submission in return for aid against the military clique. He even agreed to marry his crown prince to a Mongol princess to seal the bargain. Yet when he returned to Korea with a Mongol army at his disposal, a large part of the military faction still refused to give in. Open rebellion broke out.

Some military units held out on the offshore islands as late as 1273. But the rebellion signalled the end of the military dictatorship and the restoration of the civilian bureaucracy. By 1279 the Mongols, who were firmly lodged in north China, adopted the dynastic name Yüan and proceeded to take over the rest of China.

The Mongols allowed the Koryŏ govern-

make a getaway. He couldn't scramble over his back wall when his assailants were battering down the front gate.

In 1259, a truce was struck with the Mongols and a decade of comparative peace began. However, the military officials who dominated the government refused to capitulate and the government remained on Kanghwa rather than return to Kaesŏng.

In 1269, Kim Chun fell victim to an internal power struggle and was ousted by another military figure, Im Yŏn, who had obtained King Wŏnjong's support. Im deposed Wŏnjong in favor of a younger brother of the king, but Wŏnjong's crown prince, who had been sent to Peking under the terms of the truce with the Mongols, returned with a large

ment in Korea to remain in control, except in far northern areas and on the island of Cheju, but always subject to directions of the Yüan court. Koryŏ crown princes were regularly sent to Peking as children, compelled to marry Mongol princesses, and kept there until the death of the reigning king. In this way, the Koryŏ court was thoroughly Mongolized and neutralized.

Extracting Female Quotas

The Yüan overlordship placed a severe strain on Korea. The Mongols extracted large annual tribute—gold, silver, horses, ginseng,

Statue of Admiral Yi Sun-sin.

hawks for hunting, artisans, eunuchs, and women. A special office was set up to select girls and young widows to fill the annual quotas. In addition, Korea had to build hundreds of ships and furnish soldiers for ill-fated invasions of Japan in 1274 and 1281.

The period of Mongol domination, however, had important cultural effects. There was, for example, the transmission of ideas and techniques for others under the dominion of the Mongols. Koreans gained knowledge of astrology, medicine, artistic skills, calendrics, and cotton cultivation.

In the 14th Century, rebellions in China upset the Mongol regime which culminated in 1368 in the foundation of the Ming dynasty. There was a revival of Korean independence during these years, especially after the enthronement of King Kongmin in 1352.

Kongmin rejuvenated the government, reorganized the army, reasserted control over the northwest territories, and reorganized and enforced the civil examination system. He began in the mid-1360s to restore illegally appropriated land slaves to their rightful owners.

The great landholders proved so powerful, however, that Kongmin was forced to compromise. Eventually, he had to give up the reform program entirely. That did not satisfy his opponents at court. They had him assassinated and installed his ten-year-old son on the throne.

This was the prelude to the rise of a major new leader who swept the Koryŏ dynasty aside, Yi Sŏng-gye. Descended from a family of military leaders in Hamgyŏng, Yi distinguished himself by suppressing local rebellions and combatting Japanese pirates called *wakŏ*. He also conducted a reform program to break the power of the old landlords, reduce the influence of the Buddhist establishment, and strengthen the government.

Beginnings of the Yi Dynasty, The Rebirth of Chosŏn

In 1392, Yi ousted the king and took the throne to become the founder of his own dynasty. It survived for more than five hundred years, was Korea's last ruling house, and was a watershed in the history of Korea. The new kingdom promptly resumed tributary relations with Ming China and took the ancient Chinese name for Korea, Chosŏn.

The reformers around Yi Sŏng-gye were men who had embraced the ideas of the Chinese Confucian thinker Chu Hsi. These Neo-Confucianism doctrines gave the traditional ethico-political cult metaphysical underpinnings. It made of it a virtual religion and imbued its followers with a zealous spirit of reform. Once the new dynasty was proclaimed, the reformers intensified their drive to impose Confucian norms on Korean life.

The changes wrought constituted a re-weaving of the very fabric of society. Two examples: In burying the dead, Koreans had long practiced rituals that were an amalgam of customary and Buddhist traditions. Now these ingrained customs, including cremation, were thrust aside in favor of Confucian ancestor worship and its related rituals. Until the end of Koryŏ times, marriage customs had admitted endogamy, polygamy, and re-marriage of widows. Yi-period reforms, however, broadened the circle of kin with whom marriage was prohibited, forbade the practice of giving equal social status to multiple wives, and discouraged remarriage.

The rise of Confucianism spelled the decline of Buddhism. By confiscating land and forcing the closing of many temples, the new regime reduced Buddhism to a subservient position. It was never able to recover its former status in Korean society.

The founder of the dynasty was content to be more figurehead than dictator. Not so the third king of the dynasty, T'aejong, who came to power in 1401 after killing his youngest brother, then the heir-apparent, in 1398. Under his rule, the government was reorganized to strengthen the throne.

T'aejong's successor was Sejong (r. 1418–1450), a man considered by many to have been the greatest of Korean kings. Intelligent and scholarly, he presided over the conception of the remarkable Korean alphabet, *han-'gŭl*, and, indeed, over the flourishing of cultural activity. As an administrator, he was meticulous and indefatigable, but he was succeeded by men of lesser capacity, Munjong (r. 1450–1452) and the ill-fated boy-king Tanjong (r. 1452–1455). This unfortunate was forced to abdicate by his uncle, was imprisoned, and finally strangled. His murderous uncle took the throne as King Sejo (r. 1455–1468),

Sejo assumed direct control, intimidated his critics with purges and executions, instituted banishments, and seized property. When his reign was over, the power of the Korean monarchs again diminished and the Yi dynasty began a long decline.

Hideyoshi's Invasions And Admiral Yi's Turtle Ships

The decline of the Yi dynasty may be attributed in part to the threat of foreign invasion, which recurred in the 1590s. This time it came from Japan, newly reunified under Toyotomi Hideyoshi who, in April 1592, invaded Korea. In a month the Japanese overran most of the country.

The Koreans had little military experience on land, but at sea the story was different. Korea's great naval hero, Admiral Yi Sun-sin, was commander of a naval force of some 80 ships, based at Yŏsu. Among his fleet were a number of "turtle ships," which he used to break the back of the Japanese invasion by choking off the flow of supplies and troop reinforcements.

The "turtle ships" averaged 100 feet in length, were propelled by oars, and were faster and more maneuverable than the Japanese ships. An armored canopy studded with pointed objects made them invulnerable to enemy projectiles as well as to enemy raiders trying to come aboard. The vessels were heavily gunned, and the bow of each ship was decorated with a large turtle's head that could emit sulphur fumes masking the movements of the fleet.

From May to July, 1592, Yi's fleet met smaller Japanese ships carrying troops and supplies bound for Pusan. In eight major engagements he sank more than two hundred fifty of them. In the final naval campaign of 1592, Yi boldly took his fleet into the Japanese base at Pusan and is said to have destroyed more than half the 500 ships there.

Yi's victories, plus the growing Korean guerrilla campaign and the intervention of Chinese troops, forced the Japanese to begin pulling back. Negotiations resulted in the withdrawal of the bulk of the Japanese troops and the dispatch of Korean and Chinese envoys to Japan to conclude a settlement.

In January 1597 the Japanese renewed the war. They sent 100,000 men to punish Korea. This time, however, they met stiffer resistance from the Koreans and from the Chinese garrison. The invasion was confined to the southern provinces, but there it was waged with great ferocity.

At sea, the Koreans did not fare as well as before. Yi Sun-sin had fallen victim to court intrigues and was given only a dozen ships. Once again Yi defeated the Japanese in a series of engagements, but in November 1598, standing in the bow of his flagship, he was struck by a bullet and killed. The death of Hideyoshi in September 1598 prompted the Japanese to bring the war to a close.

Some of the Korean losses in the war were distinct assets for Japan. A number of skilled makers of ceramics were taken to Japan as captives and thousands of books were looted by the Japanese. It was also through a Korean prisoner that the tenets of Neo-Confucianism began to take hold in Japan.

Within a few decades, Chosŏn was under assault from the north. In the Manchurian highlands, the Jurchen tribes had united under Nurhachi. Sporadic attacks began along the northeastern border as early as 1583, and by the 1590s the Ming outposts in Manchuria were under pressure.

Chosŏn sided with the Chinese against the rising Manchu state but in 1627, Nurhachi captured P'yŏngyang and then took the Yi capital at Seoul. The court fled to Kanghwa Island. Under terms of a peace treaty, the Korean ruler committed his country to a Confucian-style, elder-younger brother relationship with the Manchus and he pledged aid against the Ming dynasty.

The Koreans, however, did not take their pledges seriously. In 1632 the Manchus demanded annual tribute and the Koreans issued a declaration of war.

The Manchu cavalry moved quickly and were able to block the escape route of Injo and his ministers, who capitulated on learning that the Manchus had captured Kanghwa and two hundred hostages, including the queen.

The Manchus extracted a heavy price: a tributary relationship, severance of ties with the Ming court and submission of two Yi princes as hostages. The Manchus went on to conquer and rule China as the Ch'ing dynasty (1644 – 1912).

The Sirhak: 'Practical Learning'

In the 18th Century, the Yi dynasty recovered some of its earlier vitality. Financial problems had been resolved and the reigns of Yŏngjo (r. 1724 – 1776) and Chŏngjo (r. 1776 – 1800) brought great progress.

Two important intellectual currents stimulated Korean thinkers of the late Yi period. One was the body of Western ideas flowing into Korea from China. The other was the Ch'ing School of Empirical Studies which emphasized critical reasoning. The most interesting products of these influences appeared in the works of the scholars of the *sirhak*, or "practical learning," school. *Sirhak* embraced a number of thinkers whose concerns varied widely. They had in common, though, a focus on finding pragmatic solutions to Korea's economic and social problems. They stressed inductive reasoning in their studies and had little patience with the speculative metaphysics of the orthodox Neo-Confucian tradition.

Right, during the early 18th Century scholars and statesmen such as Yi Chae were avid *Kongja* disciples.

31

WESTERNERS ARRIVE

The 19th Century was a century of crisis for Korea. Despite its longevity and its occasional brilliance, the Yi dynasty did not give Korea an efficient administration. Decades of social unrest and popular agitation in the early 19th Century, including major rebellions in 1811 and 1862, made the conservative ruling class reactionary and inward-looking. And that was a time when Korea, along with the rest of Asia, faced the challenge of an expansive and technologically superior West.

Korea's contacts with her two main neighbors, China and Japan, had been closely

tion brought the deaths of 130 Christians.

Apart from clandestine missionaries, direct contacts with the West continued to be limited until the 1860s. Korean officials, however, were badly shaken by the news that British and French troops had occupied Peking in 1860. This strengthened their determination that foreigners be excluded from the peninsula and that policy was confirmed upon the accession of a new monarch, Kojong (r. 1864–1907). He came to the throne as a 12-year-old youth who began his reign with the dowager queen as the nominal regent.

regulated and direct exposure to Westerners had been limited. Over the next two centuries, however, a good deal of information about Western learning passed into Korea which both the Chinese and Koreans declared subversive to Confucian beliefs and social order.

Despite the official persecutions in 1791, a number of Koreans embraced Catholicism. In 1794 a Chinese Catholic priest, Father Chou Wen-mo slipped into the country and began missionary work. During the next six years, the Korean Catholic community grew from three thousand to ten thousand.

Repression of Western learning deepened with the enthronement of King Sunjo (r. 1800–1834). In 1839, a new wave of persecu-

Actual power was in the hands of his father, better remembered in history by his title, Taewŏn'gun ("Great Prince of the Court"). The Taewŏn'gun, in pursuing an exclusionist foreign policy, won widespread support.

The year of Kojong's crowning also brought the intensification of Western pressures on Korea. The Russians began to demand trade and diplomatic relations but were turned down in 1866. That same year nine French Catholic priests and some 8,000 Korean converts were executed. In August 1866, the American-owned *General Sherman* sailed up the Taedong River and ran aground. The ship was burned and her crew killed. In October, the French occupied Kanghwa Island but withdrew shortly.

In 1871, the American minister to China, Frederick Low, accompanied five warships to Korea to try to open the country to trade. A clash occurred. The Americans occupied Kanghwa island where 350 Koreans and three Americans were killed before the mission was abandoned by the Americans.

Irritating the Japanese

Under the Taewŏn'gun, the seclusion policy was applied even to the Japanese who, in 1875, determined to press the issue. After a

tleground for contending powers. The rise of Japanese influence after 1876 spurred the Chinese to redouble their efforts to preserve their traditional influence. This led to a series of confrontations. In 1882 Korean army soldiers killed their Japanese instructors, burned the Japanese legation, and attacked the residences of the dominant family in the government, the Min clan of Yŏhŭng, the family of Kojong's queen.

When the rebellious soldiers went so far as to seize King Kojong, the Min clan sought help from the Chinese, who were happy to

clash between Korean shore batteries and a Japanese ship, Japan pressed upon the Korean government a treaty of friendship and commerce. It provided for the opening of three ports to trade with Japan and permanent Japanese diplomatic establishments in Korea. Kojong and his advisors did not intend to revamp foreign relations; they saw the treaty merely as the normalization of relations with a country Korea always had ties with.

Korea now became an international bat-

Preceding pages: Westerners at the Korean Court; left, early Korean lithographs— 'Corean Chief and Attendants'' and right, "Islanders of Sir James Hall group", sketched in 1817.

restore Min control. Japan won indemnity and permission to station a legation guard in Korea, but her political influence was eclipsed by the Chinese.

The Tonghak Uprising

After a Korean revolt, China and Japan agreed to withdraw their troops from Korea and not to intervene again but both countries continued to try to penetrate Korea through commercial trade. Western involvement in Korea, especially the growth of Protestant missions, also grew, sparking the Tonghak uprising in 1894 and, in its wake, the Sino-Japanese War.

The Tonghak ("Eastern learning") movement began as a religious society founded in 1860 under a philosophy that combined monotheism with the principles of Confucianism and with other concepts from Buddhism, Taoism, Shamanism, and other sources. By the 1890s Tonghak was a religious and social movement of national significance, supported by many peasants and discontented elements from the upper classes.

The troubles in the spring of 1894 grew out of a peasant rebellion which reflected the serious economic problems caused in part by foreign merchants and their influence. The government attitude provoked a large-scale armed revolt.

When the Tonghak-led rebels defeated the troops of the central government in two major battles, an appeal went out to China

for military assistance. China responded and duly notified the Japanese. Uninvited, the Japanese sent seven thousand men and warships.

The Chinese and Korean forces put down the rebellion and Japan began pressing the Korean government for a program of reform and modernization. In late July, the Japanese seized the government, occupied Kyŏngbok Palace, ousted the administration, and installed a progressive, pro-Japanese cabinet. The old Taewŏn'gun was declared the nominal head of state as regent for the king.

Soon Chinese and Japanese military units clashed and the Sino-Japanese War was on. It pitted the fading Ch'ing empire against the rising imperial power of Meiji Japan.

The Japanese dealt China a swift and startling defeat. China then formally acknowledged Korea's liberation from the old suzerain-vassal relationship.

The Murder of Queen Min

With the Chinese eliminated, the Koreans opposed to Japanese dominance found a new counterforce in the Russians. In 1895 Russia helped weaken the Japanese position by compelling Japan to restore to China the Liaotung peninsula, which was seized during the Sino-Japanese War. On the heels of this *fait accompli*, a pro-Russian faction associated with Queen Min obtained the dismissal of the pro-Japanese minister to Korea and a professional soldier, Miura Gorŏ, engineered the murder of Queen Min, reputed to be the real power behind the throne.

Then, with the connivance of the pro-Russian group, King Kojong slipped out of his place and took refuge in the Russian legation whereupon he dismissed the cabinet and replaced it with a pro-Russian one.

For a year, Kojong reigned from the legation, returning to the palace only in February 1897 when he was convinced he could do so without fear of Japanese threats. Under Russian protection, he sought to reassert Korea's independence. In October 1897, he adopted the title of "emperor" in order to claim equality with the rulers of China and Japan. At the same time, the name of the country was changed from Chosŏn to Taehan Cheguk, "Empire of the Great Han."

A novel group, The Independence Club, attempted to urge reform on the government. They founded a newspaper, the *Independent*, published exclusively in the Korean script, *han'gŭl*, rather than in the usual Sino-Korean characters. The paper became an important means of popularizing reformist proposals.

The Russians soon became a primary target of the independence Club which campaigned for independence from all foreign nations. As the club grew, its criticism of foreign encroachment and of government policies became bolder. In November 1898 the government dissolved the club and jailed some of its leaders.

The Russo-Japanese War, The Treaty of Portsmouth

As the end of the century neared, Japan and Russia maintained an uneasy truce in Korea but events beyond Korea's borders such as the 1902 alliance between Japan and Great Britain, soon began to turn the situation in Japan's favor.

The showdown came in February 1904 when Japan launched a surprise attack on the Russian fleet at Port Arthur. That set off the Russo-Japanese War. Korea had declared its neutrality, but as soon as the war broke out Japan moved into the peninsula in force. The Korean government had no choice but to authorize Japanese military occupation.

By the end of 1905, Japan's control of Korea was recognized, ending the war. In Western opinion, Japan's role in Korea was seen as one of uplifting and enlightening a backward people who had repeatedly proved their incapacity to eliminate corruption and build a modern society and government.

The next step was to get Korea's formal acceptance of Japan as her protector. To this end, Itŏ Hirobumi arrived in Seoul on

the punishment of the "Five Traitors" who had approved it. Japanese gendarmes had to be called out to suppress public demonstrations. The emperor's aide, Min Yŏng-hwan, and a former prime minister, Cho Pyŏng-se, both committed suicide.

The regulations of the Residency-General went beyond the wording of the protectorate treaty. They claimed for the resident-general the right to maintain law and order; the right to intervene in Korea's internal administration; authority to supervise Japanese officials in Korea, including those employed by the Korean government; and the power to issue ordinances.

In June 1907 Kojong sent a secret envoy to the Hague peace conference to generate international pressure for Japan's withdrawal

November 5, 1905, to persuade the Korean ruler to approve a treaty transferring partial sovereignty to Japan.

Both Kojong and his cabinet resisted, but before two weeks had passed Itŏ had convinced a majority of the cabinet to accept the treaty. It was signed on November 18 and gave Japan control of Korea's foreign relations and the right to station in Korea a resident-general to manage external affairs.

When the treaty was made public, there was an outburst of protest and demands for

Left, Korean Prince Yi Eun was commissioned as "Captain Prince Ri" by conquering Japanese; right, bronz mural at Seoul's Pagoda Park to commemorate March 1 Movement.

from the peninsula. The mission failed and in July Kojong's cabinet, apparently to forestall Japanese retaliation, forced the emperor to abdicate in favor of his feeble-minded son (Sunjong, r. 1907–1910).

At the same time, the Japanese decided to disband the Korean army, and the two events taken together touched off a wave of rioting which was suppressed by 1912. In December 1907, the treaty between Korea and Japan was revised to give the resident-general a veto over all important administrative acts, internal reforms, and appointments and dismissals of high officials. By mid-1909, the administration of justice was fully in Japanese hands. A year later the Japanese had complete police power.

Korean resistance was unflaging. One act of violence was the assissination of Itŏ by a Korean patriot in October 1909. But on August 22, 1910, another treaty annexed Korea to Japan and extinguished Korea's existence as a separate nation.

Japanese Colonial Rule Inspires the March First Movement

With annexation, the Residency-General became known as the Government-General of Chosŏn. General Terauchi Masatake, the first governor-general, began a period of iron-fisted rule during which Korean opinion

and political participation were thoroughly suppressed. Meanwhile, the Japanese were building an all-powerful, centralized government designed to exploit their new colony.

Organized resistance was completely broken by the Japanese army and policy under Terauchi and his successor, but still Korean will endured. This became evident with the March First Independence Movement of 1919, one of the most celebrated incidents in Korean history.

To take advantage of the call for the self-determination of subjected peoples being heard at the Versailles Conference, a group of religious leaders planned a non-violent protest and appeal for independence. A declaration of independence was drafted, and on the afternoon of March 1, signatories of the declaration dispatched a copy to the police and circulated others.

The Japanese were taken completely by surprise. When printed copies began to surface on March 1, the authorities did not know what to do and when large crowds began to appear in the streets, the police panicked. The peaceful demonstration turned into bloody riot. For seven weeks, public demonstrations for independence spread to every corner of Korea. Everywhere they met with the same result: brutal suppression of unarmed demonstrators by Japanese troops. It was said that as many as 7,000 were killed in the clashes or as the result of beatings and torture, and 50,000 injured.

The Japanese adopted a softer line after the 1919 uprisings. Officials and school teachers stopped wearing swords, the number of military police was reduced, but the total number of policemen continued to grow and Korean-language newspapers, which had been suppressed, were revived but was tempered by vigorous censorship.

In 1937 colonial policy turned toward the complete "Japanization" of Korea. Use of the Japanese language was made mandatory in schools and in public places, and Korean history was dropped from the curriculum. Koreans were compelled to adopt Japanese names and required to participate in Shintŏ rituals. As the war in China intensified and World War II approached, Koreans were mobilized into patriotic associations and exhorted to support Japanese expansionism. Between 1939 and the end of World War II, hundreds of thousands of Korean laborers were conscripted to fill the positions of workers drafted into the Japanese army.

Productive Exploitation

Japanese rule brought material improvements to Korea, but, as with most colonial societies, few of the improvements were undertaken with the Koreans in mind. The Japanese built highways, railroads, ports, and modern communications facilities related to strategic and defense concerns. Agricultural and industrial development took place along lines dictated by the needs of Japan's domestic economy. Where industries were built, the earnings went to Japanese, not Koreans.

The Japanese shook Korean society out of its lethargy but the benefits of the colonial period hardly offset the costs of exploitation and suppression.

Left, an 1880s Korean courtesan; right, Yi Kojong in 1898 portrait by Hubert Vos.

INDEPENDENCE/KOREAN WAR
(AFTER W.W.II)

Koreans were jubilant when Japan surrendered to the Allied powers in August 1945, but their celebrations were short-lived. Most Koreans had taken it for granted that Japan's defeat meant immediate liberation and restoration of an independent nation. Instead, Korea was once again caught in the turbulence of international politics.

At Cairo on December 1, 1943, the United States advanced the idea of a four-power trusteeship over the peninsula on the theory that Koreans would be unable to maintain a strong, stable government if left to their own

The thirty-eighth parallel was not conceived of as a permanent division of the country. However, as soon as the two occupation armies were in place on opposite sides of the line it became a barrier that no amount of negotiation was able to dissolve.

The Allied foreign ministers met in Moscow in December 1945 and agreed to go ahead with an international trusteeship, which was to direct Korean affairs through a provisional government, staffed by Koreans, for at least five years. Two protracted attempts were made in 1946 and 1947 to

devices. The British and the Russians were unenthusiastic about the plan, but did not reject it out of hand.

As the war ground to a conclusion in 1945, the Grand Alliance was already being split by the tensions that soon gave rise to the Cold War. Thus when the Russians entered the Pacific war on August 9, American leaders were concerned that the Red army might deny the United States any voice in Korea's future. To counter this possibility, Washington officials proposed that a demarcation line be drawn across the peninsula. The Russians were to accept the surrender north of that line and the Americans to the south. Under pressure to reach a decision the planners chose the thirty-eighth parallel as the demarcation line.

implement this agreement, which was bitterly opposed by most Koreans. Both attempts failed and the United States turned to the United Nations in September 1947.

In the meantime, the two occupation armies were creating the beginnings of two separate Korean states. In the north, the Russians moved ahead to establish a Communist regime that would be friendly to the Soviet Union. They recognized and worked through people's committees that sprang up immediately after the Japanese capitulation. Both Communists and non-Communists

Above, U.S. Army photo showing Korean refugees fleeing to the south from advancing armies.

worked together in the early days of the occupation. By February 1946, however, the Communists had begun to dominate politics under the leadership of the man the Russians had chosen, Kim Il-sŏng. In another two years, all pretense of coalition had ended, and the Communists under Kim were in full control.

In the south, the American army refused to recognize a rudimentary administration known as the People's Republic, which had organized hastily after the surrender. Instead, the Americans tried to retain some Japanese officials and then established a military government with American personnel as executives and Koreans in subordinate positions. The military government was barely able to cope with the chaotic conditions resulting from the collapse of the Government-General, the separation of the south from the resources of the more-industrialized north, and the influx of refugees from the Russian zone and returnees from Japan.

The American policy was to hold important political and economic decisions in abeyance until a Korean government could be formed. This, of course, required the cooperation of the Russians, which was not forthcoming. As a result there were months of drifting when action was needed and the political arena quickly became a free-for-all. There was very little middle ground. Parties and individual leaders divided along sharp left-versus-right lines, and their constant strife further complicated the work of the military government.

The Republic of Korea

The United Nations General Assembly called for the creation of a unified and independent government for all of Korea and appointed a temporary commission to oversee elections. The commission was denied entry into the Russian zone, but decided to go ahead with elections in the south. On May 10, 1948, half of Korea chose a constituent assembly to draft a constitution and elect a chief executive.

The assembly picked as chairman, and later as first president, Syngman Rhee (Yi Sŭngman), a 73-year-old conservative anti-Communist. He had returned to Korea in October 1945 after 36 years abroad agitating for Korean independence, mostly in the United States. As a young man, he had had a

minor role in the Independence Club and had been jailed for seven years as a result of his activities. He had earned a Ph.D. degree at Princeton University and in 1919 had been chosen premier of the Korean Provisional Government of expatriates in Shanghai.

Rhee was an authoritarian with scant regard for liberal democracy. Neither installed nor favored by the U.S. government, Rhee knew well how to manipulate Americans. He plied that skill repeatedly after being sworn in as first president of the Republic of Korea on August 15, 1948.

The creation of a separate government in the south prompted a similar proclamation in the north. The provisional government headed by Kim Il-sŏng became the government of the Democratic People's Republic of Korea on September 9, 1948.

The last Russian troops left the north in December 1948, and by the following June the American establishment in the south had been reduced to an advisory group. The Russians supplied arms and assistance necessary to create a formidable north Korean army, but the United States refused to provide the south with armaments beyond those sufficient for self-defense.

The Korean War

The stage was set for civil war. North Korean troops poured across the thirty-eighth parallel in strength early Sunday morning, June 25, 1950.

The American response was to assume that unless the United States acted swiftly and decisively, the forces of global communism, directed from Moscow, would soon be on the march.

In Washington, President Truman promptly ordered U.S. forces into battle and asked the United Nations to sanction his intervention. At the time, the Soviet delegate was boycotting the United Nations in protest of the seating of Nationalist China and did not return to block Truman's request. Hence, a resolution was quickly passed, placing the American action under the flag of the United Nations and calling on other member nations to render aid. Sixteen other nations eventually contributed, but half the combat troops were supplied by the United States and most of the others were Koreans. An American general, beginning with Douglas MacArthur, was always in command.

By the beginning of September, south Korean and American forces had been pushed into a perimeter around Pusan. In mid-September, however, a counteroffensive was launched and by the end of the month the front had been pushed back to the thirty-eight parallel.

With Rhee threatening to go ahead alone if necessary, MacArthur obtained U.N. authorization to push north and unite the peninsula. By the end of October, American and south Korean troops were nearing the Manchurian border. The Chinese government, however, had strongly warned the United States against going into North Korea. Tens of thousands of Chinese troops crossed the Yalu River, attacked the spread

along the line of battle. It set up a Military Armistice Commission consisting of officers from the opposing armies to administer the agreement and a Neutral Nations Supervisory Commission to monitor the truce. For three decades, the Military Armistice Commission has continued to meet periodically at P'anmunjŏm to discuss the armistice and exchange recriminations.

Korea Artificially Divided

At the end of the war, Korea lay in ruins. Millions were rendered homeless, such Koreans counted 47,000 killed, another 183,000 wounded and 70,000 missing or taken prisoner. The United Nations command lost nearly 37,000 killed, of whom 33,629 were Amer-

out U.N. forces, and drove them back. They pushed south, crossed the thirty-eighth parallel, and retook Seoul.

For the next six months, the battlefront raged back and forth and finally stabilized in an area just north of the thirty-eighth parallel. The stalemate prompted the beginning of truce negotiations in July 1951 which dragged on for two years. As agreement appeared near in the summer of 1953, Rhee, who opposed a negotiated settlement, almost sabotaged the accord by releasing 25,000 prisoners who had refused repatriation to the north. South Korea did not sign the agreement finally put into effect on July 27, 1953.

The armistice agreement created a demilitarized zone stretching from coast to coast

icans. Another 117,000 were wounded. On the northern side, total casualties, military and civilian, are estimated to have been between 1½ and 2 million.

The war dealt a fatal blow to any hopes of reunification. The creation of the demilitarized zone made the border between the two Korean states one of the most effective artificial barriers in the world, and the fighting hardened the hostility on both sides.

In the north since the war, Kim Il-sŏng has sought to construct a self-reliant socialist state based on Communist doctrines. He has skillfully steered north Korea away from total dependence on either China or the Soviet Union. Kim's political ideology is a kind of patriotic socialism revolving about a personality cult in which he is revered as the supreme leader. The domestic economy has been able to provide the basic necessities of life, but the country continues to depend on exporting raw materials and importing manufactured goods.

In the south, the period following the Korean War was one of stagnation and slow recovery, despite massive amounts of American aid. Throughout the 1950s there was little industrial growth, and the economy was plagued by shortages and inflation.

Rhee's government reflected his own authoritarian nature and his inclination to reward personal loyalty. Favoritism and corruption were widespread in the government and in the upper ranks of the military. Rhee fell in danger of being ousted in the National

out in Seoul and other cities. On April 19, police fired on a demonstration in Seoul, killing 115 persons. Rhee attempted to pacify the discontent by promising reforms, but the demonstrations continued until, on April 27, he resigned from office and took exile in Hawaii

Failure of the Second Republic

The collapse of Rhee's government was followed by a brief interim administration, and in July the constitution was changed to provide a government with a cabinet responsible to the legislature. Yun Po-sŏn won election to the figurehead position of president and took office on August 15, 1960, marking the beginning of the Second Repub-

Assembly balloting for president in 1952 and engineered a constitutional amendment to provide for popular election, which he won. Before the 1956 elections came around, he coerced the National Assembly to drop the two-term limit for presidents and was subsequently returned to office for a third term. By 1960, however, it was apparent that Rhee's Liberal party had become very unpopular.

The 1960 election was marred by fraud so blatant it could not be ignored. In March and April, massive student demonstrations broke

Left, U.S. General Douglas MacAuthur makes an inspection tour of front lines right, a north Korean general arrives for 1953 peace talk at Ṗamunjŏm on the DMZ.

lic. He chose Chang Myŏn to lead the new government as prime minister. Both were members of the former opposition, the Democratic party.

The Chang government, committed to liberal democratic rule, proved incapable of maintaining itself in power. The Yun-Chang government fell on May 16, 1961, when a military junta, seized control. The junta immediately announced pledges to oppose Communism, to respect the United Nations charter and seek closer relations with the free world, to stamp out corruption, to build a self-supporting economy, and to work for reunification. When these revolutionary tasks were accomplished, the government would be returned to civilian hands.

MODERN HISTORY

The coup leaders imposed an absolute military dictatorship known as the Supreme Council for National Reconstruction, and in July, Major General Park Chung-hee, emerged as its chairman.

Park was a 43-year-old career officer of rural origin. He had been trained in Japanese military academies and had served as a lieutenant in the Kwantung Army in Manchuria during World War II. After the war, he had entered the Korean army for serveral years, had then become a civilian intelligence officer, but had returned to active duty when the

in 1971, narrowly defeating Kim Dae-jung.

In an attempt to insure his unchallenged command of Korean affairs, Park declared martial law on October 17, 1972, and called for a program of "revitalizing reforms." At his direction, the constitution was redrawn once more, establishing a National Conference on Unification, whose membership he controlled, which functioned as an electoral college. Under the terms of the new constitution, the Conference elected Park to a new six-year term as president with no limit on future terms.

Korean War began. By 1960, he had rised to become deputy commander of the Second Army but had always remained apart from the main political factions within the army

Under Park's leadership, the military government continued to rule until 1963, when it could no longer resist pressures for a return to civilian government. With presidential elections scheduled for mid-October, Park retired from the army and ran as the candidate of the Democratic Republican party, defeating Yun Po-sŏn. He was inaugurated and the Third Republic was launched.

In 1967, Park won reelection against the same opponent, and two years lqater he secured a constitutional amendment to open the way for a third term, to which he was elected

Park's rule came to an end on October 26, 1979, when he was shot to death by the chief of his Central Intelligence Agency, Kim Chae-kyu, who claimed that he had assassinated Park in order to end dictatorship and restore democracy, Kim was convicted, along with six accomplices, and was executed.

The long-term legacy of Park's 18 years in office comprised two trends: Park's idea of Korean-style democracy placed a storng emphasis on administrative efficiency, and he presided over a series of development programs that made Korea one of the most remarkable economic successes of the 1960s and 1970s. The immediate period of transition after his sudden death, however, was a period of uncertainty and contention.

Under the 1972 constitution, the prime minster, Ch'oe Kyu-ha, became acting president, and on December 6 the National Conference for Unification, Korea's electoral college, named him to serve out Park's term.

Between Ch'oe's election and his inauguration December 21, an abrupt change occurred within the military establishment when Major General Chun Doo Huan, head of the Defense Security Command, the agency responsible for investigating Park's murder, arrested a superior, General Chŏng Sŭnghwa, who was accused of complicity in the assassination of Park. A number of other senior officers also were arrested.

After removing the army chief of staff, Chun assumed the directorship of the KCIA, Korea's national security institution. He was promoted to four-star generasl in 1979 and, in 1980, he retired from the military and focused on political maneuvering. In late August, Chun was named President by the process of indirect election set out in Park's Yushin ("revitalizing") constitution. At his inauguration on September 1, 1980, Chun promised to steer Korea through a new era of national unity and prosperity.

By October, Chun had written and adopted a new constitution, marking the beginning of the Fifth Republic. Power remained, under the constitution, primarily in the hands of the president but that power was limited to seven years for each incumbent. A National Assembly and a new electoral college were elected in early 1981 and these groups, in turn, elected President Chun to his seven-year term in March of that year.

Chun has focused governmental efforts on maintaining political stability and improving economic conditions. The National Assembly has gradually grown into a somewhat outspoken institution and "opposition" political parties have been permitted some leeway, but the president retains broad legal powers to control dissent. Student demonstrations are now tolerated (they were banned when Prime Minister Cho'e declared martial law in 1979) but they are strictly controlled and the government runs an effective verbal campaign to bar general sympathizing. An opposition party attempted to join forces with the student in late 1985 but it was met with similar abuse from the government and rejected as an ally by the students.

Korea's dramatic economic recovery has continued on course since the Park regime. The division of the peninsula in 1945 left the north with mineral assets and south with a large, unskilled labor force and agricultural resources. President Park undertook economic reform in the early 1960s with an emphasis on exports and light industry and, at the

same time, he strengthened financial institutions.

Through a series of economic plans carried out over the last two and a half decades, Korea has become (1985) the 14th largest exporter in terms of value in the world. From 1963 to 1978, real GNP rose at an annual rate of about 10%. In 1963, per capital GNP stood at $100; it is now approaching $2000.

Korea, however, is almost wholly dependent on energy imports. The drastic 1979 increase in oil prices pushed the country into a severe recession in 1980 and it was not until spring of 1983 that the economy regained its former clip. Double-digit growth is not expected to return, but the economy is still progressing rapidly.

Left, a monument at the National Cemetery; right, Lotte Hotel in Seoul.

THE KOREANS

To understand today's Koreans and their intriguing, paradoxical country; to survive potentially terminal cultural shock, and learn to get along smoothly with these fascinating people, it's necessary to give some consideration to the quetions of who they are, how they got that way, and why they act the way they do.

Seeking for the essence of the modern Korean is like peeling an onion: you strip off the thin, superficial skin of Western and American influence, shuck away a surprisingly tough rind of Japanization, carefully re-

passivity, nor does flexibility imply lack of strong individuality. The third trait, stubbornness—sometimes dignified by calling it perseverance—explains and modifies the other two.

It would be easy but misleading to make a neat generalization here and say that these three basic Korean qualities are derived from the three major outside influences, and to speak of Chinese patience, Japanese adaptability, and American stick-to-it-iveness. But it goes deeper than that: these counterpointed national themes appeared earlier than the

move one by one the thick, interconnecting layers of Chinese conditioning, probe delicately into the tender central core of archaic racial archetypes—and what is left? You don't have an onion, or a Korean: only the separate, lifeless, dissected fragments of what is, after all, a living organism: more than the sum of its parts, less than the proliferation of fluent, facile generalizations that can be extrapolated from it.

The qualities that have enabled Koreans to survive, and which have become their most strongly ingrained attributes, are primarily three: Patience, flexibility, and stubbornness. To these may be added a robust, satiric, and sometimes uncouth sense of humor.

Note that Korean patience does not mean

outside influences, it seems, and were there to be developed and orchestrated by the happenstance of proximity and event.

The Descent of Tangun

So far as it now known, the Korean peninsula was first settled by wandering tribes from central and northern Asia some 30,000 years ago. These hardy nomadic people had their own language, a variant Ural-Altaic speech related to Turkish, Hungarian and Finnish. This uniquely Korean tongue, despite a later overlay of Chinese ideographic writing and vocabulary, plus some elements shared with Japanese syntax, has remained an important factor contributing to national unity, expecially after the belated invention of an efficient phonetic alphabet, called *han'gŭl*, in the 15th Century.

The early Koreans devised a national foundation myth in which a son of heaven descended to the peninsula and mated with a bear-woman, who represented the sturdy, independent totem-animal of the tribe, producing as progeny the semi-divine ancestor named Tan'gun.

As population increased during the Bronze and Iron ages, and the people settled into sedentary occupations such as farming and fishing, their social organization developed from tribal to clan leve. Patriarchal chiefs of allied clans met in council over important issues such as war, a practice that led eventually to selection of a king who was merely "first among equals." The outspokenness and self-reliance of Koreans had taken firm root by the 1st Century B.C.

It was during this period, too, that the major influx of formative influence from China began. In addition to agricultural and manufacturing skills, there came the writing system, which brought with it classical Chinese literature. The most important borrowings from the mainland, though, consisted of religio-philosophic creeds and the social system these implied, or dictated.

Here we may be on somewhat firmer ground in seeking sources for our three characteristic Korean traits. For certainly Buddhism encouraged the cultivation of patience. Likewise, the Confucian system became in practice a pragmatic philosophy, presupposing adaptability in pursuit of advantage. And Taoism suggests a stubbornness embodied in its metaphor of water as the strongest of all elements, since it gradually wears away even the hardest stones.

With the establishment in Korea of these three interdependent systems of thought, none of which ever achieved full dominance over the others, the stage was set for the unfolding of the drama of Korean history.

Buddhism and the Golden Horde

The Silla kingdom, which first unified the peninsula under one government in 668 A.D.,

Preceding pages: Schoolgirls pass on uniforms but remain partial to hats; left, the older and wiser; above, the traditional. *hanbok* is still worn for special occasions.

is generally regarded as a predominantly Buddhist monarchy but it was actually guided by firm Confucian tenets of ritual and conduct, as was the succeeding Koryo dynasty, which assumed power in 936.

During Koryo times, the Buddhist clergy did indeed attain powerful influence in government. It was during this period too that the Mongol armies of the Great Khan swept over the country in 1213. Suffering and destruction were unprecedented, and when the Korean king sued for peace he was forced to take a Mongol princess as bride, and to

declare himself a vassal of the Khan, willing to assist the Mongols in their abortive attempts to invade Japan.

As the Golden Horde weakened and receded, it was easy to blame Buddhist ascendancy in the government for Korea's national disaster. When anti-Mongol general Yi Songgye rebelled and proclaimed himself founder of a new dynasty in 1392, one of his immediate concerns was to eradicate Buddhist power at court. Confucianism, of a peculiarly orthodox and dogmatic type, was installed in power; leading to the calcification of an already rigid social system.

Korean humor among the oppressed and ignored lower classes found oulet in bawdy, grotesque folk dramas and mask dances satirizing the effete aristocrats and the worldly cynicism of Buddhist monks.

The new dynasty started off well, however, and during the reign of the fourth monarch, King Sejong the Great (1419–1450), a cultural renaissance and some attempt at administrative reforms ushered in what many Koreans like to think of as a Utopian age.

Korea's Darkest Half Century

In 1592 and 1598, though, legions of the Japanese warlord Hideyoshi launched two successive invasions of the peninsula, bent on an invasion of China from Japan via Korea. This attempt was futile and devastating to Korea for the invading armies clashed with Chinese forces on Korean soil.

tention between a declining China and an awakening Japan, with Russia and the Western powers on the sidelines.

During the Russo-Japanese War of 1904–5, Japan consolidated 20 years of creeping encroachment upon Korea's sovereignty, and in 1910 the peninsula was formally annexed as part of the island empire.

The Japanese occupation attempted not merely annexation, but complete assimilation. The usurpers behaved with unparalleled greed, arrogance and brutality, not only in exploiting Korea's resources to a ruinous extent, but in trying to extirpate the very foundations of national identity: the language, customs and culture of thousands of years.

Unfortunately for their plans, they were up

Less than 40 years later Korea was ravaged by another invasion, this time by Manchu forces bent on overthrowing China's Ming dynasty, to which Korea maintained a tenacious loyalty.

Stunned by this double disaster into a state of near traumatic shock, Korea withdrew from all outside contacts, assuming the role of Hermit Kingdom for over two and a half centuries. Divisive feuds festered among political factions, while idealistic reformers found themselves stymied by isolation and lack of practical knowledge.

A vital new trend toward modernization and reform at the end of the 19th Century achieved too little too late to prevent Korea from becoming a helpless pawn in the con-

against on elder, tougher, more tenacious race than their own—a people armed with the ancient weapons of patience adaptability and stubbornness.

The long-dormant nationalism of Korea's intelligentsia, awakening from centuries of apathy and self-destructive bickering, arose to defy, deceive and destroy the oppressors, in ways ranging from assassination and guerrilla warfare to non-violent demonstrations and passive sabotage. The struggle was long and bitter, since the organized police and military forces marshalled by Japan were unbeatable so close to their home islands.

When Tokyo finally surrendered to the Western allies in 1945 after defeat in the Pacific War, Korea regained her independence, only to be partitioned by outside interference, and five years later endured a civil war that proved far more cataclysmic than any earlier invasion.

Koreans still find it difficult to speak of the Japanese annexation with any degree of equanimity and they shudder at the suggestion that they resemble their island neighbors. The Japanese did influence Korea in many ways—they stepped into a vacuum in social structure, political organization, education and administration —but in no way Japanese culture win the respect or allegiance of Koreans.

In fact, when Christian missionaries offered an alternative to Japanese control, many Koreans quickly took up the calling. The Japanese recogized Christianity as a sub-

separation and the frustration of having no way to alter the situation saddens every member of the Korean population. Although discussions between north and south Korea are held regularly, they bear virtually no fruit and offer the people little hope. The hostilities displayed by either government and the influence borne by the powers which support each side frighten Koreans and fill them with sorrow.

In some ways, this sorrow threatens the stability of the southern portion of the peninsula—students inevitably blame the current government for maintaining the status quo—but it also serves to strengthen the society. Koreans hold onto one another like parents do their children to fend off foreign influence and maintain their traditions.

versive force and set out to eliminate it, which only further angered the Koreans who sought to think and act freely.

Never during the Occupation did the struggle against Japan cease. Korea may have gained a railroad and accepted some ideas, but she did not lose her integrity nor take shape in the hands of Japanese sculptors.

Koreans recall with great anger the period of Japanese control but emotions today run far deeper regarding the subsequent division of the Korean peninsula. The pain of family

Left, the child on his first birthday is honored with fruit, rice cakes and cash; right bus stops are common points of arrival and departure throughout a Korean's life.

National pride and resilience results, a force far stronger than armies.

A 'Soulful Spirit' Into Kibun, Nunchi'i and Mot

As Dr. Paul Crane observed some years ago in his pioneer study of this people, entitled *Korean Patterns*, "Korea today shows many faces. The old ways of thinking remain strong in the minds of most people, regardless of their education and rank . . . a superficial overlay of Western thought patterns has changed the outward appearance of many. Because of this overlay of Western dress and manners, some mistakenly as sume that the inner man has changed."

Despite the economic urgency of importing modern science and technology, Koreans still show more concern with manner than with matter. In the words of essayist Lee O-young: "In Korea, they say there is no logic . . . instead there is emotion, intuitional insight and a soulful spirit."

Korean etiquette consists of an elaborate tissue of interdependent, formalized gestures designed to produce pleasant feelings and smooth relations. This is done by ensuring maintenance of proper *kibun* (mood or aura) through adroit employment of *nunch'i* (in-

evitably encounter when a clash of cultural values occurs. The full abrasiveness of such a clash is not felt, because the foreigner is considered in the same category as classless people, or *sangnom*: "unpersons" and outcastes who are not expected to know how to behave in a proper Korean manner, and upon whom it would be pointless to waste anger or reprehension.

From the vantage point of the foreign *sangnom*, a Korean can be seen in his best light—without all the hangups he has to deal with among his compatriots—as a courteous,

tuiting another's feelings through observation), and behaving with suitable *mŏt* (style or taste).

Somewhere along the line, amidst the maze of honorifics and the anxiety to determine whether one must talk up, down, or straight-from-the-shoulder to a given individual, any idea of truth, fairness, or brass-tacks agreement becomes distinctly secondary.

Despite the differences, most Occidental visitors receive a favorable impression of Koreans as a warm, friendly, sympathetic and cheerful people, the proverbial salt of the earth—an impression that usually remains, even after the strange experiences some in-

considerate, and tenaciously loyal friend. The Korean is gregarious, fun-loving, hearty, even bibulous; and yet remains a devoted family man, a hard worker, and a solid citizen. He is very likely highly cultivated— taxi drivers know Beethoven symphonies, schoolboys gather tasteful wildflower bouquetrs—with great respect for learning and refinement. He is fiercely nationalistic, not shallowly patriotic, and exhibits a touching reverence for the natural beauties of his mountain-riven, storm-tormented land.

You may sometimes glimpse the other side of the coin: an intoxicated Korean becomes angry or tearful, not euphoric.

Like all human beings, Koreans crave the elusive goal of security; some assurance of a plausible future for themselves and their children. They have always had less than most, and are not really confident in the signs of change. That is why their songs are sad and their poems piercingly nostalgic; it is why they try so hard to be happy, to seize the fleeting moment before it is past.

Koreans have been called the Irish of the Orient, yet the burden of their history has been longer and heavier even than that of the Irish. In the raw power of their emotional drives as well as in the calm of their patient ties with one another, and the link that binds them most firmly into the family of man.

This human family may be indissolubly united, but each link in the chain represents a

If a traveler strolls through a farming village, he may see a string of dried red peppers hung across the gateway in the stone or mud-brick wall that still proclaims each Korean's home his castle. Rather than an odd way of curing condiments, this sight proclaims the birth of a boy baby a week or less before.

Rather than simply a means of proclaiming good news (the symbolism is quite obvious; girls are announced by string of charcoal and pine, the significance of which is less apparent), the decorative peppers had a practical message to convey: a taboo on visitors. It was traditionally believed that during the first week—until the mother's lactation begins, as gynaecologists point out—the newborn child was especially vulnerable, and this would

unique, idiosyncratic national entity, with its own customs created or adapted to special circumstances. And in these differences reside the main points of interest for the traveler.

In Korea, the hallmark of nationality has for a long time probably been symbolized by family ritual. The ancient Chinese called their Korean neighbors "the ceremonious people of the east," admitting thereby that the Koreans had outdone the Sage's own people in adherence to Confucian formalities.

Left, respectful progeny gather 'round at a *hwangap* 60th birthday party in 1933. Above left, Korean bus driver; right, a Korean couple taking to the hills.

include susceptibility to bad luck or evil spirits attached, known or not, to accidental visitors.

Also during this week it was practically a ritual for the mother to consume quantities of *miyŏk-kuk* or seaweed soup, like it or not, as a restorative.

The first birthday is celebrated with a special rice cake called *susokttŏk* which is flavored with mugwort.

Marriage used to occur only after the ministrations of a matchmaker who blended astrology with canny pop psychology and sociology. Nowadays the dating game is played among the young, with rather stricter rules perhaps than in the West. Traditionally, marriage occured quite young. A girl's family sent her bedding and trousseau chest to the boy's home and the boy's family reciprocated with gifts.

On the nuptial day the bride was carried in a palanquin to the groom's house and the couple—often meeting for the first time—shared a cup of rice wine to pledge their troth.

This ritual is now seen only in staged form at folk village shows, for the ubiquitous custom of the "wedding hall" (*yesik-chang*) pervades town and country.

These marriage factories, often huge buildings with dozens of weddings going on simultaneously in various-sized chambers, provide everything from flowers to Western-style music. Crowds of friend and relatives gather in pew-like seats, with no compulsion to retain order or quiet; and children frequently scamper and shout up the aisles. The only trace of the old days remaining is the family-only room at the back where timehonored bows are performed and wine shared. The public part of the ceremony is the bridal procession, a short homily by a family and the indispensable group photography.

Government austerity regulations now forbid printed invitations as an incitement to the kind of ostenation that used to bankrupt families with numerous children to marry off, especially since it was customary to hold a reception for all guests at a nearby restaurant after the wedding. But guests still bring gifts, usually cash in white envelopes.

After marriage the birth cycle was reasonably expected to resume and keep the family busy with rituals. No further scheduled event was indicated until the 60th birthday, or *hwan'gap*, one of the most important events in any Korean's life.

The 60th birthday is celebrated with all possible pomp and ceremony. The elder sits virtually enthroned on cushions, receiving the kowtows of children and grandchildren. Behind him are low tables piled high with fruit, rice cakes, cookies, candies and other goodies set out among brass candelabra.

After the ceremony comes a feast with drinking, music, and dancing for all, including the guest of honor, to the endurance of the last one to give in.

Traditional funeral customs called for the coffined body to be placed in the house where ritual wailing went on by servants, shirt-tail relations, or paid mourners, while the family provided a convivial party resembling an Irish wake. On the third day a procession accompanied the coffin on a bier borne by laborers, fueled with frequent stops for rice wine, to the grave site, preceded by the wooden tablet (or pennant) lettered in

Chinese with the name of the deceased, which would later be enshrined in the house.

The grave would probably be located on a scenic hillside deemed propitious by the fortune teller or geomancer whose business was to select auspicious places to build or do important things. Burial would be above ground in a domed mound later planted with sod and perhaps marked by a stone stele carved with the name of the deceased.

Though such old-fashioned funerals may still be encountered in the countryside (but should not be photographed by strangers), obviously they are impractical in big cities, where the choice is cremation for the poor, burial in a crowded suburban cemetery, or a long bus ride for a funeral at a clan graveyard in a rural district.

Though the funeral completes the life cycle, it does not end the cyclical pattern of Korean family ritual, for twice a year—on the *ch'usŏk* autumn harvest holiday and in spring on *hansik* (or cold food) day, now coincidental with Arbor Day—the family members gather at the grave site from far and near, set up tables covered with fruits and rice cakes that are eaten later, and perform ceremonial bows. A cup of rice wine is ritually poured over the grave, and the rest goes to wash down the feast.

Taming The World

Although modern-day Koreans continue to practice the ceremonies of the past to show ancestral respect, they are no longer quite so superstitious about the reminisce about those forebearers whom they can recall to mind and to enjoy a few hours with their extended family. Many young people are now leaving the parental home after marriage so the traditional days of gathering are less frequent.

The streets of Seoul in this day and age look much like the streets of any international city where people wear business clothes and walk at a clip. Upon first meeting a Korean, there seems to be little mystery to his character and little contrast to the Western style. It is only after one learns to know the Korean better that his culture gradually shows through in details of behavior and thought and he will never become inapproachable. Koreans are out to tame the world and they have adapted to fit the 20th Century without letting go their heritage. It takes time to know Korea and her people; to recognize and appreciate what history took 5,000 years to create.

Right, a *harabŏji* grandfather in black horsehair hat.

PLACES

Let's take a stone for a pillow, fall into a doze.
Only at the whoop of a crane will we wake
With the lucid moon mirrored in the blue.
Above all, I endorse a calm and simple life . . .
Thus will I live, and live ten thousand years.
 —*from* The Country Life, *by*
 Cha'a Ch'on-no (1556–1615)

To see Korea, whether through a camera lens or in person, is to want to touch her. She's tough, fiery and independent—yes—but she's also gentle and warm, rich in colors and textures which flit and freeze in her golden light like luminescent butterflies a-dance over cliffs of granite.

Like other such places, Korea has to be discovered while one travels on improbable and serendipitous courses. Except for your arrival and initial days in Seoul, the magnetic center of this land between the Pacific, Russian Siberia and Chinese Manchuria, all other travels in Korea are the result of considered and curious decisions. With that pure traveling spirit in mind, move along and explore the charming "back streets" of Korean culture. Join ancient travelers in a search for early plum blossoms in the snow. Wink at a thousand-year-old Mirŭk-bul "Buddha of the Future". Rest up and drink sweet rice wine in a wayside tavern, then, in outrageous finale, marvel at the Yangju mask dancer who looks for all the world like a red beetle recently emerged from a phosphorescent cave.

The formal provinces of modern Korea, like the constantly shifting powers and borders of the ancient kingdoms of Chosŏn, defy traveling logic. They are serpentining units of space and time which appear merely as flashing roadsigns on highway blurs. Fly on—like Chollima, the legendary winged horse— past Kyŏnggi-do, Kangwŏn-do, and the north and south sectors of Ch'ungch'ŏng-do, Kyŏngsang-do and Chŏlla-do. Explore instead the gnarled pines, rocky headlands, combed burial mounds and sculpted treasures that frame this ancient Asian queen "of ten thousand peaks, ten thousand islands, and ten thousand waterfalls."

But most important, pause now and then for long looks—and feelings—of people, places and things which are Korean, and, as such, unexpected, but visible, and touchable.

61

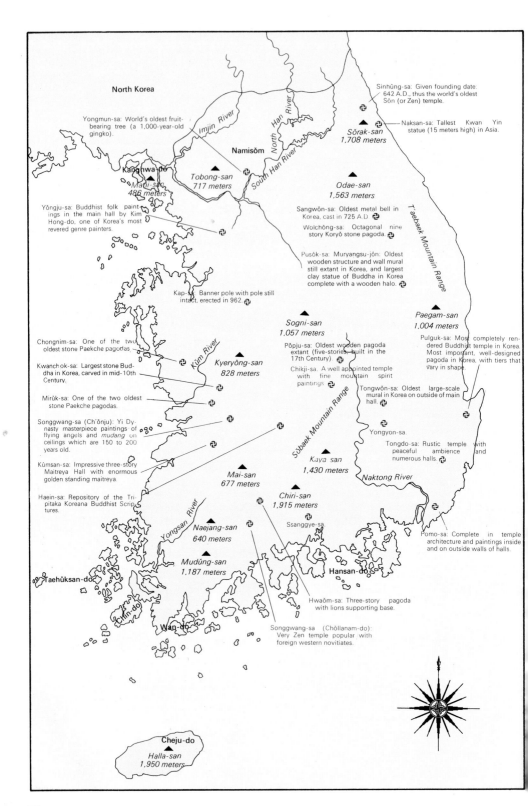

North Korea

Yongmun-sa: World's oldest fruit-bearing tree (a 1,000-year-old gingko).

Sinhŭng-sa: Given founding date: 642 A.D., thus the world's oldest Sŏn (or Zen) temple.

Naksan-sa: Tallest Kwan Yin statue (15 meters high) in Asia.

Imjin River

North Han River

Namisŏm

Sŏrak-san
1,708 meters

Kanghwa-do

Mani-san
486 meters

Tobong-san
717 meters

South Han River

Odae-san
1,563 meters

Yŏngju-sa: Buddhist folk paintings in the main hall by Kim Hong-do, one of Korea's most revered genre painters.

Sangwŏn-sa: Oldest metal bell in Korea, cast in 725 A.D.

Wolchŏng-sa: Octagonal nine story Koryŏ stone pagoda.

Pusŏk-sa: Muryangsu-jŏn: Oldest wooden structure and wall mural still extant in Korea, and largest clay statue of Buddha in Korea complete with a wooden halo.

Taebaek Mountain Range

Kap-sa: Banner pole with pole still intact, erected in 962.

Paegam-san
1,004 meters

Sogni-san
1,057 meters

Chongnim-sa: One of the two oldest stone Paekche pagodas.

Pŏpju-sa: Oldest wooden pagoda extant (five-stories built in the 17th Century).

Pulguk-sa: Most completely rendered Buddhist temple in Korea. Most important, well-designed pagoda in Korea, with tiers that vary in shape.

Kwanch'ok-sa: Largest stone Buddha in Korea, carved in mid-10th Century.

Kŭm River

Kyeryŏng-san
828 meters

Chikji-sa: A well appointed temple with fine mountain spirit paintings.

Tongwŏn-sa: Oldest large-scale mural in Korea on outside of main hall.

Mirŭk-sa: One of the two oldest stone Paekche pagodas.

Songgwang-sa (Ch'ŏnju): Yi Dynasty masterpiece paintings of flying angels and *mudang* on ceilings which are 150 to 200 years old.

Yongyon-sa.

Sŏbaek Mountain Range

Tongdo-sa: Rustic temple with peaceful ambience and numerous halls.

Kŭmsan-sa: Impressive three-story Maitreya Hall with enormous golden standing maitreya.

Kaya-san
1,430 meters

Naktong River

Haein-sa: Repository of the Tripitaka Koreana Buddhist Scriptures.

Yongsan River

Mai-san
677 meters

Chiri-san
1,915 meters

Ssanggye-sa.

Naejang-san
640 meters

Pomo-sa: Complete in temple architecture and paintings inside and on outside walls of halls.

Mudŭng-san
1,187 meters

Hansan-do

Taehŭksan-do

Chin-do

Hwaŏm-sa: Three-story pagoda with lions supporting base.

Wan-do

Songgwang-sa (Chŏllanam-do): Very Zen temple popular with foreign western novitiates.

Cheju-do

Halla-san
1,950 meters

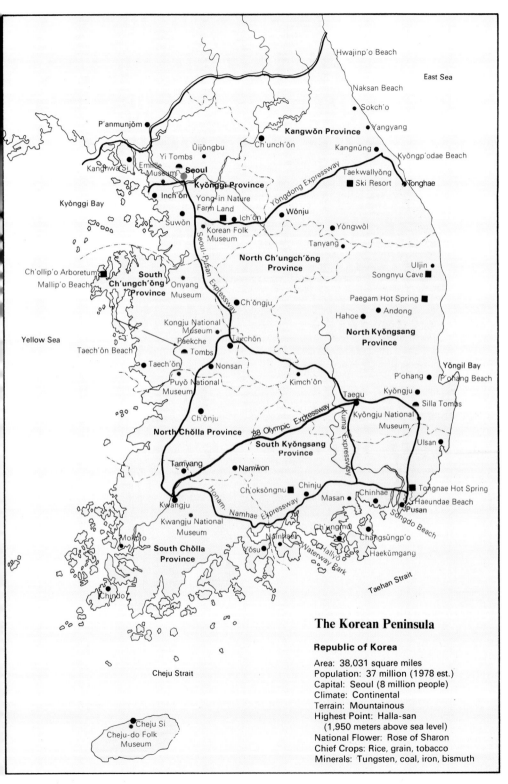

The Korean Peninsula

Republic of Korea

Area: 38,031 square miles
Population: 37 million (1978 est.)
Capital: Seoul (8 million people)
Climate: Continental
Terrain: Mountainous
Highest Point: Halla-san
   (1,950 meters above sea level)
National Flower: Rose of Sharon
Chief Crops: Rice, grain, tobacco
Minerals: Tungsten, coal, iron, bismuth

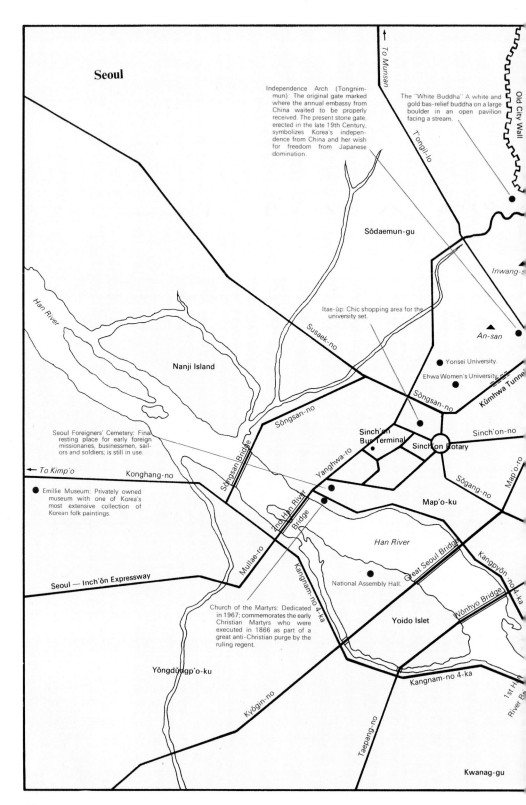

Seoul

Independence Arch (Tongnim-mun): The original gate marked where the annual embassy from China waited to be properly received. The present stone gate, erected in the late 19th Century, symbolizes Korea's independence from China and her wish for freedom from Japanese domination.

The "White Buddha" A white and gold bas-relief buddha on a large boulder in an open pavilion facing a stream.

To Munsan

Old City Wall

Tongil-lo

Sŏdaemun-gu

Inwang-s

Han River

Susaek-no

Itae-ŭp: Chic shopping area for the university set.

An-san

Nanji Island

Yonsei University.

Ehwa Women's University.

Kŭmhwa Tunnel

Sŏngsan-no

Sŏngsan-no

Sinch'ŏn
Bus Terminal

Sinch'on-no

Seoul Foreigners' Cemetery: Final resting place for early foreign missionaries, businessmen, sailors and soldiers; is still in use.

Sŏngsan Bridge

Yanghwa-ro

Sinch'on Rotary

Mapo-ro

To Kimp'o

Konghang-no

Sŏgang-no

Emillie Museum: Privately owned museum with one of Korea's most extensive collection of Korean folk paintings.

2nd Han River
Bridge

Map'o-ku

Han River

Great Seoul Bridge

Kangpyŏn-no4-ka

Mullae-ro

Kangnam-no 4-ka

National Assembly Hall.

Seoul — Inch'ŏn Expressway

Wŏnhyo Bridge

Mapo-ro

Church of the Martyrs: Dedicated in 1967; commemorates the early Christian Martyrs who were executed in 1866 as part of a great anti-Christian purge by the ruling regent.

Yoido Islet

Yŏngdŭngp'o-ku

1st Ha
River Br

Kyŏgin-no

Kangnam-no 4-ka

Taepang-no

Kwanag-gu

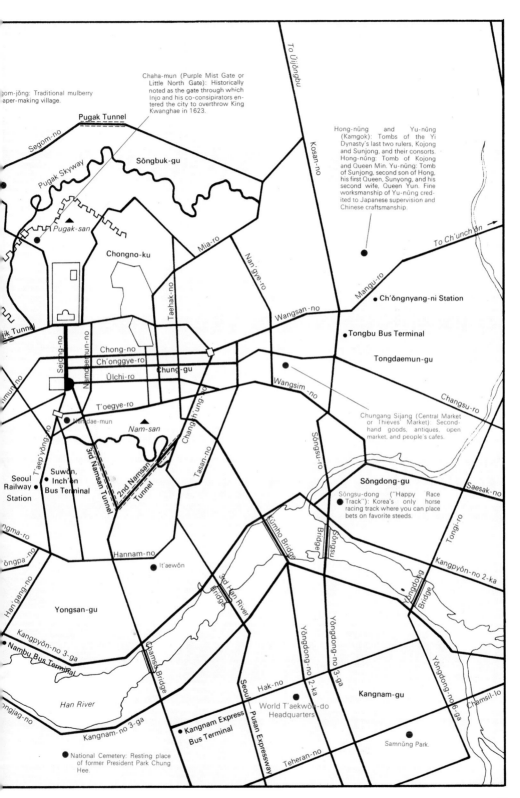

...gom-jŏng: Traditional mulberry
...aper-making village.

Chaha-mun (Purple Mist Gate or
Little North Gate): Historically
noted as the gate through which
Injo and his co-consipirators en-
tered the city to overthrow King
Kwanghae in 1623.

Pugak Tunnel

Segom-no

Pugak Skyway

Sŏngbuk-gu

Pugak-san

Chongno-ku

...ik Tunnel

Mia-ro

Nan'gye-ro

Taehak-no

Hong-nŭng and Yu-nŭng
(Kamgok): Tombs of the Yi
Dynasty's last two rulers, Kojong
and Sunjong, and their consorts.
Hong-nŭng: Tomb of Kojong
and Queen Min. Yu-nŭng: Tomb
of Sunjong, second son of Hong,
his first Queen, Sunyong, and his
second wife, Queen Yun. Fine
workmanship of Yu-nŭng credited to Japanese supervision and
Chinese craftsmanship.

Kosan-no

To Uijŏngbu

To Ch'unch'ŏn

Mangu-ro

Wangsan-no

Ch'ŏngnyang-ni Station

Tongbu Bus Terminal

Tongdaemun-gu

Changsu-ro

Sejong-no

Namdaemun-no

Chong-no

Ch'onggye-ro

Chung-gu

Ülchi-ro

T'oegye-ro

Changhŭng-no

Wangsim-no

Chungang Sijang (Central Market
or Thieves' Market): Second-
hand goods, antiques, open
market, and people's cafes.

Namdae-mun

Nam-san

Tasan-no

Sŏngsu-ro

Sŏngdong-gu

Saesak-no

Seoul
Railway
Station

Suwŏn,
Inch'ŏn
Bus Terminal

2nd Namsan Tunnel

3rd Namsan Tunnel

T'aep'yŏng-no

Sŏngsu-dong ("Happy Race
Track"): Korea's only horse
racing track where you can place
bets on favorite steeds.

Kŭmho Bridge

Sŏngsu Bridge

Tongi-ro

Kangpyŏn-no 2-ka

...ngma-ro

...öngpa-no

Hannam-no

It'aewŏn

Han'gang-no

Yongsan-gu

3rd Han River Bridge

Yŏngdong Bridge

Kangpyŏn-no 3-ga

Nambu Bus Terminal

Chamsu Bridge

Yŏngdong-no 2-ka

Yŏngdong-no 3-ga

Yŏngdong-no 6-ga

Chamsil-lo

...ongjag-no

Han River

Kangnam-no 3-ga

Hak-no

Seoul Pusan Expressway

World T'aekwŏn-do
Headquarters

Kangnam-gu

Samnŭng Park.

Kangnam Express
Bus Terminal

National Cemetery: Resting place
of former President Park Chung
Hee.

Teheran-no

67

SOUL OF SEOUL

⭕ **Points of Interest**

1 Seoul Railroad Station
2 Namdae-mun (The Great South Gate): National Treasure No. 1. One of nine gates that once led into the old city. Erected in 1396 but rebuilt twice, last time in 1962.
3 Tŏksu Palace: First built in the middle of the 15th Century. Last residence of King Kojong who died here in 1919.
4 King Sejong Statue: 15th century king who in 1446 initiated a distinctively Korean writing system called *han'gŭl*.
5 National Museum of Modern Art: Located on Tŏksu Palace grounds. Displays contemprary Korean artwork.
6 City Hall
7 Seoul City Tourist Information Service Center
8 Kojong Memorial: On the northeast corner of Kwanghwa-mun intersection; this small pavilion houses a tablet honoring King Kojong and his consort, Queen Min.
9 Yi Sun-sin Statue: Korea's favorite admiral who rose up against both domestic back-stabbing politics and Japanese attacks during the Hideyoshi invasions of the 1590s.
10 Sejong Cultural Center: Opened in 1978; this new theater for cultural events boasts a 99-rank organ.
11 Kwanghwa-mun: Originally situated at the present-day Kwanghwa-mun intersection; the gate was moved to its present position in front of the Capitol in 1968.
12 Capitol Building: Built during the Japanese Occupation in 1926 as the Japanese Government-General Building. Served as administrative headquarters for the U.S. Military Government after World War II.
13 Kyŏngbok Palace: First built in 1394 as the Seat of government for the founder of the Yi Dynasty, Yi T'aejo. Now a public park, the grounds include old Palace buildings, ponds, pavilions, the National Museum, and the National Folk Museum.
14 National Museum: Opened in 1972. Houses a superb collection of Korean traditional arts: Paekche and Silla pottery, Buddhist images, Koryŏ and Yi porcelain, Yi paintings, and calligraphy.
15 National Folk Museum: Displays traditional crafts and articles of everyday use in old Korea.
16 Ch'ŏngwa-dae (Blue Tile House): Official home of Korea's presidents.
17 Samch'ŏng Park: Panoramic view of the city from a wooded park.
18 French Cultural Center: Offers French film classics, videotapes and a changing art gallery.
19 The Space Center and Theater: An architectural curiosity and art gallery, youthful gathering center, and theater for music, dance and drama.
20 Ch'angdŏk Palace: Originally built in 1405; the best preserved of the Yi Dynasty palaces. Its 100 acres include a throne room, living quarters (Naksŏn-jae, where members of the royal family still live), and Piwŏn (the Secret Garden).
21 Piwŏn: Originally a private pleasure garden of the royal family, now a public park. Pathways meander past pavilions, ponds, streams, flowering shrubs, and trees.

22 Ch'anggyŏng Palace (Palace of Glorious Blessings): A popular place for families and couples — housing a botanical garden — newly restored.

23 National Science Museum
24 Sunggyŭn'gwan (Confucian Shrine and University): Main shrine to the Great Sage where ceremonies in his honor are held in the spring and fall. Oldest university campus in Korea, established in 1394. Adorned with 500-year-old gingko trees that turn a fiery red in the fall.
25 Tongdae-mun (The Great East Gate): One of the nine gates in the old city wall, rebuilt last in 1869.
26 Tong-myo (East Shrine): Quarter of a mile past Tongdae-mun. Dates to 1600 and is dedicated to Kwan-u, the God of War. Contains many interesting paintings and statues of Kwan-u and his soldiers.

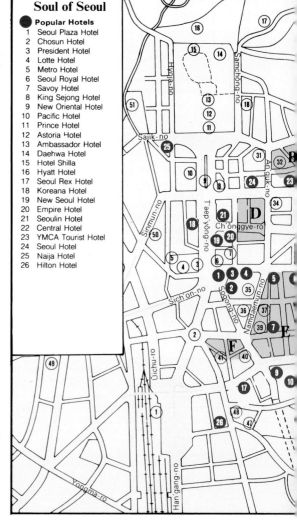

Soul of Seoul

⚫ **Popular Hotels**
1 Seoul Plaza Hotel
2 Chosun Hotel
3 President Hotel
4 Lotte Hotel
5 Metro Hotel
6 Seoul Royal Hotel
7 Savoy Hotel
8 King Sejong Hotel
9 New Oriental Hotel
10 Pacific Hotel
11 Prince Hotel
12 Astoria Hotel
13 Ambassador Hotel
14 Daehwa Hotel
15 Hotel Shilla
16 Hyatt Hotel
17 Seoul Rex Hotel
18 Koreana Hotel
19 New Seoul Hotel
20 Empire Hotel
21 Seoulin Hotel
22 Central Hotel
23 YMCA Tourist Hotel
24 Seoul Hotel
25 Naija Hotel
26 Hilton Hotel

27 Seoul Stadium

28 Baseball Field

29 Chong-myo (Royal Ancestral Shrine): Now open to the public. Houses the ancestral tablets of the 27 Yi kings and their queens. Displays of food offerings and traditional court music performed in annual ceremonies honoring them.

30 The geographical center of the old walled city.

31 Chogye-sa: Main Buddhist temple in Seoul and headquarters of the official Chogye sect in Korea.

32 Pagoda Park: On Chong-no 3-ka, the former site of a Buddhist temple, now a public park where an elaborate pagoda dating from 1466 and a monument and statue commemorating the Independence Movement in 1919 stand. A favorite lounging place for senior citizens.

33 Chong-no Bell: Not the original. The bell that hangs now in Posin-gak (Pavilion of Widespread News) at the intersection of Chong-no and Namdaemun-no was cast in 1468. One of the largest bells in the world: 2.38 meters high, 6.49 meters in circumference.

35 "Temple of Heaven": From 1897-1910 ceremonies honoring the gods of earth and harvest (formerly held at what is now Sajik Park) were observed here by King Kojong. Now only a three-tiered pavilion standing between the Chosun and Lotte Hotels remains.

36 Midop'a Department Store

37 Cosmos Department Store

38 Myŏng-dong Roman Catholic Cathedral: Built in the 1890s.

39 Central Post Office

40 Sinsegye Department Store

41 Athletic Gear Shops (Across from Seoul Tokyu Hotel)

42 Korea House: Built in 1957, renovated in 1979-80. Traditional music and dance presented to visitors. Korean food served in restaurant overlooking an oriental garden.

43 Changch'ŭng Gymnasium: Opened in 1963. National and international basketball, boxing, volleyball, wrestling, etc held here throughout the year.

44 National Theater and National Classical Music School: Where Korea's Living National Treasures in drama, music and dance practice and teach. Confucian Court instruments kept here. Performances held occasionally.

45 Namsan Tower: Command post and radio station closed to the public.

46 P algakch'ŏng: Pavilion on Namsan which Syngman Rhee had built. His statue there was toppled after his rule as president.

47 Namsan Park: Wooded park with a cable car up to its summit. This 250 meter high mountain is in the heart of Seoul.

48 Open Music Hall: Concerts occasionally held here.

49 Ahyŏn-dong: Numerous antique shops along this main street.

50 Old Russian Legation: Built in 1890, destroyed badly in the Korean War. Served as refuge in 1896 for King Kojong after Queen Min was murdered.

51 Sajik Park: Site of 14th Century altars to the gods of earth and harvest where ceremonies were held in the spring and autumn. On the slopes of the mountain ridge (Inwang-san) behind the park is the Pavilion of the Yellow Cranes, an archery range where archers using traditional bows compete.

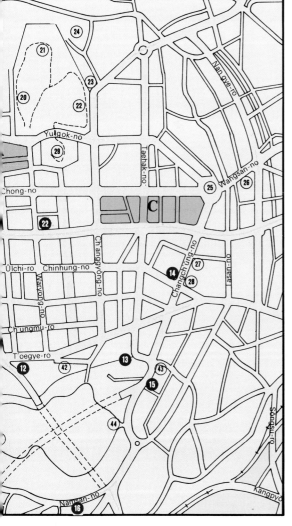

A Kisaeng Houses

B Insa-dong: Antique shops and art galleries

C Tongdae-mun Market

D Seoulin-dong and Mugyo-dong: Cabarets and makkŏlli and maekchu jip (rice wine and beer halls)

E Myŏng-dong

F Namdae-mun Market

SEOUL
'THE CAPITAL'

"If you have a horse, send it to Cheju Island; if you have a son, send him to Seoul." So an old Korean saying advises. Send a horse to Cheju Island where the grass is green and lush. Send a son to Seoul to go to school: the city swarms with thousands of students attending its twenty-odd universities and colleges. Send him to Seoul to get a job: all the head offices of any enterprise—commercial, financial, governmental—are in Seoul. Send him to Seoul for a chance at the best opportunities.

That's what Seoul is: the center of the nation, the heart of the country to which everything else is drawn. It's as if Seoul were a giant magnet attracting to itself fillings of trade and commerce, education, culture and the arts, government, politics—all the occupations of any nation. So many people, both sons and daughters, have responded to Seoul's pull that the city is now home to one quarter of the country's population. Its residents now number nearly 10 million.

If you were in downtown Seoul at 6 or 7 p.m., you would feel yourself caught up in the all too tangible and audible force field of a city at rush hour. Seoul is *the* central city and has been the capital for more than 500 years (the word *seoul* means capital), the eye, as it were, of the Korean vortex. And what better place to begin exploring such a city than at its epicenter?

Centers of the Vortex

Topographically, that center is wooded **Nam-san** (South Mountain), a 900-feet elevation that gazes across mid-town at conically shaped **Pugak-san** (North Peak Mountain). Between these peaks sprawled the old walled city. A 10-mile encircling wall made of earth and dressed stone is gone, but a few crumbling stretches on Pugak-san and Nam-san, and other restored patches that were rebuilt for tourist visibility, have survived. The original wall, however, was pierced by nine gates. Five still stand, and the two largest—**Namdaemun** (Great South Gate) and **Longdaemun** (Great East Gate)—are regal presences in the midst of the modern

Left, Seoul Tower; right, modern buildings abound in Seoul.

city's swirl. They are reminders of the capital as it was originally laid out.

Some think the center of the city is **City Hall Plaza**, the fountained square bounded on the north by **City Hall**, on the south by the **Plaza Hotel**, on the east by the entrance to **Ulchi-ro** (one of the main east-west streets), on the west by **Tŏksu Palace** (a remnant of the old dynasty that founded the city), and underground by one of the major stops of the subway line that runs through downtown Seoul. Traffic running in and out of the square from three major arteries swings round the fountain; pedestrians descend underground to cross the square through its underpasses; and, if traffic allows, you can stand in the middle of the north-south street, **T'aep'yŏng-no**, and look south to Namdae-mun and north to **Kwanghwa-mun** (Gate of Transformation by Light), the reconstructed gate in front of the 20th Century capitol building. This is City Hall Plaza—a link between the old and new.

Other centrists claim that the Kwanghwa-mun intersection is Seoul's center. This is the next crossing north of City Hall Plaza and it's dominated by a looming **statue of Yi Sun-sin**, Korea's great 16th Century naval hero. From that intersection, T'aep'yong-no runs south, **Sejong-no** north, **Sinmun-no** west, and **Chong-no** east—yes, the streets change name as they cross. Even more confusingly, the Kwanghwa-mun intersection is not directly in front of the Kwanghwa-mun gate for which it is named. That's still another long block north of here! People who believe, nevertheless, that this intersection is *the* center of the city probably think so because it is the entrance to Chong-no, the city's original main street. Yi T'aejo, founder in 1392 of the dynasty that bears his name and in 1394 of the city itself, hung a bell here, a bell that was rung at dawn and dusk to signal the official opening and closing of the city gates. Chong-no, or Bell Street, was for centuries the city's commercial street where as darkness fell vendors set up portable wheeled shops for the city dwellers to browse among.

The governmental heart of the old walled city was **Kyŏngbok Palace** (Palace of Shining Happiness); which was T'aejo's residence and seat of power, and was used by him and his successors

Racing and betting at Seoul's Majang-dong track.

until 1592 when it was burned during warfare with Japan. If you inquire more minutely, you will discover that Kyŏngbok's throneroom hall, the **Kŭnjŏng-jŏn** (Hall of Government by Restraint), rebuilt in 1867, was the very center of Taejo's governmental heart. Here the king sat to receive ministers ranged in orderly ranks before him, made judgments, and issued proclamations. The hall faces south down Sejong-no and once commanded an unobstructed view through Kwanghwa-mun to Namdaemun. This vista is now blocked by the modern Capitol building; the modern government now enjoys the vista that the old dynasty once did. A plaque of calligraphy that hangs from the gate's roof and proclaims its name is rendered in a script by Korea's late President Park Chung-hee in *han'gŭl*, the Korean alphabet. Flanking the gate are two stone *haet'ae*, mythical animals from Korean lore, which have witnessed Seoul's changes and additions ever since they were carved and placed here in the 15th Century to guard the old palace from fire.

The exact geographical center of the old city can be definitely placed, but in the name of progress it's now almost impossible to find. Just off **Insa-dong**, an area east of Kwangwha-mun known for its art galleries, art supply stores and antique dealers, is the former site of **Seoul Union Church** and its red brick rectory. This has been razed for a construction project. Immediately in front of the house stood a square granite marker enclosed by short octagonal pillars. That square of granite marked the geographical center of the old walled city. Typically enough, this particular piece of Yi dynasty history was quite ignored: neither the stone itself nor any signboard proclaimed what this spot was. This remnant of Yi history was probably carted away amid the confusion of the construction going on around it. Perhaps the city fathers will at least erect a plaque to commemorate this historic monument to a now-massive city.

Seoul Chic

Many people think Seoul's real center today is modern **Myŏng-dong**, an area of narrow alleys that starts a 10-minute walk southeast from City Hall Plaza

Fans crowd the Chamsil Stadium for a baseball game.

directly across from **Midopa Department Store**. Myŏng-dong's main thorough-fare, a one-way street, is lined on both sides by swanky shops that sell chic clothes and accessories, and it ends at the top of a low hill before **Myŏng-dong Cathedral**, Korea's grand center of Catholicism. Myŏng-dong alleyways come alive in the evening when they are crowded with after-work strollers window shopping past the fancy displays of shoes and handbags, tailor-made suits and custom-made shirts, dresses in the latest fashions, handcrafted modern jewelry, and stockings and cosmetics. But these are only the surface attractions of Myŏng-dong. Tiny upstairs and hide-away drinking houses that serve cheap liquor are already jammed with happy, noisy customers. Since Koreans always eat when they drink, many of these drinking houses display their *anju* (things you eat when you drink) in the window. Passersby are beckoned by wriggling live octopus tentacle, sizzling griddles of bean-and-onion cakes and fresh fish. A slightly more sedate crowd (perhaps they're merely richer) ducks into beerhalls for beer, peanuts and, often, a "live" entertainer, usually a popular pop singer. Indeed, Myŏng-dong can be called the emotional heart of the city, the place where the city lets its hair down to play.

Nam-san, City Hall Plaza, Kwanghwa-mun, Myŏng-dong. Perhaps it's wisest to think of Seoul as having more than one center: it's certainly a city big enough and old enough for more than one special center of interest.

Before beginning a tour of the city, however, marvel at its tenacity and adaptability. Korea's capital has literally risen from the ashes of its wartime desolation and is now rushing into the mainstream of international activity. Independent Korea has bred a people determined to improve the homeland and to gain recognition from those overseas, guarding tradition and values all the while. Seoul's noise and congestion is living proof of Korea's capability; its calm and grandeur attests to the strength of Korean culture. As you walk around the city you will feel the push of the future and the pull of the past: the essence of a soul which pumps through every artery. Indeed, Seoul is Korea's soul.

'Virtuous Longevity'

For "modern" and exploratory openers, let's start our tour of Seoul at the central and historical **Tŏksu Palace** (Palace of Virtuous Longevity), whose gate faces City Hall Plaza. Tŏksu is not the oldest of the surviving palaces—it was built as a villa toward the end of the 15th Century—but it is important for its role at the unhappy end of the Yi dynasty. King Kojŏng, who was forced to abdicate in favor of his son Sunjong in 1907, lived in retirement and died here in 1919 after having seen his country annexed by the Japanese in 1910 and his family's dynasty snuffed out after 500 years.

Among the most conspicuous structures on the palace grounds, regularly open to the public, is a **statue of Sejong**, the great 15th-Century king who commissioned scholars to develop a distinctive Korean writing system (different from the traditional Chinese characters) and officially promulgated it in 1446. There's also a royal audience hall and two startlingly European-style stone buildings with Ionic and Corinthian columns designed by an Englishman in 1909 (housing the **National Museum of Modern Art**). It's pleasant to stroll through the palace grounds—especially in the fall when its aisle of gingko trees are aflame in gold.

When school's in and the weather is good, lines of schoolchildren stream through the gate of nearby Kyŏngbok Palace. They scatter around the grounds where, paint brush and pallet in hand, canvas on easel, they work intently to capture the color of the flowers and leaves, and the charm of interior vistas once seen only by royalty and their attendants. A favorite subject is **Kyŏnghoeru** (Hall of Happy Meetings), a two-story banquet hall that was built in 1412, burned in 1592, and rebuilt in 1867 when the ruling regent had the entire palace renovated for his son, King Kojŏng. This hall extends over one end of a spacious square pond originally meant to be filled with lotus. Unfortunately, this is no longer so, but, in modern consolation, swans glide over the water and, in winter, skaters glide over the pond's frozen surface. But in July, from the shallow waters of another pond surrounding the much smaller but more

Below, a family portrait at Tŏksu Palace; right, the components of a Yi dynasty structure.

74

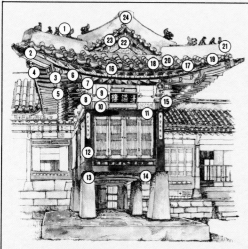

Chagyŏng Hall, Kyŏngbok Palace, Seoul

1 Clay *chapsang* animal "guardians" or "ridge beasts".

2 A false hip rafter which gives an upward curve to the eaves.

3 A true hip rafter.

4 False rafters accentuate roof curves.

5 True rafters.

6 "Jack rafters" rise to the hip rafter.

7 Girders, also called header plates or purlins, support the rafters.

8 The echindus, a square, round, or polygonal moulding that caps a post or column.

9 An architrave beam.

10 Tie-beams, or header beams, connect and bind post tops.

11 The lintel.

12 Post or column, usually of wood

13 A "one bay"

14 Raised floor to help provide air circulation.

15 Eave bracketting system in which the girder is supported by a cantilevered truss.

16 Clay and straw mortar covering wood or bamboo subsurfacing supported by the rafters.

17 Flat antefix tiles.

18 Flat tiles.

19 Round antefix tiles.

20 Round tiles covering seams between flat tile rows.

21 Decorative vertical tiles called finial plates.

22 The gablet.

23 False rafters.

24 The main gablet ridge, which accentuates this gambrel or half-hipped Korean roof.

charming **Hyangwon pavilion** in the northeast corner of the palace grounds, giant pink Indonesian lotus do rise on long quivering stems above dinner-plate-sized leaves.

The **National Museum**, opened in 1972, dominates a corner of Kyŏngbok Palace's grounds. The museum—rich in Paekche tiles, Silla pottery, gilt Buddhas, Koryŏ celadons, Yi calligraphy and paintings—showcases a panorama of Korean culture. At the rear of the palace grounds stands a **Folk Museum** which houses artifacts of everyday use and dioramas showing how they were used. Of particular interest is a modest display of metal movable type invented and used in Korea before 1234, two hundred years before Johann Gutenberg, the much-touted European "inventor" of printing from movable type.

Arabesque Walls
'Round a Secret Garden

About a block east of Kyŏngbok lies **Ch'angdŏk Palace** (Palace of Illustrious Virtue), built in 1405 as a detached palace, burned in 1592, rebuilt in 1611 and used since then as the official residence of various Yi kings, including Sunjong, the last one, until his death in 1926. The best preserved of Seoul's palaces, Ch'angdŏk has a throneroom hall surrounded by long drafty corridors leading past reception rooms furnished with heavy upholstered European chairs and sofas. In private living quarters, the furnishings are those of traditional Korea: low, slatted beds, lacquered chests and tables.

Naksŏn-jae, a small complex of buildings within Ch'angdŏk's grounds, is still the residence of descendants of the royal family: Ensconced there are an elderly aunt of Sunjong; the wife of the last crown prince, Sunjong's son (who never ruled); her son; and his wife. In the formal back gardens of Naksŏn-jae, a series of stair-stepped granite-faced tiers planted with azaleas, it is possible to feel totally isolated from the sounds of modern Seoul. From within a small raised octagonal pavilion at the top of this garden, you can imagine the royal family sitting here, gazing out over the curved roofs of the palace buildings and the arabesque walls encircling them. Under leafy tree-tops that stretch towards

National Museum at Kyŏngbok Palace.

Nam-san in the distance, you can hear court whispers and imagine the turbulence and intrigues of Korea's late Yi dynasty.

Behind Ch'angdŏk lies the extensive acreage of **Piwŏn**, the Secret Garden, so called because it was formerly a private park for the royal family. In wooded and hilly terrain, footpaths meander past ponds and pavilions and over small bridges. The most picturesque of these sites is **Pando-ji** (Peninsula Pond) shaped like the outline of the Korean peninsula. From its shore extending out over the water stands a small, exquisite fan-shaped pavilion from which Injo, the 16th king, could cast a line for a bit of quiet fishing. Piwŏn and portions of Ch'angdok Palace may be visited by joining one of several daily guided tours at the Piwŏn entrance. Naksŏn-jae is open to the public twice a year for royal ceremonies.

East one block from Ch'angdŏk lies **Ch'anggyŏngwon**, another ancient palace grounds now open to the public. Visitors may wander this park on their own and there is a lot of wandering to do—this is the largest public park within Seoul. Young couples seek out nooks in which to proceed with their courtship, families bring picnics, and elderly folk in traditional dress or new-fangled hiking gear take long, silent strolls. Across the street from Ch'anggŏngwon, lies **Ch'ongmyo**, the Royal Ancestral Shrine. This walled complex includes two long pillared buildings housing, according to Confucian requirement, ancestral tablets listing the names and accomplishments of the 27 Yi kings and their queens. Once a secluded spot, Chongmyo is now open to the public and is a favorite strolling ground for young couples. Once a year on the first Sunday in May, a traditional ceremony honoring the spirits of the kings and queens is held here. Ancient court music, not otherwise heard, rings eerily over flagstones and beyond cedar pillars as Confucian celebrants pay appropriate respects and offer proper foods and wine to each of the enshrined spirits in a ritual lasting six hours.

Honoring the Sage

The similar Sŏkchŏn ceremony is held biennially at the **Sŏnggyun'gwan** shrine located on the grounds of **Songgyun'g-**

The National Assembly building on Yoido in Seoul.

wan University to the northeast of Piwon. The Sŏkchŏn honors the spirit of Kongja, the man whose principles formed the basis of government and code of behavior in Yi Korea, Kongja, the Great Sage Confucius, is thus apostrophized in ritual prayer:

Great art Thou, O perfect Sage! Thy virtue is full, Thy doctrine complete. Among mortal men, there has not been Thine equal. All kings honor thee. Reverentially have the sacrificial vessels been set out. Full of awe we sound the drums and bells. I, the Emperor, offer a sacrifice to the Philosopher Confucius, the Ancient Teacher, the Perfect Sage. . . .

The music here is similar to that for the Chongmyo ceremony: shrill flutes, melodious stone chimes, bronze bells, heavy thumping drums and the rattle and clack of wooden clappers. Students from the National Classical Music Institute perform that accompanies this slow music. For this sacred occasion, tables of offerings representing the fruit of the land—flowers, rice, apples and pears, cups of rice wine, even an entire pig's head—are set up inside the shrine to honor the Sage and his most eminent disciples, both Korean and Chinese.

The celebrants here and at Chongmyo wear robes and insignia representing various court positions and ranks. The somewhat misogynist Sage, however, would be taken aback at a modern addition: yound women, robed in blue, assist at the formerly all-male ceremony! He would probably approve more readily of the uniformed ROTC students from the university who help keep the audience in proper order.

Sŏnggyun'gwan University is a modern transformation of the old Sŏnggyun'gwan, a national institute sponsored and supported by the Yi Court where Korea's best scholars pursued the Confucian Classics and instructed those who aspired to pass government examinations in order to receive official appointments. Students selected for enrollment here had already passed three preliminary examinations on the *Analects of Confucius,* the *Book of Mencius,* and the *Record of Rituals,* all from Chinese literature. Once enrolled, students were expected to master the *I ching* (Book of Changes), *Shih ching* (Book of Poetry), *Shu ching* (Book of

Chogye-sa devotees, Buddha's birthday.

History) and *Ch'un ch'iu* (Spring and Autumn Annals), all dating from the China of the 10th to the 2nd Century B.C., as well as numerous commentaries, expositions and the like made by scholars since then. However, these students were forbidden to study any Buddhist or Taoist works, heresies to the Confucian mind. The great state examination, held before the king himself, was made up of three parts—the composition of poetry, an exposition of the *Classics* and the writing of essays. Also, each student was compelled to follow a strict code of behavior. According to the *Hangnyŏng*, or rules governing students' lives, "Any student guilty of violating human obligations (prince and minister, father and son, husband and wife, brothers or friends), of faulty deportment, or of damaging his body or his reputation, will be denounced, with drumbeats, by the other students. Extreme cases may be reported to the Ministry of Rites and barred from academic circles for life." After all, the aim of the school was—as its name says—*sŏng*, "to perfect human nature," and *kyun*, "to build a good society." This is the dual purpose of a good Confucian education.

Candlelit lanterns, Chogye-sa.

Buddhism's Hub

The Confucian Yi court tried hard to extinguish the spirit of the Buddha throughout the country but it failed miserably. Buddhist temples abound. City temples, though, are hardly places of quiet retreat. **Chogye-sa,** founded in 1910 and the headquarters of the official sect of Buddhism in Korea, is right downtown off **An'guk-dong-no.** As the center of Buddhism in the country, it hums with activity, and on the occasion of Buddha's birthday, on the eighth day of the fourth lunar month, it becomes the hub—and hubbub—of Buddhist festivities in Korea.

On this day, in common with all Buddhist temples in the country, the courtyard in front of Chogye-sa's main hall is strung with parallel strands of wires on support poles. As dusk falls, worshipers come to the temple to buy a paper lantern and candle. The names of all the members of the worshiper's family are written on a tag dangling from the bottom of the lantern. The worshiper fixes the candle into the lantern, lights it, hangs the lantern on one of the wires,

and bows and murmurs a prayer when she's finished. Row after row of flickering candle flames illuminate the courtyard as darkness deepens. If in some stray gust of wind a lantern catches fire and burns, everyone stands aghast and mute at this stroke of ill fortune—an evil omen for the year to come. Meanwhile, within the main hall, devotees light incense on the altar before the Buddha's golden image, bow to the floor three times in reverence, and offer prayers. Everywhere the temple is thick with people. Anyone may buy and hang a lantern; so many non-Buddhist foreign residents do. Some even march in a long lantern parade that winds through downtown Seoul—an elaborate affair with floats and bands. It's a good way to try to ensure good luck for a year.

Besides these and other surviving pockets of history connected to the old dynasty, other sections of the city are interesting for more specialized reasons.

Foreigners, the Oeguk Saram

When the first Western foreigners appeared in significant numbers in Korea, they were not allowed to live within the city walls. In the 1880s, however, King Kojong permitted foreign missionaries, traders and legations to buy land in **Chŏng-dong** just inside the western wall and behind and to the north of Tŏksu Palace. Many of the structures they built still stand and are still in use: the **Chŏng Dong Methodist Church, Ewha Girls' High School, Paejae Boys' School.** All that remains of the **Russian Legation** is the ruins of a white tower near the present MBC-TV building, but the residence of the American ambassador, the **British Embassy** and an adjoining **Anglican Cathedral** are still in active use. The Cathedral is a graceful Italianate building, its quare belfry visible from City Hall Plaza over the intervening walls. The British Embassy, a red brick structure dating from 1890, "breathes," according to an Anglican bishop once a local resident, "a nostalgia for the days when Pax Britannica reigned along the China coast from Inch'ŏn to Canton."

The American ambassador's residence, behind walls and a heavy gate emblazoned with a red-white-and-blue American seal, is a low one-story

Itaewŏn's Central Mosque.

Korean-style house. Its most recent renovation added a replica of P'osŏk-chŏng, a channel in the shape of an outsized abalone shell carved from stone. In ancient times, a Silla king and his courtiers sat around the contours of the real P'osŏk-chŏng (in Kyŏngju) which was filled with running water. Through the channel floated wine cups. When a bobbing cup hesitated in front of king or courtier, it was his turn either to compose an impromptu poem or down the hesitant wine as a fine for lack of instant inspiration. A frequent result was a tipsy king and an equally tipsy court. Do you suppose the ambassador and some of his staff sit round the new P'osŏk-chŏng and ...?

Many early foreigners never left Korea, and it is the prim **Seoul Foreigners' Cemetery** that keeps and guards their bones. At the northern end of the **Second Han River Bridge,** across from the **Church of Martyrs,** it is a place for history and feeling. A headstone for Homer Hulbert, an early Christian missionary, born 1863, died 1949, reads, "I would rather be buried in Korea than in West-minster Abbey." Ruby Kendrik's

reads, "If I had a thousand lives to give, Korea should have them all." Some of the graves are American, others are English, Canadian, French, even Russian— these last marked by Orthodox crosses and Cyrillic epitaphs. Not all were missionaries. There is Arthur Gorman, born Yokohama April 9, 1884, died Seoul March 3, 1929, served in the Royal Dublin Fusileers 1915-1919. Lying now with this early foreign soldier are American servicemen from the late 1960s and early 1970s, several of them sergeants who probably retired from service here. There are also many small headstones marking children's graves.

Cruising It'aewŏn

A change of scene and spirit? **It'aewŏn.** It'aewŏn is an urban area that runs down from the southern flank of Nam-san and eastward from the fenced edge of **Yongsan Garrison**, the site of the headquarters of the Eighth U.S. Army. The main thoroughfare that bisects the army base into north-south posts similarly bisects It'aewŏn into an uphill-Nam-san side and a downhill toward-the-Han-River side. For years

Confucian dancers, Sŏnggyung-wan shrine.

that flank of Nam-san has been one of the main housing areas for western foreigners because the Korea Housing Corporation, a government agency, built and maintained western-style houses there. That idea is perpetuated, but foreigners, not all of them western, now occupy multistoried apartment buildings higher up the mountain—a location that gives them a sweeping view of the **Han River** and mountain ridges south of the city.

Imagine, however, the look of astonishment on the faces of the Buddhist monks who, for some five hundred years, kept a free hostel for travelers near here. What if they could return for a brief glimpse at the **Hyatt Regency Hotel's** mirrored facade reflecting a setting sun and passing clouds? And their reaction if they turned and caught sight of the twin minarets of an onion-domed mosque below? What would they make of the muezzin's call to afternoon prayer?

Centuries back It'aewŏn was used as a stopover point for visitors to the capital. Then, during the Japanese Occupation, Japanese troops were housed here. These soldiers were replaced after the Korean War with American soldiers stationed at the adjacent Yongsan base and Korean merchants moved into the thoroughfare to cater to soldierly needs.

Today, It'aewŏn merchants attract shoppers from civilian ranks as well, and visitors hail from all over the world. By day, bargain-hunters swarm through the hundreds of clothing, eelskin, brassware, shoe and antique stores where they stock up on Korean-made goods.

By night, It'aewŏn attracts as many young Koreans as it does foreigners. The neons light up and the music begins— this short, 1.5-kilometer strip is now home to literally hundreds of bars and discotheques which rock until the break of dawn. Alcohol pours freely here and cross-cultural marriages often get their starts in the packed It'aewŏn clubs. Older Koreans blame It'aewŏn for the Westernization of Korea's youth, particularly of the young ladies who now partake of beer and tobacco without hesitation, but the Koreans hold their own against the foreigners. It'aewŏn is a place to play, yes, but it is also the place where many foreigners learn to appreciate the Korean temperament and vice versa.

Suburban Seoul City snow-scapes.

Chinatown

For years there was a special section of the city for the Chinese—as there is in almost any sizable city outside of China. This "Chinatown" was behind the Plaza Hotel, but the construction of that hotel and other forms of city renovation razed much of the old area and scattered the Chinese around the city. Nowadays what remain as parts of a Chinese "section" are the **Embassy of the Republic of China,** Chinese middle and high schools, and, in a side alley on the fringe of Myŏng-dong, a Chinese temple.

Once a year on a spring day determined by the lunar calendar, Chinese residents offer an all-day performance of Chinese opera here in the temple. The day celebrates the birth of the Chinese goddess of progeny. The performers are amateurs who practice weeks to produce the high-pitched voices required by this kind of music. The audience is Chinese (few Koreans know about this piece of Chinese culture in their midst), and sometimes you can even glimpse an elderly woman with bound feet. Of course, there are Chinese restaurants everywhere in Seoul—with fare ranging from awful to delicious, usually depending upon the cheap to very expensive price. Latest reports say, however, that these days many young Chinese are leaving Korea (though born here they are not Korean citizens) to go to Taiwan for college and to pursue Chinese lives there.

By government designation Seoul is officially Seoul T'ŭkpyŏl-si, the Special City of Seoul. (Seoul is one of two "Special Cities"—Pusan is the other. The designation indicates that the city's administration is of rank equal to that of provincial governments.) Seoul Special City extends today far beyond the now vanished walls of the original confines of Seoul. It encompasses some 614 square kilometers—most of that in an area that sprawls north of the Han River (which flows west to the Yellow Sea through about 40 kilometers of the city proper).

Despite this seemingly large land area, the city is everywhere crowded. In 1968, Patricia Bartz reported in her book, *South Korea,* that the population density of the city in certain areas is up to 77,500 persons per square mile in the most crowded area, **Map'o-ku.**

Chang-kyungwon in winter.

Ku, Dong and Ka

Administratively, Seoul is divided into 17 wards (*ku*), with each *ku* again segmented into various precincts (*dong*). A *dong* is an area of considerable size, but the term is often used simply to identify where you live or where you're going. People hoping to share a taxi ride, for example, stand at the side of the street shouting, "Hannam-dong!" "Tonam-dong!" "Yaksu-dong!" and other etcetera dongs at passing taxis.

Only downtown, in fact, will you hear the names of certain streets used regularly. It's handy, however, to have some idea of which streets these are. The east-west streets include: **T'oegye-ro** which runs east from **Seoul Railway Station** and follows the northern foot of Nam-san until it joins Ulchi-ro beyond **Seoul Stadium; Ulchi-ro** which runs east from City Hall Plaza (west from City Hall Plaza runs another main artery, Seosomunro; **Chong-no**, which from Kwanghwa-mum intersection runs east to Tongdae-mun and far beyond; **Sinmun-no** which runs west to **Sŏdaemun** (this is the West Gate, but no gate now stands there); and a block south of Kwanghwa-mun intersection is **Ch'ŏnggyech'ŏn,** which runs east in the shadow of the elevated **Samil-lo** expressway.

The north-south streets are: **Namdaemun-no** which curves northeast from Namdae-mun until it intersects Chong-no (where its name becomes An'gukdong-no); and **T'aep'yŏng-no,** which runs from Namdae-mun north to the Kwanghwa-mun intersection where its name becomes Sejong-no. (A word to those who may be confused: The Chinese character for "road" is romanized *-no, -ro, or-lo* according to the ending of the preceding word to reflect how it is properly pronounced.)

Getting Around

To say to a taxi driver that you want to go to Chong-no is not enough, however. Each of these thoroughfares is longitudinally divided into areas roughly corresponding to blocks, called *-ka;* each *-ka*, in turn, is numbered sequentially from where the street begins.

Behind the ancient gates, the thinking at the Korea University is right up to date.

Chong-no 1-ka, for example, is an area extending from Chong-no's beginning at Kwanghwa-mun intersection to the next major crossing where it meets Namdae-mun-no and where the great bell that used to signal the closing and opening of the city gates now hangs. The subway line, however, is the handiest means of public transportation for this heavily traveled route. It begins underground at Seoul Railway Station, curves beneath Namdae-mun, turns north to Kwanghwa-mun (running under T'aep'yŏ–ng-no), then turns east under Chong-no.

If you want to go shopping at the **Nagwón** arcades, get off at Chong-no 2-ka; if you want to go to the movies at the **Picadilly Theater,** get off at Chong-no 3-ka; and if you want to plunge into the flurry of **Tongdae-mun market,** get off at Chong-no 5-ka or 6-ka. From Tongdae-mun, the subway continues east for several miles before terminating at **Sóngbuk-dong** station. It also runs south from Seoul Railway Station across the **First Han River Bridge** and out into the southern suburbs as an above ground electric train (that continues, depending on which line you catch, as far west as Inch'on, or as far south as Suwón).

Outside of the downtown area, the name of a *dong* is what's necessary to identify where you live or where you want to go. Although each *dong* is further divided into units of a few households called *pan*, people living in a particular neighborhood often refer to it as "our village," a concept not necessarily identical to the government's *pan* or *dong*. The urban neighborhood village is typically a maze of small alleyways and side streets.

A visiting western urbanologist once wrote, "If you imagine pouring some water onto a pile of large rocks, the pathway found by the water between the rocks, as it flows to the ground, is somewhat similar to the way streets exist in Korean neighborhoods." Partly for this reason, knowing the address of a particular house does not guarantee that you will find it—at least, not quickly. Addresses are given as such-and-such *ku,* ku-and such-and-such *dong*, and a house number. And house numbers seldom follow in numerical sequence;

Market-places specialize in everything from food to clothing.

rather, they are assigned according to when the house was built. Number 111-3 need not be next to or across the street from Number 111-4; it may be up the alley and kitty-corner from the dry cleaner's instead. As a result, a conversation such as the following is typical:

"It's my birthday. Come over on Satuday."

"Sure. Where do you live?"

"In Samch'ŏng-dong."

Samch'ŏng-dong? Oh, yeah. I know where that is."

"OK. Take the No 104 bus and get off at the Sam'ch'ŏng-dong stop. Go past the dental clinic on the corner to the second alley and turn up there. When you come to a drug store, turn left and ...."

"Wait, wait ... Here's a piece of paper. Draw me a map."

All Koreans get a lot of practice in drawing maps. Not that they don't wander around lost a good deal of the time; they do anyway. And looking for a house in a tangled web of alleyways is not made any easier by being faced with stone or concrete walls—behind which the house you want may be invisibly sitting.

Everything You Want

The life of an urban villager, especially that of the housewife, revolves around the local market. Though Korean households have refrigerators these days, the housewife (or housemaid) still shops every day for the basic ingredients. **Tonam-dong** market is typical. This market lies along both sides of a roadway which shoppers on foot share with bicycles, hand carts and an occasional motorcycle delivering goods. The shops are more like open stalls because few of them have fixed doors. In the morning, a shopkeeper takes down his metal shutters and sets out platforms displaying his goods. Sellers of one commodity tend to cluster together, so you'll find a neat segregation of products: fruit sellers are ranged in a double row down one roadway, then all the fish dealers, all the grain stores, all the vegetable stalls, all the umbrellas, all the dresses and skirt... and so on.

The Tonam-dong market also includes a large two-story building which on the first floor features open shops selling ready-to-wear clothes, household goods; accessories, cosmetics, kitchen

Economic success both pleases and shocks.

ware, plastic goods, textiles in a rainbow of colors, and a whirl of patterns. The proprietress of a textile shop is often a seamstress who, after you pick out the material you want, will whip out her tape measure and measure you up, down and around for a set of *hanbok*, traditional Korean clothes, that will be ready in a few days. The second floor of the building, meanwhile, is quarters for the shopkeepers and their families. For the shopkeepers don't just work here in the market; they also live here with spouses and children. Preschool children scamper underfoot intent on their games in the midst of shoppers and bicycles and hand carts. And they become fascinated spectators if a shopper happens to be a foreigner strange to the neighborhood.

Makkŏlli and Kimch'i
In A Local Sul-jip

In the evening when business slows down, another aspect of market life unfolds; the *sul-jip* or drinking house. A *sul-jip* should not be thought of as a bar, cocktail lounge or beer hall, though those too certainly abound in the city. Rather, a *sul-jip* is a mini-restaurant and social hall. Indeed, a stranger could pass through the market unaware that behind a tiny sliding door is a narrow room with four small oil drum tables, a cluster of tiny stools, and space for 16 customers sitting (and up to three standing at a counter).

Here the men who live and work in the market gather—they and their friends—for a few after-work snacks and bowls of *makkŏlli* rice wine. A certain amount of *makkŏlli*-nipping leads to loud singing (accompanied by banging metal chopsticks against the edge of a table)—and so unwinds another working day in a Seoul marketplace.

In the late fall, special neighborhood markets are set up to sell the ingredients necessary for that staple of the Korean diet, *kimch'i*. A foreigner wandering through one of these markets would be amazed at the mountains of Chinese cabbage, towering stacks of giant white radish, bins of powdered red pepper and anchovy sauce, and the fierce bargaining going on over the price of enough ingredients to make *kimch'i* to last a family through the winter.

To carry her considerable load of vegetables home, the proper Seoul housewife hires a *chige* man, a figure not yet vanished from the Seoul scene. He carries strapped to his back a *chige*, a large wooden frame in the shape of an A which is well-designed for transporting large, cumbersome loads. The housewife leads the way home, *chige* man following, and then beings the timeless Korean task of chopping her ingredients up and pickling them in brine—a process that transforms cabbage, radish, garlic and red pepper into *kimch'i*.

If you're really into fish, try the fish market—Susan Sijang—in Karakdong just across the Chamsil Bridge. Fresh fish on ice, crabs waving their claws about, squid trying to slither away, and fat and succulent shrimp all promise gourmet experiences. But you'll have to get there in the wee morning hours before dawn if you want to compete with those who have come here to get supplies for their own fish stalls in neighborhood markets.

Any foreign visitor to Seoul should venture into a proper market, if not one of the neighborhood markets, then certainly into one or both of the great central markets downtown. Take the previous description of Tonam-dong market, multiply it by fifty, and you

Seoul station, Namdaemun-ro.

have **Namdae-mum Sijang** (Great South Gate Market) located east of the gate itself); then take **Namdae-mun** Sijang, multiply it by another fifty and you have Tongdae-mun Sijang (Great East Gate Market), a large area that stretches south of Chong-no 5-ka and 6-ka.

At either place you can find almost anything you want, and, perhaps, many things you'd rather not find.

Feast your eyes on the silk market in Tongdae-mun Sijang—stall after stall of brilliantly colored silk and synthetic brocades, a truly dazzling display. Then feast your stomach at the fruit stalls where you'll find not only "ordinary" fruits in season—apples, pears, grapes, strawberries and peaches—but also here and there a handful of black cherries or a box of wild raspberries.

Among the fish, some of which are kept flappingly alive in shallow tanks of water, you may come face to face with an eight-foot octopus hanging from a hook or red slices of beefy looking whale. Even a hammer-head shark! You'll find other disturbing exotica too: a tubful of long-necked turtles trying very hard to escape through their chicken wire enclosure; a stack of dog carcasses ready for delivery to restaurants specializing in *posin-t'ang*, a heavily spiced dog meat soup especially popular, would you believe, during the "dog days" of August.

Labyrinthine Arcades

Although these great markets undoubtedly contain anything you'd want to buy and would find if you searched long enough, the city offers other somewhat more convenient if less colorful shopping places: modern department stores—**Midop'a** on Namdae-mun-no opposite the entrance to Myŏng-dong, **Cosmos** and **Cheil** in Myŏng-dong, and **Sinsegye** on Namdae-mun-no opposite the **Bank of Korea**; the above-ground shopping arcades—the Nagwŏn at Chong-no 2-ka, the four-block-long arcade that runs (changing name as it crosses a street) north-south between T'oegye-ro 3-ka to Chong-no 3-ka; and the luxury hotel shopping arcades in the **Chosun, Lotte** and **Plaza** hotels all just off City Hall Plaza.

Underground labyrinthine shopping arcades lie invisibly beneath some of the city streets: the **Sogong Arcade** runs

National Dance Company, the Sejong Cultural Center.

from under the corner of the Plaza Hotel, turns left at the Chosun Hotel and continues as far as the basement of the Cosmos Department Store in Myŏng-dong; the **Hoehyon Arcade** starts in front of the **Central Post Office** (kitty-corner from the Bank of Korea on Namdae-mun-no) and runs up to T'oegye-ro; and other mini-arcades exist where pedestrain underpasses allow room for a few stores. These arcades offer clothes, jewelry, calculators, typewriters, cameras, and souvenir items, including reproductions of antique porcelain.

'Mary's Alley'

Left, pagodas are common at palaces and temples; right, traditional detailing at historic sites.

Above ground, specialized shops tend to run along together in a row — a hangover from market days, perhaps. Barbells, volleyballs and other sporting goods can be found at any one of the half dozen stores under the shadow of **Seoul Stadium** (what could be a more appropriate location?) at Ŭlchi-ro 7-ka; Buddhist rosaries at the shops near the entrance to Ch'ogye-sa; and puppies and brightly painted dog houses along T'oegye-ro 4-ka and 5-ka. Hub caps and car seat covers? On a street connecting Ch'ŏng-gyech'ŏn 5-ka with Ŭlchi-ro 5-ka. Men's tailored suits? Along Namdaemun-no north of Ulchi-ro, in an area called Kwang-kyo. And antiques? Ah, antiques.

The time-honored location for antique dealers is **Insa-dong** along a narrow street called by foreigners "**Mary's Alley**" that leads south from **An'guk-dong Rotary** to **Pagoda Park**. (Who Mary was now nobody remembers.) Some good shops offering fine Koryó celadon, Silla pottery and Yi furniture are still flourishing there, but many have fled to other sections of the city, notably to **Ch'onggyech'ón 8-ka.** Ch'ŏng-gyech'ŏn is well worth a visit even by someone who isn't in the market for antiques. It's actually part of **P'yonghwa Sijang** (Peace Market), itself an extension of Tongdae-mun Sijang.

Although some of the antique stores face the street, others lurk in back alleys snuggled between tiny restaurants, junk dealers, and blaring tape and record stores. Some vendors spread their wares on blankets on the ground. It's a real bargain hunter's challenge. Who knows, the hunter may even *find* a bargain.

Other favorite antique haunts are Ahyŏn-dong and It'aewŏn.

Korean Alpiners

Shopping can be a recreation, but Koreans enjoy many other forms of play, too. For instance, sports. Most Korean men and boys are sports buffs, and to further stress the point, Seoul has three sports arenas to satisfy their lust for organized athletic competitions: **Seoul Stadium** for baseball and soccer, **Ch'angch'ung Field House** for volleyball and boxing, and the new **Olympic Sports Complex** in Chamsil, south of the river. When a Korean athlete or team competes in a televised international event, traffic in the city virtually comes to a halt. People are indoors or congregated in front of a TV shop window watching—and cheering or moaning.

Sports have gained in popularity recently with the coming of the Olympics to Seoul in 1988. Koreans inevitably ask foreigners for their views on the Olympics and relate, with great pride, the extensive preparations currently in progress in Seoul. Korea is eager to show the tens of thousands of visitors expected in 1988 how quickly the country has grown and how strong it will become in the future.

Age-old Korean martial arts such as *t'aekwŏn-do*, *hapki-do*, and *yu-do* are taught in schools and centers nationally, and these days around the world. A favorite *t'aekwŏn-do* viewing spot is the **Yuksamdong World T'aekwŏn-do Headquarters** across the Third Han River Bridge.

Korea's unofficial sport for young and old alike is hiking and trekking year-round, probably because 70 per cent of the country is mountainous. In the fall, hikers wearing alpine gear can be seen lined up to board buses out of the city to assault the nearby mountain peaks on Sunday mornings. They are a strikingly colorful and eager lot decked in hiking boots, long colorful socks, sturdy pants and windbreakers, and backpacks stuffed with the makings of a cook-out lunch. A hat or cap with a jaunty feather tops off the costume. (Koreans are among the greatest hat wearers in the world. The members of almost any group out on an excursion can be readily recognized by their identical caps.)

A favorite and easy peak to scale among Seoulites is **Tobong-san,** which is just northeast of Seoul. Once on top the mountain, hikers let loose with not-so-Alpine-like haloos and yahoos vaguely akin to a yodel.

Other Forms of Recreation

While hiking may be the most popular outdoor recreation, tennis is not far behind. Tennis courts can be found all over the city, and Koreans play not just in the summer but on into the winter.

Picnicking elsewhere in the world usually involves just a leisurely meal. In Korea, however, it is a recreation especially popular during the spring and fall. Friends, fellow office workers, and family carry with them not only food and drink but also, if the picnic grounds permit, a *changgu* (an hourglass-shaped drum) to set the rhythm for singing and dancing—essential entertainment to rouse the spirit. (Unfortunately, modern youth display a tendency toward guitars with portable amplifiers.) Among the few picnic grounds in the city limits, those on the slopes of Nam-san and **Chŏng-nŭng Valley** in the northern part of Seoul draw the most people. It is common to see a club of middle-aged women in long flowing Korean dresses out for an afternoon. At some point, they will relax and form a circle and dance to their *changgu,* waving their arms gracefully and turning slowly and rhythmically. With their full skirts billowing, they look like pastel flowers blowing in a passing breeze.

At the end of the day, everyone wends home. Some, not yet surfeited, dance down the mountainside. The dancer may be a gray-haired grandma. Once past her sixtieth birthday, a woman is freed of many Confucian restraints, and now she can drink and smoke in public. And dance.

Seoul After Dark

After the sun sets, Seoul's pleasure seekers have a considerable amount of entertainment at their disposal. They can go to the movies. A theater-goer can choose a locally produced feature (usually either a historical drama or a modern melodrama) or a subtitled American or European film (though some imported films are from Hong Kong's prolific studios). Although the censors are more lenient these days, nudity on the screen is either blurred or cut.

In addition to the many movie houses, Seoul boasts about a dozen little theater groups. Many of them rise and fall rapidly, but a few—notably the Silhŏm, Minye, Munyae and Space Theatre troupes—have managed an existence of some years; a couple even have their own small theaters. These groups produce works by both Korean playwrights and plays in translation by such writers as diverse as Woody Allen, Neil Simon, Harold Printer, and Ionesco.

A music lover can have his fill in Seoul. Today's typical Korean likes Occidental music most whether his tastes are classical or popular. Korean preference in western classical music tends to the tried and true—Beethoven, Brahms, Tchaikovsky—and opera. Someone once said that the country appears to be made up of thousands of aspiring Italian tenors. Truly, Koreans are often splendid musicians as the international successes of such people as concert violinists Chung Kyung-wha and Kim Young-uck or the Kim Sisters, a pop vocal group, attest. Concert goers will pay high prices to hear these artists or touring foreign performers but tend to neglect the talent of local performers—except for Korean pop singers who are quite popular among the young.

These artists can perform in either of two luxurious concert and theater halls: the **National Theater** on the slopes of Nam-san or the new **Sejong Cultural Center** in the middle of the city opposite the **American Embassy** on Sejong-no. Both halls include a large main auditorium and a smaller one for more intimate performances. The Sejong Center, which opened in the spring of 1978 with a great festival of imported artists including the Royal Ballet from London, is a true musical and architectural marvel. It even houses a ninety-nine rank organ, the first of its kind in Korea and one of very few in Asia.

The National Theater, supported by the government, is the home not only of its own drama group but also of the National Symphony, the National Ballet, the National Opera Troupe, and the National Traditional Performing Arts Troupe. The National Classical Music Institute is also located there. It offers scholarships to children through high school to study and perform traditional Korean music and dance. Foreigners also

Camera club outing with traditional subjects.

enroll here for special classes. The Institutes' faculty and students perform at important ceremonies and traditional rituals. Thus, there are many stages presenting a variety of cross-cultural performances.

Nightlife

If our pleasure seeker is of a somewhat different stripe, he can indulge himself in other kinds of music and dance at Western-style nightclubs and discotheques. All of the first-class hotels in Seoul have discos, the best of which are at the Chosun Hotel (**Xanadu**) and the Hilton (**Rainforest**). It'aewŏn, of course, is the main area for nighttime romping and the list of clubs here is incredibly long. For a chic, private atmosphere, It'aewŏn regulars go to **Rumors,** located next to the Crown Hotel but by far the most popular everyman's club is **Sportsman's** smack in the middle of It'aewŏn.

If our pleasure seeker is a tippler (some do say the national sport is not hiking but drinking), where he goes to tipple depends on his pocketbook. Most will choose the *sul-jip* where life is convivial and the drink cheap. More expensive is the beer hall where a demure hostess may, or may not, sit down with him and his friends to pour the beer, light cagarets, and engage in *repartee*. In a cabaret (a beer hall with a live band), a hostess is available for a fee and will do all of the above plus dance with the customer.

If our night wanderer is especially well-heeled, he may, with a group of friends or, more likely, a group of business acquaintances, seek out a *kisaeng* house. These luxurious establishments, the equivalent of Japan's geisha houses, are located mostly in side streets or suburbs. Here, too, female companionship comes with the fee, which will be exorbitant, but the food, decor and costuming—though not always the entertainment—tend to be authentically traditional. The girls in a *kisaeng* house these days are seldom the highly cultivated *artistes* of the old days, but they have developed comparable skills in helping the tired businessman relax.

A step between the *kisaeng* house and the cabaret is a kind of small, discreet place you wouldn't know was there unless you already know. Inside are rooms furnished with western chairs and sofas

Sparkle and shine warm the atmosphere at Seoul's Lotte Shopping Centre.

and large central coffee tables to hold bottles and glasses and plates of *anju*. Again the female companions come with the fee, but the dress and drink (Scotch, usually) and decor are western—perhaps an adaptation of the old to modern times.

For the truly determined tippler, one last watering-hole stands between him and home: a tent pitched along the side of an alleyway. Lit by a carbide lamp, or kerosene tapers, these one-man operations offer *makkŏlli* and *anju* (bean-and-onion cakes, clams, eel, slices of home-made sausage, or, in winter, whole broiled sparrows). A trestle counter may or may not have small stools for customers to perch on, but by this time of the evening customers would be better off simply leaning against the counter anyway. These cozy tents appear like magic only late at night and, a few minutes before dawn, up and trundle away.

After Work Soap Operas

Of course, our man in the city may not be a pleasure seeker at all. He may merely go home right after work, though

National Assembly resembles a planetarium.

going home right after work is not the common practice for the male office worker or businessman. (One could suspect that if he is home early it's because he's broke and all his friends are broke, too.) But if he does go straight home, he and his wife and his children probably settle in front of the TV set to choose from among four channels—five, if anyone wants to practice English by watching the U.S. Army's station, AFKN-TV—and all now broadcast in color.

Korean programs include sports, game shows, variety shows (Korean comedians are among the world's best at slapstick), historical drama and tear jerker "home dramas"—the equivalent of the West's soap opera adapted to modern Korean family life. It's possible, say some foreign residents, to get quite caught up in the ups and downs of the Kim family as it struggles with the problems generated by all the personalities in a large extended family: grandpa, grandma, married son who's failing in business, his long-suffering wife (no children yet), their married daughter and ne'er-do-well husband (at least one cute grandson, though), a rebellious unmarried son in college (he's in love with an unsuitable girl), a pert unmarried daughter in high school (*she* had better not be in love with anybody), and the nosy neighbors and poor relations from the country who have come to visit for a month or so.

A Way of Life

In Seoul—as in real life everywhere—the social interaction is clearly visible to all, for a good deal of living goes on out of doors—even right downtown. Walk up an alley that curves off T'aep'yŏng-no behind a government office building. In almost any weather, except the coldest and the rainiest, there'll be a boy out washing one of the cars parked along the alley (he's hired by the car's owner and runs this enterprise as a regular concession); a few drives lounging against a wall (they're professionals employed by the car owners); a man with a pullcart full of small things useful to cars and drivers, such as feather dusters, sets of screw drivers, plastic buckets, white cotton gloves; a woman tending a coal briquette fire to roast small sweet potatoes or ears of field corn or chestnuts for the passerby; and a pair of shoeshine boys who hail the passing foreigners with a cheerful, "Hey, shoeshine!"

These boys make regular runs into office buildings where they gather up the shoes of people who want them shined, and leave behind slippers for the temporarily unshod to pad about in. At the end of the alley on the right is a man with a cart whose top folds down to display a selection of hand tools, tape measures, rolls of plastic tape, razor blades, shaving cream in aerosol cans. Next to him is a cart with magazines in Korean and English for sale, then a glass-fronted stand on wheels displaying cigarette lighters, lighter fluid and flints. At the mouth of a side alley is a paperback bookstall, titles in English. At the end of the alley to the left is, in season, the calendar seller; and opposite him sits the key maker in a tiny doorless cubbyhole. At the furthest corner where this alley turns and joins another rests the cobbler who will hammer on new heels, sew up sandals, and attach uppers to lowers—all while you wait more or less comfortably seated on a very small stool.

The New Seoul

It's heartening to know that these small enterpreneurs have not yet been banished from the very heart of the city. Seoul's city fathers have been allowed these small and industrious businessmen to trade on the sidewalks of the new Seoul, that part of the city south across the Han River. There, rising forests of multistoried apartment building complexes are lined with newly planted saplings, children's playgrounds and shopping arcades, and, here and there, lit at night by carbide flames, are the same ubiquitous handcarts loaded with tangerines and chewing gum, dried cuttlefish and peanuts. And even here the *yŏnt'an* man pulls his cartload of coal briquettes through the streets to deliver a family's household heating fuel supply.

Yŏnt'an is a major item in any household; it's the main fuel for heating the *ondul* lacquer floor with flumes underneath it and it used to be the source of heat for cooking new Seoul apartments are fueled for cooking with liquid propane gas). Even off duty, the *yŏnt'an* man's occupation is clearly visible: black dust clings to his hands and swipes across his face.

In contrast to the older residential sections of Seoul on the north side of the

A shop in the Joongang market of Seoul.

94

river, the old neighborhoods of diverging alleyways, these southern sections of the city, spreading out from the foot of bridges newly constructed across the Han, are carefully gridironed, their streets ruled into right angles. Here dwellers buy everyday necessities in "proper" stores—modern supermarkets where onions come prepackaged in plastic bags. To some, these beige and gray complexes (**Chamsil, Hyŏndae, Yŏngdong, Yŏido**) seem lacking in color and charm; yet even they offer a kind of beauty, a beauty revealed at night by a drive east along the north bank of the Han River from the First Bridge. Across the black water, these facades of tall apartment buildings make a wall of patterned light that shimmers in the reflecting river. The bridges become ribbons of light flung across the water as streamers of automobile head-lights mark the passage of traffic between the old center of the city and its new southern sector.

City Streets

Many of those automobiles are driven by that exemplar of the city: the taxi driver. One rapidly develops ambivalent feelings toward taxi drivers. Frustration and hostility are easily aroused when a taxi driver won't pick you up or take you where you want to go, especially if it's rush hour.

But if you're a foreign passenger and you speak a little Korean or the driver speaks a little English, watch out. You're in for a torrent of questions about your place of origin, how long you've been in Korea, your age, your marital status, what you do for a living, when you plan to leave the country. One young American woman, after providing the information that she's twenty-eight, has been married for six years and doesn't have any children, has been told by no fewer than five taxi drivers that it's time she had a baby!

Sometimes all a foreigner has to do is get in a cab, answer the question, "*Ŏdiekaseyo?*" (Where are you going?) with a three-syllable response, "*Hannamdong,*" and he's told, "*Han'gung-mal-ŭl chal hasimnida!*" (You speak Korean very well!)—an opinion delivered in tones of pleased surprise. Then he's deluged with questions and comments in

Kids find balconies and stairwells the best part of modern apartments.

Korean that he can't understand. The attitude of the driver who finally realizes that his passenger knows no more than the three syllables he said is very likely to be one of injured disappointment.

Another feature on the city streets is a fleet of butterscotch-colored "call" taxis which one can phone for service. The fare is higher than that of the ordinary taxi, but call taxis are air conditioned.

An increase in the number of automobiles, especially private sedans, in the city has been far too rapid during recent years for the streets to accommodate them, and this press of vehicles creates traffic jams most foreigners groan about. Like, most large cities, Seoul is congested. Traffic snarls at the slightest excuse—such as an eighth of an inch of rain. And snow. The Korean driver is much maligned and, indeed, Korea reports one of the highest accident injury and death rates in the world, but it is possible to learn to cope with the traffic—whether as a driver or as a pedestrian. Just watch everything all the time.

Streets Abloom
On Holidays

Among the people passing on the street, men will usually be dressed in western clothing; so will most of the women. Only a few wear Korean dress except on traditional holidays (Ch'usŏk—the Autumn Moon Festival—and Lunar New Year's holiday) when the streets seem to bloom with the sheen of silky reds, greens, yellows, blues, pinks and purples. Modern Koreans, especially the women, are highly style-conscious and tend to dress carefully and well, even for casual outings. Acceptable dress standards, however, remain conservative—no shorts (except on workmen and children) or backless dresses on the summer sidewalks.

A walker around Seoul is sure to be detoured by some busy construction project: a mammoth office building or hotel, repairs to the street or to the flagstone sidewalk, excavations for new underground shopping centers, walkovers, underpasses or elevated highways. The city changes shape rapidly around the old palaces and gates.

Tabang Society

Congestion is a problem even indoors. Try sitting in a *tabang*, (tearoom), for instance. Although there are more than three thousand *tabang* of various sizes in the city, finding a seat in a popular one will be the first hurdle. *Tabang*, where more coffee than tea is served, are popular for their convenience as meeting places. Here friends meet friends to spend an hour or so in talk or as a preliminary to going somewhere else, business associates meet to negotiate a deal, prospective bride-and-groom couples meet under the eye of their family and friends. Each *tabang* tends to specialize in a certain clientele—university students gravitate toward some, businessmen to others—largely in response to the kind of music the tearoom offers. A disc jockey in a glassed-in booth, often labeled the "Music Box," will play customers' requests through a typically excellent stereoloudspeaker system. The mix of loud conversation and loud music can be cacaphonous.

The central government, responding to complaints about over-crowding, noise and pollution, is pushing for decentralization, ordering the universities to find themselves new campuses south of the river, flinging new bridges across the Han at almost every bend. It has even moved itself out of the city to a certain extent—the ministries of justice, science and several others have relocated to areas outside of Seoul.

All the complaints about the city are well-taken, yet. . . Yet it is alive, it is invigorating, it is exuberant. There's an almost palpable air of well-being, expanding prosperity, swelling confidence. You can feel it in the pace of the city. Koreans seldom stroll in the city streets; their step is brisk and purposeful—thus the bumping and jostling. When a signal light turns from red to green, the driver in the car behind you impatiently honks his horn. He wants to go *now*! Lights burn late in office buildings; businessmen work 10 or 11 hour days then jet off to Tokyo, New York, Abu Dhabi. Even Seoul's children, beneficiaries of growing affluence, have little idle time—they literally swarm through the streets after school on their way to music lessons, swimming lessons or painting lessons.

Seoul, the city, is vibrantly alive.

Right,
Chong-no
sidewalk.

SEOUL AREA
DAY TRIPS

Beyond Seoul's secure city walls there are numerous day outings one can go on to get away from the hustle and beep of urban life. Stroll down to any bus, subway or train terminal, set off in virtually any direction from Seoul, and you'll be amazed at the classical intrigues which await you only minutes outside this sprawling city.

Ancient castles, artworks, massive mounded tombs, hot springs, charming pine glens, moon-watching pavilions, strawberry fields, pottery villages, and even a lion and flamingo park "for the kids" pop up like apparitions at improbable bends in a country road. Do as Koreans do: Simply follow a travel instinct until it leads you to a stream filled with plum blossoms, or a meadow bursting with pink cosmos blossoms and singing grandmothers. Picnic anyone?

The following Seoul day trips are but a few fun and educational excursions we'd like to recommend as worth your time, energy and enjoyment. For further infor-

mation on how to get to these places or their general area, please refer to the transportation section of the Guide in Brief.

Historic Battlements
To the North and South

• **Namhansansŏng, the South Han Mountain Fortress,** is a popular weekend hiking area about 30 kilometers southeast of Seoul proper. This grand highland redoubt—with some eight kilometers of stone walls, some of them seven meters high in places—was originally built about 2,000 years ago during Korea's Paekche dynasty. Most of the fort's now visible structures, however, date to the 17th and 18th Centuries, when the fortress served Yi kings of that period as a retreat from invading Chinese armies. In 1637 Namhansansŏng was the site, following a month and a half long siege, where King Injo, the 16th Yi monarch, surrendered himself, some 14,000 of his men, and in the end, Korea, to a huge Manchu invasion force. This spectacular place is located just east of **Sŏngnam,** and may be reached via National Route 3 (enroute to Kwangju), or

Train conductor, Kimch'on.

through Sŏngnam off the Seoul-Pusan Expressway.

• **Pukhansansŏng, the North Han Mountain Fortress.** This fortress and the preceding one, Namhansansŏng, are the two major ancient fortresses in the Seoul area. This one, which is similar in design and setting to Namhansansŏng, is located above the sprawling northeast suburbs of Seoul along the high ridges of **Pukhan Mountain.** Pukhansansŏng was first built during the early Paekche period and at various times fell into martial disuse. Following severe attacks during the 16th Century by armies of Ch'ing China, the Yi King Sukchong refurbished its battlements. These same walls were partially destroyed during the Korean War, but have since been restored to honor their historic importance. A neat village has bloomed alongside a stream in the crater-like center of the fortress, and meadows and small forests on its less-populated fringes are favored picnic sites. On the road back to Seoul, if you take the northern access highway, look carefully to your left and right. You may see shamanistic **spirit posts** (a rarity these days) peeking out at you through the brush and pines.

Rolling Dice, Tomb-Hopping

• **Walker Hill Resort.** Thousands of mind miles away from country idylls, but nevertheless a lovely spot from which to view Seoul over a proper martini, is the well-known Walker Hill Resort complex. This nightlife area of Las Vegas-style revues, gambling (in the **Sheraton-Walker Hill Casino**), and resort amenities is located above Seoul's eastern suburbs, the swank **Seoul Country Club,** and a picturesque bend in the Han River. From Walker Hill's glittering lounges and gardens, you can see Seoul's city lights twinkling in the urban west. Walker Hill was named after Gen. Walton H. Walker, former Commanding General of the U.S. Eighth Army, who was killed in action during a major Korean War campaign in this area.

• **Kwangnŭng.** The impressive Confucian-style burial tombs of King Sejo (r. 1456–1468), the 7th Yi king, and his wife, Queen Yun Chŏn-hi, are probably the most aesthetically and idyllically located tombs in the Seoul area. These monumental mounds are located about 28 kilometers northeast of Seoul and just past Ŭijŏngbu (a town and military camp

Traditional tombsite guardians, Taenŭng.

made famous in the American movie and television serial "M*A*S*H"). The tombs are hidden in the thick of a forest of old trees which shade trickling streams and wide greenswards ideal for a picnic.

• **Hŏninnŭng.** These tombs of the 3rd and 24th Yi kings lie in the southeast skirts of Seoul in Naekok-dong and near a green belt area where melons, strawberries, eggplant, peppers, corn, and rice are cultivated. In late spring, summer and autumn, shady fruit stands are set up in fields so people can sit and enjoy refreshing breezes, sunshine and fresh-from-the-earth fruit before hiking up to the nearby Hŏnnŭng, the tombs of King T'aejong (1367–1422) and Queen Wonkyŏng (1364–1420), and Innŭng, the tombs of King Sunjo (1790–1834) and Queen Sunwŏn (1789–1857). All of the tombs are guarded by granite statues of the monarchs' royal subjects and by fantastic animal sentries. Hŏninnŭng's grounds are well-manicured, and the area's classical tomb settings make this a popular area for the filming of historical kung-fu movies. If you are in Korea on May 8th, you may want to attend a formal *chesa* (ancestor worship) ceremony conducted annually at Hŏnnŭng by Yi dynasty descendants.

• **Yong-in Farmland.** An African safari, American zoo, and Korean amusements come improbably together at Yong-in Farmland, a recreation complex on the north side of National Highway 4 (enroute to Kangnŭng) about 34 kilometers southeast of Seoul. Behind a 1,634 acre curtain of pine, chestnut, walnut, paulownia, and other hardy trees, one can amuse oneself with a Korean-style lion safari; a 163-acre nursery with 1,200 kinds of rare plants; a 41-acre tree park of apples, plums, pears, peaches, grapes and 14 other fruits; and the advertised "fancy performances of wild pigs and flamingoes." If that range of rural fantasies doesn't suit you, there is also a 1,000-meter jet coaster ride, a fishing pond, and other such thrills.

Shopping for Pots

• **Ich'ŏn.** The soulful pottery kilns of two of Korea's finest potters are about 70 kilometers south of Seoul near Ich'ŏn (also just north of National Highway 4). In **Sukwang-ni, Sindŭng-myŏn,** four kilometers north of Ich'ŏn proper, you can observe Koryŏ celadons being created by

Kitsch vendor, Ŭijŏngbu.

ceramics master **Yu Kŭn-hŭng,** or you can marvel at **Ahn Dong-o's** Yi dynasty whiteware as it's pulled hot from his traditional kilns. These gentlemen's fine work can be purchased on the spot or in prominent ceramic art galleries in Seoul. At the other end of the potting spectrum, you will find, here and there in the greater Ich'ŏn area, row upon row of the ubiquitous shiny, brown, tall and oblong **kimch'i pots.** These utilitarian wares are hand-thrown and fired in adobe huts. After a day of pot-shopping, languish in the hot springwaters that burble into the **Ich'ŏn Spa Hotel** before returning to Seoul.

• **Tobong-san.** If after visiting all the above, pent up energy has you wanting to climb up mountains, consider scaling Tobong-san, a pleasant peak just five and a half kilometers north of Seoul. The hike to this summit takes an hour or longer, depending on your serendipitous pace. You may want to linger enroute next to a clear stream or pool, or, if you're a camera buff, photograph the odd rock formations up there. Or—if Buddhist spirits move you—you may wish to trek along one of several diverting paths in and around Tobong-san to the temples of **Mangwŏl, Chŏnjuk,** and **Hweryŏng.**

• **Yangju** The Yangju *pyŏlsandae* masked dance drama is performed in this small village just north of Ŭijŏngbu. Traditional performance times are during *Tano* (a spring festival held during the fifth lunar month, usually in May), on *Ch'usŏk* (an autumn festival in the eighth lunar month), and sometimes for the convenience of visiting cultural groups. This particular folk drama originated in Kyŏnggi Province. According to Yangju villagers, about 200 years ago a troupe from Seoul was invited to perform in Yangju, but broke their engagements several times to perform elsewhere. Instead of enduring more cultural disappointments, the villagers decided to produce their own show and patterned it after the Seoul masked dance drama. Since then, Yangju's versions have become extremely popular, and now people from Seoul travel to enjoy this little village's semi-annual performances.

Such *sandae* plays originally were performed only for Yi dynasty royalty. But about 1634, during the reign of Yi King Injo, this masked dance drama was discontinued in the court and became enter-

Kimch'i pottery, Ich'ŏn.

tainment for commoners. To this effect, the entertainment draws heavily from the villagers' perspective of life.

The performance begins with a parade around the village by the various characters dressed in full costume and mask (made of paper or gourd). It's rather a colorful and surreal sight to see a monk, a lotus leaf "spirit of heaven," a winking spirit of earth, an acupuncturist, a shaman witch, an aristocrat's concubine, a monkey, police inspector, and 14 other characters (who play some 32 roles using 22 masks) parading past the turkey coops and vegetable gardens in this rural town.

A sacrifice to the spirits is conducted shortly after the parade ends at the dance site. Offerings of wine, fruits of three colors, rice cakes (*ttŏk*), pigs' legs, and an oxen's head are presented and then eaten by the performers—to set them in the right, jolly mood. Then the day's play begins in an open-air, grassy area beneath a mountain north of the village. It lasts for several hours. The play satirizes an apostate monk, the *yangban* (aristocrats), corrupt government officials, and other lofty and fallen people while weaving in contemporary editorial comments. This performance has become a type of "gridiron" show in which persons and institutions worthy of skewering and grilling are roasted with satire that often evokes howls of laughter. There is also audience participation. Metal bowls of *makkŏlli* rice wine and *ttŏk* rice cakes are passed around in the audience (which sits in a broad circle around the performers), and when the various characters say something the audience agrees with, the audience calls out, *"Ŏlch'i, chalhamnida"* ("That's right; well said"). It is advised to attend these masked dance dramas with a Korean friend who can translate the jokes for you. (For further information, see this book's section on Korean music and dance.)

• **Korean Folk Village.** A morning excursion 28 miles south of Seoul to the Korean Folk Village near Suwŏn will give you a full day to tour the 240 homes, shops and other attractions in this authentically rendered Yi dynasty village. Visit ceramic and bamboo shops, drink rice wines in a wayside tavern, then join the daily staged wedding procession of a

Stylized "spirit post" guardian, Korean Folk Village.

traditionally costumed (and transported via palanquin) bride and groom who are trailed by a colorful, whirling farmers' dance band. Even in a day you may not be able to see the wealth of fascinating exhibits in this sprawling museum. The privately-funded folk village is open from 10 a.m. to 5 p.m. seven days a week.

If even more time is on your hands, consider one of the following day trips which involve greater distances and time, but which provide experiences equal to the effort:

The 'Flower Fortress' Due to Filial Love

• **Suwŏn**—the easy-going capital of **Kyŏnggi Province**—is an old fortress city about 51 kilometers south of Seoul in the vicinity of **Mt. Paltal.** Suwŏn's name, which means "water source" or "water field," derives from its location in an area which was traditionally known for its fine artesian wells.

These days Suwŏn is renowned for its recently restored castle walls and sup-

port structures, and—in a tastier realm—for its luscious **strawberries** (called *ttalgi* in Korean). The city is also famous for its *kalbi*, or barbequed short ribs, but it's the late spring through summer strawberries that come to most Korean minds when you mention the word Suwŏn.

The city can be quickly and easily reached by regular electric subway trains from Seoul City Center, or by just as regular buses from the Kolon Express Terminal in Cho-dong.

The first thing you'll notice about the city are its massive fortress walls, gates, and other historic architectural facilities which meander for 5,520 meters around the old city proper. Construction of these structures began during the reign of King Chŏngjo (r. 1794–1796), the 22nd Yi monarch, who established the Suwŏn fortress in memory of his father, the Yi Crown Prince Changjo. Prince Changjo had been the innocent victim of a mid-18th Century court conspiracy in which his father, a senile, disillusioned king, unjustly condemned him to be locked in a rice box until dead. Years later this daffy king died and his grandson, Chŏngjo,

Suwŏn's southside city gate.

proceeded to prove his father's innocence and honor his memory with the building of Suwŏn fortress.

Chŏngjo wanted to move the Korean capital from Seoul to this new Suwŏn site, but because of various personal and political problems, he was never able to accomplish that kingly feat.

Chŏngjo created a beautiful fortified city here—complete with proper parapets and embrasures, floodgates, observation platforms and domes, parade grounds, command bunkers, cannon stands, and an archery range. Chŏngjo's original fortress, known as the "Flower Fortress," was heavily damaged by weathering and by bombing during the Korean War, but in 1975 the Korean government undertook a major restoration of his dream city. This project took 4 years, 5 months, and w3,286 million before it was completed, but the beautifully finished product was officially dedicated on November 29, 1979.

These impressive new walls and other structures will look even better once they've weathered a bit, but even in their pristine state they are a fascinating redoubt and an invitation to a circle city stroll. One particularly lovely spot near the **North Gate, Changan-mun,** is a strikingly landscaped reflecting pond, **Yong-yŏn,** which sits below an octagonal moon-watching pavilion called **Panghwasuryu-jŏng.**

This meditative spot was ordered created by the aesthetically inclined King Chŏngjo when he initiated his Suwŏn fortress-city master plan in 1794. These days it's a gem of a place much-favored by neighborhood *harabŏji,* grandfathers, who sit inside its gabled cupola lighting long-stemmed pipes, drinking sweet rice wine, and bouncing patriarchal thoughts off nearby castle walls. The whole classical effect is officially labled "The Northern Turrett."

If after a hike around the "Flower Fortress" it's fresh strawberries and cooling wine you crave, bus or taxi to the popular **Agricultural Green Belt area** in Suwŏn's west suburbs near the modern **Agricultural College of Seoul National University.** There you can eat basketsfull of blood-red and juicy sweet strawberries—and grapes during the summer and fall—at umbrellaed tables next to the patches and vineyards from whence they came.

Yongju-sa

Thus sweetly sated, visit one of these other Suwŏn area sites:

• **Yongju-sa**, a Buddhist temple which, like the Suwŏn fortress, was also built by King Chŏngjo in his father's memory. Yongju-sa, "The Dragon Jewel," rests in a rural, piney area about a 20 minute bus ride south of Suwŏn's mid-town South Gate. Built in 1790 on the site of an earlier Silla dynasty temple (dating from 854), Yongju-sa's grounds boast, among other attractions, a seven-story stone pagoda, a 1,500 kilogram Koryŏ-era brass bell, and in its main hall, a superb Buddhist painting by the Yi genre painting master Danwŏn Kim Hong-do.

Yongju-sa is a popular place to visit at the time of Buddha's birthday (celebrated on the 8th day of the 4th lunar month, usually in late April), when pilgrims from miles around arrive here bearing candle-lit paper lanterns and prayers for good fortune.

Just west of the temple, in a properly serene setting, are the **mounded tombs** of King Chŏngjo and his beloved father the Crown Prince Changjo (Sado Seja, the "Ricebox Prince"). Chŏngjo posthumously awarded his father the title "King Changjo," and according to his wishes, he lies here forever with him.

Fiery Sogni-san:
'Escape From the Vulgar'

• **Sogni-san National Park.** This mountain retreat in North Ch'ungch'ŏng Province is superb any time of the year, but is most favored by discriminating Korea weekenders in the autumn when its trees are burning with color. Oaks, maples and gingkos try to outdo each other in their autumnal radiance reminiscent of New Hampshire or Vermont at their most fiery. As one romantic Korean travel writer once wrote of Sogni-san: "The tender green for spring, abundance of forests for summer, yellow leaves for autumn, and snow for winter—all deserve appreciation."

Indeed, since ancient times Sogni has been a preferred resort area, and appropriately, *Sogni* means "escape from the vulgar." To achieve this Sogni escape, travel from Seoul to **Taechŏn City** by train, then transfer by bus or car through **Okch'ŏn** to the Sogni area. You can also reach "escape from the vulgar" by motoring directly by car or bus from Seoul

Monk farmers, Pŏpju-sa.

via Ch'ŏngju City. It's about a three hour motorcar journey one-way.

After passing through Ch'ŏngju City and beginning an ascent to idyllic Sogni, you will enter the steep and curve-filled **Malti Pass** which serves as an unwinding transition from urbanity to nature at its crispest.

Just beyond a glassy reservoir, on your final approach to the Sogni highlands and Sogni village, your local guide will no doubt point out the most distinguished tree in Korea. This is an old pine on the left side of the road called the **Chong-ip'um Pine,** so named because the Yi King Sejo (r. 1456–1468) granted this hoary fellow the official bureaucratic title of Chong-ip'um, a rank equivalent to that of a cabinet minister. Legend and history note that this humble tree was granted that distinction because it lifted its boughs in respect one day as King Sejo and a royal entourage passed by. The pine's politeness was duly rewarded by the flattered king.

Just beyond this ministerial pine is the final approach to **Sogni-dong,** a mountain village famous for the semi-wild tree **mushrooms** cultivated in this area and sold in roadside stands. Seoulites *who*

know try to arrive in Sogni village at lunchtime, when they can enjoy a fabled Sogni mushroom lunch. Such a lunch can feature as many as six completely different mushroom dishes served with a dizzying array of side dishes, *kimch'i* and rice. Be sure to buy a bag of these tender air-dried morsels for later munching at home.

The 'Biggest Buddha'

Following this mushroom overdose, proceed uphill to Sogni-san's biggest attraction, **Pŏpju-sa,** a large temple complex dominated by a massive **Mirŭk Buddha of the Future** fashioned of modern poured cement. This 88-foot image, completed in 1964, is often identified by tour guides as "the biggest Buddha in Korea."

This sprawling temple complex was first built at the base of Mount Sogni in the 6th Century, shortly after Buddhism had been carried into Korea from China. Records note that work began in 553 during the 14th year in the reign of the Silla King Chinhŭng. The original founder and spiritual master was the

Pŏpju-sa and her concrete Buddha.

high priest Ŭisang, who had recently returned home from studies in India. Ŭisang contributed several Buddhist scriptural books to Pŏpju-sa's first library.

Author-historian Han Ki-hyung, a former assistant editor of the *Korea Journal*, writes in a research story about Pŏpju-sa that this temple, "one of Korea's oldest," reportedly was "renovated during the reigns of Kings Sŏngdŏk and Hyegong (702–780). This can be confirmed by observing the stone buildings of the temple surviving to date."

"The temple was protected," Han says, "by the monarchs of not only the Silla dynasty but also the Koryŏ and Yi dynasties. In the sixth year (1101) of King Sukjong's reign (in the Koryŏ era) the king gathered 30,000 priests from all over the country to pray for the health of ailing Royal Priest Ŭich'ŏn. In the Yi era, King Sejo (1456–1468) presented the temple with large tracts of paddy, grains and slaves, and Kings Injo (1623–1649), Ch'ŏljong (1849–1863) and Kojong (1864–1906) had the temple renovated."

Remnants of this favored temple's days of spiritual grandeur can be found on all parts of the compound. Consider for practical openers the famed **Ch'ŏlhwak**, a massive iron rice pot which was cast in 720, during the reign of Silla King Sŏngdong, when some 3,000 priests were living—and eating—here. This grand mess facility is 1.2 meters high, 2.7 meters in diameter, and 10.8 meters in circumference. These days you'll find perhaps only two per cent of that number of gray-robed, sutra-chanting monks, so the pot's utilitarian purpose is no more.

Perhaps the most celebrated historical treasure at Pŏpju-sa is the five-story **P'alsang-jŏn**, or **Eight Image Hall**, which rises in symmetrical splendour above the complex's roomy main courtyard. As Han notes: "This five-story building, presumably reconstructed during the second year of King Injo's reign (1624) in the Yi era, is a rare architectural work for Buddhism not only in Korea but also in China, and can be compared with a similar five-story pagoda at Nara, Japan."

Other Pŏpju-sa curiosities include a large deva lantern surrounded with relief bodhisattvas, a second stone lantern supported by two carved lions, and, outside the temple, a large "ablution trough"

Resident
devotee,
Pŏpju-sa.

carved in the shape of a lotus. To the left side of the main entrance you'll also find a huge boulder that has come to life with a serene Buddha sculpted into a wide and flat facade.

If such art over-boggles your mind, head for the surrounding hills which are laced with excellent hiking trails. A view of the Pŏpju-sa complex from one of Sogni-san's upper ridges is just reward for any huffing and puffing it takes to get up there.

Plum Blossoms in the Snow

• *Realm of the Immortals.* Cornelius Choy, founder and president of the Korea Art Club and a longtime conductor of countryside tours sponsored by the Korea Chapter of the Royal Asiatic Society, suggests that visitors and Seoulites alike spend at least one late winter day in the area north of Seoul he calls the "Realm of the Immortals." Go there if you can, Cornie advises, when plum blossoms—the year's first flowers—begin to bloom in forests and ravines that are still dusty with snow. Or as the ancients advise: "Do as amused immortals do: Whenever the boredom and frustration

of a long winter indoors becomes too much for them, they put on their cape and hat, tell the attendant to saddle the donkey, and *go out in the snow looking for plum blossoms.*"

This journey through a painted screen will take you on Highway 43 north of Seoul between two popular hiking mountains: **Tobong-san** and **Surak-san.** Tobong-san, the rocky, harsh-looking mountain on the west side of the road, is said to represent the male gender, while the curved and flowing Surak-san on the east side is said to personify female qualities. Beyond this broad pass your vehicle will take you through **Ŭijŏngbu,** the "City of Ever Righteousness."

Further north, the terrain becomes yawning canyons and ravines. Beyond **Tong-du-ch'ŏn,** turn at the highway into the **Soyo Mountains** and make the short hike to **Chachae-am temple,** a place famed as the testing ground for a monk's celibacy. Ornately carved dragons—snarling out from each corner of this quaint temple's eaves—may seduce you inside, where you'll find a pair of tempestuous carved dragons writhing on the ceiling. A spouting waterfall and narrow gorge with a stream complement this little canyon.

Sambuyŏn, the "Dragon Waterfall".

An even more exciting waterfall and river scene is located much further north in the **Sinch'ŏlwŏn** area. (Because there are several military checkpoints in this area close to the 38th parallel, it is suggested that foreigners join the Royal Asiatic Society's tour if possible.) A massive granite boulder, **Kosŏk**, nicknamed "**The Lonely Rock**," sits in the **Imjin River** and invites clambering up to its pine-studded brow. Legend says that this rock rolled in from the East Coast and decided to rest at this lovely turn in the fast-flowing river. A recently constructed pleasure pavilion overlooks the rock and the river's noisy rapids, and local boatmen may be hired for a ride through the narrow river canyons which jut to the north.

A Feisty Carp

Due south of this "Lonely Rock"—in a deep canyon and off a steep dirt road—is the little known **Sambuyŏn** or "**Dragon Waterfall.**" You'll see local villagers fishing for carp in pools above the falls. This is an appropriate pastime, because in these parts—and in oriental mythol-

ogy—the carp and dragon are distant and legendary relatives.

The carp is regarded by Koreans as a symbol of strength and perseverance, and one famous story in national lore is about a carp who persistently tried to climb up this strong waterfall. On the 100th day of his attempt, this feisty carp succeeded (with the help of gods) to scale Sambuyŏn and as a reward he was magically turned into a powerful dragon. These falls, however, are easy for humans to climb (a splendid path runs through a stone tunnel to the right side of the falls). And you don't have to worry about being turned into a dragon once you get to the top.

On your way back to Seoul, you may want to picnic and recuperate at **Sanjŏng Lake**, an artificial lake resort built by Japanese engineers during Japan's colonial occupation of Korea. The lake is a popular skating spot in the wintertime, and most of the year it's a fine area for hiking and relaxation. Watch for the large colorful tents which serve as dance halls, and while hiking 'round this picture-perfect reservoir don't hesitate to sip wine or sample the many tasty goods being sold by lakeside vendors.

Domestic
tourists,
Sanjŏng
Lake.

INCH'ŎN, PORT-OF-ENTRY

In the recent jet age, travelers from the West invariably begin Korea adventures at Seoul City's Kimp'o Airport. But in the old days—before stretch-bodied aircraft with swept wings—most travelers put in at Seoul's chief seaport, Inch'ŏn. Inch'ŏn—which until the 1880s was a sleepy fishing village called Chemulp'o—was for a long time the only Korean place foreigners were allowed to visit.

Westerners, of course, were not officially allowed into "The Hermit Kingdom" until 1883, but when they did receive royal permission, usually for purposes of trade, Inch'ŏn was the popular port-of-entry. Today, Inch'ŏn is a booming harbor and Korea's fourth largest city.

For many years after Korea opened her Inch'ŏn gate, this harbor developed a lively port-to-port relationship with China. Appropriately, an old "Chinatown," which today is but a reminiscence, sprang up along the waterfront to cater to homesick compradores and seamen from the Celestial Kingdom.

The number of trading ships calling at Inch'ŏn has increased with every passing year, and consequently the 38.9 kilometer stretch between Seoul proper and the Port of Inch'ŏn has become the most important sea, road and rail supply route in Korea.

Operation CHROMITE

Because this is a strategic port, several important battles have been fought in and around Inch'ŏn since ancient times, but in the current century Inch'ŏn has become most well-known as the place where General Douglas MacArthur, Commander of U.S. Pacific Forces, directed a brilliant amphibious landing which turned the bitter Korean War around for southern Korea and its allies.

That landing, code-named Operation CHROMITE, began at dawn on September 15, 1950. Historian David Rees writes in his important book *Korea: The Limited War* that "The successive objectives of the operation called for the neutralization of Wolmi-do, the island controlling Inchon harbour, a landing in the city, seizure of Kimpo Airfield, and the

Local dockworkers and fishermen, Inch'ŏn.

capture of Seoul." MacArthur's subordinates argued fiercely against their commander's plans to attack this vulnerable harbor with tricky tides and a narrow entrance, but always confident MacArthur contended that, "The very arguments you have made as to the impracticabilities involved will tend to ensure for me the element of surpise. For the enemy commander will reason that no one would be so brash as to make such an attempt."

MacArthur was right—and the rest of the story is military history at its swashbuckling best. At 6:33 a.m. on the September 15 D-Day, elements of the 5th Marines poured ashore at Inch'on, as Rees writes, "to meet only scattered shots. The flag was raised on Radio Hill, dominating Inchon harbour, at 0655, and the whole of this 105-metre high feature which had caused the planners so much worry was taken by 0800." U.S. Marines began a bloody advance towards Seoul, and after 12 more days of hellish fighting took that devastated capital. As Rees recalls: "Surrounded by hills blazing with napalm and huge benevolently smiling posters of Stalin and Kim Il Sung, the Stars and Stripes at last floated over the shattered fifth city of Asia."

Today, Radio Hill, now commonly called Freedom Hill, looms over an earnest seaport abustle with international trade; but atop the hill, jaunty in sculpted khakis, is a 10-meter high statue of the much-revered General MacArthur.

The fastest and easiest way to get to MacArthur, who stands atop Freedom Hill facing the Yellow Sea and with a pair of binoculars gripped in his right hand, is to take the Seoul Subway train due west through industrial suburbs and rice fields that sprawl alternately between Seoul and the setting sun.

Flagstone and Cobble
In Korea's 'San Francisco'

Once you arrive at Inch'ŏn-dong station—take a cab or hike up to Freedom Hill above this town of steep streets ("The San Francisco of Korea," say some romantics) and endless ocean terminals. The ocean view from up there is, well, overtly industrial, but sea breezes are crisp, and, besides the statue of MacArthur, you'll find a whitewashed replica of America's Statue of Liberty and a charm-

After a day's fishing, it's time to pack up the gear.

ing moon-watching pavilion from where you can sometimes see a spectacular red fireball sun dropping through container cranes and ships' riggings into an amber ocean.

The walk down from Freedom Hill through old Inch'ŏn is a pleasant one which should serendipitously follow gravity and your nose down cobble and flag-stoned by-ways and stairs past some of Korea's most distinctive verandahs and storefronts.

There is, however, only one deluxely priced hotel in Inch'ŏn. This is the Olympos, which dominates a lower city promontory over the sea and attracts high-rollers to its Lido nightclub, gambling casino, European grill and roomy swimming pool. This hotel has some 200 rooms available for the sleeping, but if your budget leans toward or yearns for a more Korean experience, there are several yŏgwan (inns) here and there among Inch'ŏn's hills and dales.

Popular nearby diversions include seafood dining on one of the area's land-linked islands, either Wŏlmi-do (Moon Tail Island) or Sŏwŏlmi-do. Both isles are partially made of reclaimed land and are famous for their gourmet plates of raw fish and other earthy delicacies from the deep. During the summer, various off-shore islands become favored Korean resort destinations. Once you reach one of these isles you can bake on white sand beaches or wallow in lovely man-made lagoons rimmed by colorful cabanas and bathing beauties. There also are several smaller resort hotels in this area, particularly near big Songdo Beach south of the city.

Follow an Ajumŏni
To the Fishmarket

Travelers also enjoy visiting the big public seafood market on the southern side of Inch'ŏn's tidal basin. Ask for the *Yonan Pudu O-sijang* (fish market) and any *ajumŏni* (housewife) will send you on your way to this massive covered market next to a small sheltered harbor full of fishing trawlers. Inside three huge quonset huts and under hundreds of dangling electric lightbulbs you'll find every sort of sealife you ever dreamed existed. A number 26 bus will take you from downtown Inch'ŏn near the Olympos hotel directly to this interior marineland marketplace.

Salted fish.

KANGHWA-DO,
ISLE OF REFUGE

Mysterious, prehistoric men left strange, unexplainable sculpture here. Tan'gun, the founding father of Korea, built an altar on this island's highest peak. The Tripitaka Koreana Buddhist scriptures were carved at a temple here. And Koryŏ and Yi dynasty kings sought refuge on this island from invading Mongol and Manchu armies.

This historic place is **Kanghwa-do,** an island about 50 kilometers northwest of Seoul and across the narrow **Yŏmha Strait.** To visit this rural island, catch an express bus at Seoul's Sinch'on Rotary, and in about 90 minutes you'll be mingling with Kanghwa town's market folk.

Kanghwa town proper is small and easy-going—just the right size for pedestrian tourists who like to putter around marketplaces and in handicraft shops. Korea's finest rushcraft weaving is meticulously done on Kanghwa-do, so in local shops you'll find numerous baskets, woven into fun shapes, colors and sizes. You'll also discover fine floor mats and doorway hangings which are woven so tightly they let summer breezes in while filtering out pesky warm weather mosquitos.

Another kind of weaving—silkweaving—is also done in this town. And to that effect you'll hear the sound of machines clacking out reams of silk as you walk along Kanghwa's streets and footpaths.

Follow your ears to the **silk factory** (off the main street on the road opposite the bridge fronting the marketplace). Since visitors aren't allowed inside for tours anymore, take a long look instead at a **bronze bell** hanging idly inside a small slatted pavilion next to the factory. Cast during King Sukchong's reign (1674–1720), this bell used to toll at 4 a.m. to signal the opening of Kanghwa's city gates, and again at 8 p.m. to close the gates. When French troops stormed the city in 1866 to seek revenge for the execution of several French Roman Catholic priests, they attempted to haul this 3,864 kilogram (about 8,500 pounds) bell to their ship, but the French couldn't manage the carrying of it into captivity.

At the top of this same road is the restored **Koryŏ palace** where King Ko-

Inland poplars, Kanghwa Island.

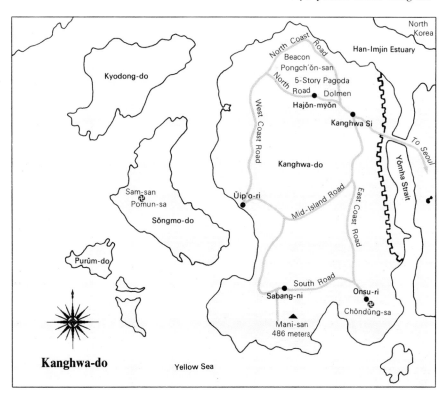

Kanghwa-do

jong lived in retreat during his unsuccessful 39-year-long resistance against invading Mongol hordes during the middle of the 13th Century.

From the Koryŏ palace, catch a taxi up to the neatly restored North Gate, **Pungmun,** for a view of the distant blue mountains of **north Korea.** On a clear day you can see for several miles across the **Han-Imjin Estuary** and into the forbidden and Communist north.

On the way back down to town, ask your driver to stop along the road and send you down a narrow footpath which leads to Korea's oldest and most unique Episcopal Church, **Kam Tok Kyohwe.** This Christian structure, built in 1900 by Bishop Charles Corfé about 10 years after his arrival in Korea, harmoniously combines Christian, Taoist, and Buddhist elements in its overall design. The front gate of the church is decorated with a large, paisleyed Taoist symbol; the church, constructed of wood, is classically Korean in its interior and exterior architecture; a bodhi tree, an old Buddhism-related symbol, was planted in the church's main courtyard at the time of the church's dedication; and atop the roof is a Christian cross trimmed with fluorescent light bulbs which show *the way* at night.

A Prehistoric Dolmen

After seeing this eclectic shrine site, catch a bus at the main terminal and head northwest of Kanghwa town to one of the most mysterious sculptures in Korea. The scenery along this roadway is dominated mostly by fields of ginseng protected by low thatched lean-tos, and typical Kanghwa farmhouses and grain silos are decorated with contemporary folk art. This "art" is in the form of meticulous sheet metal sculpture attached at the upturns of eaves and along corrugated metal rooflines. Here and there you will see brilliantly painted sheet metal cranes, lotus blossoms, airplanes, and other such symbolic and surrealistic roofcraft.

About three kilometers outside of town, down a dirt path behind a chicken farm, is a primitive stone sculpture constructed of three large, flat boulders. Archaeologists have identified this as a **northern-style dolmen** (in Korean, *chisong-myo* or *koin-dol*)—a sacred tomb or altar—which dates back to paleolithic times. Life goes on around it as it stands undisturbed in the midst of peppers, tobacco, and ginseng.

'Flowers of Youth'

Further down the bus line, in **Hajŏn-myŏn,** there is another old but less-visited stone sculpture. It is a **five-story pagoda** *(sŏk t'ap)* that was once a part of a Koryŏ temple. The temple is gone but the pagoda stands hidden in a pine forest. If you do seek out the pagoda, which is about a kilometer's walk from the main road past farmhouses, you might also wish to scale **Pongch'on-san,** the high hill behind it. Hikers are promised a panoramic view of the Han-Imjin Estuary and an opportunity to stomp around the ruins of an old **stone beacon tower.** This tower supported one of 696 beacon fires lit during the Yi dynasty to relay national security messages to Seoul. It was rendered obsolete when the telegraph was introduced in 1894.

Now travel back in time to the Three Kingdoms Period. On the southern end of Kanghwa-do (take a bus to **Onsu-ri** from town), about 16 kilometers south of Kanghwa town, is one of the oldest temples in Korea, **Chŏndŭng-sa,** the "Temple of the Inherited Lamp." **Chŏndŭng-sa** was named for a jade lamp presented to the temple by a Koryŏ queen. Formerly called **Chinchong-sa,** it was built in 381 A.D. by a famous monk named Ado. Legend has it that the wall surrounding the temple, however, was constructed by three princes to fortify the monastery. Thus the fortress was named **Samnangsŏng,** or the "Castle of Three Flowers of Youth."

The friendly monks here may invite you to share a vegetarian meal with them or guide you to some of the remaining **Tripitaka Koreana** sculptural woodblocks carved during the 13th Century. It took 16 years to carve the Buddhist scriptures on these blocks, a monumental task done in hopes of preventing a consuming Mongol invasion. (Most of the Tripitaka blocks were moved to Haein-sa west of Taegu to protect them from the Mongol invasion that eventually overwhelmed Korea.)

On the temple grounds is an **iron bell** about 1.8 meters tall. It was cast in 1097 during the Northern Sung dynasty in a typical Chinese style. Despite its foreign origin, the bell has been designated a national treasure. Before departing from Ch'ŏndŭng-sa, examine the architecture and unique ornamentation of human images engraved on the eaves of **Taeŭngjŏn Hall.** This particular design style was popular during the mid-Yi dynasty and is rarely seen anymore.

Tan'gun's Altar
And the 'Eyebrow' Buddha

Two-and-a-half kilometers southwest of Chŏndŭng-sa is the small town of **Sangbang-ni** and the site of **Tan'gun's altar** on nearby **Mani-san.** It is an arduous climb (almost 500 meters up) to the summit where ambitious hikers can get a sweeping view of Kanghwa-do and touch the spot where an important Korean legend was born. Some archaeologists claim Tan'gun's altar is no more than 400 years old, which would date it considerably younger than Tan'gun who, according to popular myths, descended to earth from heaven about 2333 B.C.

One last significant excursion that takes the better part of a day is a trip to the "Eyebrow Rock" Buddha at **Pomun-sa** on the neighboring island of **Songmodo.** This pilgrimage starts with a quick bus ride to **Uip'o,** a small fishing village on the west coast. Foreigners may be asked to show their passports in order to ferry across to the westward island. The ferry ride is a brief ten minutes, but the bus ride from the landing on the opposite side to Pomun-sa is about 45 minutes on a bumpy dirt road. The island is serene and carpeted by endless fields of rice, punctuated here and there by pointed churchhouse steeples.

Pomun-sa is a neatly restored 1400-year-old temple. It overlooks the light blue Yellow Sea and strangely-shaped islands that dissolve into the horizon. Behind the temple, carved into the mountain, is a stone chamber with **22 small stone Buddhas** enshrined in individual wall niches behind an altar. The Buddha statues are said to have been caught by a fisherman who was instructed by a monk in a dream to enshrine them here. Steps lead further above this stone chamber through junipers. At the end of a steep, heart-thumping hike is the massive concave "Eyebrow Rock" Buddha sculpted into the granite mountainside. He blissfully overlooks the rice fields, Yellow Sea and setting sun below.

Pomun-sa's 'Eyebrow Rock' Buddha.

P'ANMUNJŎM, ON THE DMZ

During the economic boom of the past decade, and midst the apparent tranquility of life in suburban Seoul and rural Korea, visitors have found it hard to believe that—after nearly 30 years of ceasefire and a Korean War truce agreement— the threat of an all out war still hangs over this "Land of the Morning Calm."

However, the danger is all too real, and to acquaint overly-optimistic tourists about this potentially volatile situation, the Korean government and United Nations representatives have in recent years sanctioned one of this country's— and indeed one of the world's—most unusual tourist outings. This unique visitor attraction is a day trip to **P'anmunjŏm,** the site of a small farming village which was obliterated during the Korean War.

P'anmunjŏm is also the historic place at Korea's **38th parallel** where American and South Korean representatives of a special United Nations Military Armistice Commission have been holding periodic talks with north Korean and Chinese negotiators to mutually supervise a ceasefire truce that was signed here on July 27, 1953. That truce agreement formally divided Korea into north and south political sectors and put an uneasy end to the bloody Korean War.

Geographically, P'anmunjŏm sits in a wide valley just northwest of the broad **Imjin River** and about 56 kilometers (35 miles) due north of Seoul.

Cartographically, and thus politically, Panmunjŏm also straddles land near the end of Korea's demilitarized zone (**the "DMZ"**), a demarcation line about 4,000 meters wide which serpentines 243 kilometers across Korea's waist between the Yellow and East (or Japan) seas. This truce camp is the only point of official contact between north Korea and the free world. This is also a heavily mined, barricaded and patrolled "no man's land" fit only for well-armed soldiers, a few hundred brave native farmers, and, ironically, several formerly endangered species of birds (such as the spectacular Manchurian crane) which have flourished within the "protected" confines of the DMZ since it was declared off-limits to most humanity in 1953.

Truce talks posturing, P'anmunjŏm.

'Truce or Consequences'

Truce talks have droned along here—as of 1980 more than 400 official meetings had been held—and though little is usually accomplished during most negotiations, they have often provided a convenient forum for the discussing and defusing of potentially provocative military or political issues. This role has proved crucial at times. "Korean DMZ Is the Scene of Truce and Consequences," stated a headline over an October, 1979 front page story about the truce talks in *The Asian Wall Street Journal.* In the dispatch which followed, reporters Seth Lipsky and Norman Thorpe explained Panmunjŏm's importance:

"These talks aren't," they wrote, "part of the so-called North-South dialog, where the issue is the reunification of Korea. Such talks are conducted by others, when the political stars are properly aligned. Instead, these talks are about maintaining what could be the most important truce in the world. It keeps a total of one million troops at bay on either side of this line, where a clash—by accident or misunderstanding—could trigger a world-scale confrontation in minutes."

The two journalists noted further that the truce talks, though often written off as hum-drum events by most media, have "proved remarkably effective" since they began in July, 1953.

"Many credit this truce mechanism," they wrote, "with helping to defuse major potential crises, such as when the North Koreans captured the U.S. spyship *Pueblo,* when Communist agents attacked the Blue House residence of South Korea's [late] President Park Chung-Hee, when two American soldiers were killed in a clash stemming from a disagreement over the pruning of a nearby tree, or when North Korean antiaircraft fire downed an American CH47 Chinook helicopter that strayed north of the DMZ."

Odd incidents such as the above still continue to happen when tempers flare, or when spies become bold, so Panmunjŏm continues to serve as a strategic and important truce buffer between the north and south sides of Korea.

The actual place where the talks take place is a simple barracks-like shed which is split exactly in half at the north-

American observer.

south demarcation line. Negotiators sit on either side of a table covered with green felt (which also exactly straddles the DMZ). On one end of the table is the red, white and blue yin-yanged and tri-grammed flag of the south, and at the other is the green and red-starred standard of the communist north.

Visitors aren't allowed to visit Panmunjŏm during actual negotiations, but on off days, if weather and the political climate are conducive, you can book a tour to P'anmunjŏm, "Freedom" or "Truce Village," and the DMZ by contacting the Korea Tourist Bureau office at the Koreana Hotel, or by making arrangements for the same tour through agents stationed at most of Seoul's luxury hotels (see Guide In Brief section for details). As of 1979 the cost of such a tour was about U.S. $13 round trip. That fee included lunch at a U.S. Army cafeteria within the demilitarized zone.

Your P'anmunjŏm-bound tour bus courses due north of Seoul on national **Highway 1** and follows wartime history through plains and valleys that were the heavily bunkered scenes of massive military advances, retreats and more advances during the Korean War and even during ancient Mongol invasions. This area is green and lush during the summer, but when winter chill sets in its beauty is bleak and brittle. Or as author James Wade describes this region in his book *West Meets East:*

"North of Seoul the Korean landscape is austerely beautiful in late winter. A light dusting of snow sets off the dark dots of rice stubble in frozen paddies and the lonely clumps of thatch-roofed farm houses. The steel-gray horizon, rimmed with jagged, ice-streaked mountains, recedes before the noisy jeep as it rumbles past the rail terminal city of **Munsan-ni** and approaches the Imjin River, with its symbolically narrow and precarious **"Freedom Bridge."** Suddenly you realize that the bleak new chain of mountains looming up not so far ahead is in north Korea."

In the old days, your motor-car or train would have paused at Munsan town, then continued on to P'yŏngyang and perhaps north and west through Manchuria to Peking. But these days all south-to-north journeys end at a DMZ village called **Taesŏng-dong** (which means **"Attaining Success Town"**), a community of ex-refugees who have opted to resettle in their native habitat,

and, of course, at the "end of the road," Panmunjŏm.

Taesŏng-dong, called by the U.S. military "Freedom Village," sits about a half mile from the P'anmunjŏm sheds where the truce talks are conducted. The villagers sometimes have to endure the indignity of propaganda being yelled at them over loudspeakers mounted on the north side of the DMZ, but life generally goes on here in much the same way it does in other parts of the Republic of Korea.

Once you reach the exact P'anmunjŏm talks site, you will be escorted around a heavily guarded sector formally called the **Joint Security Area.** You will be taken on a tour of the **Conference Room** where the truce talks take place, and from atop **Freedom House,** an ornate Korean-style pavilion, you'll be treated to a rare, panoramic view of **north Korea,** a place often referred to as "the world's most sealed-off society."

This government-sponsored tour usually takes place twice a day, and often your tour leader will also schedule an additional field trip, an official military briefing, and an American-style lunch as part of the tour package.

North Korean observers (below), and right, American sentries at the DMZ.

NORTH HAN RIVER LAKE COUNTRY

When a Korean is fraught with wanderlust—when he or she feels like hiking into that beauty which inspired classical brush paintings—he or she dons an alpinist's hat and heads northeast to the Republic of Korea's finest collection of rivers, lakes and mountains. They go to the land, as tourist brochures note, "Where Men and Mountains Meet."

This is the great northeast province of **Kangwŏn-do,** where in a single day a happy wanderer can bask on a lake or seaside beach, and—following a morning of catching resort rays—can hike through crisp mountain mists to a 15th Century Buddhist shrine scooped out of a granite cliff.

For centuries Korea has been referred to as *"sam ch'ŏn li kŭm su kang san,"* or the land of "3,000 *li* of rivers and mountains embroidered on silk." And in Kangwŏn-do, for miles in either direction—from the North Han River Valley to the demilitarized zone and the East Sea—this adage rings true. Here you will

indeed find a superb tapestry—delicately shaded with silken green rice terraces, swaths of amber grain, and pointilist vegetable patches that wind hither and thither along cold blue rivers and craggy mountain passes.

Probably the most picturesque journey of the above genre is the so-called "road to Sŏrak-san and the northeast coast" which takes you north of Seoul on a zigzag course of modern highways, inland waterways and dusty but pleasantly spectacular mountain roads.

This adventure—by bus (from Seoul's Chŏngnyang-ni station), or car—moves in a northeast direction on Highway 46 through mild mountains and along and across the snakelike North Han River and its valleys.

Glassy Lake Country

Several river and lakeside resorts have sprung up here and there along the highway from Seoul to Ch'unch'ŏn. If you see a turn on the river to your liking, stop and linger a day or two according to whim, but if you'd like a suggestion of where to stay, consider **Nami-som,** an island in the middle of the Han River near a

Boating piers, Ch'unch'ŏn Lake.

quaint highland town called **Kapyŏng.** This particular journey is about an hour's drive north of Seoul, followed by a 10-minute ferry ride to Nami-sŏm, where you can rent a small house or cabin and become one with splashing rowboats, cooing cuckoos, falling chestnuts and whooshing pines. Wake up early and wait patiently as the rising sun slowly but surely burns morning mists out of the little valleys which surround Kap'yŏng, lovely Nami-sŏm, and the Han River.

About 20 kilometers further north (a journey you can make by leisurely ferry from Nami-sŏm if you've got the time), you'll round a hill and descend into **Ch'unch'ŏn,** a convenient resort city for Seoulites who like to get away from it all for a day or week to enjoy some of the country's finest, if not *the finest,* lake country. Freshwater fishing, swimming, sailing, and water-skiing are readily available at several colorful resort piers which rim roomy **Ch'unch'ŏn Lake** and other sky blue waterways in the area.

In **Ch'unch'ŏn,** where violet, yellow and green rose cabbages landscape a series of cute mini-parks, you can follow your nose in a number of watery and earthy directions. Pause at **Ethiopia House,** an improbable teahouse which sits above candy-striped boathouses bobbing on glassy Ch'unch'ŏn Lake, and ponder adventurous alternatives over a bottle of beer.

Some folks ferry hop around Ch'unch'ŏn through narrow river gorges to charming riverside villages, sandy beaches, waterfalls (the Kukok Falls near Nami-sŏm are a favorite), and jade green swimming pools that have never been reached by a car or train. Others browse through East Ch'unch'ŏn's **Koryo Silk Factory**—the only "handmade silk" factory in Korea—where bright bundles of silk drying in the sun will dazzle your wandering eyes. Still others continue due north to **Hwach'ŏn** and the even more remote **Paro Lake** north of **Samyŏng Mountain.**

But probably the most popular local tour after a cooling respite along Ch'unch'ŏn's lakebanks is a visit to the nearby **Soyang Dam** and its attendant **Soyang Lake.** On the north side of this concrete monument to engineering and hydroelectricity (sometimes called "Korea's Boulder Dam") you'll find a colorful boat docking area, the **Soyang**

Rose
cabbage,
Ch'unch'ŏn.

Pavilion, where a road-weary traveler can leave land and embark on a tour of Korea's most splendid inland waterway. Lake Soyang is hyperbolically, but not unbelievably, called by some Korean travel writers "the largest lake in the Orient made by man."

Whatever Soyang's claim to environmental fame, from this pavilion you can proceed for many cool miles on a gliding cruise toward the Sŏrak Mountains and the northeast coast.

The Princess and the Snake

A sidetrip favored by travelers not pressed for time is a brief (about 15 minutes) diversionary cruise by open air launch to **Ch'ŏngp'yŏng-sa,** an ancient Buddhist temple (about 20 minutes hike and a mile and a half above a sleepy floating dock and restaurant) a few kilometers north of Soyang Pavilion.

This Buddhist retreat provides deliberate solace seekers with a simple escape from asphalt and beeping buses. A well-kempt trail to Ch'ŏngp'yŏng-sa rises easily—but steeply and steadily—along and above a tinkling and rocky streambed until you reach a waterfall and piney crags which sometimes come alive at dawn and at sunset with the om-azing harmony of sutras being chanted by resident devotees of the Lord Buddha.

Lakeside residents, who ply you with a ready supply of hot toasted cuttlefish, mandarin oranges, O.B. beer and aquamarine bottles of *soju* whiskey, are never too many hiking puffs away, but their sales pitches are quiet and unobtrusive—in keeping with the serenity of this lovely hike cum pilgrimage. (And the woman who manages the floating restaurant and souvenir shop just north of the boat dock will cheerfully mind your baggage while you huff to the temple.)

It will cost you about 200 won to enter this Buddhist center of desirelessness and non-attachment, and on the back of your ticket, in han'gŭl, you will be informed:

"This temple originated 1,600 years ago. A Chinese princess of the Tang period visited here to rid herself of a snake. She brought three bars of gold for the expense of rebuilding this temple, in hopes of losing the snake. At this time the gate of the temple was struck by lightning in the midst of a severe storm. The snake vanished, so the temple was renamed 'Revolving Door' from this incident."

Dragon guardian, Ch'ŏngp'yŏng Temple.

That ticket story is understandably perplexing, but only adds to Ch'ŏngp'yŏng-sa's mystique. Art historian Jon Covell theorizes that this story about the princess and a snake indicates shaman influences creeping into Buddhism. Another theory supposes the temple was the refuge-headquarters of a tantric, or erotic, Buddhist cult. Whatever its origins, you'll find your visit to Ch'ŏngpy'ŏng-sa rewarding if only to see its fine outer wall murals—which include, among other themes, an unusual Kwanseŭm holding a willow branch, a finely-executed Oxherding Series and a well-focused tiger panel.

Meanwhile, back on Lake Soyang, you can motor back to Soyang Pavilion near the massive dam, then catch one of many regular commuter specials (these are covered craft with a breezy after-deck) for the hour and 20 minute glide to a rural docking point just south of isolated **Yanggu** town. The surrounding mountains, which are ablaze with amber and roseate trees in the crisp autumn, are reflected by glassy Lake Soyang, and remind one of similar situations in New Zealand or the American Northwest. At the Yanggu area dock you can transfer to

a bus or taxi and proceed through hills and farm plots to sleepy Yanggu town.

At Yanggu, which lies in a pleasant valley only a few miles south of the demilitarized zone between north and south Korea, there are a number of good *yŏgwan* inns, restaurants and all the other amenities of small town Korea. From here there are also regular buses which race through corn and cabbage country to **Inje**, the "gateway town" to the spectacular Sŏrak Mountains area.

The 32.5 kilometers of mostly dirt roads between Yanggu and Inje offer bracing country airs and quaint rural scenes at every turn: here and there are timber and thatch rest pavilions, golden corn clusters drying in the cold glare of a clear autumn day, neat shamanist shrines dedicated to good harvesting, and, leaning against haystacks, kerchiefed and pantalooned mountain maidens puffing on long-stemmed pipes. Your bus or car will progress in lurches along pleasantly meandering stream beds and through mist-shrouded gullies until it drops down to the wide **Soyang River** bed, **Highway 44**, and Inje town on the river's sandy west bank.

Lake
Soyang.

SŎRAK-SAN, 'SNOW PEAK MOUNTAIN'

Sŏrak-san, the "Snow Peak Mountain," is now more formally known as the **Sŏrak-san National Park.** And as the name hints, this "Snow Peak Mountain" is not just a lone mountaintop. It's actually a series of peaks in the mid-section of the spectacular **Taebaek Sanmaek,** or "Great White Range," Korea's most prominent geographical region.

This panoramic backbone of South Korea's northeast province of **Kangwŏn-do** is one of those much-publicized "tourist destinations" which live up to the hyperbole and public relations written and spoken on its behalf. The Sŏrak area is indeed a mountain wonderland, a living nature scroll, and you'll understand after a visit why early Zen (or *Sŏn*) Buddhist monks chose this region to sit and work at becoming one with the universe.

There are several convenient ways to get to the Sŏrak area from Seoul. The quickest is by Korean Air Lines domestic aircraft to **Sokch'o** (about 40 minutes

flying time), then by bus or taxi to **Sŏrak-dong** (add another 20 minutes). You can also train to or bus to the terminal fishing town of Sokch'o.

Korea oldtimers aren't in such a hurry to get to this place. They prefer, as outlined in the preceding North Han River section, to enter Sŏrak slowly, from the country's scenic interior, and drift into the area's magic on newly paved, winding roads which meander through the wilds of **Inner Sŏrak.**

Inje, the renowned "Gateway to Inner Sŏrak," is as good a place as any to begin this exploration. But even in Inje town you'll have to decide which of two scenic ways you'll take to traverse the Sŏrak range. One route, called the **Southern Route,** goes through the **Han'gye-ryŏng Pass;** and the other, the **Northern Route,** serpentines through two back mountain passes, the **Chinpuryŏng** and **Misillyŏng** passes, before descending into Sokch'o on the East Sea. Most first time and veteran travelers prefer the Southern Route, both for the comfort and scenery. But if you're up for a bit of "roughing it," head north.

The Southern Route from Inje wends its way through "Inner Sŏrak,"

The summit of sorak (preceding pages), and left, swaying footbridge to Flying Dragon Waterfall.

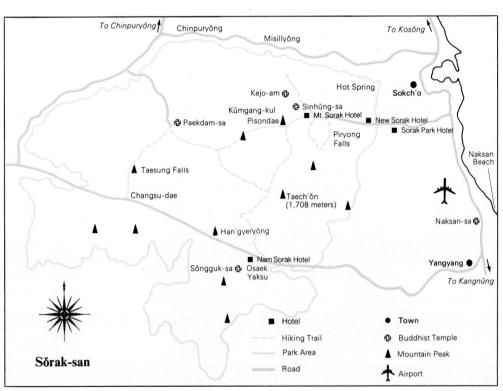

To Chinpuryŏng   Chinpuryŏng
Misillyŏng
To Kosŏng

Kejo-am
Hot Spring   Sokch'o
Sinhŭng-sa
Kŭmgang-kul   Mt. Sorak Hotel
Paekdam-sa   Pisondae   New Sorak Hotel
Sorak Park Hotel
Piryong
Falls
Naksan
Beach
Taesung Falls
Changsu-dae   Taech'ŏn
(1,708 meters)
Naksan-sa
Han'gyeryŏng
Nam Sorak Hotel   Yangyang
Sŏngguk-sa   Osaek
Yaksu   To Kangnŭng

Hotel   ● Town
Hiking Trail   Buddhist Temple
Park Area   Mountain Peak
Sŏrak-san   Road   Airport

Naesŏrak, through the southern fringes of "Outer Sŏrak," Wesŏrak, until you emerge at lovely Yangyang town on the turquoise blue East Sea. You'll be traveling from Inje to Yang-yang on a meandering, newly paved road that enables you to take in the gorgeous sights in expressway comfort.

En route you'll encounter (at Chang Su Dae) numerous nature trails (abloom in the spring and ablaze in the fall), veil-like waterfalls, red-bellied frogs, cripple creeks, and (at Osaek Yaksu) mineral water springs famed for their therapeutic properties. Some travelers like to pause at Chang Su Dae and hike up to the Taesung waterfalls (which can range in fall from a rush to a trickle), then course onward and upward to Paekdam-sa, a charming Buddhist temple smack in the interior of Inner Sŏrak. Both hikes are good for the soul after the traffic of Seoul, but be prepared—with warm clothes, good walking gear, food and drink—if you plan to camp overnight in these desolate parts.

Further east on the Han'gye Pass road, at the very top of this spectacular pass, you can begin yet another trek—this one all the way to the top of Sŏrak's supreme peak, Taechŏn-bong, the third highest mountain, at 1,708 meters (5,604 feet), in Korea. If prepared for such adventure, you can navigate onward and enter the Sŏrak-dong resort complex by its back door. However, again be advised that this 11 hours of steep zig-zagging through beautiful nature can be dangerous during the icey and very slippery winter months.

The Osaek Yaksu medicinal springs at the far east end of the Han'gye Pass road are well worth a stop and recuperative soak, but if you're feeling fit without the benefit of such therapy, you may want to rush on down to sea-level to a grand seafood meal at Yangyang, Naksan or Sokch'o. Appetite thus satisfied, and mind and body braced by cool breezes off the East Sea, you are now ready to tackle Outer Sŏrak and her well-equipped bands of happy mountain wanderers.

The 15-minute bus ride from the sandy East Coast into Sŏrak Village is a grand transition from beach cabana chic to mountain resort cool. One moment you're sniffing at raw sea fish and clams arrayed 'neath your beachside umbrella, and only moments later you're in a piney

lodge considering hot buttered rums and steamy pinenut soup.

Thanks to Koreans' almost religious dedication to proper hiking, camping and enjoyment of the great outdoors, and the government's far-sighted investment in this wilderness area, the Outer Sŏrak-Sŏrak-dong resort complex has become one of the finest woodsy places in Korea, indeed in the world, for leisurely hiking and dining alfresco. Nature strolls here can accommodate everyone— from the most languid non-hiker to an aggressive rock-climbing fanatic. There's even a modern cable car that will carry less aggressive outdoorspersons to a properly catered promontory where they can meditate on **Pisŏn-dae,** a famous rock structure called the **Flying Fairy Peak.**

However, once you've settled in to one of Sŏrak-dong's many inns or hotels— which range from deluxe hotels to simple *yŏgwan* inns—your biggest problem will be to decide which of Sŏrak's many possible mountaineering-excursion themes to pursue.

On the road to inner Sorak

A large and detailed information sign just below the charming **Sŏrak-san Tourist Hotel** offers a few suggestions, but for openers let us suggest the following Sŏrak area frolics:

'World's Oldest Zen Temple'

Before you head into the bush, stroll up the main flagstoned and fir-lined path which leads to **Sinhŭng-sa,** an ancient Sŏn (or Zen) temple originally built near its present location in 652 A.D. The first Sinhŭng-sa, then called **Hyŭngsong-sa,** or the "Temple of Zen Buddhism," was destroyed by a forest fire in 707, rebuilt in 710, burned again in 1645, and finally rebuilt a third time at its present location in 1648.

"If the signboard date at Sinhŭng-sa is correct," writes Zen and oriental art authority Dr. Jon Carter Covell, "then Sinhŭng-sa is the oldest Zen temple in the world. Nothing in China or in Japan is of this age, not by many centuries."

Just before you reach the temple compound proper, you'll pass (on the right side of the cobble path) a neatly kept and fenced-in cemetery full of unusual **bell-shaped tombstones** erected to honor formerly illustrious Zen monks who spent much meditative time in this area.

In the temple itself, which sits on a pleasant little bluff with a superb view of the surrounding mountains, you'll pass through lattice doors carved and painted in a floral motif and come eye-to-eye with a standard **Amit'a Buddha** flanked by **Kwanseŭm** and **Taiseiji** bodhisattvas. Of a more light-hearted interest, you will also be confronted, to your spiritual hilarity, by "the two crazy idiots of the 7th Century"—**Han San and Sup Duk** (known in China as Han Shan and Shih Te)—who grace the temple's northern wall. These absurd, grimacing and "crazy" fellows are often found in such spiritual surroundings, where they temper our overly-serious lives by laughing at the absurdity of existence.

Sinhŭng-sa offers even more such fantasy, some of it drawing on combinations of shaman, Taoist and Buddhist imagery. Consider the creatures which are half-tiger and half-leopard, and the writhing dragons, cranes and bats—all brilliantly painted on the ceiling. Or the drawing on the main hall's rear wall which shows a Zen patriarch offering his severed arm to a higher-ranking Zen master.

With that Zen mind-full, continue up this spiritual pass and path to the **Kejo Hermitage** about three kilometers onward and upward along a singing stream bed.

Kejo Hermitage, a subsidiary of the mother Sinhung Temple, is partially built into a granite cave at the base of **Ulsan-bawi**, a spectacular granite formation that dominates this part of the Sŏrak area. Like much of Sŏrak, and like the famous **Diamond Mountains** due north of here, Ulsan-bawi's face is rich with anthropomorphic images. And indeed, about halfway up to the Kejo Hermitage, an enterprising fellow with a high-powered telescope sells lingering peeks at one particularly erotic formation at Ulsan-bawi's mid-section. Price per peek: 50 won.

The hermitage is identified by a bright red Buddhist swastika carved and painted over an entrance arch. A narrow and cool corridor leads to the cave interior where you'll find a superb altar where candles burn before a small but exquisite golden Buddha. When monks are inside this ancient niche, chanting sutras and clacking wooden bells by flickering candlelight, the effect is Zen Buddhism at its most poignant.

Distant temples are accessible only by foot.

Fronting the Kejo Hermitage and Ul-san-bawi is another geologic curiosity which has become a major tourist attraction over the years. This is the famed **Rocking Rock,** a massive boulder which rocks back and forth in its secure place when given a solid nudge. Being photographed in front of this tipsy ball of granite is a touristic must.

If you enjoyed your ramble to the Rocking Rock, then perhaps you're ready for a more exerting trek—this time to the **Kŭmgang Cave** above the aforementioned **Flying Fairy Peak** (Pison-dae).

The hike to Pison-dae, a vertical rock that juts heavenward at the entrance to an extremely picturesque gorge, is easy enough, and at every lovely turn you'll find yourself gawking at the beauty of chill pools, small waterfalls, and, in the autumn, fire red maples and golden gingkos. "In Canada you'd have to do a lot of bushwhacking to see country like this," commented a visitor from Vancouver. Another hiker squealed with joy when he rounded a granite boulder and found a smiling grandmother selling cooling bowls of *makkolli* rice wine and *moru-jip,* a beverage made from the ber-ries of a local plant related to the grape.

From this restful camp at the base of Pison-dae, serious Buddhist pilgrims head up a smaller path to **Kŭmgang Cave,** which is located near the top of Pison-dae and requires a serious genuflection to exercise. After negotiating 649 stairs (yes, we counted them) to reach this charming cave-shrine, your heart will be pounding in your head, but the extraordinary view from up there— and from a halfway point promontory— will be your earthly reward. If you want to commemorate this trek, there's usually a young fellow at the cave entrance who makes a living selling Buddha medals to which he adds your name and the date you conquered the Flying Fairy Peak. Inside the cave is a small gold Buddha surrounded by burning candles, incense and small food offerings.

Meanwhile, back at the Sŏrak-dong base camp, other hikers have opted to visit the **Flying Dragon Waterfall** (Piryŏng) at the top of a lovely gorge below 1,345-meter high **Hwachae-bong.** This **peak** used to be a tough hike, but the government built a fun suspension bridge across the narrow gorge and stream that leads to the Flying Dragon.

The famed 'Rocking Rock'.

THE EAST COAST

Snow country and a ski resort. High-land hot springs overlooking rice terraces and pine forests. The bluest waters and whitest sand beaches in Korea. Stalactite and stalagmite-filled caverns. Even massive, computerized industrial complexes.

Korea's **East Coast,** home of all the above, does indeed live up to travel brochure pronouncements that this is "A Land of Contrasts." As in any country, that promotional cliché is true, but in Korea it is quite properly applicable to this broadly curving coastal region between her 36th and 39th parallels.

At the southern end of this arc are **P'ohang** and **Ulsan,** recently created industrial cities where steel, automobiles and ships are manufactured at astonishing production rates. And to the north, along postcard-perfect pine bluffs, inland lagoons, and cabana-dotted beaches, are seaside retreats which have been favored by hedonistic Koreans since ancient times.

You can begin your tour of the East Coast at several points up and down the East Sea, but probably the most central place to use as pivot point for travel is **Kangnŭng,** the major city in east **Kangwŏn Province.** This city of more than 80,000 people is easily reached by train or bus, but the most interesting way to make the 228 kilometer journey from Seoul is by private car.

A motorcar cruise to Kangnŭng—south on the **Seoul-Pusan Expressway,** then east on the **Yŏngdong Expressway**—will allow you the time you would need to explore both famous and obscure "tourist attractions" enroute to the East Coast.

Tune your car radio in to a popular Korean music station, fasten your seat belts, and enjoy a Korean highway at its best. This journey along broad expressways cuts a grand swath through cute Saemaul (New Community Movement) villages with turquoise, tangerine and chartreuse rooftops; glassy rice paddies that reflect neatly marching poplars; pine green hillsides that from a distance look like the backs of well-combed sheep; and busy logging camps in the bends of timber-clogged rivers.

Preceding pages, fishing village, Ullŭng-do; below, a village south of Kangnŭng.

If children are along you may want to stop at the **Yong-in Farm Land and Lion Country** at the very early part of the journey; but if they aren't, you may be content to stop and sniff the fragrance of a roadside acacia forest. Koreans like to soak white and pale yellow acacia blossoms in alcoholic spirits (usually in *soju* or *chŏngjong*), then (after a month or so of soaking) take this spirited essence to a scenic region such as this for a day of sipping and poésie.

Once you get into more mountainous areas, notice the unusual pointy-topped silos of Korean design, bright ears of corn drying along rooftops, and hops plantations which are distinguished by the lacy network of string trellises built to support these twining vines from which *maekju* (beer) evolves. These are subsidiary hops plantations of Korea's old Oriental Brewery.

Land of 10,000 Buddhas

One "road-to-Kangnŭng" detour you must make is just beyond little **Chinbu** village (about 40 kilometers west of Kangnŭng). This sidetrip carries you along paved and dirt roads to **Mount Odae National Park,** a charming mountain area and the location of two of Korea's most well-known temple complexes, **Wŏljŏng-sa** and **Sangwŏn-sa.** The road to 1,563 meter high **Odae-san** is literally dotted with tiny hermitages, Zen meditation niches, and other impressive remnants of Buddhism which date to the 7th Century and Korea's impressive Silla dynasty.

Because cool Mongolian winds and warmer air currents off the East Sea meet in this mountain region, the lush and pine-covered peaks of Odae-san often are wreathed in cool, shifting mists which sometimes give the area an eerie or other-worldly aura when patches of sunshine appear and disappear in improbable shifts and intensities. It is no wonder that early Buddhist masters in Korea chose this place as a prime meditation spot.

"According to an old mountain legend," says a passage in the 13th Century book *Samguk Yusa,* "it was Chajang Pŏpsa who first called Mt. Odae the abode of Buddha." Chajang, a famous monk, reportedly was sent to Odae-san by a Chinese monk who told him that he would find 10,000 Buddhas in the Odae

Monks at Sangwŏn-sa, Odae-san.

area. In a subsequent vision, a dragon told Chajang that the mysterious Chinese monk was actually the Munsu Buddha, so:

"In the seventeenth year of T'ang Chen-kuan (643)," the *Samguk Yusa* reports, "Chajang climbed Odae-san in order to see Munsu Buddha, but due to a thick fog which veiled the whole mountain in darkness for three days he returned to Wŏnyŏng-sa, where he met Munsu Buddha in person."

We can't guarantee you'll see the Munsu Buddha but chances are you will encounter much of the same dark fog Chajang did, and you too can retreat—after a day of fascinating hikes—to the area of a temple, now called Wŏljŏng-sa, which was built by Chajang in the Munsu Buddha's honor.

Wŏljŏng-sa, which sits on the southern fringe of Odae-san about eight kilometers off the expressway, is a sprawling temple complex distinguished by a superb nine-story **octagonal pagoda** and an unusual **kneeling Buddha** sculpture. The tiered pagoda, which rises 15.2 meters, is capped with a sculpted lotus blossom and a bronze finial of intricate design; the kneeling Buddha, meanwhile, has

well-weathered features, and (because of an unusual cap he's wearing), looks much like a European tin soldier. Both national cultural treasures are located in front of Wŏljŏng-sa's main hall within a grassy plot protected by a low iron fence wrought in a continuous swastika motif.

Along a riverbed road which snakes up to the higher reaches of Odae-san, you'll see occasional shrines and memorials to monks who've lived and died in this region over the centuries. One forest clearing contains several tall stone stupas, most of them notably phallic in design, which are said to contain the cremated remains—*(sarira)*—of famous Buddhist masters.

Even higher up, just east of Odae-san's main peak, and about 200 meters off the road at the end of a pine-bordered pass, is Sangwŏn-sa, another temple established by Chajang. According to an information board there, Chajang built this temple in 646 A.D. during the reign of the Silla Queen Sŏndŏk. Zodiacal images adorn its walls, and in a wooden pavilion on the grounds is a large bronze bell said to be the **second largest bell in Korea** (the largest being the Emille Bell at the Kyŏngju National Museum). This

Sari-ra (reliquaries) Odae-san

particular Silla bell, also the oldest known bell in Korea, is 1.7 meters tall and reportedly was cast in 725 during the reign of the Silla King Sŏngdŏk.

Schussing, Korean-style, In the Dragon Valley

Perhaps another 12 kilometers east and just south of the Yŏngdong Expressway is another highlands area with a decidedly different aura. This is the **Taekwallyŏng mountain** region where Korea's most modern and well-equipped ski resort is located. Throughout the Taekwallyŏng area are various ski spots with names such as **Talpanje, Chirmae** and **Third Slope.** Most are located in the vicinity of a small town called **Hwoeng-gye,** but the newest and favorite slopes have been developed in a place called **Yongp'yŏng,** or the **Dragon Valley.**

This **Dragon Valley Ski Resort** sprawls over 52 acres, features three newly completed slopes, and is equipped with chairlift systems, snow-making machines, a ski school, ski rental facilities, and even lighting facilities for night skiing. Chairlifts carry schussers to the top of both intermediate and beginner slopes.

Longer runs are being developed up the sides of the area's **Golden Dragon, Silver Dragon** and **Palwang** (1,458 meters high) mountains, but as of the 1980 season the longest ride, down Taekwallyŏng's 957 meters high **Mt. Twin Dragon,** offered a major headwall drop of about 50 meters that quickly tapered off into a series of cheerful bunny slopes.

Looming over this snow complex are two first rate hotels cum ski lodges, the **Dragon Valley Hotel** and the **Hotel Ju Won.** These lodges offer comfort-seekers both Western and Korean-style accomodations, plus a "Chalet Grill," billiards lounges, discotheque, heated swimming pool, archery range, tennis courts and rifle range for non-skiers and warm weather visitors. But if these places aren't your style, there are also private villas, *yŏgwan* inns and a large dormitory facility in the area which can be rented at single, double or group rates.

Just a few more kilometers east of the turnoff to the Dragon Valley and ski country the Yŏngdong Expressway begins to narrow somewhat. Then, after negotiating one last mountain rise, the **Taekwan Ridge,** you will begin a final, zig-zagging descent to Kangnŭng town

Tano festival visitors, Kangnŭng.

through the famous 99 turns of the Taekwan Pass. On a clear day the view from the top of this awesome granite cliff provides a fine first-impression of Kangnŭng and the deep blue **East Sea.**

Kangnŭng is a sleepy seaside town rich in traditional architecture and hospitable people. Its always been known as the key trading and terminal point in this part of Korea, but has also gained local fame as the site of an annual Tano spring festival (held on the 5th day of the 5th lunar moon, usually in May) that takes place on the banks of a wide river that divides the town's north and south sectors. This Tano celebration is rich in shamanistic dancing, religious rituals and general merrymaking which attract country folk from the seaside and mountains to its colorful tents, sideshows and outrageously colorful carnival atmosphere. It's a true local people's event.

Confucian Reflections
on Rising Moons

The Kangnŭng area abounds with precious distractions worth anybody's touring time, but perhaps the most prominent are:

• A classical Confucian academy and shrine—**Hyangkyo and Taesungjŏn**—in the northwest suburbs of Kangnŭng on the grounds of the **Myungnyun** middle and high schools. This hilltop structure, which was built in 1313, destroyed by fire in 1403, then rebuilt in 1413, has low, brooding rooflines and tapering colonnades typical of Koryŏ dynasty structures in other parts of Korea. Rooms on either side of this old academy's main hall are filled with boxed spirit tablets that are opened every year when Confucian *chesa* ancestral rites are held here.

• **Kyŏngp'o-dae Lake** and **Kyŏngp'o-dae Beach.** This resort just a few kilometers north of Kangnung has long been a popular Korean recreational spa. Waters off Kyŏngp'o-dae Beach are often busy with zig-zagging speedboats and sailing craft, and on shore are numerous tented seafood restaurants where you can choose your lunch swimmingly fresh from gurgling saltwater tanks. Korean tourists like to buy bundles of *miyŏk* (seaweed for soup-making), dried cuttlefish, and other exotic delicacies from women vendors who ply their trade on this colorful beach.

Ski tot, the Dragon Valley.

Just inland of this beach scene—past the clutter of hotels and inns, and rows and rows of shops which sell touristic kitsch souvenirs—is mirror-like Kyŏng-podae Lake. This fishing lake dotted with lovely islets used to have pleasure pavilions set like jewels on its every shore. This was where local *yangban* aristocrats met with friends or lovers to sip wine, compose poems and watch sunsets and moonrises over the nearby T'aebaek mountain range. As an old saying sings, from the old **Kyŏngp'o Pavilion** on the lake's north shore "you can see the rising moon reflected in the lake, in your bowl of wine, and in your sweetheart's eyes."

If such images keep you in a romantic and classical mood, head back across the lake toward Kangnŭng, detour northwest a bit, and cross a series of rice paddies by footpath until you reach the 99 *k'an* living compound, Confucian academy, lotus pond and pavilion built during the 18th and 19th Centuries by members of the prominent Yi Ku family clan. This complex is as perfect an example of a *yangban* Yi dynasty living compound as you'll find anywhere in Korea. And what makes it even better is that the Yi family still lives in the main house, just as

their ancestors have for the past two centuries.

This compound is picturesque in the white winter—when snow trims its curved roofs, mud and tile walls and cozy thatched servants' quarters—and in the summer—when giant pink Indonesian lotus blossoms rise out of their shallow pond like sleepy dragons.

Black Bamboo Shrine

Another fine Confucian place, this one about four kilometers north of Kangnŭng, is **Ojuk-hŏn** (Black Bamboo Shrine), birthplace of the prominent Confucian scholar-statesman-poet Yi I (1536–1584). Yi I, more popularly known by his pen name Yulgok (Valley of Chestnuts), was one of a select group of Neo-Confucianists who became quite powerful during the 16th Century. Among positions he held were royal appointments as Korea's Minister of Personnel and War and Rector of the National Academy.

One biographical sketch notes that Yulgok was an infant prodigy who knew Chinese script at the age of three, "and when he was seven he already composed

Kwanseŭm-posal (Bodhisattva of Mercy), Naksan Temple.

poems in Chinese. At the age of nineteen he entered the Diamond Mountains and was initiated in Buddhism, but soon abandoned it for the study of the philosophy of Chu Hsi."

To honor Yulgok's example and memory, the Korean government has in recent years completely restored and rebuilt his birthplace site. This memorial, on the west side of the road to Yangyang and Sokch'o, is a prim compound rendered in the cheerful yellow favored by the ministry in charge of national parks and memorials.

Ojuk-hon, which has the aura of a shrine (proper clothes must be worn here, and smoking, gum-chewing and photography are not allowed in the vicinity of Yulgok's memorial tablet house), is a memorial not just to Yulgok, but also to his mother, Sin Saimdang, who was revered during her lifetime as a fine calligrapher and artist. Various calligraphic scrolls by Yulgok, his mother, and other members of this Yi family are on display in a small museum at the rear of the Ojuk-hŏn compound. Also on view, and well worth a cultural pilgrimage to this shrine, are several original paintings by the talented Lady Saim-

dang. Her precise and flowing studies of flora and fauna are superbly executed.

Before continuing north from this site, marvel for a moment at the fine stand of **black bamboo** which bends in a garden between the museum and Yulgok's house. Then look west toward nearby pine forests and consider the following stanzas from Yulgok's famous poem *The Nine Songs of Mt. Ko* (as translated by Peter H. Lee):

Where shall we find the first song?
The sun lances the crown rock, and
Mist clears above the tall grass.—
Lo the magic views far and near—
Calling my friends I would wait
With a green goblet in the pine grove.

Proceed north past such sun-lanced rocks, pine groves and the shocking blue East Sea towards **Yangyang, Naksan, Sokch'o, Hwajinp'o,** and, at the northernmost reaches of Highway 7, the sleepy fishing village of **Taejin.**

Just above Yangyang, on the southern skirts of Sokch'o, you'll find what is probably the most charming and impressive religious site in this part of Korea. This is **Naksan-sa,** a Buddhist temple complex originally established at this site by the Silla high priest Ŭisang in 671

Cabanas,
Hwajinp'o.

during the 11th year of Silla King Munmu's reign. The main hall and support structures were rebuilt in 858, burned down during the Korean War, then rebuilt again in 1953 by Gen. Hi Hyong-kun and his men.

According to a story board, the high priest Ŭisang prayed here for seven days on a 15-meter high rock by the sea. He wanted to see Avalokitesvara (the God of mercy), the story notes, "but in vain."

"In despair he threw himself into the sea and then Avalokitesvara appeared, gave him a rosary made of crystal, and told him where to worship him. Thus Wŏntŏngp'o-jŏn, the main hall of this temple, was built on this spot." Another version of this story notes that Ŭisang "became a Buddha himself when he saw the image of the Maitreya Buddha rising from the sea in front of him following his seven day prayer toward the sea."

However long Ŭisang prayed or whatever he saw emerging from the deep, this temple stands in his and Buddha's honor. Several national treasures are housed in Naksan-sa's halls, towers and pavilions. The first item you'll notice is a splendid stone gate, **Honghwa-mun,** built during the reign of King Sejo (r. 1455–1468), who once prayed here. Probably the second most impressive structure is a **seven-story Koryŏ pagoda** that stands 6.2 meters high in front of the main hall. Its gleaming finial is composed of finely wrought treasure rings, a fortune bowl and a treasure jewel. Third, but certainly not least, is a large bronze bell, called **Pŏmjong** with four raised bodhisattva images. It was cast in 1496. The bell— 1.6 meters high by a meter in diameter— is inscribed with poetry and calligraphy by the famous poet Kim Su-on and the calligrapher Chŏng Ran-jong.

A Merciful Apparition

On Wŏntŏngp'o-jŏn's sea side, dominating all natural and man-made items in the area, is a 15-meter high white granite statue of Buddhism's **bodhisattva of mercy,** known in Korea as the goddess **Kwanseŭm-posal,** in China as Kwan Yin, and in India as Avalokitesvara (though Avalokitesvara is an earlier male counterpart). This particular Goddess of Mercy faces the southeast atop a six-foot granite pedestal and open lotus blossom.

The massive statue, the work of Pusan sculptor Kwŏn Chŏng-hwan, was dedi-

Ŭisangdae fishermen.

cated on November 5, 1977. According to Ch'oe Wŏn-ch'ŏl, then chief priest at Naksan-sa, an old priest appeared to him in a 1972 dream and told him where and how to place this statue. Following this apparition, Ch'oe reported his dream to the religious affairs board of the Chogye-jong Order headquarters in Seoul. After considering Ch'oe's vision, the board decided to proceed with the project. Some six months of hard labor and 700 tons of granite stone were required to complete his and Kwŏn's inspired sculpture.

"From the day when the granite standing bodhisattva was solemnly dedicated, Naksan Temple went into a thousand-day prayer for national peace and security," reported a dedication day story in *The Korea Times*.

From this statue, which stands like an ancient beacon of hope on this quiet and rugged coastline, continue north past Ŭisang-dae and its tiny pink lighthouse to Sokch'o town. (See the preceding travel story regarding a detour you can make in this area to the Mount Sŏrak National Park area.) Sokch'o, an important northeast coast fishing port, has long been a hopping off point for seaside resorts to the north.

Private and government enterprise have developed several sand beach areas north of Sokch'o, but the all-time favorite languishing spot is **Hwajinp'o Beach** about halfway between Sokch'o and the demilitarized zone. Korea's presidents have traditionally maintained summer villas here, as have other persons who appreciate comfort and beauty.

Most travel beyond Sokch'o is on dirt road, but such bumps, curves and dust slow your highway mind and make this fine coastline excursion even more special and memorable. Along the way are several quaint fishing villages, exotic inland lagoons quackingly alive with fish and waterfowl, and broad, dune-like beaches as fine as any you'll discover in California. End of the line—and as far north as you can go in southern Korea—is **Taejin,** a friendly little town of tiny streets, people who are pleasantly surprised to see a foreigner this far off the beaten path, and one of the most colorful fishmarket docks in Korea.

'Underground Diamond Mountains' And Other Points South

The going used to be tough from Kangnŭng southward, but with the re-

Uisangdae.

cent completion of the smooth East Coast Expressway all the way to P'ohang, traveling in these parts is now sweet and easy. Among sights and sites not to miss along the southeast coast are:

• The strangely beautiful **Sŏngnyu Cave** just south and then inland from **Uljin** town. **Sŏngnyu-gul,** which is actually a proper limestone cavern adrip with bizarre stalactites and stalagmites, is, as one tour leader describes it, "a spelunker's delight." The easiest way to get there if you don't have a car of your own is to catch a local bus from Uljin and travel eight kilometers south to the Sŏngnyu-gul bus stop. From there the cavern is about a two kilometer walk west on a dirt path or road across attractive rice paddies and along a curving riverbank.

At the cavern site, even early in the morning, you'll find uniformed guides, a complete curio shop, a lovely pavilion overlooking the chill river, and little Korean-style cafes where you can either cool off or warm up, depending on the season.

Inside the 470-meter long cavern, which arches in a ragged crescent from a narrow stoop entrance to its final exit, you'll discover red, blue, yellow and white spotlights playing off weird limestone formations. Sŏngnyu-gul's caretakers over the years have given nearly every stalagmite, stalactite, grotto and pool a proper or whimsical name: There's "The Upside-Down Diamond Mountains," "Cloudy Rock," "The Secret Room of a Nymph," and statues of "St. Marie," "The Maitreya Buddha," and "Santa Claus." There's even a phallic, fluted, and spot-lit "Love Ball" that towers over a 30-meter deep "Dragon Pond."

According to brochures about the cavern, it is a quarter of a billion years old. During the Hideyoshi invasions, it is written, sacred Buddha statues from a nearby Sŏngnyu Temple were secreted away in these "Underground Diamond Mountains." However, according to another source, during this time some 500 local residents who hid in the cavern from Hideyoshi's invaders starved to death when they were discovered and the Japanese sadistically blocked Songnyu-kul's narrow entrance.

• **The Paegam Hot Springs.** Approximately 30 kilometers south of Uljin is **P'yŏnghae,** a quiet farming town where

Seafood, Taejin.

you can book a taxi or chance a bus to Korea's picturesque **Paegam Mountain and Hot Springs.** We say chance a bus, because the irregular buses that crawl up to the Paegam springs on a rocky and dusty road through beautiful highlands country are invariably overcrowded with people, animals, and domestic goods. Taxis, though more expensive, are your best ploy. Once there you can rest and recuperate in some of Korea's most re-knowned mineral baths. (See the feature section story about Korean pleasures for more details about the Paegam-san health spa.)

The Land of King Ju

• **The Juwang Mountains.** Korea hands who like to travel and seriously *get away from it all* journey to the **Mount Juwang National Park** due west of Yŏngdŏg and southeast of **Andong** via **Chŏngsong.** This 720-meter-high East Coast mountain in north Kyŏngsang Province can usually be reached only by country bus; but according to visitors who have made the effort to get there, the trip is well worth the bouncing hassle. Consider the following comments made by traveler Cornie Choy in a recent memo mailed to members of the Korea Art Club:

"Juwang-san, the Mountains of King Ju, stood before me—an Oriental landscape painting on a folding screen. The tiny country inn a friend had told me about is perfectly situated on the grounds of an old Buddhist temple, a clear running stream in front of it. Beyond is a hermitage where only Buddhist nuns live—and all around us are towering granite peaks. My small room in a mud-walled, thatch-roofed hut is rustic, clean and simple . . .

"Eager for a walk, I set out, taking my time, following footpaths thru silent fragrant autumn woods whose leaves display their bright farewell, and along the sides of deep gorges with dragon waterfalls and fairy bathing pools the color of jade . . . By noon, I am deep in the mountains making my way up a rocky path which leads thru a narrow gorge where the sun never shines. As I come out of the gorge, I find myself in a quiet sunlit valley. There, hidden away from the rest of the world, is a lone Buddhist hermitage. Looming all around it, like fearless guardians, are the awesome peaks of **Nahan-bong, Mirŭk-bong, Kwanseŭm-**

bong, Chichang-bong, Piru-bong, and **Pirot-bong**—all named after loyal disciples of Buddha.

"Approaching the hermitage, I notice the hermit monk—young, handsome and proud—chanting sutras to the rhythm of the wooden **mokt'ak** which he strikes . . . He invokes in me the following beautiful poem written by a Buddhist monk:

"Reach out your hands to me, Oh Buddha./With your mother-gentle hands of skyblue celadon, embrace this breaking and falling reed./Lower a thick warm rope to this soul sinking into the darkness./I am longing for you Lord./ Like the white foam which rises to the brim of the seas./Distill my longing into a single ruby bead . . . "

• **Pogyŏng-sa.** In the foothills of **Naeyon-san,** about 15 kilometers north of Pohang, is Pogyŏng-sa, a temple that offers a long history and a hike to a nearby pool and waterfall. A Western-style *yŏgwan* down the road to the right is a good spot to stay overnight. It offers a picturesque view of the mountains and is within Buddhist drumbeat range of the temple. If you can sleep with one ear alert for the early morning drum-call to prayer, you might want to repair outside for the sight of a sunrise and birds leaving nocturnal perches. The only human sounds you may hear will be your own stirring about and distant sutras being chanted by monks celebrating all life on earth.

The Chinese Mirrors of Madung and Pumran

Once sleep is washed from your eyes, stroll over to Pogyŏng temple. Just before reaching the temple proper, you will see a walled-in hermitage. Next to it is Pogyŏng-sa where monks hold retreats for lay Buddhists. According to the sign posted at Pogyŏng-sa, this temple was built during the Silla dynasty when Buddhism was first introduced to Korea. At that time, priests Madung and Pumran returned from China with the new religion and two faceted mirrors. One mirror had 12 facets and the other had eight. The eight-faceted mirror was given to Priest Ilcho, one of their disciples, who was told that if he went eastward, he would find a deep pond in Chongnam-san on the east coast of the Silla kingdom. If he threw the mirror into the water and filled the pond with earth and built a temple there, Buddhism would flourish.

The eight-faceted mirror is said to be buried under Pogyŏng-sa's **Choggwang Hall.** Fine Buddhist paintings are hung in Choggwang-jŏn and Taeung-jŏn, but what distinguishes this temple from most others is its backdrop of numerous waterfalls that streak the mountains which form this lush valley. There is a rather easy hike along the trail beside the temple to a clear pool, and further to 11 other waterfalls where you can—if you will—enjoy a cool summer splash.

• **P'ohang.** At the southern end of your East Coast adventure looms P'ohang, a seaport and resort area that since 1968 has been the apple of Korea's industrial eye. This is because P'ohang is the location of the model **P'ohang Iron and Steel Company, Ltd.** (POSCO), Korea's successful producer of industrial steel and its by-products. This monument to Korean industry rises like a fiery sculpture along the rim of **Yongil Bay** and the East Sea.

By 1978, 10 years after its dedication on April 1, 1968, POSCO was producing an estimated 5.5 million tons of crude steel for domestic and export purposes. By 1981, plant executives predict,

Blue-green Ullŭng-do visions.

POSCO will be cranking out up to 8.5 million tons. To achieve these goals, the Korean government has created a veritable workers' city, called **POSCO Village,** to support POSCO's steelworkers, their dependents, and the Korean economy.

If you're further interested in the fire and drama of ore-melting, blast furnaces, and bloom, slab, ingot and coil casting, tours can be arranged by contacting the Korea National Tourism Corporation or the POSCO public relations office.

Ullŭng-do: Away From It All

• **Ullŭng-do.** Few foreigners venture out to this island 268 kilometers northeast of Pohang. Indeed, because of its location Ullŭng-do is one of Korea's best-kept secrets. But, look out—the word is getting around as tourism to this island is now being promoted by the government.

Some of the best sights and travel experiences in Korea are on this island, which is about halfway between Korea and Japan (and is the farthest east one can go and still be in Korea). Embark on the *Han II Ho* speedboat ferry in P'ohang (see the Guide in Brief section on trans-

portation to outer islands), and six hours later you'll be strolling into To-dong town on Ullŭng-do's southeast coast. (Another proposed ferry from Imwŏn in Kangwŏn province may be in operation. Check with tour agents.)

A diverging footpath into town takes you past children and adults sitting and lying outside' their homes on straw mats. On warm summer nights they relax on these mats while chit-chatting with neighbors. Clapboard walls without windowpanes flimsily divide the outside from the indoors during the warm season. Also, as recently as 1978, there were no cars nor a paved road in use, and the air was extremely seaside fresh. Because there were no glaring streetlights, the stars were brilliantly visible. All that, however, is changing with the construction of a 'round-the-island road.

There are many yŏgwan in town— almost all of them without locks on the doors; Ullŭng-do, in fact, has long had a reputation for having no thievery. A few of the yŏgwan fronting To-dong Harbor have rooftop decks where one can sip a sunset beer and watch fishermen dock their boats. Meals, which include freshly caught seafood, can be ordered at most yŏgwan or cafes.

Behind the town and up a path towards the rugged mountains and forest is a mineral water fountain that spews out of a stone-carved turtle's mouth set in the mountainside. Foreign visitors like to splash a bit of Johnny Walker "on the rocks" and mix into this fresh mineral water. The island's freshwater is very soft (as you'll find out when you bathe), and it's also pure enough to drink straight from waterpumps.

Bat Caves, Chuk-do Beef
And Night Squidfishing

To get a 360-degree view of Ullŭng-do, hike up 984-meter-high Sŏnginbong, the island's highest peak. Set off at daybreak and you'll be high among the clouds by mid-morning and back down just as the sun's heat becomes oppressive.

To circle the island, you can either hike 40 kilometers across valleys and along the coast (which takes three days) or hire a boat. Either way, you'll find coves with bat caves (in Korean, pakkwi-kul) and sun-toasted beaches with warm clear water.

The beach at Wata-ri on the east coast features a freshwater falls that rushes into a saltwater pool. Stop for a morning swim at this beach, shower under the falls, and boat across to Chuk-do, a flat-topped islet jutting out across the water.

Approach this island from the south side, then scale its steep hillside. The hike up the steps to the top may seem arduous, but the men on this island actually carry calves on their backs all the way up to this island's highland farm. The fattened, corn-fed cattle are then lifted off the island by rope onto barges and sent to Ullŭng-do to be eaten. Chuk-do beef is renowned as the tastiest and tenderest in Korea. Four families who live on this small island mountaintop also raise watermelon (which some say is the sweetest in Korea), and the young, thin bamboo growing here is used for stretching out and drying squid in Ullŭng-do. Large mulberry leaves are grown here, too, for silkworm production on the mainland. Indeed, though the island is small, there is even room for a camelia forest which blooms in early to late February. Next to the camelia forest are palownia trees— the only tree, according to Korean mythology, on which a phoenix will land.

All along Ullŭng-do's coast, steep mountainsides drop straight down to a sea which is a most unusual, clear shade of blue—like liquid blue laundry bleach. Women divers with heavy lead weights tied to their waists bring up catches of seacucumbers, lobsters, crabs, abalones, prawns, and other shellfish.

Off the northeast coast is a sea grotto of unique, craggy candlestick rock formations with nesting sea birds. The northernmost rock, called Kongam, has a hole through which you can boat.

On the southwest side of the island, just north of Namyang, is T'aeha-dong, the landing site of the first Koreans to migrate to this island a thousand years ago. A children's shrine, which may be locked, is maintained in this town. Nearby is Sat'ekam beach, a cove with warm, calm waters ideal for swimming.

Climax your Ullŭng-do experience with a squid-fishing expedition. Squid fishermen set off at night, and once at sea they light up a string of bright lights across their boats to attract the squid. The brightly-lit squid boats bobbing in the dark are a memorable sight.

THE WEST COAST

A journey down Korea's West Coast—with occasional side trips inland—provides fascinating nature sights and cultural insights into the southwest provinces of Kyŏnggi-do, the Ch'ungch'ŏng-dos, and the Chŏlla-dos.

Korea's jagged West Coast, cut by the whimsical Yellow Sea, is dotted with myriad peninsular islets floating offshore, and bordered by sandy beaches overlooked by quiet pine glens. Along this coast village fishermen and seasonal beachgoers regulate their activities according to tidal changes, because the tide differential is so extreme. In certain areas at low tide, the Yellow Sea exposes vast mud flats 17 to 25 feet offshore—a distance second in tide extremes only to the Bay of Fundy in Nova Scotia.

To reach the West Coast, head south from Seoul on the Seoul-Pusan Expressway, otherwise known as the Kyŏngbu Expressway, then veer west and southwest on Highway 21 into the lush, terraced valleys and rolling hills of Ch'ungch'ŏngnam-do,

Onyang Stopover

Travelers enroute to the coast may find Onyang, about 18 kilometers west of Ch'ŏn-an on Highway 21, to be a refreshing stop along the way. A hot spring and Hyŏnch'ungsa Shrine, which is dedicated to Korea's great 16th Century naval hero, Admiral Yi Sun-sin, have long attracted visitors. But since the Onyang Folk Museum in Kŏngok-ni opened in October 1978, tourist traffic to Onyang has increased. Touted as having the best all-around collection of Korean folk art in the world, the privately-owned Onyang Folk Museum has more than 7,000 traditional Korean folk articles on display—only a portion of the vast collection Kim Wŏn-dae has accumulated over the past 20 years. Three diorama display halls depict the life and traditions of Koreans with authentic household articles, work utensils, and religious, recreational and scholastic items.

Primed after a stimulating hot bath, a pilgrimage to Admiral Yi's shrine, and insights into Korean culture, head westward to Mallip'o Beach and Korea's largest arboretum.

Flora Koreana

Nature lovers may flee to popular Mallip'o Beach on the western tip of a peninsula which flares into the Yellow Sea like a snarling dragon. Just north of Mallip'o Beach lies Ch'ŏllip'o, another kind of haven for flora and folks fond of flora. On a 200 acre sanctuary, more than 7,000 varieties of plants, almost exclusively of temperate climates, thrive on a stable climate, the longer springs and autumns in this part of Korea, and on the fog and mist which provide a natural water sprinkling system. The Ch'ŏllip'o Arboretum is nurtured and owned by Carl Ferris Miller, a naturalized Korean originally from Wilkes-Barre, Pennsylvania, who's lived in Korea for the past 37 years.

Some of the plants in Miller's arboretum are indigenous. Others were imported from around the world. There are, for example, two varieties of magnolia indigenous to Korea at Ch'ŏllip'o, and 180 paxa variety from elsewhere. The entire magnolia family, however, accounts for 800 members. Hollies have been hybridized at the arboretum; there are presently 450 hollies.

Among the many botanical wonders flourishing in Miller's arboretum are such rare species as the *Glyptostrobus lineatus,* a conifer from southern China, and *Magnolia biondii* from north central China.

Although Ch'ŏllip'o is a private arboretum, Miller welcomes persons who are genuinely interested in plants, who have a respect for nature, and who can resist picking flowers and cuttings without permission.

'The Beach'

Veteran westerners in Korea have long favored the West Coast's Taech'ŏn Beach, or Taech'ŏn-dae, as a spring through fall resort haven. This fun spot, about 14 kilometers from the town of Taech'ŏn, can be reached by bus or train and car from Seoul.

As you near Taech'ŏn town, fields of yellow barley—the staple added to rice or boiled into drinking tea—cut bright yellow swaths across the summer rice terraces. Taech'ŏn is a lush agricultural area, but it's also well-known in Korea for its coal mines in surrounding hills which contribute the base fuel from which yŏnt'an, or charcoal heating briquettes, are made. Other industries are salt-making and cuttle-fishing.

"The Beach," as locals refer to Taech'ŏn-dae, is actually unofficially divided into two sectors—a northern stretch called "KB," or the "Korean Beach," and a southern stretch called the "Foreigners' Beach." This was originally a Christian missionaries' resort, and indeed, many Taech'ŏn homes are still occupied by missionaries or their descendants, but now also by members of Seoul's diplomatic and banking corps, and by a more *nouveau corps* of wealthy Korean business and government leaders.

The Korean Beach—where discos and wine houses co-exist with sleepy fishermen's huts—is a non-stop boogie scene during the peak summer season. But the well-manicured foreigners' beach maintains a residential dignity.

During spring through fall the foreigners' sector of Taech'ŏn-dae is reminiscent of northern California's coastline, what with its piney bluffs, rocky back bays, and offshore isles. On a clear day, you can see for nearly 40 miles across the Yellow Sea in the direction of China and toward the good-sized island of Wŏnsan-do.

Kongju and Puyŏ, Paekche Capitals .

Further inland from Taech'ŏn, away from frolicking surf and missionary resorts, lie the ancient towns of Kongju and Puyŏ. To get to these towns, it is necessary to return to the Seoul-Pusan Expressway.

Kongju is about 35 kilometers southwest of the expressway on Highway 36. It was once the capital of the Paekche Kingdom until the capital was moved south to Puyŏ. Both towns have regained the limelight in the 20th Century because of Paekche relics which have recently been excavated in the central and southeastern provinces of Korea.

In Kongju, a national museum was dedicated in 1972 to house relics found around town. Almost half of the 6,800 display items were excavated from King Muyŏng's (r. 501–523) tomb. As you browse past Muyŏng's gold crown ornaments, his exquisitely engraved bronze mirror, and other Paekche articles, remember that it was this same craftsmanship which was taught to the Japanese by emigrant Paekche artisans.

From Kongju, head further southwest (some 50 kilometers) and deeper into Paekche history and legacy to Puyŏ on the curving Highway 23. Along the way, pause at Kap-sa temple on the outskirts of Kyeryŏng-san National Park.

Paekche historical remains abound in Puyŏ. For openers, there is in a park near the entrance to town a seated stone Buddha and a five-story stone pagoda—one of three left from the Three Kingdoms Period. Other relics are displayed in the Puyŏ National Museum. Prehistoric stoneware vessels, shamanistic instruments, gilt-bronze and stone Buddhist statues, gold and jade ornaments and other treasures attest to the development and excellence of Paekche craftsmen, who were influenced by central Asian and North and South China artists. Much of the stonework is damaged due to the Silla and T'ang China attacks that brought this dynasty to its end.

The Puyŏ museum building is a curiosity that was designed by a Korean architect according to traditional Paekche lines, which were adapted by the Japanese. Indeed, the modern rendition looked so Paekche in style that it was criticized for its Japanese resemblance.

Paekche legacy extends itself beyond the museum. Along the serene Kŭm River at Paengma-gang (White Horse River), remnants of the grandeur and the fateful fall of the Paekche kingdom of some 1,300 years ago are preserved. Picnic perhaps on the flat rock (Nan-sok, Warm Rock) on the riverbank at Saja just as the Paekche kings used to. On the opposite side of the river is the picturesque Nakhwa-am (Rock of the Falling Flowers) bluff with a pavilion on its brow. Tradition says that the T'ang Chinese general Su Ting-fang lured a protective dragon out of the river with a white horse's head, and thus was able to cross the river and conquer Puyŏ. Out of loyalty to their king and to preserve their dignity, court women jumped to their deaths from Nakhwa-am into the river. As recorded in some Korean epics, they looked like falling blossoms as their colorful *ch'ima-chŏgori* dresses billowed in their deadly flight.

From these Paekche visions, head southeast along Highway 23 to Kwanch'ok-Temple outside of Nonsan and to one of the most impressive Buddhas in Korea. (Kwanch'ok-sa is also accessible from Seoul via the Seoul-Pusan and Honam Expressways).

The Ŭnjin Mirŭk

As you scale up the stone steps on the P'anya hillside to **Kwanch'ok-sa** (**Temple of the Candlelights**), all the superlative descriptions you've ever heard regarding the **Ŭnjin Mirŭk**—the thousand-year-old, largest standing stone Buddha in Korea—stir you with anticipation. Your curiosity is piqued when, at the top of a flight of stairs, your first glance at the Ŭnjin Mirŭk is through the clear, horizontal window of the temple (if the temple doors are open). All you can see of the "Buddha of the Future" is its face—its eyes peering back at you through the holy sanctum.

The "Standing Stone Kwansaeŭm Maitreya" in its totality is awesome. Its disproportionate massiveness, extended earlobes, crown, and large hands formed in a mudra all suggest a higher evolved spiritual being. Its face, however, which is scrubbed clean occasionally, has flat features and exotic, almond eyes, not unlike the Koreans, and exquisitely sculpted toes—all of which give it human qualities.

Situated in the rear of the temple courtyard, the Ŭnjin Mirŭk stands sedately at the foot of a stand of dwarf maple and scrub pine.

Also included at Kwanch'ok-sa are a five-story stone pagoda, lantern, and altar which were constructed while the Ŭnjin Mirŭk was being sculpted.

From Nonsan, as one heads along the old road to **Chŏnju**, one passes the **Nonsan Army Basic Training Camp** near **Yŏnmu**. This basic training camp is the largest in Korea, and almost every young male in the country has been trained here at one time. Three years ago, however, another camp was opened in Chŏnju.

Continuing southward on Highway 23, your vehicle passes through several small villages and various monuments to the past. In **Kŭm-ma** (**Gold Horse**) village, just past an open-air granite carving shop, there is a gracious poplar carriage road and rivulet that cuts through a field. About a hundred meters down the right side of this road, one of two pairs of banner stone posts which once belonged to a temple entranceway remains. Across the road from these stone posts is the oldest stone pagoda in Korea, **Mirŭk-sa** (originally named **Wanghŭng-sa**). This granite tower was built during the

Paekche period around 600–610 A.D. by King Pŏp and his successor-son, King Mu. It stands 13.5 meters high, and is large enough for the curious to walk through. Formerly either seven or nine stories, it was partially destroyed by lightning during the reign of Silla King Sŏngdŏk (r. 702–737). The pagoda was reinforced with cement in 1915 during the Japanese occupation, but today the six remaining stories of the pagoda are surrounded by rubble. Workmen reconstructing Mirŭk-sa in 1965 discovered a unique gold plate with Buddhist scriptures and other treasures.

Two more sculptures lie along the country road south toward Chŏnju. The first outside Kŭm-ma village are a pair of stone mirŭk standing on grass mounds facing each other some 200 yards apart across a rice field. They are said to be about 120 years old, but their purpose remains a mystery. Between them the Honam Plain stretches without a mountain in close proximity. The second sculpture is **Wanggŭng Tower** which is in the middle of a field. Some say it was once in the palace of the Mahan dynasty, but most historians claim it was originally placed at this site as part of the

remains of **Ch'esuk** temple which was built during the end of the Unified Silla period. This five-story granite tower is about nine meters high and three meters wide, and its grounds are still tended to by a gardener despite its seclusion.

Along the Honam Expressway to Chŏnju, mountains and hills roll endlessly in every direction. Considered the "rice bowl of Korea," Chŏllapuk-do is a veritable cornucopia of food. In the late spring, rains water the fields, and the farmers can be seen bent over, planting rice together in even rows. The Korean curve motif is everywhere in this pastoral scene—in subtle curves of terraced rice paddies, the rolling curves of mountains, hills and burial mounds, and the up-curved roofs of traditional farmhouses.

Chŏnju City, Paper and Pi Pim Pap

Chŏnju, which is 93 kilometers south of Seoul, is the provincial capital of Chŏllapuk-do. It is the ancestral home of the descendants of Yi Song-gye, founder of the Yi dynasty, and is famous for paper products (fans, umbrellas and proper papers), *pi pim pap,* and food in general.

Burial mounds, Chŏnju.

Papermaking was introduced to Korea by the Chinese about 1,000 years ago. The Koreans, however, became so adept at this fine craft that both Chinese and Japanese calligraphers came to favor Korean papers over their own.

Technology has encroached on the handmade papermaking industry, but in Chŏnju villagers still actively perpetuate this tradition in their homes and in makeshift factories. The sound of new paper pulps swishing in water rises out of windows, and in backyards white sheets of paper hang like drying laundry.

Despite modernization, papermaking is still best done by hand. Fibers of the *Ttang* tree, mulberry stems, bamboo (all brought from other areas in Korea) and other flora are stripped and cooked into a soft pulp and then bleached in a soda solution. They are then transferred to a large wooden and cement vat. Rectangular bamboo mat screens suspended from resilient bamboo poles are dipped in and out of these pulp-filled vats, and—with a rhythmic finesse that has made this process a fascinating sight—a sheet of sopping wet paper is eventually sieved onto the bamboo screens.

The entire process may be observed at

Oh Dong-ho's factory at the end of Chŏnju's main street—just before a small bridge and to the left along a red brick wall.

A variety of paper in various textures and colors is available in Oh's paper and antique shop in town called Koryŏ Tang, "The House of Meaning Taste." In Oh's paper stocks are *unhyang-ji* of coarse mulberry, a basic wrapping paper; *whason-ji* for brush painting; *chang-ji* ("paper of a thousand years") from the *ttang* tree for calligraphy; *chang p'an-ji* for *ondol* floors; *ttae ju-ji*, algae paper; *chuk-ji*, bamboo paper; *p'i-ji*, bark chip paper; and recycled paper made from various secondary papers. If you have trouble finding Oh's paper place, ask a local to direct you to Pungnam-mun, Chŏnju's ancient south gate. "The House of Meaning Taste" is very near this entrance.

Ah, but ask any Korean what Chŏnju is *really* famous for and the answer will be *"Pi pim pap*—don't leave Chŏnju without tasting the state-of-the-art in this food form." At the famous, long-established Han Il Kwan restaurant (progenitor of the two Han Il Kwan branches in Seoul), the *pi pim pap* comes with the

Papering a screen, Chŏnju.

rice deliciously mixed with soy sprouts and topped with broiled and sliced meat, fern bracken, strips of boiled squid, bluebell roots, toasted sesame seeds, pine nuts and a sunny-side-up egg. And that's not all. This savory dish is further accompanied by a bowl of beef broth and side dishes of cool seaweed and onion soup further spiced by at least five different kinds of *kimch'i*.

Indeed, even at the simplest Chŏnju restaurant expect to see amazing foods piled up at your table, in some cases *at least* as many as 20 different side dishes. When in Chŏnju, don't be shy—eat!

Before leaving town, however, be sure to visit the private antique shop-museum **Chŏn Bok T'uk San P'um Ch'ŏn** run by Chŏn Jin-han. It is located near the **T'o Chŏn (Provincial Central Headquarters)**. Chŏn's family collection must be one of the most superb in Korea. It includes traditional Korean masks, Silla ceramic pieces, woven goods, and fine antique jewelry.

A Chŏnju city bus or taxi will get you out to **Songgwang-sa,** a fine Buddhist temple between Chŏnju and **Mai-san.** Located in a corner of a quaint village that produces *onp'an-ji* paper for *ondol*

floors, Songgwang-sa offers the jaded temple seeker some of the finest mineral color murals in Korea. Flying fairies and *mudang* (sorceresses) are painted directly on to the walls and ceiling of this temple. These 150 to 200-year-old artworks were rendered in earthy and warm greens, orange, blues and yellow. Its characters posture and prance as if they were part of a modern animated film. Carved wooden fairies, wispy as clouds, are suspended from the ceiling above three enormous gilded maitreyas. Even the main altar is splendidly wood-carved.

Horse Ears
And Frozen Fairies

The winding road on to **Mai-san, Horse Ears Mountain,** is a joyful cruise in its newly paved condition. There are charming and classical sights at nearly every highway turn. Just five minutes outside of Chŏnju, for example, you will see on your left side a series of hills covered with hundreds of traditional Korean grave mounds. This is an unusually crowded pre-Christian-style cemetery. A few kilometers further, a splendid Bud-

Admiral Yi duplicates and friend, Chŏnju.

dha can be seen enshrined in a large granite bluff. All along this 34-kilometer haul eastward and up and over the **Chinan Plateau** to **Chinan**, you'll see farmers who are out planting rice in the late spring, and, at other times, tending plots of hay, tobacco, onions and ginseng.

The famous Mai-san "Horse Ears" are not visible until you get quite close to Chinan town. There, over to the right yonder, they spring up from behind a large knoll above a meandering riverbed. From Chinan, lovely Mai-san is but a three-kilometer cruise southward through an oak forest where mushrooms are cultivated under clusters of short logs leaning against trees.

As everything in Korea has its divine or mythical reason for existence, the two Mai-san peaks are no exception. Legend notes that before Mai-san was created, two fairies—one male, the other female—once lived there. They were enjoying their respite on earth when one day their heavenly creator called for them to make their ascent back home. He warned them to let no mortal eye witness their flight, so they carefully planned their departure for the next full moon night. This was so the moon could

The pagoda works of Yi Kap-yong, Mai-san.

light their path to heaven.

The chosen night was overcast, so they decided to wait until dawn, an escape deadline decreed by their creator. As the two fairies were ascending to heaven, however, they were spotted by an early-rising housewife. They looked back at this eagle-eyed mortal, and instantly they were transformed into stones and fell back to earth as the two curious peaks of Mai-san. Moral: Don't procrastinate. If you are curious as to which frozen-in-place fairy is which, the peak to the left is called **Sut Mai** (Male Horse Ear) and the one to the right is **Am Mai** (Female Horse Ear).

A Hermit's Stone Vision

Once you reach Mai-san, your expedition has just begun. The hike through narrow **Chŏnghwang Pass** between the two horse ears is a stair-climbing, heart-thumping rise up 132 steps. Up there, near **Hwaŏm Cave,** you can rest a while and enjoy a panoramic view of Chinan and environs. Continue into a little valley on the south side of the ears, veer to your right (while negotiating another 181 steps in segments) and you will soon find

yourself at one of the most bizarre Buddhist temples in Korea. Built by the hermit monk Yi Kap-yong, this **T'ap Sa (Pagoda Temple)** religious site is an amazing collection of stone pagodas, some of them 30 feet high. All were skillfully built without mortar and have stood in surrealistic splendor in this narrow valley since the early part of this century. The Spanish architect Gaudi would weep with joy if he could return to life and study hermit Yi's architectural fantasy. The path past these "Shaking Pagodas," as some of them are titled, continues through the steep mountains to other temples such as **Ŭnsu-sa, Kŭmdang-sa** and **Isan-myo Shrine,** all about a kilometer walk away.

A white statue of the Hermit monk Yi sits comfortably at the foot of his Mai-san temple complex. Yi holds on to a wooden walking staff and stares west toward the rising sun that bathes him, his narrow valley home and his zany pagodas with amber light of morn.

A crackerbox *yŏgwan* at T'ap-sa's base offers accommodations to the weary body and soul not keen to rush back to civilization.

Kŭmsan-sa (Gold Mountain Temple)

on the western slope of **Moak-san,** is reputedly the most beautiful temple in **Chŏllapuk-do.** It is approximately 21 miles southwest of Chŏnju. Take the old Highway 1 heading southwest from Chŏnju towards Kwangju, and some 16 miles later, just north of **Wŏnp'yŏng-ni,** veer eastward along a side road that will lead up to Kŭmsan-sa.

The pathway to the temple entrance is graciously adorned with a line of cherry trees and Himalayan pine (*Nakyŏp song* "Falling Needle Pine") and a three-tiered pool off to the right side of the path. This quarter-mile walkway induces a meditative calm which prepares the traveler for Kŭmsan-sa itself.

First built in 599, Kŭmsan-sa was rebuilt in 766 by High Priest Chinp'yo Yulsa during the Silla dynasty and enlarged in 1079 (during the Koryŏ period) by High Priest Hyedŏk Wangsa. The complex was burned during the 1592 Hideyoshi invasion, then finally rebuilt in 1626. Today, its main hall, **Mirŭk-jŏn,** stands three stories high, making Kŭmsan-sa the tallest temple in Korea. This spaciousness is devoted to housing 10 designated cultural assets from Silla, Paekche, and Koryŏ periods.

Rice-planting, Chŏllanam-do area.

Mirŭk-jŏn, a worship hall for the god Avalokiteswara, is one of these 10 treasures. (One of the three surviving buildings at Seoul's Kyongbok Palace is a replica of Kŭmsan-sa.)

Inside Mirŭk-jŏn, an enormous golden Maitreya (Buddha of the Future) stands 39 feet tall, holding a red lotus blossom in its left palm. It is flanked by two smaller, crowned bodhisattvas, Taemyosang and Pŏphwarim. Below the statues, behind the wooden grill, a stairway leads down to the Maitreya's feet. One may walk down these steps (going towards the left side of the Buddhas, please) to kiss the candlelit Maitreya's feet and make an offering.

Next to Mirŭk-jŏn, above the left slope of the hill, is a stupa made of stone and a six-story granite pagoda where a monk's body minerals are enshrined after cremation. The pagoda's roofs are flat and subtly curved at the corners, in traditional Paekche style. The roofs to all of the temple structures, in fact, were never measured with anything but the eye.

In Taejŭng-jŏn worship hall behind 1,200-year-old wood-carved doors which survived the 1592 Hideyoshi invasion, a gold-gilt Sakyamuni Buddha sits peacefully with a mandala around it—a rare embellishment.

In the second largest hall, the Nahanjŏn Buddha sits with 500 sculptured disciples, each exhibiting different facial expressions. Several other treasures and sights are scattered around the temple grounds. On the way back down the path, there is a broad Zelkova elm tree. Large and branching, it is renowned as a fertility tree. If one throws a stone up the tree trunk and the stone doesn't fall down, legend says that person will soon have a child.

'Inner Sanctum' Mountain

From Kŭmsan-sa, traverse tobacco fields along the main tributary road here and rejoin the world's mainstream and traffic on the Honam Expressway bound southwest for Naejang-san National Park. In this national park an entry tunnel of red maple trees paints fiery fall colors on the reflective faces of visitors.

The journey up to Naejang (Inner Sanctum) Mountain National Park near Chŏng-ŭp is a peaceful prelude to a pilgrimage to Paegyang Temple. Up here, in maples and mist and steep mountain

passes, you will find a pleasure pavilion placed aesthetically onto a massive and living scroll. Enjoy this spot, then press on.

Upon reaching the Paegyang (White Sheep) Temple you will already be properly inspired and in the mood to consider this place and its Sŏn, or Zen, Buddhist origins. Originally built in 632 A.D., Paegyang-sa was then called Paegam-sa after Mount Paegam. Sŏn master Hwangyang Sŭro Sa renamed it Paegyang-sa in 1574. Despite its reclusiveness this temple befell malevolent forces four times— twice it was destroyed by invaders. It was rebuilt a fifth time by Sŏn master Sangmanam Taejongsa in 1917. In its present form it sits like a jewel in the midst of mountain foliage that seems to be afire during late autumn. An aged and lonely bodhi tree broods in the temple's main courtyard.

Just outside of Paegyang-sa enroute to the city of Kwangju, the Changsŏng Lake and Reservoir seems to stretch endlessly through the mountains like a wide river. From here it is about an hour's drive to Kwangju via Honam Expressway. The landscape is a continuum of hills and mountains—here and there a burial mound cut and manicured into a piney slope.

Tamyang,
Bamboo To Go

One of the most revered plants in Korea is bamboo, called tae-namu (or great tree) in Korean. It is splintered into chopsticks, carved into spoons, harvested for its delicious tender shoots, and immortalized in paintings and poetry.

The center of bamboo growing and craftsmanship in Korea is Tamyang, north of Kwangju on the main highway. And the best time to visit Tamyang is on market day, which falls on days which end with the number 2 or 7. The market is held along the Paekchin Riverbank. Across the river is a bright chartreuse bamboo forest. The bamboo is usually not cultivated longer than three years, as its purposes are not for construction, but specifically for basket weaving. Villagers bring these utilitarian objects down from their nearby village homes on market day, which starts at around 9 a.m. and peters out by 3 in the afternoon. Straw and bamboo mats and by-products are sold near the market above the riverbank.

The country's foremost *sok'uri* bamboo basket weaver lives in Tamyang. He is 79-year-old **Kim Tong-yon**. Though he carries the lofty title of Living National Treasure, his Tamyang abode is most humble and simplistic. He lives next to a bamboo forest which he cultivates for his craft's needs.

Kim works sitting cross-legged on a porch with the dependable though primitive implements he's grown accustomed to using over the decades. His calloused hands dexterously manipulate his tools like fingers: a strip of old cloth wrapped around a forefinger serves as a thimble, and his strong teeth grab and hold the bamboo strips while he scrapes them clean and thin.

The *sok'uri* basket Kim specializes in is a traditional yellow and maroon bamboo basket which was used in olden times by rich landowners to house gifts for the king. Of his baskets, a visiting European weaver once commented that only a computer or a person who has woven for more than 60 years could create Kim's basket patterns working at the steady continuous pace he does. It takes Kim three to four days to complete a basket, and only he and a younger villager whom he has taught are capable of doing this intricate weave. He has a waiting list of patrons eager to purchase his baskets, which are spiraling in value each year.

Kwangju:
Tea For You

Kwangju, the ancient provincial capital of **Chŏllanam-do**, is a low-key city. At night, in many areas of the central city, vehicular traffic ceases and streets become pedestrian malls busy with strolling townfolk.

Kwangju competes with Chŏnju for honors such as "best food in Korea" and "the most food served in Korea." This is because in the past wealthy landlords established gracious food standards, and also because the lush Honam Plain in Chŏllanam-do has agriculturally helped supply that gourmet reputation. Also, the country's best *ch'ungchŏng* (barley and rice wine) and *makkŏlli* (a simpler form of rice wine) are served here with a dizzying array of *anju* (drinking snacks) which make a veritable dinner out of a drink.

Mudŭng (Peerless) Mountain hovers like a guardian over Kwangju City. A resort area has been created at its base among acacia trees and beside a whispering stream. Along Mudŭng's right flank are two factory buildings which are used for tea production during spring and autumn tea-harvesting seasons. A tea plantation previously owned by the famous turn-of-the-century Yi dynasty artist Ho Paek-nyŏn (and now cared for by Buddhist monks) sprawls next to Mudŭng's **Chung Sim (Pure Mind) Temple**.

Perhaps tea has helped purify the minds of local monks. A monk at Chung Sim-sa explained recently that in Korea green leaf tea was traditionally the preferred brew of only monks and scholars. They believed this tea purified their blood and stimulated them so that they could resist sleep and study until early morning. It must work, because even today Mudŭng-sa monks cultivate *chon sol*—"Spring Snow" tea—on slopes adjacent their temple.

The small *chŏn sol* leaves must be cut at a very early growth stage and then steamed and dried nine times in the early morning dew and mist (intense heat or cold spoils the delicate leaves). This is a very particular and tedious tea-cultivation process which apparently only Buddhist monks can patiently manage. The tea, which smells of aromatic persimmons, is said to aid digestion and whet the appetite.

The two-story **Kwangju Museum** was built specially to house Yuan dynasty booty that was discovered in a sunken 600-year-old Chinese ship in the Yellow Sea in 1976. This archaeological find is exhibited on the ground floor gallery. A map there illustrates the spread of Chinese-influenced Yuan dynasty kilns throughout Eastern China down to Hong Kong, across to Korea's west coast, and on to Japan, Tenega Island and Okinawa. Among the finds are early 14th Century Luang-Ch'uan wares—including celadon vases with two rings and a peony design in relief, cups shaped like flowers, and a celadon druggist's mortar and pestle. Many of the art objects are in perfect condition.

Upstairs on the second floor is a gallery of Chŏlla Province treasures which includes Neolithic Korean relics from Taehŭksan-do, 11th to 14th Century bronze Buddha bells, Yi dynasty scroll paintings, and white porcelain.

The golden Mirŭk-bul (Buddha of the Future) Kŭmsan-sa, Moak-san.

ANDONG, HAHOE AND PUSŎK-SA

Take a side trip inland from the East Coast's pleasurable beaches, ski resort, phenomenal caves, and hot springs to Andong, where Yi dynasty *yangban* (aristocrats) still walk down the streets. Andong has become synonymous with *yangban* since the Andong Kwŏn clan served in high government positions during Korea's last dynasty.

Stately Harabŏji

The hour-long ride on Highway 34 westward from **Yŏngdŏg** to Andong—or the six-hour-long, roundabout train ride from Seoul—begins to get interesting as your bus or train enters the outskirts of Andong town. The monotony of hills and grain fields and modern Saemaul cement villages is broken by several sturdy, warm, wooden houses with white rubber *komusin* (Korean shoes with upturned toes) lined up outside lattice doors on the *maru* (wooden porch).

Andong is full of small surprises and ironies. Expect to see stately *harabŏji* (grandfathers) dressed in *hanbok* (traditional Korean clothes), and sporting horse-hair hats, top-knots, horn-rimmed glasses, and wispy beards, strolling around town. Although the 20th Century has encroached on this provincial town with a multi-purpose dam and concrete architecture, a few *yangban* manors have managed to survive through the ages with a traditional graciousness and charm. These houses are easily recognized by their roofs of charcoal-colored tile which curve upward over thick wooden beams, white and cement-covered mud walls, windows and doors of paper and wood, a hard wooden *maru*, and weathered wood railings that surround the house. Above the front entrance, a signboard in an ancestor's finest calligraphic script proclaims the dignity of the dwelling. These old-time houses preserved into this time are not without modern trappings. You will now spot electrical wiring and an ubiquitous television antennae.

An ironic juxtaposition of buildings in the heart of town has placed the **Andong Taewŏn Buddhist** temple at the foot of a knoll which supports the classical Cath-

Preceding pages, two Confucian country gentlemen, Andong; and, below, riverboat navigator, Hahoe.

olic **Sŏngdang Church,** built of red brick with a white cross atop its spire.

Outside of the town is a seven-story brick pagoda, **Ch'il Ch'un Chŏn T'ap,** with United Silla era relief engravings of god-generals and devas. This pagoda is thought to be the "oldest, biggest pagoda (still standing in its entirety) in the country." It sits on a dirt lane next to a mid-Yi dynasty government building. You'll find both in **Sinse-dong** along the railroad tracks.

Tosan Sŏwŏn, Thousand Won Academy

An epitome of Confucianism that shouldn't be missed while in the Andong area is **Tosan Sŏwŏn Confucian Academy.** The academy is a 28-kilometer inter-city bus ride north of Andong, and a two-kilometer walk down a winding paved road that overlooks a peaceful blue lake and green rice paddies.

Tosan Sŏwŏn was initiated by Yi Whang (1501–1570) (a.k.a. T'oegye, Tŏng, T'oedo and Ch'ŏngnyangsanin), one of the foremost Confucian scholars of Korea and once Chief of Confucian Studies and Affairs. The name Tosan Sŏwŏn was given to the academy in 1575 by King Sŏnjo. The government also later acknowledged Yi Whang and his academy by depicting both on the commonly circulated thousand won note.

Confucianism is no longer instructed at Tosan Sŏwŏn, but one can stroll through the hallowed **Tosan Sŏdang lecture hall** at the main entranceway, see the wooden plates that were used for printing lessons in the **Kyŏngchanggak archive,** and study some of Yi Whang's relics—his gnarly walking cane and books of his teachings rendered in his personal calligraphy. The wooden, tiled Yi dynasty house behind the academy and over the ridge has been the abode of Yi Whang's descendents for the past 16 generations.

An older institution, and one which is still very much alive with followers, is the **Pongjŏng-sa Buddhist temple,** 16 kilometers northwest of Andong city. But perhaps a more awesome sight is the 12.38-meter-high **Amit'aba Buddha** carved on a mammoth boulder on the mountain at **Chebiwŏn,** five kilometers from Andong enroute to **Yŏngju** on Highway 5. This Buddha, which dates back to the Koryŏ dynasty, stands on

Andong's Amit'a Buddha.

single lotus petals. Its robe and hands are carved into a massive granite boulder, and its head and hair are carved of two separate pieces of rock set into holy place. A stone pagoda sits higher on the slope among gnarled pines.

Charming Hahoe:
Yangbans and Thatch

A purer essence of Yi dynasty architecture and rural life has been maintained for the past 500 years in an isolated hamlet called **Hahoe**. This village is a half-hour ride southwest of Andong. During the Yi dynasty Hahoe was celebrated for its literati, military leaders, and for a form of mask dance drama that evolved there. These days, it is appreciated for its rustic, traditional aesthetics.

Hahoe is certainly off the beaten track, which has helped to keep it traditional. The Andong inter-city bus makes infrequent round-trips as far as **Chungni** (about four kilometers north of Hahoe). Be advised to take a taxi or wait at a bus stop at the western fringe of town for a privately-run bus to **P'ungsan**, which is 16 kilometers west of Andong. P'ungsan is your last glimpse of paved Korea; the zigzagging eight kilometer dirt road to Hahoe passes Chungni, cutting through grain and vegetable fields, and, finally, the bus deposits you in 16th Century Korea. Earthen thatched huts, larger *yangban* manors of wood and tile, the surrounding T'aebaek Mountains, and the serpentine Naktong River which bends around Hahoe, speak of a Korea that is warm, hearty, and strongly rooted in tradition.

The dirt path that wends around the hamlet is inlaid wtih chips of ceramic and tile. Cows are tethered in the front yard, chewing on hay. Under the tiled and thatched eave of each home is a row of fermented soybean (*twoenjang*) patties drying in the sun. *Chige,* or A-frames used for carrying heavy loads, lean against mud walls. In all its natural, raw beauty, Hahoe is perhaps the most picturesque village in Korea. It's the real thing, which is why Korean filmmakers use it as a set in many historical movies.

Admittedly, there are a few modern obstructions; even the oldest house, said to be around 550 years old by the local museum curator, is equipped with a large refrigerator on its hard wooden *maru*. Also, television antennae sprout on its lichen-covered tile roof, and electrical wiring creeps along its walls.

Across the path from this *yangban* manor is a museum which imitates Yi architectural lines and is painted in bold Saemaŭl colors. This museum honors an educated 16th Century aristocrat from Hahoe, Yu Sŏng Yŏng. Yu competed with the famous Admiral Yi Sun-sin for court favors during the Japanese Hideyoshi invasions of the 1590s, and eventually became the king's prime minister. Yu's voluminous books of genealogy, various personal articles, and government documents are displayed in the museum. The Yu clan remains the most influential in Hahoe.

But probably the most glaring visual obstruction in Hahoe is an off-white cement school building. It stands out most noticeably when seen from the top of the hill across the river. The school was a Saemaŭl Ŭndong (New Community Movement) project. The Hahoe villagers vetoed future Saemaul developments, and with the blessing of certain government officials, managed to keep their hometown in thatch. The hamlet is far from the eyes of most foreigners. In fact, seldom do foreigners ever come to Hahoe, so don't be surprised to find the

The Floating Rock, Pusok-sa environs.

local folk staring back at you with as much curiosity as you exhibit toward them.

At Pusŏk-sa, The 'Floating Rock'

Another place that is not too accessible but really shouldn't be passed up while in the Andong area is Pusŏk Temple about 60 kilometers due north of Andong along Highway 5 and a long, bumpy road. Pusŏk-sa (Floating Rock Temple) was established in 676 by High Priest Ŭisang, who returned to Korea from China with teachings of Hwaŏm Buddhism. It is said that Ŭisang's former lover reunited with him in the form of a huge granite "floating rock." She later transformed herself into a stone dragon and buried herself under the main hall— her head beneath the gilded-clay Buddha and her tail 60 feet away under a stone lantern—so she could help protect Ŭisang's temple. That same legendary "floating rock" still hangs protectively— and precariously—outside Pusŏk-sa's main hall.

Despite the dragon-in-residence and floating rock protectors, the temple was burned down by invaders in the early 14th Century. It was reconstructed in 1358. Fortunately, however, it was just beyond Hideyoshi's destructive reach in the 1590s, so the famed Muryangsu-jŏn (Eternal Life Hall) main hall has been preserved to this day. This hall is considered to be the oldest and most classical wooden structure in Korea. Its Koryŏ architectural style is said to have been influenced by Greek artisans through India, and this structural theory is evidenced by the way the hall's main support pillars gradually taper off at the top and bottom.

Predating the temple by at least 50 years and complementing its Koryŏ architecture is a nine-foot tall gilded-clay sitting Buddha, the only one of its kind in Korea. Also, Pusŏk-sa's interior Koryŏ paintings of Buddha and the Four Kings are considered to be the oldest wall paintings in Korea outside of ancient tomb art. This is one of the most inaccessible temples in Korea, but for the serious traveler and student of ancient culture, Pusŏk-sa is one of the more rewarding detours he or she can make while in this country.

Thatching a rooftop, Hahoe

KYŎNGJU CLASSICS

General Points of Interest

1 Anap-ji (Duck and Geese Pond): Lavish garden where later Silla kings received foreign diplomatic emissaries; now only a fourth of its original size.
2 Ch'ŏmsŏng-dae Astronomical Observatory
3 Folk Museum
4 Golf Course
5 Hwangsŏng Park
6 Hwarang (Flower Youth) House: Concept brought forth from Silla days when select youths were trained and educated in the martial arts and Buddhism to serve the country.
7 Kŭm Ho Kak Kisaeng House
8 Kyŏngju National Museum
9 Myŏnghwal Fortress
10 Na-jŏng: Shrine to Hyŏkkŏse, the first Silla ruler.
11 Panwŏl Fortress site
12 Pŏsŏk-chŏng (Abalone Stone Pavilion) and "Wine Cup Floating Pool"
13 Sŏkbinggo (Ancient Ice Storehouse)
14 Sunghye-jŏn: Ancestral shrine of the royal Kim clan.

Buddhist Points of Interest

1 Ch'ilbul-am (Seven Buddha Hermitage): Excellent Buddhist stone relief carvings.
2 Hŭngnyun-sa (Flourishing Wheel Temple): Legendary site where Buddhism was first introduced to Silla by the Priest Ado in the early 5th Century.
3 Paengnul-sa (Chestnut Curd Temple): Simple temple which dates back to the 7th Century. The Yaksa Yorae (Buddhist of Medicine) in the Kyŏngju Museum was sculpted here by a T'ang Chinese refugee artist.
4 Pori-sa (Enlightening Awakening Temple): Built in 886. Several striking Buddhist stone relief carvings.
5 Pulguk-sa (Buddhist Country Temple): Built between 514 and 539. The temple's foundation is constructed of stones that were fitted together without use of a mortar.
6 Punhwang-sa Pagoda: Built in 634 of stone shaped like bricks. Only three of the seven or nine tiers of the original pagoda remain.
7 Sŏkkuram (Stone Cave Hermitage) Grotto: Designed by Silla Minister Kim Tae-sŏng, who also designed Pulguk-sa.
8 Three Stone Buddhas of the Amit'a Buddha and two attendants.

Confucian Points of Interest

1 Soak Sŏwŏn (West Peak Confucian Hall): Established in the 16th Century in honor of scholar Ch'oe Ch'iwon, Sŏl Ch'ong and Kim Yusin.

Tombs

1 Kwoe-nŭng: Perhaps the tomb of King Wonsŏng (r. 785-799)
2 O-nŭng: Tombs of Silla kings Hyŏkkŏse (r. 57 BC — 4 AD), Namhae (r. 4 AD — 24 AD), Norye (r. 24 AD — 57 AD), and Pasa (r. 80 AD — 112).
3 Sam-nŭng: Tombs of Silla kings Adala (r. 154 — 184), Sindŏk (r. 913 — 917), Kyŏngmyŏng (r. 917 — 924).
4 Square Tomb of Kim Tae-sŏng, Silla architect of Pulguk-sa and Sŏkkuram.
5 Tomb of Queen Chindŏk (r. 647 — 654)
6 Tomb of King Chinhŭng (r. 540 — 576)
7 Tomb of King Chinp'yŏng (r. 579 — 632)
8 Tomb of King Chŏnggang (r. 886 — 888)
9 Tomb of King Hŏndŏk (r. 809 — 826)

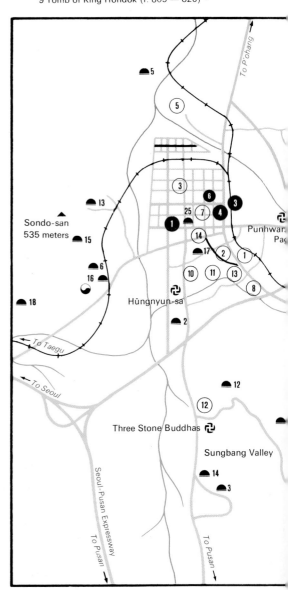

10 Tomb of King Hongang (r. 875 — 886)
11 Tomb of King Hyoso (r. 692 — 702)
12 Tomb of King Ilsŏng (r. 135 — 155)
13 Tomb of Kim Yu-sin, Silla General (595 — 673)
14 Tomb of King Kyŏngae (r. 924 — 927)
15 Tomb of King Munsŏng (r. 839 — 857)
16 Tomb of King Muyŏl (r. 654 — 661)
17 Tomb of King Naemul (r. 356 — 402)
18 Tomb of King Pŏphŭng (r. 514 — 540)
19 Tomb of King Sinmu (r. 839)
20 Tomb of King Sinmun (r. 681 — 692)
21 Tomb of Sŏl Ch'ong, Confucian scholar (late
    6th Century).
22 Tomb of Queen Sŏndŏk (r. 632 — 647)
23 Tomb of King Sŏndŏk (r. 702 — 737)
24 Tomb of King T'alhae (r. 57 AD — 80 AD)
25 Tumuli Park: Includes the tomb of King Mich'u
    (r. 262 — 284) and the Heavenly Horse Tomb.

Tourist Stops

1 Bus Terminal
2 Kyŏngju Tourism Agency
3 Kyŏngju Railroad Station
4 Post Office
5 Tourism Center

Kyŏngju Hotels

1 **Bomun Lake Hotel**
2 **Bulkuksa Hotel Shilla**
3 **Kolon Hotel**
4 **Kyŏngju Chosun Hotel**
5 **Kyŏngju Tokyu Hotel**
6 **Kyŏngju Tourist Hotel**

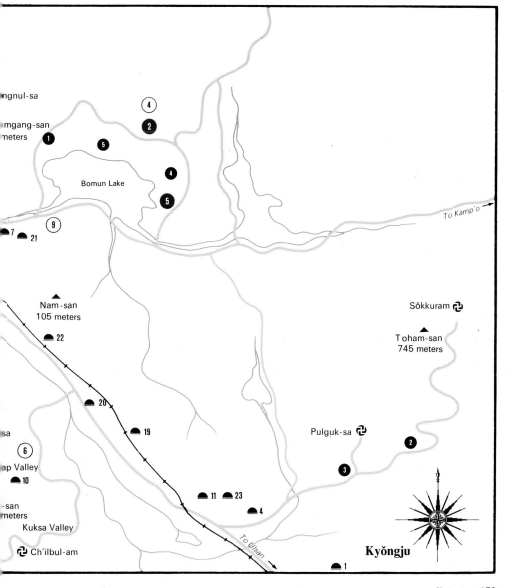

KYŎNGJU

It's the massive burial mounds—brown and dusted by frost in the winter, and carpeted with a dark-green nap in the summer—which punctuate any visit to **Kyŏngju.** Like so many camel humps rising here and there in populated and rural areas, they dominate all other physical realities in this riverine valley between Taegu and Pusan. Even the sweeping **T'oham Mountain Range** that hovers west of here is temporarily forgotten as one motors through this busy town. The mounds, memorial tombs known as *nŭng* to Koreans, represent for now and all time the glory that was Silla, and the wonders one can behold —and which wait to be unearthed for our amazement—in the Kyŏngju area.

Opulent Shaman Kings

Kyŏngju, the capital city of **North Kyŏngsang Province**, was well known to Asia's ancients as Kŭmsŏng, the home of powerful and opulent shaman kings. Today, it's an easy-going resort town where rice cultivation and tourism are more important than wars of conquest. Its distinction as a one-time seat of power, however, cannot ever be forgotten. One can't even wander aimlessly around this sprawling mountain-bounded vale without stumbling across dozens of important cultural sites. This 214-square-kilometer valley is literally dotted with 1st to 8th Century and later burial tombs, tired pagodas, fortress ruins, granite standing and relief sculptures, palace grounds and other remnants of the rich Three Kingdoms Era. The particulars of ancient Silla's history are discussed in earlier sections of this book, but even if you haven't bothered to brief yourself, a short tour of the Kyŏngju sites will prove to be a very knowledgeable and an inspirational one.

Art historians and archaeologists understandably indulge in superlatives when writing of Kyŏngju's manmade treasures:

"The monuments of Silla's greatness preserved in the Kyŏngju Branch Museum and scattered in the vicinity of the town provide material for the study of the art and the whole civilization of two epochs of great importance in Far Eastern history. Together with other objects of artistic and historical interest to be found here and there over the peninsular, they deserve thorough study and a prominent place in the art history of the world," wrote archaeologist-historian Helen B. Chapin in 1948.

Chapin was supremely impressed, but she was writing nearly 30 years before the most amazing of Kyŏngju's treasures had even been excavated.

A later commentator, Evelyn B. McCune, author of *The Arts of Korea, An Illustrated History*, noted 31 years later that ceramics, precious wrought metals, paintings and stone sculptures recently unearthed in the Kyŏngju region have introduced the world 'to the sophisticated art of refined shamanism.' Modern Korea is experiencing a growing awareness of its cultural heritage that is emerging, ghostlike, from these recent finds.

The enthusiasm of both art historians was unanimously underscored by international art critics who had never even been to Korea when several exquisite, but never before publicized, Silla pieces were shown in a spectacular exhibit, "5,000

Kyŏngju's Tumuli Park moundscape.

Years of Korean Art," which began touring the United States in 1979. Dominated by the porcelain, granite, gold and jadeworks of ancient Kyŏngju-Silla, it catapulted Korea into Asian art chronicles.

Entire books have been written about this scattered open-air museum called Kyŏngju, but in deference to the sheer number of sites one can visit here, we will briefly review some of the most important. Many of these locales beg you to spend days, even weeks, exploring, but even a day's time will give any traveler much to consider and reserve for future, more detailed visits. For Kyŏngju cannot be fully appreciated in a day.

The Sillan Tombs at Tumuli Park. In this unique 152,000 square meter "park" on the southeast side of Kyŏngju are located some 20 tombs of varying sizes which were originally heaped into place as early as the mid-1st Century. Until quite recently, this restored, landscaped and lamplit complex of mounded graves was just another neighborhood in Kyŏngju, but when private individuals and government archaeological teams began to find literally thousands of important items here, the area was cleared of homesites and designated a national museum and park-site of major historical importance. The restoration of Tumuli Park was begun in 1973, and the complex was offically dedicated and opened to the public for viewing in 1975.

Jade Tiger Claws And a 'Heavenly Horse'

The largest of the tombs, that of King Mich'u (r. 262-285), has been identified in ancient chronicles as the "**Great Tomb**". However, a secondary tomb, the socalled **Ch'ŏnma-ch'ong**, or "Heavenly Horse" or "Flying Horse" tomb, is probably the most well-known gravesite in Tumuli Park (sometimes called the Tomb Park). This tomb, about 27 meters in diameter and 12.7 meters high, was excavted in 1973, and in its collapsed wood and stone burial chambers were found numerous important treasures—including sets of gold and jade tiger claw earrings, a solid gold, 125-centimeter long belt-girdle with dangling gold and jade ornaments, a 32-centimeter-high gold foil crown embellished with 58 carved jade pieces, and an unglazed stoneware pot ornamented with

a dragon's head and turtle's body.

More than ten thousand objects were discovered in this unknown king's tomb, but the most celebrated find was a painting of a galloping, winged horse. This flying horse study, the first early Silla painting ever discovered, was painted onto a birchbark saddle flap in white and vermillion and bordered by a rococo frame. (For further information on this piece see this book's section on Korean art.) Visitors to this tombsite can now literally walk into the tomb, which has been scooped out and converted into a domed glass, metal and concrete gallery. On display here are a detailed diorama-model of the tomb's burial chamber, photographs of the actual excavation in progress, and more than 100 excavated Silla pieces. Many of the most important treasures are safely displayed in larger national museum structures at Seoul and at the nearby Kyŏngju Museum.

Kyŏngju National Museum

The Kyŏngju National Museum. As the editors of the informative book *Ko-rean Art Seen Through Museums* have written, "The National Museum in Kyŏngju is, so to speak, actually a museum within a museum." The phrase is apt, because so many of Kyŏngju's treasures are in the open air where they can be seen, touched, experienced. But in this vast and modern compound on the eastern skirts of Kyŏngju you can see some of the finest of more than 80,000 items unearthed during recent and old-time digs in this area: metal work, paintings, earthenware, calligraphic scrolls, folk art objects, weapons, porcelains, carved jades, and gold, granite and bronze sculptures wrought in shamanist, Buddhist, Taoist and Confucian motifs.

Among important pieces here is the huge bronze **Emille Bell**, The Divine Bell for the Great King Sŏng which is one of the world's oldest (cast in 770 A.D.) and largest (weight, about 20 tons; height, about 3.07 meters; diameter, about 2.3 meters) bells. This Buddhist bell, which originally hung in a pavilion at nearby **Pongdŏk Temple**, is embellished with four relief devas who kneel facing each other on lotus blossom cushions. It is said that the bell's sonorous tones can be heard

Mask dance images by a Kyŏngju maskmaker.

176

40 miles away on a clear day. The bell's name, it has been written, comes from an ancient Silla term, pronounced Em-ee-leh, which literally means "mommy". The bell was given this name because its sound resembles the voice of a lost child crying for its mother.

Pulguk-sa

Pulguk-sa. This sprawling temple complex about 16 kilometers due east of Kyŏngju on the western slopes of Mt. T'oham is one of the oldest surviving Buddhist monasteries in Korea. First built during the reign of Silla King Pŏphŭng (r. 514-539), Pulguk-sa, "Temple of the Buddha-land," is also Korea's most famous temple. Its renown comes not from its age or size but probably because it stands, flawlessly restored, as a splendid example of Silla-era architecture in a spectacular hillside setting lush with manicured stands of pine, plum, peach, pear, cherry and cryptomeria trees. It also enshrines some of the country's and Korean Buddhism's most important national treasures.

Wonderfully stone-crafted steps and bridges carry the visitor on an uphill stroll to the broad granite block terraces on which this pristine temple compound stands. Almost all of the hand-painted wood structures on these terraces are of recent Yi dynasty construction, but most of the stone structures, pieced together of large granite blocks fitted without mortar are original. The architect credited for this stone masterwork, Kim Taesong, also supervised the construction of the nearby Sŏkkuram Grotto, an annex to Pulguk-sa and one of Buddhism's most-celebrated shrines. Architect Kim directed his design and structural skills during the reign of King Kyŏng-dŏk, the 35th Silla king (r. 742-765), at the period when Pulguk-sa underwent several major modifications and restorations.

Entering Pulguk-sa
On Blue and White Clouds

Two double-tiered stone staircases, the **Sŏkkye-mun**, used to lead pilgrims and tourists up and Pulguk-sa proper. The larger, 33-stepped staircase to the

Contemporary neo-Sillan dancers at a tourist revue.

right has been given two names, one for its lower flight (called **Chŏngun-kyo**, the Blue Cloud Bridge), and the other for its upper flight (**Paegun-kyo**, the White Cloud Bridge). The smaller, left-side staircase, meanwhile, was similarly named. Its lower flight is called **Yŏnhwakyo** (Lotus Flower Bridge), and the upper flight is **Ch'ilbo-kyo** (the Seven Treasure Bridge). The Blue Cloud and White Cloud bridges terminate at an entrance gate called **Chala-mun**, while the Lotus Flower and Seven Treasure bridges climb up to secondary entrance gate known as **Anyang-mum**. Both are grand entry-ways, but these days tourists and devotees alike have to enter the temple via new stairways and gates on the left and right sides of the temple.

On the interior side of Anyang-mum, is the **Kuknak-jŏn** hall where you'll find a bronze **Amit'a-bul**, or Buddha of the Western Paradise and Boundless Light. This delicately sculpted Buddha's features have been gilded in recent years by Pulguk-sa's tidy monks.

Through the small **Chong-ru** entry pavilion, is Pulguk-sa's main worship hall. **Taeungjŏn**, and an expansive courtyard dominated by two unusual and impressive multi-tiered Silla pagodas. The smaller (8.3 meters high) of the two pagodas is called the **Sŏkka-t'ap**, and the larger (10.5 meters hight) pagoda is known as the **Tabo-t'ap**. Legend says these neighboring pagodas were built by Asa-dal, an esteemed artisan who came to Silla from Paekche.

Both stone pagodas (which have been considerably restored in recent years) are considered premier examples of such Silla pagoda construction. Inside a niche on the left side of the Tabo-t'ap you'll spot a small growling lion sitting on a neat lotus pedestal. He's Tabo-t'ap's (the many Treasured Buddha's) guardian.

The Sŏkka-t'ap structure appears less amusing, but a reliquary time capsule of great historical and artistic value was found inside this pagoda in 1959. As a government survey notes, "The relics in cluded a*sarira* box containing gold images of Buddha and a scroll of Dharari sutras, the oldest Buddhist literature of its kind remaining in the world today. The inscriptions engraved on the cover of the relic box says that in 706 A.D. King Sŏndŏk placed within the pagoda

four *sarira* (remains of Buddha or high priests), a gold Amit'a figure, and a volume of sutras in memory of three deceased royal family members—King Sinmun, Queen Mother Simok T'achu and King Hyoso."

In this couryard's Taeung-jŏn hall is an image of **Sŏkkamoni**, the Historic Buddha, who is flanked by appropriately subservient bodhisattvas and other disciples of the Lord Buddha.

Other Pulguk-sa structures and objects deserving meditative attention are the nine-pillared **Musol-jŏn** hall, the compound's oldest and largest structure; the **Viro-jŏn**, which houses a **Viroch'ana Buddha** found clutching his right forefinger in an overtly sexual Diamond First mudra; and **Kwanŭm-jŏn**, a hall which is home to a 10th-Century wooden image of **Kwanseŭm Posal**, the popular Bodhisattva of Mercy known to Chinese Buddhists as Kwan Yin. Nearly all of the halls are painted in the gay, day-glo colors and designs popular in contemporary *Yi Dynasty nouveau* building circles.

A Perfect Buddha

Sŏkkuram, The Stone Cave Hermitage. This Pulguk-sa annex, several winding kilometers northeast of Pulguk-sa proper, has become a major pilgrimage site for practitioners and students of Buddhism and Buddhist art. Sŏkkuram is a grotto temple, set among pines and maples, which enshrines a white granite Sŏkkammoni Buddha image considered by some art historians to be the most perfect Buddha image of its kind anywhere. Unlike grotto temples in other parts of Asia, Sŏkkuram was not carved out of a granite hillside or built inside an existing cave. Rather it's an artificial chapel built of large stone granite blocks placed on a summit. Following a pleasant hike through a lower woods and an ascent up a flight of stairs, the visitor to Sŏkkuram will enter as classical a Buddhist shrine as he would ever expect to see in the Far East.

A Multi-headed Goddess

The basic Sŏkkuram structure consists of a square antechamber and a round in-

Pulguk-sa

A typical Korean Buddhist temple is made up of many shrines which are often housed in several special halls. In the layout of its compound, Pulguk-sa, like many things Korean, is both typical and unique. The arrangement of halls and courtyards, the selection of icons, the emphasis placed on particular architectural details — all reflect the varied beliefs and styles of the temple's original builders and many renovators. However, most temples of comparable size will include the fundamental shrines found here. Among important structures at Pulguk-sa are:

1 *Yoñhwa-kyo* and *Ch'ilbo-kyo* entry bridges

2 *Ch'öngun-kyo* and *Paegun-kyo* entry bridges

3 *Anyang-mun* gate

4 *Chaha-mun* gate

5 *Chong-ru* passageway

6 *Kuknak-jön* hall with its *Amit'a Buddha.*

7 *Sökka-t'ap* pagoda

8 *Tabo-t'ap* pagoda

9 *Taeung-jön* hall which houses a *Sökka Buddha*

10 *Musol-jön,* or old meeting hall

11 *Viro-jön* (Viroch'ana hall)

12 *Kwanŭm-jön* (Kwanseŭm-posal hall)

For more detailed information please see the feature section article on Korean Buddhist iconography.

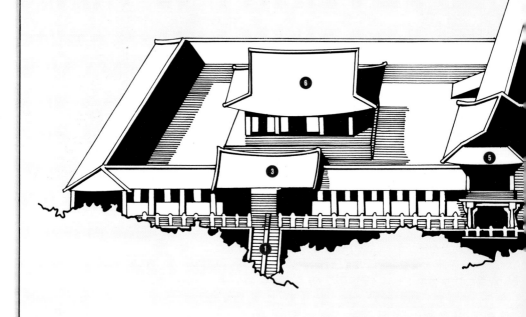

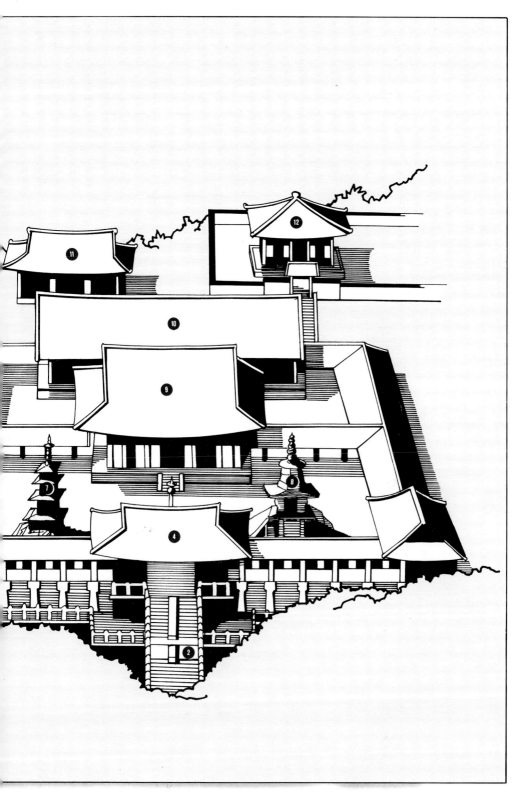

terior chamber with a dome-shaped ceiling. As you enter the chapel you will first pass stone images of the **Eight Generals**, each representative of one of the Eight Classes of Beings. Then come a pair of wild-eyed and ready gate guardians in typical *t'aekwŏn-do* fighting postures. Specifically, they are set in a *sipsu*, or "10 hands" posture, and a *palsae*, or "picking fortress out" posture.

Next are the **Four Deva Kings**, Guardians of the Four Quarters. A pair of these directional deities cavort on either side of the main passageway. All are framed in the radiant aura of haloes, but they also are depicted in the act of stomping on little threatening demons. These devas are usually found in a painted or wood-carved form at the main entrance to Korean Buddhist temples.

Inside the main chamber is **Sŏkkamoni**, sitting in maximum repose on a lotus dais. At his forehead is a typical protuberance, and atop his head are neatly cropped spirals of curly hair. Facing the grotto's entrance and the East Sea, the Buddha Sŏkkamoni sits with his right hand palm downward over his right leg.

This is the mudra position referred to as "Calling of the Earth to Witness." The left palm, meanwhile, faces up in a proper meditation pose.

Cavorting on walls of the inner chamber are relief sculptures of the **Ten Great Disciples** and **Eight Great Bodhisattvas**. The most curious of these is an 11-headed Avalokitesvara, or **Kwanseŭm Posal**, who has been placed on the back wall of the Sŏkkuram rotunda directly behind the Sakyamuni Buddha. This Goddess of Mercy is unusual becuase 10 of her heads have been placed into a crown atop her head. Art historian Chapin explains this multiplicity:

"An Old legend explains the eleven heads: formerly endowed with only one, the Compassionate Lord grieved so deeply over the sufferings of creatures that his one head split into eleven fragments, whereupon his spiritual father, the Buddha Amitabha, picked up the shards and placed them on his son's head where they grew each into a separate head. Thus, the Bodhisattva's power to see and relieve suffering was multiplied eleven times."

In ancient times, men would try to compose a poem before their teacup floated around this waterway.

While the individual sculptures may be matched by some of those in the cave temples of China, nevertheless the chapel as a whole is unequalled in the art of the Far East.

Ch'omsŏng-da. This astronomical observatory tower, one of the oldest structures in Korea, was built during the reign of Queen Sŏndŏk (r 632-647), Silla's 27th ruler. Astronomers question just how the tower was used, but they point with intrigue at the following coincidences: 365 stones, the number of days in a calendar year, were used in its construction; and there are 12 rectangular basestones, plus 12 separate levels of stones above and below a central window. Could this constructional recurrence of the number 12 imply the zodiac, or the number of months in a year? This telescope-shaped tower probably served several generations of Silla geomancers who attempted to foretell astrological fates in this historic region.

P'osŏk-chŏng (The Abalone Stone Pavilion). The world's hedonists have a particular fondness for this site just east of the old road to Pusan. This place received its name from the shape of a curving, stonerimmed ditch which was cut in the ground next to a pleasure pavilion used by Hŏn–gang, the 49th Silla king. This serpentining ditch was a large board game of sorts which involved the drinking of wine and the impromtu composition of poetry. Nearby stream water was channeled in and onto its waters were set afloat cups of wine. A guest was challenged to compose a proper poem before his cup made a floating round of the channel. If he didn't compose a satisfactory poem, he had to chug-a-lug his entire bowlful of wine and try again, and again, and . . According to ancient chronicles, it was great royal parlour fun.

The Bomun Lake Resort Complex. The Korean Government says in its promotional brochures: "If the tourist has time or inclination for only one sidetrip outside of Seoul, Kyŏngju should be the choice." With that thought in mind, the Government has created what is probably the most complete resort complex in Korea—the Bomun Lake Resort, a sprawling playland about six kilometers east of Kyŏngju proper.

Ready for the ceremony.

Three deluxe class hotels had sprung up on sprawling Bomun Lake's shores. A 900-seat convention hall, 18-hole golf course, a folk arts amphitheatre and a lakeside marina with a posh clubhouse are but a few of the amenities which await Kyŏngju tourists who stay at Bomun Lake. The Korea National Tourism Corporation's master plan for this area sees an eventual hotel capacity of 3,000-plus rooms. All new structures are being built "Silla-style" in keeping with this grandiose KNTC master plan.

If even more time is on your side consider hiking to the top of **Namsan,** South Mountain, above the valley's **Namsan Village.** There, perhaps an hour of huffing and puffing away, you'll find amazing Buddhas and attendant bodhisattvas etched into sheer granite boulders and cliffs. All look east, like the Sŏkkuram Buddha, toward the rising sun.

Kyŏngjuophiles also strongly suggest that visitors are not to miss a visit to **Kŭm Ho Kak,** Kyŏngju's most opulent and traditional *kisaeng* house; or a respite at **Anapji,** a beautifully landscaped duck and geese pond-park which was a favourite idyll of Unified Silla kings.

Also high on the Kyŏngju *must do* list is the impressive **tomb of General Kim, Su-yin,** which is rimmed by superbly carved stone zodiac figures; the **Punhang (Famous Emperor) Temple** with the oldest datable pagoda in Korea; and perhaps first before all, **O-nŭng,** the serene five mounds memorial park on the south side of Kyŏngju where, tradition says, Silla's first, second, third and fifth kings, and first queen, are buried. At this site is a fine memdorial hall, **Sungjong-jŏn,** dedicated to Silla's first ruler, pak Hyŏkkŏse (57 B.C.—3 A.D). The memorial hall was erected by Kim Yŏng-jo, the 21st Yi King, in 1759.

Still haven't seen enough Silla era Buddha images? Then head for **Pagoda Valley** on the eastern slopes of Nam-san, or the so-called **Buddha Valley** just north of T'ap Valley, or the **Kuksa Valley** east of Namsan, or the more remote **Sungbang Valley.** This litany of place names and their resident treasures grows longer and more awesome with every passing lunar year—and every new discovery—in Kyŏngju.

Korean star chart (below) of the type probably used by astronomers who studied the heavens in Kyŏngju's Ch'omsŏng-dae astral observatory (right).

184

THE HISTORIC
SOUTH CRESCENT

In 1592, the Japanese warlord, Toyotomi Hideyoshi, dispatched 150,000
troops to begin an ambitious assault on
the Chinese Empire. Korea had the bad
fortune of being in the way and of being
loyal to China. When the Korean government refused to grant Japan free access across its frontiers, the Japanese dis-
posed with courtly etiquette and
proceeded to fight their way through. After six years of war, they finally retreated, failing to conquer China, but
thoroughly devastating Korea. Thousands of Koreans were killed or taken to
Japan as slaves, vast tracts of crucial
farmland had been razed, the country's
social order was in shambles, and much
of Korea's great cultural legacy was destroyed or stolen. Nearly four centuries
have passed since this tragedy, yet all
along Korea's southern coast monuments and memorials remain to keep
alive memories of this Imjin War. The
dominant theme in this area of the country, despite more recent wars and
wrenching transitions, is still the Japanese invasions.

Taegu: Apples and Industry

The logical starting point for a swing
through Korea's southern crescent area
is **Taegu,** the capital of **North Kyŏnsang
Province.** Taegu serves as a clearing
house for a variety of produce harvested
in this agriculturally rich province and is
an industrial center as well. The definitive product of this city, however, is apples. This may seem an odd claim to
fame, but the Taegu apple is a state-of-
the-art fruit, deservedly renowned
throughout Asia.

Though at first glance Taegu may appear to be at best a half-hearted attempt
at a city or an overgrown village, a closer
inspection reveals it to be a uniquely Korean compromise between urban and
rural extremes: It is big enough to offer
good hotels, restaurants and 20th Century entertainment, yet small enough to
retain a relaxed ambiance that is all but
lost in Seoul or Pusan. Few of Taegu's
buildings are so imposing as to obstruct
the view of the surrounding mountains.
Streets are dominated by pedestrians

Preceding
pages:
Autumn
around
Sŏraksan;
below, the
view from
the field is
rapidly
changing
color.

rather than machinery. And traditionally styled clothing is still very much in evidence, especially (for no apparent reason) in the environs of **Talsŏng**, a massive earthwork fortress dating back to the prehistoric Sam-Han era.

Talsŏng was originally constructed of several artificial hills in the middle of the broad plain that is now largely filled by Taegu. Presumably these hills supported a Korean variant of the motte-and-bailey forts once common in Europe. Late in the 14th Century, at the end of the Mongol occupation and the beginning of the Yi dynasty, the fort was enlarged and stones were added to its existing earthworks. In 1596, during the Imjin War, the fort was again enlarged—to its present circumference of 1300 meters and height of four meters. The fort is now a popular park, complete with a small zoo that includes several claustrophobic lions donated by the local Lions Club. The entrance to Talsŏng is a favorite meeting place for the city's senior citizens, who lounge amiably along its cobblestone walkway, traditionally sartorial in pastel silks and cotton voile.

West Gate Market, one of the largest and oldest in the country, is just a short walk away, across from **Tongsan Hospital.** The narrow alleys of the market are lined with cauldrons of noodle soup billowing steam, mobile vendors with carts devoted exclusively to such specialized merchandise as sewing needles and arcane mousetraps, and clustered networks of permanent stalls dealing in even more mundane necessities.

Redolent Pharmacopoeia

Yak-chŏng Kol-mok, "medicine alley," is the site of one of Taegu's more notable sensory delights. The street is a center for wholesale purveyors of traditional medicines. A stimulating barrage of scents ooze out of buckets and boxes of prepared pharmacopoeia and wafts up from exotic herbs drying on woven mats set out in the sun. The precise blend of aromas shifts gradually as one meanders down this pungent street. Indeed, mere pedestrian inhalations will probably relieve you of any afflictions of the nasal passages—or soul. Should simple breathing prove ineffective, there are several licensed herbalists who are able and willing to prescribe healing brews.

Taegu also has its own brand of

Many of the original city gates still remain.

nightlife which, if lacking the polish of posher establishments in Seoul, is well-endowed with enthusiasm. Most after hours partying in Taegu is conveniently centralized in several blocks near the "old station" at the center of town. Standing with your back to the station, expensive "businessmen's entertainments" are to your right; on your left are casual rock-and-roll clubs and wine stalls. Adjacent to the latter is one of the city's larger markets. At night the two merge in a spirited confusion of side alley vendors, eclectic shop fronts, blasting nightclub bands, and throngs intent on entertaining themselves.

Start your Taegu evening with a sidewalk snack of steamed crab, or, if you dare, raw sea cucumbers. Continue with dinner in a smoke-billowing *pulgogi* house or in an inexpensive but elegant western-styled restaurant, then move out to explore such tantalizers as the **Theatrical Beer Hall** or one of many ubiquitous and raucous *makkŏlli* bars.

For tamer daylight diversions there is **Su-song Reservoir** on the southern outskirts of the city. In winter the reservoir's ice is crowded with skaters, most of whom seem to be primarily engaged in falling down, though some soar by with regal grace on racer skates. A few children uphold tradition by squatting on small planks fitted with runners and propelled by child-powered wooden-handled picks.

Rented rowboats replace skates in summer, whereupon suitors display their naval aptitude by dodging excursion boats which are busy transporting less athletic adventurers to a small island in the middle of the reservoir. The umbrella tables of outdoor restaurants contribute to a carnival atmosphere, as do mechanical swings and miniature ferris wheels.

Taegu has several other recreational areas: **Tong Chon Resort** and **Mangwuli Park** are out past the new train station, on the **Naktong River** where the Communist attack that began the Korean War was finally halted. **Apsan Park** includes a cable car ride up to the summit of **Ap Mountain** for a panoramic view of the **Taegu plain.** Near the old train station is Taegu's small **Central Park,** which contains two reconstructions of old government buildings. The original structures were built in 1601 as part of a complex of administrative buildings which remained in use until 1965.

Icecapades at Su-song Reservoir.

Back Road Bussing

In addition to the train station and the highway bus terminal adjacent to it, Taegu has four depots for back-road buses, one for each of the cardinal directions. Indeed, Taegu is a convenient hub for travel to any number of fascinating spots down south.

These buses serve remote villages and mountain hamlets out of range of highway express buses or trains, and in many of these places foreign visitors are still a considerable surprise. Goats, chickens, and pigs on their way to market are often included among the passengers. Disembark with them and their owners and you'll be rewarded with a rare glimpse of a genuine village market day. Transistor radios and plastic serving trays may now be bartered for livestock and vegetables, but such rural events have yet to lose their timeless appeal.

The annual cycle of village life fluctuates between intense periods of field labor and long stretches of off-season leisure. The days begin early in any season. Rise at dawn and follow the *makkŏlli* merchant on his delivery rounds to village taverns. A cluster of children outfit-

Local folks on the road to Haein-sa.

ted in their school uniforms hurry through the morning fog to schoolyard chores. Farmers lash wooden plows to the backs of bullocks and lead them out to rice fields. Women gather at the village well to pound laundry with wooden bats. And the resounding toll of a brass gong announces a funeral. Join the stragglers in the procession led by a bier laden with paper flowers and you will witness a remarkable blend of solemn ritual, mourning, and carefree frivolity as the deceased is escorted to the netherworld. On festival days, such as Ch'usŏk and Lunar New Year's Day, everyone gathers to dance to the pulsing rhythms of hourglass drums and clanging gongs. There are no strangers on a country festival day: exhibit the slightest touch of whimsey and you will be accosted, festooned with brilliant ribbons, plied with liquor, and dragged into a frenzied dance.

Back road buses are cheap, crowded, and not especially comfortable; but, except for a possible stiff back, they offer a low risk gamble for anyone inclined to exploration. Pick a destination at random (place names ending in "sa" are safest, as they promise a temple at the very least), stock up on emergency provisions,

and try your luck. A cultural experience is guaranteed.

Taegu Area Temple-hopping

The Sŏ-bu-ju-c'ha-jang (West Depot) will get you to Yong-yŏn-sa, a tiny temple perched high in the mountains with an exquisite set of guardian deva paintings, miles of hiking trails, cordial inns, and an invigorating stream for bathing.

The bus to Ŭnmun-sa from Nambu-ju-ch'a-jang (South Depot) is a challenging, but rewarding, test of stamina. After enduring several hours of some of Korea's most jarring dirt roads, you will be left at a dead end town consisting of a gas station, a single inn and restaurant, and a few dozen farm houses, including some handsome examples of traditional folk architecture. The path to the temple follows a meandering stream through a spacious pine forest. The surrounding mountains harbor several small hermitages. Set in an open field, Ŭnmun-sa is a restful sanctuary for a community of Buddhist nuns, who go about their work and worship unperturbed by occasional visitors who drift through to enjoy the scenery or to study the many fine paintings adorning her temple walls.

Chikji-sa, easily reached from Taegu via Kimch'ŏn, is a gem of a temple, recently repainted in an entrancing blend of blue, magenta, and gold. Exquisite figures and landscapes embellish virtually every available external wall space and Chikji-sa's shrines are populated with a bewildering array of finely carved statues. A quick stroll through the temple grounds is likely to induce a giddy overload of visual stimulation, but taken slowly Chikji-sa is a rare pleasure. Unfortunately, the beauty of the temple, and of the forested mountains rising above it, has not escaped general notice. Only in off-season months may it be enjoyed in appropriate serenity, but even in the bustle of crowds of snapshooting hikers Chikji-sa is well worth seeing. It is one of several temples associated with Samyŏng Taesa, who was both a Buddhist saint and a military hero.

Samyŏng was born in the town of Milyang in 1544. His family was of the yangban class and he was well-educated in the Confucian Classics. After losing both his parents, Samyŏng left his home to wander in the mountains. He eventually made his way to Chikji-sa where his study of Zen led to his attainment of

Chikji-sa.

enlightenment. He became chief priest of Chikji-sa in 1574.

Needles and Noodles

Soon after, he set out wandering again and met Sŏsan, the most prominent Korean Buddhist master of the period. According to an apocryphal legend, they engaged in a contest of magic. Samyŏng began by arduously transforming a bowl of needles into noodles. Sŏsan received the bowl, promptly turned it upside down, and needles crashed to the floor. Samyŏng's next feat was to stack eggs end-to-end vertically, several feet into the air. Sŏsan followed suit, but started from the top. Samyŏng responded by turning a clear blue sky to a thunder storm and challenged Sŏsan to return the torrential rain to the sky. Sŏsan calmly met the challenge and added his own flourish by transforming the ascending droplets into a flock of birds. Duly humbled, Samyŏng asked to become a disciple of the greater master.

Several years later, the Japanese invasion began and Sŏsan emerged as the leader of a voluntary militia of monks, which eventually grew to a force of 5,000. Sŏsan was too old to participate in battle, so he appointed Samyŏng as field commander for his militia. Under Samyŏng's command, Korea's warrior monks earned a reputation for their fierce courage and played a major role in repulsing the Japanese.

Samyŏng is particularly admired for his courage in venturing into the Japanese headquarters camp to attempt a peaceful solution to the deadlocked war. Although this first attempt proved a failure, he later traveled to Japan, secured the release of 3,000 Korean hostages, concluded active hostilities, and opened the way for a resumption of peaceful relations between the two countries.

After the war, Samyŏng retired to nearby **Haein-sa**, where he died in 1610, at the age of 66.

Haein-sa's Ancient Library

Ritual drums thunder down through the mist-wreathed **Kaya Mountain**, temporarily silencing the clack of prayer knockers and the hum of chants. The smoke of cooking fires mingles with the delicate aroma of incense as the monks of **Haein Temple** prepare a meal of unpol-

Entrance to Haein-sa's library.

ished rice, mushrooms and mountain herbs. Undoubtedly the most rewarding of Korea's more accessible temples, Haein-sa is still isolated enough to be a calm, meditative haven; yet it is only an hour from Taegu by bus, and more than adequate accomodations are available within easy walking distance of the temple grounds. The scenery of **Kaya-san National Park,** beautiful in any season, is stunning in autumn, with craggy peaks and languid streams surrounded by fiery maples and oak.

Haein-sa houses the **Tripitaka,** a collection of more than 80,000 wood blocks engraved with Buddhist scriptures. This vast library was completed in 1251, during the Koryŏ dynasty, after nearly two decades of labor. It was a mammoth task undertaken twice: a first set, carved as a plea to the Buddha for aid against invading Khitan tribes, was destroyed by Mongols when they took their turn at invasion. Retreating to virtually impotent exile on Kanghwa Island, King Kojong ordered the creation of a second set in hopes of inducing an avataristic intervention against the Mongols. It is difficult to assess whether the King's hopes were justified or not: the Mongols finally departed in 1382 due to the collapse of their dynasty in China.

The Tripitaka library was moved from Kanghwa-do, which was too near the capital for safety, to Haein-sa early in the Yi dynasty. The building which now protects the wood blocks was constructed in 1488. It was designed with an adjustable ventilation system to prevent deterioration of the precious blocks. A much more recent concrete structure utilizing an array of modern devices to ensure a controlled environment was intended as a new and improved replacement. However, it utterly failed preliminary tests and now sits neglected within smirking distance of the more efficacious old library.

One of the first statues you are likely to encounter in the temple complex is not a gilt deity, but a curious self-portrait of a monk carved in wood and painted true to life. The figure sits in apparent rigor mortis in a glass case in Haein-sa's small museum, surrounded by displays of elaborate embroidery and remnants of the temple's past. More typical statues are to be found in the compound's numerous shrines, including an imposing 18th Century trinity (with Virochana at altar cen-

Choongmoo Harbor, Kyungsang-nam-do.

ter) in the main hall. Outstanding among the paintings along the inside walls of this hall is a mural depicting scenes from the life of Buddha. It is crowded with tiny figures painted in exquisite detail.

In common with most of Korea's major temples, Haein-sa has a flock of hermitages scattered through the surrounding mountains. All are a meditative lure to exploration.

Sacks of dried wild mushrooms spill out into the streets of the local "resort" town and in several restaurants you may indulge in a fungi eating spree in a semi-private *ondol*-heated room. While most of the town's inns are adequate, albeit a bit mundane, there is a virtual palace located on a low hill at the western edge of town traditionally styled with massive pine timber construction and wood-floored hallways.

The Port of Pusan:
Huffing Tankers and Fish Mongers

Wedged between a range of mountains and the sea, the big port city of **Pusan** is a raucous melange of masts, loading cranes and buildings; honking cabs, train whistles, and the throbbing air horns of passing ferries; suited businessmen, deck hands, navy cadets and fish mongers. Tiny punts propelled by the sweep of a single sculling oar slide through the shadows of huffing tankers. Urban gentlemen in tidy angler outfits toy with their delicate bamboo poles, waiting patiently for nibbling minnows, and scruffy trawler crews unload the day's catch of squid and dog sharks. Dockside fish market matrons hawk 12-inch abalones, brilliant orange sea apples, deep sea clams, and fishes of all sizes, shapes and colors.

For those willing to dare the murky water of Pusan harbor, **Songdo Beach** is just a stone's throw southwest of **City Hall**. Even if you prudently abstain from swimming, it offers an interesting alternative to staying in town, as there are several inns and hotels with a uniquely Pusan flavor. Somewhat cleaner waters are available at three sandy beaches to the east of the city. The most popular is **Haeun-dae**, which has good hotels and a properly bustling resort town.

A few small Buddhist temples are scattered around town and two large, important ones are within easy reach by bus or taxi. **Pomo-sa**, the closer of the two and

Modern apartment complexes are attracting more and Koreans.

the headquarters of the Dyana sect, is a mountain temple a few kilometers from **Tongrae Hot Springs.** The courtyards of the temple are well-landscaped and in traditional Korean style—with trees, stone lanterns, relics, and a pagoda dating back to the Silla dynasty.

Korea's Largest Temple

T'ongdo-sa is about half an hour to the north along the highway to Taegu. The road leading to the temple is a long, slow incline snaking alongside a boulder-strewn stream, sheltered by a forest whose name means "pine trees dancing in the winter wind." Engraved Chinese characters embellish the rocks, some of them huge and scattered among the gnarled bases of staid pines.

With a total of 65 buildings, T'ongdo-sa is Korea's largest temple. Many of the buildings are dispersed throughout the surrounding mountainside, so the temple does not appear especially expansive on first encounter. However, virtually every major Buddhist deity is honored in a separate shrine in the central cluster of buildings, an unusual largesse even for so large a temple compound. The buildings themselves comprise an unusual variety of exceptional architecture, some left pleasantly unpainted or faded to the muted brown of weathered pine. Clustered around several courtyards, T'ongdo-sa is guarded by a massive quartet of wooden devas, each towering figure rendered in vivid and intimidating detail. Inside, one fine mural depicts Chi-jang's boat which escorts the deceased to paradise.

In addition to the many fine statues housed in the shrines, an excellent collection of artwork is on display in the temple museum. Wood block prints are available for purchase.

According to legend, T'ongdo-sa was founded in 646 by a Korean religious leader named Cha-jang who traveled to China in search of a truth capable of saving his nation. There he experienced a miraculous visitation by a holy being who presented him with relics of the Buddha, including his yellow robe. Cha-jang returned to Korea to create his temple, naming it "T'ong-do," which means "salvation of the world through mastery of truth." The gifts received in his vision are preserved in a stone monument in the temple.

Due east of T'ongdo-sa, on a separate

Traditional homes still house many Koreans.

highway running north from Pusan to Kyŏngju, is the urban antithesis of these two vestiges of Korea's heritage: **Ulsan** is an exemplar of the "economic miracle" of modern Korea. One of the centers of Korea's industrial network, Ulsan is a concrete and steel concentration of petroleum refineries, heavy industry, shipyards, and power plants.

The first South Coast city to fall during the Hideyoshi invasion was Pusan, but throughout the war sea battles were waged all along this jagged coast. Near the main nightlife district of Pusan there is a small park, made conspicuous by an imposing tower which dominates the city's skyline. The park contains two statues; one is a high-kitsch representation of a dragon, the legendary king of the sea; the other is of the patron hero of the south coast: **Admiral Yi Sun-sin.** It was largely his staunch patriotism and military skills that prevented the Imjin War from becoming a total disaster for Korea.

Admiral Yi Country

Admiral Yi was born in Seoul in 1545. Eight years later, his father, a Neo-Confucian scholar who preferred poverty to politics, moved the family to Asan, a remote town near Onyang, to escape the high cost of living and political intrigues of the capital. Though he disappointed his father by choosing a military career, Yi is credited with a thorough knowledge of the Classics and a legendary adherence to the stern tenets of Confucian rectitude. Twice stripped of all titles and rank as the target of factional conniving, he reputedly endured humiliation and accepted reinstatement with genteel grace.

In 1591, four years after the first of these incidents, Yi was appointed fleet commander for the eastern coast of Chŏlla Province. One year later the Japanese invaded. In less than a month they had overrun the country, routed the untrained and ill-equipped Korean army, and occupied the capital. Only the ingenuity and prowess of the Korean navy and, later, the assistance of China prevented Korea from becoming the first acquisition of a Japanese Empire.

Admiral Yi quickly became the bane of the Japanese navy, which gradually disintegrated in a series of Korean victories, climaxing in a stunning naval rout at

The port of Pusan is busy year-round.

Hansan-do, near Ch'ungmu. During these battles Yi introduced his famous turtle-ships. Generally regarded as the first iron-clad warships in the world, the heavily armed and highly maneuverable turtleships were virtually impervious to the limited firepower of the Japanese navy, whose ships carried only token cannon.

Later in the war, Yi suffered his second demotion, and the Korean navy was turned over to a rival, Wŏn Kyun. Under Wŏn's command the Navy was promptly decimated. Yi was hastily pardoned and asked to resume command of the admiralty, but his once powerful navy now consisted of only 12 ships. Exhibiting a remarkable blend of strategic genius and gall, he led his paltry fleet in an assault of 133 Japanese ships and won. This astonishing victory revived the dwindling Korean resistance, marking the turning point of the war. Less than a year later, as the Japanese were attempting to retreat from their debacle without further loss, Yi was mortally wounded by a stray bullet in the last battle of the war (fought in the narrow strait of Noryangjin). Concerned that his death might interfere with victory by demoralizing his men, Yi ordered that his body be concealed until the fight was over.

Noryangjin cuts between the mainland and the island of Namhae, at the western end of the scenic Hallyŏ Waterway. To the south is Yŏsu, the site of one of Admiral Yi's major naval bases and now an industrial and resort town. To the east are Ch'ungmu and Hansan-do.

An 'Uncommon' Voyage

. Regular ferries run from a terminal behind Pusan's City Hall throughout the Hallyŏ Waterway to Ch'ungmu and Yŏsu, to the port cities of Masan and Chinhae, and to the island of Kŏje-do (see Guide in Brief). The terminal has two entrances, one marked "Tourist," the other "Common." Unless circumstances permit or require only a hasty trip, free of surprises, join the commoners. In the tourist section you may book passage on a sleek hydrofoil which will get you to your destination promptly, in a seat, and dry, but salt spray fogs the windows, the ride is reminiscent of a plane in heavy turbulence, and, well, why bother?

The common boats are slow, noisy, lacking in seats and other amenities, and inclined to lurch a bit in high seas. But they are also a lot of fun. Libations are liberally dispersed and everyone has a grand time singing, gambling, cajoling passing fishermen to toss up a portion of their loot, supervising the always chaotic loading and unloading of passengers and protesting livestock, or enjoying the scenery, which slides by slowly enough for each subtle nuance to be fully absorbed.

The waterway is sheltered from the open sea by hundreds of islands which are the ancient peaks of an inundated mountain range. Submerged valleys have become countless secluded harbors, many of them now crowded with the vibrantly painted boats of fishermen and divers, and to the north of the waterway are Masan and Chinhae, the two urban ports of the area. Masan is a gritty industrial city, struggling to catch up with its new status as a Free Port. Chinhae, smaller and more spacious, is a naval station famous for the cherry trees that swath the city with blossoms each spring.

Charming Ch'ungmu

Ch'ungmu is deservedly the most popular local destination out of Pusan. The

Buddhist lamp at T'ongdo-sa.

dock of this still rustic resort town is small, but always busy with ferries returning from neighboring islands, small private fishing trawlers, tourist excursion boats, and all manner of hired craft which take watersportsmen out for an afternoon of fishing or skindiving. Ch'ungmu's marketplace begins on the dock, where catches are sold directly from piers, and continues a considerable distance into town, where local specialties such as traditional horse-hair hats, reed baskets and, of course, all kinds of fishes are available.

The many tidy restaurants in town serve a variety of seafood and that's about all they serve. Clams, oysters, soft-shelled crabs and unidentifiable mollusks are thrown into everything, to the delight of those who have an appetite for submarine curiosities and to the horror of those who don't.

There are plenty of inexpensive inns and on **Miruk Island** to the south there is a modern tourist hotel. Near the hotel, on the north slope of a mountain which dominates the island, is **Yonghwa-sa**, a tiny temple with an unusual set of appropriately diminuitive altar paintings. **Kwan-ŭm Hermitage**, a short walk

away, has a lawn instead of a courtyard, a recent but handsome stone gate, and careful landscaping which manages to convey a sense of serenity, despite the incongruity of stone lanterns wired with electric lightbulbs.

Ch'ungmu was indirectly named for Admiral Yi; *Ch'ung* ("loyalty") and *mu* ("military valor") were borrowed from a title conferred on the Admiral posthumously. There are several memorials to him in the area, including a concrete scale model of his base on **Hansan-do**. The largest of the mainland memorials is at **Ch'ungyol-sa**, a shrine where Yi's sword and other weapons and gifts he received from the emperor of China are on display.

On the way to Ch'ungmu, you will pass between the mainland, to the North, and the island of Kŏje, to the South. **Kŏje-do** is Korea's second largest island (after Cheju) and one of the most beautiful areas of the country. The ferries to Ch'ungmu stop at several of the larger towns on the northwest coast of Kŏje-do. With careful scheduling it is possible to spend much of a day exploring the isolated beaches, hillsides, and pastoral towns of the island, catch a ferry (or bus)

Ch'ungmu Harbor.

and arrive at the more accommodating Ch'ungmu by evening. The harbor town of **Changsŭngp'o,** serviced by its own ferry from Pusan, is the island's main eastern port, but it's hardly more than a village if compared to Ch'ungmu or other area "cities." This is a good place to get the feel of a tiny Korean coastal town, and is also a good point of departure for a hiking and camping outing. Excursion boats may be hired to **Haekŭmgang,** a striking camelia-covered rock outcropping off the island's southern tip. Haekŭmgang, undercut with anemone-infested caves, may also be reached from Ch'ungmu by hired boat. Ferry service continues west from Ch'ungmu to **Samch'ŏnp'o** and Yŏsu and shuttles run from Yŏsu to the islands of **Namhae** and **Odong,** both of historic and scenic interest. Odong is covered with camelia and bamboo and was known as a place where bamboo arrows were made for Admiral Yi's fighting men. Namhae is connected to the mainland by a red suspension bridge that crosses the strait of Noryangjin where Yi was killed.

Buses connect Namhae, Yŏsu and Samch'ŏnp'o to Chinju, one of Korea's most enchanting and least visited small cities. The **Nam River** runs through the center of this city. In early morning mists, ghostly anglers squat along the shore with the patience of statues, and elderly gentlemen in traditional dress stroll along the winding walls of **Chinju Castle,** bringing the distant past breathtakingly close. Even the perfectly mundane concrete traffic bridge that crosses the river takes on an air of timelessness. Ancient legends memorialized within the castle seem at least as pertinent as morning news.

Patriotic Chu Non-gae

Chinju Castle was attacked in one of the first battles of the Imjin War. After an heroic defense by the Korean army assisted by a civilian militia, the attack was repulsed, and a planned drive into Chŏlla Province was thwarted. Less than a year later, the castle was the site of an equally heroic defeat after ten days of fierce fighting. The Japanese celebrated their victory with a banquet in **Ch'oksongnu,** a spacious pavilion within the castle. One of the Korean women brought in to provide entertainment was Chu Non-gae, a *kisaeng* hostess whose patron, a

Fishing vessel, Kŏje Island.

200

Korean military official, had died in the battle for Chinju. During the banquet Non-gae lured one of the Japanese generals to the edge of the cliff between the pavilion and the Nam River. There she threw her arms around his neck and dove into the river, dragging him down with her to a patriotic and much-celebrated suicide-assasination.

Non-gae's selfless courage is commemorated now, nearly four hundred years later, in a special ritual held on the last day of lunar June at a small shrine built in her honor above the rock from which she jumped.

The walls of *Chinju Castle* and *Ch'oksongnu* have been tastefully reconstructed and several shrines, temples and pavilions are preserved within the castle grounds. The most imposing structure is Ch'oksongnu, which is raised on stone pillars to provide a pleasant view of the Nam River below. A small gate leads to the cliff where Non-gae lured the general to his (and her) death. Evidently the river was either considerably deeper then or the general a remarkably poor swimmer, or they were killed by hitting the rocks along the shore and not by drowning. A peculiarly Korean form of graffiti embellishes the cliff — names (presumably of Non-gae's posthumous admirers) carved into the rock-face.

Off to one side of Ch'oksongnu is the small shrine in Non-gae's honor. In it is her portrait. A group of attendants keep candles and incense burning every day of the year.

Chinju is one of few Korean cities that has developed into small urban centers without losing their individual identity or rural ambiance. Wander through the narrow streets, browse in the clusters of tiny shops, visit one of the several small temples scattered around town, or spend the day simply—rowing a rented boat around Ch'inyang Lake or enjoying the amusements of an ancient lakeside resort town.

Fifty miles southwest of Chinju, the town of **Hadong** sprawls alongside the **Sŏmjin River** running down from **Chiri Mountain**. Regular buses follow the river upstream to **Kurye**, a small city on the southern edge of **Mt. Chiri National Park**. The highest mountain of the **Sobaek Range**, Chiri-san is a stark jumble of snow-covered peaks in winter, cool and lush in summer, and brilliant with turning foliage in autumn. The area is a

Koje-do
fishtraps.

popular challenge for experienced hikers and a favorite haven for Buddhist monks. There are many small temples tucked in the valleys of the mountain and two major ones—**Hwaŏm-sa** and **Sanggye-sa**—are both easily reached from Kurye.

Hwaŏm-sa was founded in the Silla dynasty. A 15-foot stone lantern, the largest in Korea, is preserved from that period on the temple grounds. The dominant structure of the temple is the imposing two-storied "Awakening Emperor Hall," **Kakhwangjŏn**, which was built in the 18th Century and named in honor of the Chinese Emperor whom legend credits with funding its construction. There are several pagodas in the temple area, including one which bears four stone lions representing the cardinal emotions: love, anger, joy, and sorrow.

A Sacred Skull

According to legend, Sanggye-sa was founded by Priest Sambŏp in 723 during the Silla dynasty. Sambŏp dreamed of becoming a disciple of the great Buddhist master of the time, Hui-neng, a patriarch of the Tsaochi sect of Chinese Sŏn Buddhism. Hui-neng, however, died before this dream could be realized. Sambŏp found some consolation in studying transcriptions of Hui-neng's discourses which had been brought to Korea. This motivated him to visit Kaiyum Temple in China, where Hui-neng's skull had been preserved. While there, Sambŏp bribed a priest at the temple into giving him the revered skull. Returning to Korea, Sambŏp eventually made his way to Chiri Mountain where he built a shrine for his pilfered relic. This shrine gradually developed into Sanggye Temple.

Tea was introduced to Korea from China during the Silla dynasty and cultivated in plantations on the slopes of Chiri-san. An ancient tea ceremony ritual has virtually disappeared in recent years, but some attempts are now being made to revive it. All that remains of the plantations of Chiri-san, however, are wild tea plants that may still be found growing on the mountain's slopes.

K'ogusu is a week-long spring festival, generally celebrated in mid-April, peculiar to this area of the country. No one now seems to be quite sure what the festival signifies, but it is resolutely celebrated anyway. Hordes of celebrants,

Monks heading into the temple.

predominately women, descend on the temple nearest their village fully armed with instruments of revelry. Rising sap is gathered from the forests and brought to the temples to be drunk as a guarantee of continued good health. Sustained by this and other elixirs, villagers sing and dance in the temple grounds.

For Love of Ch'unhyang

Continuing north from Kurye around the base of Chiri-san, you will come to the ancient city of **Namwŏn**, birthplace of Ch'unhyang, the favorite heroine of Korean literature. It is not known whether her birth was more than a literary event, as no proof of Ch'unhyang's actuality exists. However, the story of her life is set in Namwŏn and has had sufficient effect on Korean life and thought for quibbles to be immaterial.

"Ch'unhyang-chŏn (The Story of Ch'unhyang)" is a simple, romantic tale. Mong-nyong, the son of an aristocrat, falls in love with Ch'unhyang, the daughter of a *kisaeng*. The two are secretly married. Soon after, Mong-nyong's father is transferred to a government post in the capital and the two lovers are separated. A lecherous governor is appointed in Namwŏn who is determined to add Ch'unhyang to his roster of lovers. Remaining faithful to Mong-nyong, she flatly refuses to comply with the governor's wishes. She is promptly imprisoned and beaten under the personal supervision of the enraged governor. Meanwhile, Mong-nyong is appointed Royal Inspector of Chŏlla Province. He soon hears of Ch'unhyang's maltreatment and comes to rescue her and punish the governor. The two lovers return to Seoul where they of course live happily and prosperously to a grand old age.

Ch'unhyang's staunch fidelity is still revered and her story is an essential part of Korea's literary legacy. She is honored in Namwŏn with a shrine and an annual festival held on the eighth day of the fourth lunar month, roughly mid-March by Western reckoning.

Confucian Chunghak-dong

Hidden in a high valley on the eastern face of Mt. Chiri is **Chunghak-dong**, one of a few villages which have been granted permission to abstain from Saemaŭl Un-

Korea's cherry blossoms brighten the early spring.

dong, the "New Community Movement." The colorful concrete rooftiles, ersatz chalets, paved roads, electricity, and plumbing that have redefined most Korean villages have not affected Chunghak-dong—though "monoleum," a soft, flexible linoleum in vogue in Korea, has infiltrated onto some porches and living room floors. The formal courtesy of Confucianism is meticulously observed in Chunghak-dong. Unmarried men still wear their hair in single long braids, and education is still conducted in the old Yi dynasty style—the teacher wearing his horse-hair hat while lecturing on the Confucian Classics to his students (who sit cross-legged on the *ondol* floor dressed in traditional white *hanbok*). Visitors are obliged to impose on the hospitality of village residents, as no inns or restaurants are available, and the trip to Chunghak-dong is difficult enough that so far protective isolation is still possible in this timeless place. It is reached only after two jostling hours by bus from Hadong and an arduous three-hour hike. Like most of Korea's best experiences, a visit to Chunghak-dong is an earned reward, reserved for a fortunate and persistent few.

So-so Mokp'o

To the south of Kurye is the city of **Sunch'ŏn**, with regular bus service to **Songgwang Temple**. One of the three largest temples in Korea, Songgwang-sa is a sprawling complex of buildings and courtyards. It is the center of Sŏn Buddhism, the Korean version of Zen, and is the only temple in Korea with western monks and nuns in permanent residence.

Originally a small hermitage built during the Silla dynasty, Songgwang-sa was expanded in the 12th Century after Pojo, a Sŏn Master, settled there with his followers. A tiny, intricately carved, wooden statue of the Buddha, believed to have been carried by Pojo in his travels, is preserved in the temple. The temple includes a number of architectural treasures. The oldest is the four hundred year old **Kuksajŏn**. One unique feature of Songgwang-sa is the pair of arched, covered bridges spanning a shallow stream at the temple entrance.

At the southeastern extreme of the Korean peninsula is the port city of **Mokp'o**, a drab shipping town with few indulgences for the frivolous visitor.

Mokp'o's docks abound in coarse vignettes: six-foot sharks for sale in a fishmonger's shop, a trawler festooned with gaudy banners, sulking ponies hitched to cartloads of produce, blubberous hogs screeching in protest as they are hauled ashore.

The major pastime distraction of this city is the interesting view from **Yudal-san**, a craggy twin-peaked mountain which cuts into the center of the city. Several miles of winding pathways allow visitors to earn a vista in corresponding proportion to his or her particular degree of health or ambition.

These entertainments aside, Mokp'o is chiefly of interest as a point of departure. A variety of more or less seaworthy craft offers access to a significant number of Korea's 3,000 islands. A poor man's cruise to **Cheju-do** is available, taking seven hours to reach its destination. And eight hours to the west of Mokp'o is **Hong-do**, the "Red Island," named for the pink hues of its rock and famous for the imposing, contorted rock formations that line its coast. The bleak beauty of this isolated island is a regular feature of calendar photographs, but the arduous ferry ride and lack of accommodations there discourage all but the most dedicated travelers from attempting a personal encounter. Food and lodging are available on **Huksan Island**, from which a private boat may be hired to Hong-do.

Chin-do Isle:
Canines and Spirits

Considerably less demanding is a trip south to **Chin-do**, a large island only two hours from Mokp'o by ferry. Chin-do is famous for its rare and unique breed of dog and a unique style of shamanism. A pedigreed Chin-do-*kae* has a short, nearly white coat of fur with a touch of ochre along the inner curve of its characteristic arched tail. An annual Chin-do dog show is held in the autumn, billed in the English-language press as a "beauty contest." In one recent show, 90 pedigreed Chin-do dogs competed for the grand prize: a refrigerator.

Among the rituals peculiar to the shamanism of Chin-do is the *Sik-in kut,* or literally, a "ceremony to wash out the soul of the dead." Participants dress entirely on white *hanbok* and gather at the shore to cleanse the soul of a departed relative. Free of worldly taint, the soul is placed in a miniature boat and sent off to heaven.

Women divers in Jeju Island, Korea

CHEJU-DO, 'OVER THERE'

In a 1975 jet-set travel article about "undiscovered worldwide tourist destinations," *Newsweek* magazine nicknamed **Cheju-do** the "Island of the Gods" and raved about its people, culture, seafoods, climate, beaches, golf courses, horseback riding, challenging hiking trails, sportsfishing grounds and volcanic peaks and craters. Later, in 1980, *The Asian Wall Street Journal* headlined a story about Cheju-do with: "Korea Hopes to Transform Tranquil Cheju Island Into Bali of North Asia." The Korean Government, however, has long preferred to call Cheju-do "Korea's Hawaii" and "The Hawaii of the Orient."

Whichever sobriquet you choose for Korea's biggest and most famous island, such descriptions completely debunk stereotypical visions of this country as a land of frozen mountain passes and howling Siberian winds.

Though logic would argue the contrary, there are indeed uncanny geographical similarities between Cheju-do and the Hawaiian isles. On this egg-shaped island, which lies about 150 kilometers south of Pusan in the channel between Korea and Japan, offshore waters are 'of the same aqua-turquoise color as Hawaii's. And these colors in turn lap against the same type of black lava shelves, jagged outcroppings and steep cliffs which rim Oahu, Maui, Kauai and the Big Island of Hawaii. Also, cloud-wreathed **Mt. Halla** (which at 1,958 meters is the highest mountain peak in Korea) is a dead ringer for either famous Haleakala Crater on Maui and/or the active volcanic peaks Mauna Kea and Mauna Loa on the Big Island.

Cheju can't (as can Hawaii) advertise that its deep fissures and frozen lava swirls are the products of still active volcanoes, but it can boast to be home of the world's longest known lava tubes—**the Snake and Manjang caverns** located at **Kim Nyŏng** between **Cheju City** and **Sŏngsanp'o.** The Manjang cavern, the longer of the two tubes, is 6,976 meters long with a diameter that ranges from 3 to 20 meters. (During the summer tourists can join local guides on lamplight tours of these caverns filled with bats,

Preceding pages, the village of Mosuip'o, Cheju-do, left, *haenyo* on photo-plate.

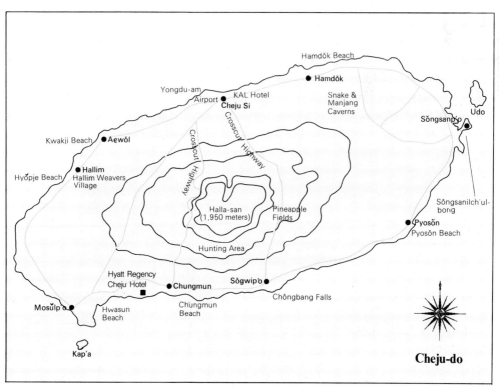

Cheju-do

spiders, centipedes and unusual lava formations; but you are advised to wear warm clothes because temperatures drop to a soggy nine degrees centigrade and cooler inside.)

Probably Cheju-do's most distinctly Hawaiian-like phenomena are man-made structures. Particularly similar is a network of low walls of lava rock construction which lace the Cheju countryside. These walls, which from the sky look like irregular, wind-torn spider webs, border pastures and garden plots throughout the island, and many are almost exact replicas of lava rock walls which flow hither and thither in rural Hawaiian areas.

However, due to Cheju's temperate locale—at north latitude 33 degrees 20′ and east longitude 126 degrees 30′—and the absence of coconut palms (though there are pineapple fields)—these romantic comparisons to Hawaii and Bali must end. Once winter sets in, icy offshore winds knife across Cheju-do and shatter all Polynesian allusions. And though the average monthly temperature from June through September is a balmy, semi-tropical 22° to 27° centigrade, this pleasant level dives to an average of 7° to 10° degrees centigrade from mid-November through March.

Yes, "The Hawaii of the Orient" gets cold, but despite occasional temperature changes and sometimes fierce winds, this splendid island—which since ancient times has been renowned for its winds, women and stones—is worth any traveler's detour. When weather gods are cooperating, Cheju-do is one of Asia's great vacation idylls.

She can be easily reached—either by ferries from Pusan or Mokp'o, or by regular Korean Air Lines flights from Seoul or Pusan—but before you hop over, consider the island's unusual history.

Yang, Ko and Pu

According to Cheju myths, the original inhabitants of this island were three male demigods—**Yang, Ko and Pu**—who emerged from three holes in the ground (called **Samsong Hyŏl**) located at **Cheju City**, about 300 meters distance from the **KAL Hotel**, Cheju-do's only (at 21 stories) high-rise building. These male progenitors were hunters and fishermen who had the good fortune to later meet three princesses who brought with them

Rape (mustard) blossoms at Sŏgwip'o.

grains, livestock and other forms of agriculture. Yang, Ko and Pu married these princesses and thus was Cheju society born. The births and meetings of these original Cheju ancestors are celebrated on special feast days every April, October and December by natives.

Until about 1,000 A.D., however, Cheju, like many other detached island places in Asia, survived in relative isolation. Frederic H. Dustin, a longtime Chejudo resident who in 1975 authored *An Introduction to Cheju-do,* a booklet about Cheju-do's history, geography and mythology, writes that it wasn't until about the end of Korea's Koryŏ Dynasty (918–1392) that Cheju was influenced by off-island events.

Tambulla, Do-i, T'amlla

It was during the reign of Koryŏ King Kojong (1214–1260), Dustin notes, that Cheju received its present name. *Che* means simply "across" or "over there," he writes. And *ju* in earlier times referred to an administrative district. Therefore, Cheju is the *do*, island, in the district over there. Previously the island was variously known as Tamlla, Tambulla, Do-i,

Tanna and T'amlla, the latter appearing to be the most common in historical references.

In the 13th Century, after the Koryŏ kingdom of mainland Korea had been subjugated by Mongol invaders, Chejudo became a Mongol possession for about 100 years (from 1276 to 1375). Professor Sang Yong-ick of the Cheju National University reports that during this time the armies of Kubla and Genghis Khan "used Cheju-do as a bridge to invade Japan." One Japan invasion by Kubla Khan, according to Professor Sang, involved 33,000 men and 900 vessels, many of which were constructed of wood milled from trees on Mt. Halla.

These Mongol conquerors permanently altered Cheju ways. As Professor Sang notes, "Language and habits were greatly changed. The present day dialect (unlike the languages spoken on the Korean mainland) is a direct result of influence by the Mongols (and) until very recently, it was still possible to find leather hats, fur clothing and fur stockings of Mongol style in use in mountain areas. Through the Mongols Cheju (also) became a stock-raising area. Cheju became a famous breeding area for horses

Sŏngsanp'o

... (and) Buddhism was brought to Cheju by the Mongols along with temples and statues."

'Abounds in Horses and Cattle'

The first Westerners to visit and tell the outside world about Cheju-do (and Korea proper) were Dutch sailors who shipwrecked at **Mosŭlp'o** on Cheju's south shore on August 16, 1653. These men—of the Dutch ship *Sparrow Hawk* enroute from Batavia to Taiwan and then Nagasaki—had ventured into fierce Cheju-area winds, which, according to survivor-author Henrik Hamel, "blew so boisterously, that we could not hear one another speak, nor durst we let fly an inch of sail . . ." In a later account of the shipwreck off Cheju (which the Dutch named Quelpaert, after a type of Dutch sailing vessel), Hamel said of this place:

This Island which the natives call Sehesure, lies 12 or 13 Leagues South of the Coast of Corea, and is about 14 or 15 leagues in Compass. On the North side of it is a Bay, where several Barques lye, and whence they sail for the Continent, which is of very

dangerous Access to those that are unacquainted with it, because of several hidden rocks, and that there is but one place where Ships can Anchor and Ride under Shelter for in all other places they are often drove over to the Coast of Japan. The Island is all encompass'd with Rocks, but abounds in Horses and Cattle, which pay great Duties to the King; so that notwithstanding their Breeds of Horses and Herds of Cattle, the Islanders are very poor, and despis'd by the Inhabitants of the Continent. In this Island there is a Mountain of a vast Height, all cover'd with woods and several small Hills which are naked, and enclose many Vales abounding in Rice . . .

Hamel's is a 330-year-old description which, except for the occasional streetlamp, automobile or bus, endures to this day in Cheju-do's rural areas. It's a very early description of a North Asia Eden, but despite such good publicity, Cheju-do didn't become known as a premier Asia tourist destination until about two decades ago.

Author Dustin recalls that it wasn't until 1958—an incredibly late explorato-

Fisherman, P'yŏng-dae-ri.

212

ry date by contemporary tourism standards—that the first "really significant" group of tourists descended on Cheju-do. Dustin, 47, was a member of that initial tour, which was led by Carl F. Miller, a Bank of Korea executive. Dustin quotes Miller as saying of the 1958 visitation:

> Over a hundred people went, by boat of course since there were no commercial planes then, and the occasion was considered so important that the governor and the mayor of Cheju City met the ship. There were no hotels so we rented all of the seven or eight inns in town, staying three nights. We also took over two bath houses, one for men and one for women, with runners to guide visitors to them through the unpaved, unlighted streets.

That idyllic Cheju-do situation has changed considerably. The island is now criss-crossed and circled with paved streets and highways and dotted by hotels and *yŏgwan* (inns). And at the KAL Hotel in Cheju City you can even retire to a proper casino for high-stakes games of chance.

Massive Pleasure Complex

Perhaps the greatest evidence that Cheju-do has been "discovered" are government plans to develop a future resort complex at **Chungmun Beach** on Cheju-do's south shore. Plans for this lovely sand beach below emerald rice terraces and seacliff waterfalls call for the building of a massive pleasure complex which would one day include 10 hotels, six Korean-style inns, three motels and 130 villas (for a total of 2,860 rooms); three shopping centers; a tourist center with restaurants, bars and stores; a Korean "folk village" visitor center; a marina for fishing, sailing and other sorts of pleasure boating; and fresh and saltwater bathing facilities.

A simple drive around Cheju-do, or a cruise along one of the two crosscut highways which skirt Mt. Halla's west or east slopes, are both worthwhile. But whichever course you choose, you'll soon find yourself driving past pine forests, tangerine orchards, pineapple fields, mushroom caves, dancing waterfalls, bizarre rock formations, and rural charms that will draw you yet deeper into Cheju-do's calm and beauty.

Beachside restaurant, Chungmun Beach.

Among island attractions one shouldn't miss are:

• Any of Cheju-do's superb beaches. Favorite crescents of sand are located at **Hyŏpje, Kwakji, Hamdŏk** and **Sŏngsan** along Cheju's upper half, and at **Hwasun,** the aforementioned **Chungmun'** "and **P'yŏson** in the south sector. Most of these spots feature superb seafood restaurants, gaily-painted tent cafes, and rentable recreational facilities.

Korea's 'Emerald Isle'

• The **Hallim weavers village** on the northwest shore. At this quiet spot, where you'll see sheep grazing on rolling hills, you'll find the **Hallim Handweavers** complex where Koreans trained by Columban Roman Catholic priests and nuns are creating some of the finest Irish woolens outside of Ireland. This village's unusual cottage industry was begun in the early 1960s by one Father Patrick J. McGlinchey who imported about 500 Japanese and New Zealand sheep to this natural grazing spot reminiscent of "The Emerald Isle."

At the Hallim Handweavers factory you can watch Koreans shear sheep, then wash, card, spin, warp, thread, weave, check, tenter and steam raw wool into a weavable product. And following the clacking of looms, you can buy superb woolen sweaters, ponchos, caps, mittens, skirts, scarves, blankets and berets (also sold at their Seoul shop in the Chosun Hotel). Only traditional Irish patterns are created by Hallim's industrious "Irish of the Orient."

• The series of **waterfalls** on both the east and west sides of lovely **Sŏgwip'o Town.** The strong **Chŏngbang Falls** right in Sŏgwip'o town is often referred to as "the only waterfall in Asia that plunges directly into the sea."

• The *tol-harubang,* or grandfather stones. These carved lava rock statues, 52 in all, are seen on all parts of Chejudo. However, nobody's quite sure what to make of these phallic fellows with funny smiles. Anthropologists say they probably represent legendary guardians which once flanked the entrances to Cheju's largest townships. Other scholars compare them to mysterious statuary found in some parts of the southern Korean peninsula, Tahiti, Okinawa, Fiji and even Easter Island.

Sŏngsanp'o

Good places to study these images up close are at the entrance to the **Samsonghyŏl Museum** in Cheju City or in front of **Kwandok-jŏk-jŏng** (a 15th Century pavilion, and the oldest standing building on Cheju-do, which faces Cheju City's main square). If you find these *tolharubang* fellows charming, miniature lava rock reproductions are for sale at tourist shops throughout the island.

The Haenyo,
Deep-diving Sirens

• Koreans suggest that you also see the curious **Yongdu-am,** or "**Dragon's Head Rock,**" on the sea in Cheju City's western suburbs near Cheju's main airport. According to Cheju legends, this dragon descended from Mt. Halla and, upon reaching the sea, was petrified in place.

Probably the most dominant memories one will have of this island after a proper tour will be pictures of its famous diving women, awesome Mt. Halla, and, if you visit in the springtime, brilliant fields of rape that paint broad yellow splotches across Cheju-do's pasturelands.

Cheju-do's diving women, called *haenyŏ*, have long been a symbol of this island and its purported matriarchal culture. They are immortalized in folk songs, contemporary promotional brochures, as plaster-of-Paris sculptures, and on postcards, souvenir pennants, cups, plates and *ad trinketum*. Indeed, these hardy and amphibious females, whose free-diving exhalations pierce the air with oxygen-releasing shrieks and whistles, have been celebrated for centuries by Chejudoites and Korean mainlanders alike.

When sea and weather conditions are favorable, scores of the *haenyo*, who range in age from teenagers to wrinkled grandmothers, can be seen bobbing offshore between free dives for seaweed, shellfish and sea urchins. In their slick and black ankle-to-neck wetsuits, face masks and snorkels, they look more like members of a navy demolition team than the sexy sirens they're supposed to be, but they are still the favorite target of every camera-bearing tourist who visits Cheju-do. But remember to ask for permission before photographing the *haenyŏ*, because they often are camera shy or want to be reimbursed for their bathing beauty modeling.

Left, a real life diving woman, Right, a Cheju City tol *harubang*.

정
靜
KEEP

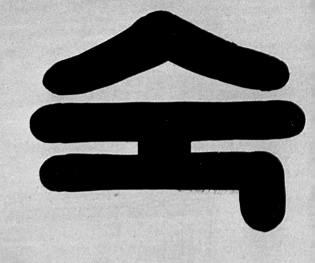

QUIET

RELIGION

"... Confucianism makes love and right-eousness its basis. By a life of virtue, and by keeping the Five Commands blessed there-by ... Taoism has to do with purity and by means of water and fire lifts its subject to a place of refinement where the spirit sloughs off its outer shell and guards only the essence; ... living in the world and yet not of the world ... Buddhism dwells in the regions of silence ... With all sensations of the mind and body cast aside as worthless, and zero as the objec-tive attainment ... it grows brighter and clear-er in mind as the body decays."
—*17th Century Korean Scholar
Hong Man-jong*

Such was the literati's view of Korean religion three hundred years ago. It was complicated to analze then, and so it is now:
It is Easter Sunday at Seoul's Myŏngdong Cathedral. Elderly Korean Christians receive respectful bows from their juniors in the never-dying tradition of Confucius prior to entering the vestibule of this grand and gothic church. Matrons dressed in brightly colored hambok embroidered with Taoist symbols sell Easter eggs and candy to anxious children in the plaza below. Meanwhile, bald-headed Buddhist monks in gray robes pass by the entrance to the cathedral compound, and across the street a fortuneteller consults manu-als in order to advise an aging woman on her future—to the best of his shamanist know-ledge.

Most East Asian countries adhere to a spiritual mainstream, but Korea denies a sim-ple religious label. Strong traditions of sha-manism, Confucianism, Taoism, Buddhism, Christianity and other various religions in-fuse Korean society. Though many Koreans ascribe exclusively to one religion, they also allow all of the country's spiritual beliefs to play an occasional role in their lives.

If one were to peer into the souls of Korean people, one would find fascinating elements of shamanism, the folk workship of a panth-eon of household, village and animate and inanimate forces in nature. (See the shaman-ism article in this book for further details).

Koreans, like other Asian people, maintain

Preceding pages: A trilingual plea for silence; A "thousand Buddhas" at Chikji-sa near Kimch´ŏn; left, Prince Yi Kyu and desendants of Yi dynasty royal families honor their ancestors in Confucian rites at Chongmyo Shrine.

ancient traditions such as the *kut*, or exorcising ceremonies. These practices have not been fully institutionalized into a religion but shamanism has been kept very much alive in Korea—as in the deification of *Sanshin*, a non-Buddhist Mountain God, who has found his way into special shrines found within the courtyards of Buddhist temple complexes.

Shamanist elements have also worked their way into Confucian ceremonies dedicated to *Sajik*, the "Gods of Land and Harvest." Indeed, until the end of the 19th Century, such ceremonies took place throughout the country, even during royal rituals.

The veneration of Tan'gun, the mythical founder of the Korean race and civilization, has earned government backing as a means of instilling greater patriotism. Tan'gun was the

doctrines of Lao-tze and advocating simplicity, selflessness, etc." Taoism has been practiced in Korea for more than 1,300 years, but active examples of its presence are rare these days.

Though Taoist texts were often studied in the past, and though some of Korea's Buddhist temples temporarily served as Taoist temples, few remnants of early Taoist art survive today, save for the occasional Taoist statement on a Yi dynasty genre painting. A few other strong symbols of Taoist legacy are the ubiquitous Chinese characters for longevity (*su*) and blessings (*pok*) which serve as decorative motifs on clothing, bedding, jewelry, and other such items.

Taoism achieved its greatest height in Korea during the Unified Silla dynasty (668-

central figure in a Taejŏng cult which declined to near extinction by the 15th Century. The cult may be generically separated from shamanism proper but in actual practice it is inseparable from the shamanist world.

The casual visitor to Korea will often see sprinkled throughout the countryside carved and painted shamanist posts depicting an ancient general "of the heavens" and his companion female general "under the earth." These posts are placed outside of villages to repel evil spirits.

Korea's Taoist Way

Taoism, according to *Webster's*, is "a Chinese religion and philosophy based o the

918 A.D.). Practitioners aren't so dedicated today but Taoism is experiencing something of a renaissance as a number of modern, synthesizing religions draw upon its teachings. Koreans as a group have never the Chinese, but they have recognized the readings of Lao-tze and Chuang-tze as being complementary to Buddhist and Confucian thought.

Buddhist Theocracy

When it comes to the arts and innovative thought, Buddhism stands out as one of the most important of this country's cultural fountainheads. This religion stresses finding a practical and moderate way towards self-actualization while on earth. In ancient times

Buddhism split into a number of spiritual schools but the two largest—Hinayana and Mahayana—earned the most converts outside of India. The Mahayana school—which preached that any practical method towards teaching salvation is generally acceptable—eventually entered China from the west along the ancient Silk Route. This widely sectarian form of Buddhism, with its easy acceptance of local deities as a means of drawing the masses to the temples for an eventual study of more orthodox doctrines and practices, proved much to the liking of the Koreans.

Buddhism entered the northernmost of Korea's three kingdoms, Koguryŏ, in 372 A.D. Though Chinese ancestor worship had been commonly accepted for some time, Buddhism became Korea's first sophisticated,

period.

During the following Koryŏ dynasty (918–1392), temples became Korea's centers of learning and Buddhist monks enjoyed privileged roles within the society. Wŏnhyo, one of Asia's greatest thinkers, dominated intellectual and religious arenas both inside and outside of Korea. The most important Buddhist achievement during that time was the carving of some 80,000 woodblocks to print and preserve the *Tripi taka Koreana*, one of the world's most complete collections of ancient Buddhist scriptures. The blocks are preserved today in Haein temple southwest of Tacgu in the Mt. Kaya National Park. These blocks are regarded as one of the greatest achievements of world Buddhism and Korean culture.

truly institutionalized religion. The Paekche (18 B.C.–661 A.D.) and Silla (57 B.C.–631 A.D.) kingdoms to the south gradually accepted this new faith as they recognized the political, cultural, and philosophical merits of a Buddhist theocracy.

It was the Kingdom of Paekche that transmitted Buddhism to Japan. Silla eventually conquered the entire peninsula, Buddhism flourished, and a new height in Korean culture was reached under the Buddhist government of the Unified Silla (661-918 A.D.)

Mirŭk-bul sits in opulent serenity at Kŭmsan-sa in Chŏllapuk-do; right, modern Confucianists at Changmyo Royal Ancestral Shrine during May observances.

As the Koryŏ dynasty slowly degenerated the major philosophical force to emerge was Confucianism. Confucianism became a growing force in Korea, and eventually its adherents called for an all-out government reformation. In 1392 the Yi dynasty (1392–1910) was established by T'aejo or "The Great Founder." From that time on Buddhism fared poorly under the attacks of Neo-Confucian court scholars. An occasional Yi kîng would look favorably on the religion, but Buddhism was basically driven from Seoul's courtyards of power and into mountain retreats. The social status of monks often was degraded to that of itinerant entertainers and prostitutes. Only in recent times have the Buddhist monks and nuns been able to recover any significant gains in prestige.

While Buddhists took a very active part in Korea's struggle against the Japanese occupation during the first half of this century it was, ironically, the Japanese who encouraged the revival of modern Buddhism in Korea. However, it was definitely in Japan's interest to strengthen all cultural similarities between the two nations. And at the same time, the Japanese installed a variety of sects from Japan that allowed monks to marry and otherwise change Korean Buddhism.

Today, the traveler will regularly spot many of the more than 30,000 grayrobed monks and nuns who come from all levels of Korean society. Buddhism is Korea's largest single religion. Indeed, the religion is so strong that in 1975 the Republic of Korea

carnation, with an accompanying perspective of a cyclical nature of history and phenomenae, gives Koreans an introspective view of the universe.

A Confucian Empire

Confucianism has become a way of life in Korea. Confucius— or *Kongja*, as the Koreans refer to him—was never a breaker of traditions but a conservative reactionary who called in print for a return to China's "Golden Era," the early days of the Chou dynasty (1112 B.C.–256 B.C.). Consciously or unconsciously, his greatest innovative moment came when he proclaimed that the ultimate measure of political success was not simply sheer might but a ruler's virtue and his peo-

government recognized Buddha's Birthday as a national holiday. This popular festival is fervently and joyously observed throughout the nation.

In viewing Buddhism in modern-day Korea, one will find that its influences are subtle but pervasive. In the thought patterns of Koreans, for example, the principle of "karma", or "cause-and-effect," allows many to take a passive view of the world. The individual who is caught by the negative effects of some past action may justify his or her problem as being out of his or her control.

Another element of Korean Buddhist psychology is "Creation, Staying, Destruction and Nothing." This concept of rein-

ple's contentment. Confucius was the region's first and greatest moralist.

Confucian codes, which encourage harmony in relationships—from that of the Emperor with Heaven down to that of a mother with child—became the social and cultural keystone of more than 800 years of Korean history.

While there are traditions and records of various forms of Confucianism, or Confucian-like religions entering Korea as early as 550 B.C., these initial movements were not necessarily Confucian. Confucianism never really made serious headway in staunchly Buddhist Korea until about 896 A.D. when it was reported that a Korean named Ch'oe Ch'i-won passed the highest

Confucian examinations in Peking.

As Buddhism became more and more corrupt under the protection of the Koryŏ dynasty, a call for a more moral form of government began to gain great appeal among Korea's dissident intellectuals. In 953 A.D. a Chinese Confucian scholar, San Gen took office under Kwangjong, the fourth Koryŏ king. Under San Gen's leadership, Confucian Examinations or *Kwago*—exactly like those administered in China, were introduced into Korea's bureaucratic qualifications system.

Kwago became the backbone of a solidly Confucian Korean society. The system had its base in local primary schools that nearly every community of any size supported during the Yi dynasty. Through a series of examinations, any male—but actually almost

these examinations free of favoritism. Upon completion of compositions, for example, a court scribe would copy the manuscript so that detection of the examinee's identity would not be possible by judges. Furthermore, a *nom de plume* was affixed to the rolled papers, and when they were delivered for evaluation, the examinations were thrown over a high wall so that the judges could not even see who was throwing the compositions. Later on, though, even this foolproof system was corrupted and success could be obtained through a secret exchange of wealth. During the later years of the *Kwago* system, which ended in 1894 with the era-changing Kapo Revolution, corruption had become so widespread that the best of scholars refused to take the examinations.

always those of the artistocratic *yangban* class—could eventually rise to enter one of the four colleges. Each school admitted 100 students, but only 200 students could pass the triannual *Kwago* examinations.

Secretive Examineers, Neo-Confucianists

In the beginning, according to the late religious authority Charles Allen Clark, a great deal of energy was spent on keeping

Left, an 1880s Presbyterian missionary, Rev. Samuel Moffett with new Christians; right, a 1980s Sam Moffett in Korean film role in which he portrayed his grand-father.

During much of the Koryŏ dynasty Buddhism and Confucianism survived side-by-side and were generally complimentary to each other. This peaceful coexistence, however, began to change when the philosophies of the great Neo-Confucianist, Chu Hsi, entered the Koryŏ court in the 12th Century.

The Neo-Confucianists were able to unify and synthesize various Confucian theories into a more homogeneous and dynamic form of political philosophy. They denounced Buddhist practices as wasteful and injurious to the state. Furthermore, Neo-Confucian philosophies found royal favor in the court of T'aejo who militarily usurped political power from the koryŏ court. He astutelyd recognized the necessity for a new, integral political philosophy to solidify his power. With the revolutionary support of the Neo-Confucianists he quickly gained absolute political control of Korea.

Initially, Neo-Confucian philosophies devised by Chu Hsi were innovative and dynamic. However, Chu Hsi's followers soon regarded his complete logic as more than a practical and ethical way of life; they saw his work as an all encompassing venue of truth. Soon, the following of his doctrines to the letter became the standard fare in Chinese political circles, and this dogmatic adherence to tradition suffocated much of the Chinese thought and culture which preceded it. This was even more true in Korea. The Koreans introduced inflexible precepts of Neo-Confucianism into almost every aspect of

towards "family first" are all well-practiced ideals which have been only modified during "modernization" and "Westernization" of the past 50 years.

Confucianism today is a dilemma within Korean thought; it's a tradition upon which their culture must be based, but it is also a tradition whose precepts often stifle genuine, innovative thought. It is a 2,000-year-old philosophy, lifestyle, and institution that is desperately trying to find a tolerant place in contemporary Korean society.

Christian Korea

So far this review has discussed religious forms one might expect to encounter in an Oriental country—shamanism, Taoism,

daily life.

Today Confucianism thrives more in Korea than in any other nation. And though Confucianism has been greatly discredited since the turn of the century by both foreign and domestic intellectual movements, its basic values and premises still dominate the lives of all Koreans. Ancestor worship continues to be practiced much as it has been for more than a thousand years. In Korea even an "old fool" is first and foremost an "elder," To rebel against the word of an elder is to invite social censure—a conservative and powerful force which is very effective in Korea's small and closed society.

Confucian deference to age, respect for those generically superior, and responsibility

Buddhism and Confucianism. However, first time visitors to Korea often gaze with wonder at the many purely Christian church steeples and crosses that punctuate populated skylines. More than 6 million people, or 16 percent of South Korea's population are avowed Christians.

When Yi T'aejo set up his new capitol in Seoul and instituted a new political system throughout the peninsula, Buddhism was tossed out of the spiritual picture and Neo-Confucianists began dominating Korea's royal centers of powers. As mentioned ear-

Above, Buddhist dancers wearing stiff hemp hats whirl as the ancients did during recent ritual staged for modern Seoul spectators.

lier, the Neo-Confuicanists succeeded in creating an almost too ideal state which eventually stagnated into a bureaucracy.

Shamanism, the spiritual soul of the Han people, was frowned upon as being uncouth and Buddhism was denounced as frivolous and blamed for the demise of the previous Unified Silla and Koryŏ dynasties. But Confucianism in the end promised nothing more than a better society based on an ideal historical model. There was little of spiritual substance available to the masses.

Christianity entered Korea's spiritual vacuum in 1592 the date of Hideyoshi's invasion of Korea from Kyushu, Japan. One of his two generals, Konishi, was a Christian in command of Christian-Japanese troops who was given the unenviable assignment of storming through Korea enroute to do battle with the Chinese Enpire.

Traveling with Konishi's Christian *samurai* were two Jesuit priests—one Japanese and the other a Spaniard named Gregario de Cespedes. Because Koreans of that time were less than interested in being converted to a foreign religion, these two priests had to restrict their missionary work to as yet unconverted Japanese troops. Aided by Chinese troops, the Koreans eventually were able to drive the invaders—and their Western religion—out of the country. Surviving Christians who made it back to Japan eventually met martyrdom or accepted apostasy during later purges of Christians by Japanese rulers.

A number of scholars—particularly those of the *Sirhak* (Practical School) movement—learned more of this peculiar Western faith during diplomatic missions to Peking where emissaries of Christian nations were stationed. But only a few looked upon Christianity with anything more than casual curiosity. Eventually some studies of the religion were written in Chinese and a few of these books were brought back to Seoul as intellectual curiosities.

In 1777 a young scholar named Yi Tukso joined a group of friends at a mountain temple to study various schools of thought: Among the works they brought with them was a book on Roman Catholicism. Yi appreciated the ideas espoused in this book and soon was using all his influence with the Korean court to secure other books on the religion. He quickly realized, as he became more committed to this new religion, that for the new faith to grow he would have to convert an influential family. This he accomplished through the conversion of the politically influential kwŏn family of Yangŭn. Shortly afterwards, the town of Yangŭn became the first Christians began to refuse to perform ancestor sacrifices, the prestuge if a number of them required the government to take decisive action. By the end of the 18th Century in Korea, but already hundreds had been arrested and tortured for leaving the national Confucian religion.

Later, a number of Chinese and European priests smuggled themselves into the country, but most were betrayed or gave themselves up to Korean authorities, when they attempted to stop the persecution of Christian brethren. Missionaries—both foreign and native—were allowed at various times to preach their religion but still, Christian Korea had to endure at least four major periods of persecution.

By 1849 there were some 11,000 Roman Catholics (led by 12 French priests) in Korea. In 1864 King Kojong came to the throne and advocated a reign of tolerance towards the Christians. His policy was to play Catholic France against his encroaching neighbor, Orthodox Russia. By 1866, though, the young king was forced by his staunchly conservative court to order the greatest and last of Korea's Christian persecutions. Seoul's Bishop Simeon Francois Bereneux and three French priests were seized and on March 8, 1866 led to a public execution ground above the Han River. At this spot, appropriately named Chŏltu-san, or Chop Heads Mountain, they were decapitated by sword. During the next three years some 8,000 people were put to death.

Of three surviving French priests who individually escaped to China via small boats, one, a Father Ridel, was largely responsible for introducing Korea to another form of Western civilization—the military.

Ridel returned to Korea as an interpretor with a small armada of French ships. This task force vainly tried to establish contact with the Korean government to demand satisfaction for the Christian slayings. When it became apparent that the royal court in Seoul was ignoring them, a small force of 150 men decided to take on a badly underresti-mated unit of Korean tiger hunters at a monastery fortress. After suffering a severe mauling, the French forces retreated. The French retreatd back to their Chinese ports and Korea entered a reinforced—if brief—final period of isolationism

Today a Church of the Martyrs stands next to the Second Han River Bridge in Seoul to mark the spot where the first French priests lost their heads. The second floor serves as an interesting museum and memorial to the thousands of Korean Christians who were killed for their religion.

Missionary Waves

Protestantism first touched Korea's shores in 1832 in the guise of one Charles Gutzloff who had commissioned a Bristish ship to take him to the south coast of Ch'ungch'ŏng Province. There, he quickly distributed a supply of bibles among the villagers, met some local Catholies, then departed as suddenly as he had arrived.

The first *substantial* contact of Protestantism occurred with the arrival in Korea in 1884 of Dr. Horrace N. Allen, who also served as the U.S. Minister to Korea. Allen was soon followed by waves of missionaries of all creeds, in particular by successful Presbyterian and Methodist groups.

The Protestant missionaires came at a most opportune time to proselytize their faith directly to the masses. Their additional knowledge of Western technology—and a dedication to establishment of schools—made them a very attractive influence.

Missionaries—both Protestant and Roman Catholic—later made substantial contributions to the Korean independence movement and the anti-Japanese resistance. And through on-going institutions such as the Royal Asiatic Society, missionary families have done much to educate the outside world about the *real* Korea. Through the founding of a number of higher educational institutions such as Ewha and Yŏnsei universities in Seoul, these families have contributed much to Korea's development.

Today, Christianity plays a disproportionate role in power circles, considering its small percentage of the Korean population. Christian leaders can be found at the highest levels of society, probably because of their historic headstart in local education.

While one may encounter almost every brand of Christianity in Korea, Christianity here has a distinctly fundamentalist flavor. More moderate sects (such as Presbyterians and Methodists) include among their flocks large numbers of fervent devotees who would probably feel quite out of place in similar congregations in the West.

Because some 11 million Koreans belong to a wide variety of "minor" religions, mention of some here is necessary. Undoubtedly the most colorful of Korea's native religions is Ch'ŏndo-kyo, a cult founded roughly 100 years ago by an impoverished scholar. After he had experienced a vision calling him to lead mankind in the ways of heaven, Ch'oe Che-u started a religion and a movement that brought Korea to the attention of the world. Ch'oe's followers' belief in *Hananim* (God) and a use of magical symbols caused the government to suspect they were part of the Catholic movement. Ch'oe argued that his was not of the *Sŏhak* (Western Learning or Catholicism) School but of the *Tonghak* (Eastern Learning) School. In 1866 the government decided otherwise and Ch'oe lost his head with the Catholics.

In spite of this setback, Ch'oe's religion continued to gather strength among Korea's southern peasantry as their only viable form of representation of the declining Yi government. In 1893 a band of "Tonghaks" approached the court in Seoul and petitioned the government to remove its ban on their religion. If this was not done, the delegation said, its followers would slay all foreigners whose presence was responsible for the confusion which result in the Ch'ŏndo-kyo persecution.

Shortly afterwards, a man named Chŏn "Noktu" (Little Beans) Pong Chŏn captured the leadership of this religion. The Tonhaks organized a revolt that quickly spread through much of the southern third of the nation and a panicked court requested military aid from China. The Chinese responded as requested, but they were in clear violation of a treaty with Japan that required prior notification before any movement of Chinese troops into Korea. Consequently, the Japanese seized this opportunity to send troops into Korea, crushed the rebellion in the south and moved northward to engage the Chinese. In a short time, Japan was recognized as a world power because of its victory in the Japanese-Chinese War.

Today, the religion continues its synthesized faith by adhering to a goal of, in the words of the founder, "fusing into one the ethics of Confucianism, the awakening to nature taught in Buddhism, and the cultivation of energy as espoused by Taoism."

One of the more religious developments in modern Korea has been the introductin of Muhammadanism. The teachings of Muhammad never made a real impact until 1950 when Turkish troops arrived to fight for U.N. forces. In 1955 a teacher and a handful of Korean followers formed the nucleus of a Korean Muslim movement, and in 1960 the Korean Muslim Federatin was founded with a Korean as its leader.

Today, statistics for the number of Korean Muslims varies greatly but the group is attracting attention for its efforts to establish a true Muslim community.

Western-style Easter egg baskets are as common in Korea as they are in other Christian places, location: Seoul's Myŏngdong cathedral.

Korean temple art is as bewildering as it is beautiful. Demons crouch under the heavy burden of roofbeams, sword-wielding guardians put off anyone with ill intent, and serene Buddhas hold meditative poses under the staring eyes of a hundred scowling faces. Figures and legends are depicted in an array of colors and distorted imagery foreign to the Western eye.

The confusion of touring foreigners who attempt a more than

ple context and help you to enjoy Korea's subtle and fantastic Buddhist heritage.

Temple Protocol

While common Occidental sense is usually sufficient, the practice of a few finer points of temple protocol should guarantee you a friendly reception and also lead you to an increased awareness of an appreciation for the religious commitment typical of

eaves of shrines, the photographing of temple interiors is another matter. Almost always you will be politely forbidden to photograph the main icons, but if people are not engaged in prayer, you might be allowed to photograph secondary religious artifacts. Always ask permission, because some of the most beautiful artwork is strictly off limits to cameras—not only for religious reasons but for protection of the artwork itself.

casual look at Korean temples can be attributed to more than cultural ignorance, because the temples vary in design from sect to sect, temple to temple, and opinion to opinion. The sheer number of Buddhist temples, more than 2,000, has helped increase exponentially this number of variations, as have historial and other such factors.

Still, there are figures, paintings and shrines common to all Korean temples, and their ancient and contemporary icons and ideas are quite accessible to persons new to Korea and Buddhism. The following guide will help you identify common figures and shrines in their tem-

most temple residents. When you meet a monk or nun, they often will pause before you, bring their hands together, and bow. Be sure to come to a full stop and return this respectful greeting. Don't stand or crouch in the doorway of a shrine. Either take a quick look inside and move on or remove your shoes and enter.

Various paintings and altars line the walls of most shrines. These items are there for the seeking and resident monks and nuns are usually flattered when a visitor wishes to take a closer look. However, though you should feel free to photograph exterior pagodas, courtyards, bells, drums and the walls and

Guardians

Whether they be mighty wooden statues or paintings of the **Four Heavenly Kings**, or simply two figures painted on gate doors, the first images one encounters at a Korean temple are guardians.

If a temple is not particularly grandiose, it is usually the two gate gods one must push past to enter the temple grounds. In Korean they are called **Kŭm-gang-sin-ch'ang**. These deities prevent evil spirits from entering temple precincts. Their symbolic attributes are abundant. In China they are called **Heng** and **Ha**. They boast the power to send forth deadly rays of light, one from his nostrils giving forth the sound "heng" and his partner from his mouth with the sound "ha." The mouth is the door of the face, and, symbolically, Ha's open mouth indicates that the temple is protected whether the doors are opened or closed. The two gate gods protect on another level as well, that of wisdom over ignorance, for they represent two forms, feminine and masculine, openmouthed and closed, of the **Vajra** god who is a symbol of indestructibility and of the sharp edge of wisdom cutting through the most solid ignorance. The guardian gods, therefore, represent a spiritual confrontation with oneself.

was setting out to beg. The Guardian Kings all rushed to present him with bowls made of precious stone. Sŏkkamoni refused them. The Guardians then offered him bowls of ordinary stone. Accepting them as more suitable to his position, Sŏkkamoni piled the four, one atop another, and, miraculously, they became one vessel.

The Four Heavenly Kings, or **Guardian Kings**, all bear a fierce countenance and trample the opponents of Buddhism under their feet. Each of the Four Guardian Kings represents one of the cardinal directions.

The guardian of the North, **Ta-mun-ch'ŏn-wang**, holds a pagoda or tower. The tower re-

The Guardian of the West, **Kwang-mok-ch'ŏng-wang** holds a dragon in one hand and a jewel in the other. The original meaning of these symbols seems to be lost in obscurities of the ages, but there are varying, interesting theories. It may help Westerners, when considering dragons, to refer to their experience with the snake as a symbol because the snake can represent evil (sin) or good (wisdom), and the dragon, in different contexts, is equally diverse. On the one hand we see Kwang-mok-ch'ŏn-wang, in an obvious show of strength, keeping the dragon and jewel apart. On the other hand, numerous dragons, especially those incorporated among

Especially when exploring one of Korea's larger temples, one is likely to find, in addition to the two gate gods painted on the doors, the **Four Heavenly Kings**, housed in their own gate structure. In statue or painted form, these figures are imposing, often as much as 15 feet tall. These protector gods are of Hindu origin, and are said to have helped **Siddhartha Gautama**, the Indian prince who became Buddha, to escape from his father's house by each taking hold of one hoof of Siddhartha's horse and lifting him over the palace walls. In another legend, Siddhartha (at this point in his life called **Sŏkkamoni**: Prince of the Sŏkka Clan)

presents a particular type of reliquary stupa and draws its symbolism from it. The stupa consists of three basic parts: the base, which represents the earth, the dome, which represents heaven, and a connecting piece, or cosmic axis.

Chon-chang-ch'ŏn-wang is the Guardian of the Southern quarter. One may identify him by the sword he bears, usually poised for action. He is reputed to have the power to multiply his sword so that he may always outnumber his opponents.

Chi-kuk-ch'ŏn-wang guards the East. He is easily spotted by the lute he holds, the strings of which control weather phenomena.

the eaves of temple shrines, have a big, round jewel smack in their jaws. According to some, these two dragons are essentially different. The dragon which holds the jewel in its mouth is in truth a divine being capable of taking on the form of a dragon and flying through the heavens. The jewel set in its jaw means that the world can go on. The dragon that the guardian holds, however, is not a spiritual being but simply a dragon, capable of flying, but not quite all the way to heaven. The dragon as a beast is fierce, huge and mighty, but held in the guardian's hand is kept from stealing the jewel and appears weak and small as a garden snake.

The Four Guardians should be looked for in the corners of temple murals where variations may be observed between Koryŏ and Yi style paintings. Even within the history of Korean Buddhism the objects which the guardians hold have changed. (There is even dispute as to which guardians govern which quarter of the world.)

Regardless of iconographic variations, one may identify the guardians by their everpresent battle dress and imposing facial expression. Their variety in appearance only serves to provoke thought and make us more aware of their function. They forever remain routers of evil

all beings who call on him. He assists them by admitting them to his Pure Land where they will know no hindrances to achieving enlightenment. Pure Land is no different from Pure Mind, the state in which one is free from illusions.

Sometimes it is almost impossible to know if one is looking at a figure of Amit'a-bul or Sŏkkamoni-bul because their faces are so similar and their *mudra* (symbolic hand gestures) are often the same. Each is generally depicted as the central figure of a trinity. When trying to discriminate between the two, it is helpful to be able to identify the images which flank the central figure. For example, if the

which represents the perfection of wisdom, and, therefore, resembles the Law of Buddha.

Sŏkkamoni-bul

Sŏkkamoni is the title given to the historical Buddha, Siddhartha Gautama, who lived in the 5th Century B.C. Some or all of the P'alsang-do (Eight Paintings from Sokka's Life) are frequently found painted on the outside of temple shrines. One may follow Siddhartha through the process which brought him to enlightenment. Often pictured are: his birth in the **Lumbini** Gardens, his childhood bath in the fire of nine dragons, his meditation in the Himalayas, his strug-

demons and protectors of Buddhism and Buddhist doctrine.

Amit'a-bul

Amit'a-bul emanates from the meditation of the primordial Buddha. He is the Buddha of Infinite Light and governs the Pure Land, or Western Paradise. In India, where Buddhism began, people felt relief from the extreme heat of day when the sun reached the western sky. Thus, Amit'a-bul's paradise came to be associated with the west. Appropriately, he sometimes wears the color red.

Amit'a-bul has vowed to save

side figures are Kwanseŭm-posal and Taese-ji-posal, the central Buddha is Amit'a-bul. **The Temple of Supreme Bliss (Kŭngnak-jon** in Korean) houses this celestial trinity. Amit'a-bul often holds his left hand in the mudra of "fulfilling the vow," the palm turned outward in a gesture of offering. This mudra is found most often in standing figures. When he is seated, the left palm is often simply held face upward in the lap. The right hand is raised, granting an absence of fear. There are three variations of this right hand gesture: the thumb touching the index, middle, or ring finger. The thumb and index finger form a circle

gle with *Mara* (the devil), his enlightenment under the Munsu and Pohyŏn and represents the unifying principle of each pair.

Trinities

Buddhist trinities are composed of three buddhas; three bodhisattvas; one buddha and two bodhisattvas; one buddha and two historical personages (usually *arhats*); or one bodhisattva and two historical or mythical personages. In addition to specific attributes, emblems, and mudra, there are some simple ways of discriminating generally between buddhas and bodhisattvas.

232

Boddhisattvas are sometimes adorned with jewelry and crowns while buddhas generally are not. Though there are certain celestial trinities of three buddhas, one can often identify bodhisattvas by their secondary position in a trinity, relative to the main image. It should be noted, however, that bodhisattvas, though they appear to be secondary in position and stature, are not negative or inferior. Instead, the buddhas are more positive and true.

Buddhas bear the "thirty-two marks," some of which are easily spotted. Examples are the tightly knotted black hair; protuberances on the head; white, curled hair at the center of the fore-

head; long earlobes (without earrings); and three rings, or creases, around the neck.

Certain basic configurations are apparent in the composition of trinities of images. One combination is known as the **Three Holy Ones:** Amit'a-bul attended by **Kwanseŭm-posal** and **Taesaechi-posal**. The two bodhisattvas are emanations of the compassion of Amit'a-bul. Taesaechi is a bodhisattva of power. He symbolizes perfect activity and often holds a lotus flower.

Although Sŏkkamoni-bul is commonly less popular than either Amit'a-bul or Chijangposal, he still holds a prominent place in temple art. As the cen-

tral image, he is flanked by one of several pairs such as: Amit'a-bul and **Yaksa-yŏrae-bul**; his two favorite disciples, **Ananda** (representing intellect) and Kasop (representing experience); or **Mirŭk-bul** and **Chekara** (who is the first of the earthly buddhas). When the Trinity consists of Chekara, Sŏkka, and Mirŭk, it is the Trinity of the Past, Present, and Future Buddhas.

Munsu-posal (seated on a lion when a solitary figure) and **Pohyŏn-posal** (seated on an elephant when solitary) also frequently attend Sŏkkamoni. Munsu is bodhisattva of *prajna* (essential wisdom; knowledge of the true, non-dualistic identity of the world). **Pohyŏn** is a bodhisattva of power and love, *karuna*. Prajna is identified with the intellect and with unification, while karuna is emotion and multiplicity.

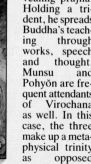

Munsu often holds a sword with which he severes earthly attachments, revealing prajna. Holding a trident, he spreads Buddha's teaching through works, speech and thought. Munsu and Pohyŏn are frequent attendants of Virochana as well. In this case, the three make up a metaphysical trinity as opposed to the historical trinity of Sŏkka, and his disciples, Ananda and Kasop.

Virochana is sometimes depicted with **Sŏkkamoni** and **Yaksa**, composing the Trinity of the Preciousness of the Law of Buddha.

Ch'il Sŏng

Ch'il Sŏng, the **Seven Star Spirit**, has his roots in Taoism and shamanism. The Great Bear Constellation, which is Ch'il Sŏng, is visible year round, partly accounting for the great reverence with which he is regarded. Ch'il Sŏng is thought to control both good and bad fortune.

On the left hand side of the

Main or **Hell Hall**, a large painting of Ch'il Sŏng is sometimes hung. The painting is colorful and impressive. It contains many figures and festive scenes. Presumably, when Buddhism came to Korea, people assumed that their beloved Ch'il Sŏng was in fact another manifestation of the compassionate Buddha. Seven Buddhas, one for each star, run in a row along the top of the painting. The seven stars pictured as Buddhas demonstrate the incorporation of originally shaman concepts into Korean Buddhism.

Some large Korean temples have an entire shrine dedicated to Ch'il Sŏng. In this case Ch'il Sŏng is depicted economically in one statue. Like Yaksa, he holds a medicine cup in his left palm which rests on his left knee. In his other hand he sometimes holds a lotus flower. In addition to the statue, he is further depicted in seven paintings, one of each star deity, which are found on the walls of the shrine. In keeping with Ch'il Sŏng's celestial nature, to the left and right, respectively, of the central Ch'il Sŏong are figures of Ilkwang and Wŏlkwang who also attend Yaksa. Ilkwang's crown has at its centre a red sun, Wŏlkwang's, a white moon. Both hold lotus flowers.

Tongjin-posal

The **Sin-chung-tan**, a painting featuring **Tongjin-posal**, is commonly found in Korean temples. Its frequent presence, however, in no way seems to make its meaning well-known. The only point on which most people agree, Buddhists included, is that most people don't know much about the Sin-chung-tan.

Depending on the size of the temple, and consequently on the number of halls or shrines therein, the Sin-chung-tan is found in any one of many buildings.

Depicted in the Sin-chung-tan are approximately 12 to 20 figures. The central images is of **Tongjin-posal**, who is easily identified by his elaborate headdress which resembles a fan of feathers. One of a number of beings who guard the doctrine, Tongjin-posal is the bodhisatva who protects the *Saddharmapundarika*, the lotus of the True Law. One of the teachings of this scripture, also known as the Lotus Sutra, is that truth is communicated not only by words, but also by gestures and silence.

One interpretation of the Sin-chung-tan is that the figures surrounding Tongjin represent beings who are well-acquainted with the Three Refuges, Gems, or Jewels: Buddha himself, his teaching (*Dharma*), and the Buddhist community of monks (*Sangha*). These personages or divinities, officers in the sense of those who keep things in their proper order, help spread the word of Buddhist truth. If they keep the Law well, they will rise to the level of bodhisattva, in this case Tongjin, in the next life.

Some people consider the figures depicted in the Sin-chung-tan to be historical personages such as **Confucius**, or lesser deities like the kitchen god. The four, or sometimes five, figures at the base of the painting or to the sides of Tongjin-posal, are clearly guardians. Varying from painting to painting, these protector gods carry an assortment of weapons, magical wands, and other symbolic objects. The sword is the most common attribute-object and has already been discussed in reference to the Guardian of the South. One of Tongjin's guardians usually carries a rolled-up scroll, representing the doctrine which he protects. The lance and trident are often present as symbolic arms against evil. The trident's three prongs resemble and are symbolic of fire, an exorcising agent. The three lines also symbolize, in keeping with the Sin-chung-tan's theme, the Three Refuges, Gems, or Jewels mentioned above. From Tantric and Lamaistic Buddhism comes the notion that the trident possesses the magical power to overcome demons. The shaft of the lance, spear, or trident is identified with the cosmic axis of the universe, the pillar which supports and separates heaven and earth.

The bow and arrow are also common attribute-objects. The arrow is considered to be another weapon against evil. Appropriate to the Sin-chung-tan, the bow and arrow are believed to keep one alert to the precepts of the Law. Pictured in one hand of the guardian are the bow and arrow which together symbolize love, concentration, and wisdom.

San-sin

Every Korean temple has a place for **San-sin**, the Mountain Spirit, whether it be a painting and small altar set up in one of the larger halls, or, as is most often the case, a small separate building. San-sin is not depicted in statue form, but instead is always painted.

As belief in mountain spirits preceded Buddhism's entry into Korea, San-sin is not a Buddhist conception. However, with the spread of Buddhism, it came to be suggested that San-sin had been a bodhisattva all along. San-sin is particularly popular among women asking for sons. Visitors to most temples pay their respects to San-sin.

The paintings of the "Mountain Spirit" all follow the same basic pattern: an old man seated with, or sometimes on, a tiger. Because tigers were a constant threat in mountainous areas, their ferocity came to be associated with powerful spirits. The Mountain Spirit is not exclusively the old man or the tiger, rather he is both. Perhaps the tiger's presence also suggests the close relationship in geomancy between mountains and tigers. The old man and tiger are commonly pictured in a deep valley with a stone cliff on the right.

Tok-söng-in

Tok-söng-in is commonly known as the Lonely Saint, though his name translates more precisely as "he who is alone and holy." Tok-söng-in is not a historical personage or a paradigm of isolation. He represents in the *Mahayana* (Northern School) tradition of Buddhism what the *arhat* represents in the *Theravada* (Southern School). The *arhat* is a holy person, perfect being, a disciple of the *Buddha Sökkamoni*. Tok-söng-in is a timeless being, a reminder that one should not seek enlightenment outside of oneself, for, "alone and holy," he is enlightened within.

Mahayanists are wary of the illusion of the ego appropriating external self-definitions. Tok-söng-in urges us to seek the Buddha within. Demonstrating Chinese iconographic and cultural influence, a young manservant is sometimes present holding tea, a platter of fruit, or a fan.

The Ox-Herding Paintings

The Ox-Herding Paintings (called **Simudo** in Korean) were conceived by Buddhist *Bodhi Tree*, scenes from his preaching career, and his eventual death and passage into *nirvana*.

Sometimes a painting can be found of Sökka descending on a white elephant from the **Tusita Heaven** (Heaven of the Satisfied), where he dwelled as a *bodhisattva*, to be incarnated on this earth. The term bodhisattva is made up of *bodhi* (perfect wisdom) and *sattva* (a being who never hesitates; one determined, who lived in perfect harmony). Bodhisattvas are not models to be imitated, but are manifestations of the infinitely renewed compassion of the Buddha. Their presence helps the devotee to see his or her inherent purity and perfection. On the popular level, bodhisattvas are, above all, compassionate beings. They are capable of passing into *nirvana*, but have deferred their own passage in the hope of helping those in need. Some have vowed to remain bodhisattvas until all beings are saved. Others, like Sökkamoni, are destined to become buddhas (*bul* in Korean) on their earth and help humans by teaching.

When Siddhartha was about to proclaim his Buddhahood, he was warned that evil demons would attack him. Siddhartha claimed that he could suppress them by this *bodhi* (perfect wisdom) knowledge. He pointed to the ground and called to the gods of the earth to rise up and kill the demons. In that decisive moment he called on the earth as witness to his enlightenment and made the transition from bodhisattva to buddha.

The mudra of "touching the ground," which is most often associated with Sökkamoni-bul, demonstrates his lordship over the earth. When the figure is seated, the hand hangs over the knee, palm inward, pointing with one finger, or the whole hand, towards the earth. When this mudra is absent from a statue of Sokka, inviting confusion with Amit'a-bul, it can be helpful to pay particular attention to the painting set behind it. 'Backdrop' paintings serve the purpose of providing a suitably religious environment for the statues, but, because they depict the same central figures, they also hold iconographic clues. Though the mudra of "touching the ground" may be substituted with another gesture on the statue of Sökka, very often the corresponding painted figure holds his hand toward the earth and thus may correctly identify Sŏkka.

Mirŭk-bul

Mirŭk-bul is the Coming or Messiah Buddha. He lives in the Tusita Heaven where he waits until his time to appear on this earth arrives. Mirŭk-bul is the fifth and final Buddha of this evolutionary cycle. (Sŏkkamoni was the fourth). He is the embodiment of love and compassion.

Paintings of Mirŭk-bul are virtually non-existant, but statues of him are still extant. They were particularly popular during the days of the Three Kingdoms and devotees carried miniatures of this Buddha in their robes.

Mirŭk-bul is most easily identified when in the "posture of reflection." He sits with his right elbow resting on his right knee. His right foot or ankle is on his left knee. The left hand rests on the right ankle or foot. His head is slightly inclined, suggesting contemplation. The index and middle fingers of his right hand are slightly inflected and just touch the face.

Many large statues in Korea are called Mirŭks, but there is speculation about their true identites. The famous **Ŭnjin Mirŭk**, for example, is thought by many actually to be a depiction of **Kwanseŭm-posal**.

Legend tells us that Mirŭk and Sŏkka were great friends together in the Tusita Heaven. In good spirit, they challenged one another, each betting that he would study the hardest and learn the quickest and be the first to come to earth to serve humankind. They would know who was ready first by the lotus which would bloom in front of the winner. The lotus bloomed in front of Sŏkka, so he preceded Mirŭk in coming to this world.

Kwanseŭm-posal

Kwanseŭm is the bodhisattva of mercy. Although her predecessor and Indian counterpart, **Avalokitesvara**, is clearly male, she is most often depicted as a female by today's artists. A bit of moustache is visible on Kwanseŭm in some contemporary paintings, but these works are generally of an old style. In her Buddhist context, Kwanseŭm's sex is irrelevant. She should be considered not as a sexual being, but as a form of meditation on celestial forces.

Avalokitesvara was born from a ray of light which emanated from Amit'a-bul's right eye. Thus, as Avalokitesvara's counterpart, Kawnseŭm is undeniably linked with Amit'a-bul. Appropriate to this relationship, Kwanseŭm assists those who request access to the Pure Land.

Kwanseŭm's name means Hearer of Cries, and she is often pictured with her head slightly inclined as if listening to the pleas of the suffering. Because she has 42 principal emblems and many forms, a variety of representations are common. She is frequently pictured with a vase and willow spray. The vase contained *amrita*, nectar of her compassion. The willow branch represents her ability and willingness to liberally sprinkle "sweet dew" on the afflicted. The willow, which has long been considered to have medicinal value, also symbolizes her role as a healer. She is often shown near water, suggesting her island paradise, *Potala*. In paintings she wears white clothing and, like other bodhisattvas, is sometimes adorned with jewelry, including a crown.

Kwanseŭm also assumes a thousand-eyed thousand-armed form (demonstrating Indo-Tibetan influence in her genesis), yet another indication that she is able and willing to aid the afflicted. Her eleven-headed and nine-headed forms often accompany her multi-limbed depictions and remind us of her all-accepting and all-inclusive nature. In her eleven-headed form the left three heads bear an angry countenance; the right three, a serene smile; the three at the back, an expression of compassion; the front and largest face exudes serene equilibrium; and the eleventh face, at the very back, is laughing: a testimony to her wisdom. Situated at the apex of the multi-headed Kwanseŭm, a head or miniature Buddha represents the bodhisattva as an emanation of the *bodhi* knowledge of Amit'a-bul.

Yaksa-yŏrae-bul

Yaksa-yŏrae is the Healer or Medicine Buddha. He provides relief not only from disease and misfortune, but also from ignorance, which Buddhists consider to be the ill to which the flesh is most susceptible.

Usually bodhisattvas, not buddhas, hold attribute-objects. The alms bowl and the medicine

bowl (which evolved as a symbol from the alms bowl) are exceptional. Sak-yamuni and Amit'a hold the alms bowl, or sometimes hold their hands in a mudra suggestive of holding the vessel, and Yaksa holds the medicine bowl.

The alms bowl is one of the very few personal possessions of Buddhist monks. It represents the sincere offerings of believers and the humility of monks.

The bowl, as a receptacle, is related to the reliquary stupa mentioned earlier in relation to the Guardian of the North. The shape of the stupa is both a depiction of the order of the universe and reminiscent of the form of the seated Buddha. The stupa has come to be identified with Buddha himself. By association, the bowl too has become a symbol of the essence of Buddha, the essence of the universe.

Images of Yaksa closely resemble those of Amit'a-bul except that Amit'a-bul is usually golden, while Yaksa is almost always white. Though Yaksa usually holds the medicine bowl in both hands, he sometimes holds it in only one hand, the left. In this case, Yaksa's right hand assumes the mudra of the "absence of fear" which, although certainly appropriate to his role as a healer, is usually associated with Amit'a-bul.

the left hand "diamond finger." The "diamond fist" is formed by making a tight fist with the thumb at the center. The "dimond finger" is the left index which is inserted into the right hand fist. The mudra of the "knowledge fist" dispels darkness. One of Virochana's names is **Diamond Buddha**. The diamond represents the supreme strength and duriability of Buddhist Knowledge.

The left index represents the world of sentient beings, the surrounding right hand, the protection of the world of buddhas. Generally the left hand refers to the passive pole and the right, the active. The left represents the physical plane and the right

have expanded, usually to ten pictures, on the fundamental idea of illustrating the Zen training of the mind by the metaphor of tethering an ox.

The progressive whitening of the ox indicates the gradual awakening of the oxherder to his true nature. The original series ended with an empty circle. In an effort to dispel the frequent misunderstanding of Buddhism's "enlightenment" as mere emptiness, or inactivity, later teachers decided to continue the series to include the oxherder's return to the world.

With typical casualness, Korean Zen (Cho Sŏn Sect) temples only sometimes have the series, and the ones who do dis-

Virochana

Virochana is the Buddha who spreads the light of Buddhist Truth in every direction. He is the Center, Buddha Incarnate, the Original Teacher, Virochana is the embodiment of Truth and Knowledge. As is the case with all buddhas and bodhisattvas, Virochana is not exclusive of other buddhas but represents a particular aspect of origin and center.

Depictions of Virochana show his hands in one of several mudra. A common example is the mudra of the "knowledge fist." This mudra is made up of the right-hand "diamond fist" and

the metaphysical. This mudra is a divine representation of the passions, and a comment on the intensity with which one aspiring to Truth pursues that Knowledge. The mudra represents the union of the sexes with Virochana as the procreator.

Virochana is sometimes enshrined in his own building called the **Great Light Hall**. He is usually unattended when in his own shrine. Found in other halls, he is the central figure of a trinity. He is attended by Sŏkka and Yaksa or teachers in China as far back as the Sung Dynasty. Originally there were only five paintings in the series, but through time different teachers

play perplexing variation in the order and number of paintings.

Searching for the Ox illustrates the separation of the herder and the ox, and the former's seeming violation of his true nature. The oxherder is dissatisfied with his environment, he is subjected to passions, and desire for possessing a satisfactory self-definition and fear of losing that identity have him in a vulnerable position and a painful predicament.

Seeing the Footprints illustrates the awareness gained by the oxherder that somehow all is as it should be, that there is the possibility of transcending his pain. He cannot yet distinguish the truth, but he has a preliminary understanding of the origin of his pain. Though he is unable to see the ox, the ox's presence is known.

Preceiving the Ox illustrates the oxherder's realization that nothing exists outside of himself, and, therefore, that "himself" as an individual entity is non-existent. He is comforted by the loss of objective perception. The herder is free from the need to defend his objective self-definition. D. T. Suzuki, a renowned Japanese Zen master, tells us that at this point the ox is perceived in the same way that one knows the presence of salt in the ocean, that is not distinguishable as an idividual entity.

Catching the Ox illustrates the struggle which is the result of incompletely transcending aggression. The oxherder has laid hands on the ox, but has not developed the energy to keep it under his control. He knows his ego to be untrue, but the ego (attempting objectification of the self) struggles to control the herder.

Taming the Ox illustrates the oxherder's determined and concentrated efforts to attain *bodhi* despite his still prevalent vulnerability to confusion, for the ox and herder are not yet one. The herder must keep his whip ready to prevent the ox from wandering, just as the student of Zen must discipline himself to prevent his mind from wandering.

The ox, properly tended, is pacified. When the fuel of passions is burned, the fire is forgotten. The oxherder is pictured **Riding the Ox Home**. The oxherder's concentration is not subjected to the calls of the world. His mind may no longer be deceived, but instead has begun to engage in truly creative activity. He may not be led astray. With a joyful heart, he meanders home.

The Ox Transcended/The Ox-Herder Alone illustrates that the ox was never real. Not only has the ego no chance of gaining control, but there is no longer even a notion of an individual mind to be eluded by the ego. The light of *bodhi* shines. The oxherder is no longer born, and no longer dies—the phenomena that previously caused so much pain. He is unborn.

The Ox and Herder Transcended illustrates by the empty circle the closure of the slightest remaining distance, which is yet an infinite separation, between mind and self. With the non-existence of dualism, Buddhism cannot be exclusive or inclusive. At this point, it is not a path to be followed, but a truth to be lived. The oxherder no longer follows, but knows the immediacy of *Bodhi*.

Reaching the Origin, one is not enriched by anything external. It is apparent that one was never in fact enriched, but was eternally pure and compassionate. There is only a "source" or "origin" in the sense of eternally present, inexhaustible serenity.

In the World the awakened, enlightened being follows no example. He is what he knows to be true and projects his Buddha-nature to those who need him.

Chijang-posal

Almost without exception, Korean temple compounds include a **Myŏngbu-jŏn, Chijang-posal's Shrine**. The Myŏngbu-jŏn is an interesting and colorful building containing depictions of the Buddhist hells and heavens.

The central figure is **Chijang-posal**, the bodhisattva of the nether world. Chichang is greatly loved by Mahayanists for his commitment to remain at the level of bodhisattva until no more people suffer in hell. Chijang is usually bald, or has closely cropped hair (the surest clue to his identity when he is present in a painting of many figures) and holds in one hand a staff or a sistrum, and in the other, a jewel (the jewel of mystical material previously discussed in connection with the Guardian of the West). When held by Chijang (and occasionally by Kwanseŭm-posal) the jewel is interpreted as the "wish fulfilling gem," a magical jewel which grants all selfless requests. Chijang is usually flanked by one of two sets of figures: two guardians of the Underworld, **Tomyŏng-jonja** and **Mu-dok-kwi-wang**, or **Yama** and Chijang's mother from his former earthly existence; whose place he offered to take in the lowest hell.

On each side of Chijang and his flanking pairs stand five of the **Ten Judges**. The Judges are in statue form, either standing or seated, and are approximately four feet tall. Some more elaborate halls contain, interspersed among and in addition to the Ten Judges, many smaller statues of celestial deities.

The Judge who receives the most attention is Yama (**Yŏmma-tae-wang** in Korean). He is considered to be the most powerful of the Ten and, as previously mentioned, sometimes occupies the prestigious position beside Chijang. Yama, a deity borrowed from Hinduism, is the **Lord of Death**. Various Hindu texts describe him as splendid, others as ugly and deformed.

Behind each of the Judges is a painting of the territory each governs. The ten territories (six belonging to common people and four to bodhisattvas) are not only to be thought of as places the deceased must traverse, but should be considered allegorically, as either levels of existence or stages in an individual's life.

The Heaven-Bound Boat, **Panyayong-sŏn**, although not necessarily found in or around the Myŏngbu-jŏn, is mentioned in this context because one of its principal occupants is thought by many to be Chijang-posal. The boat is headed for Kŭngnak (paradise). Chijang encourages the passengers to persevere, while Amit'a-bul, the Buddha of paradise, keeps watch at the bow.

Final Note

The *dhyani*-bodhisattvas and buddhas number together ten. They are the five bodhisattvas of meditation and their prototypes, the five buddhas of meditation, who in turn are born on this earth as human buddhas. They rule the ten directions (the four cardinal, four intermediate, zenith and nadir) and symbolize the principle characteristics of *bodhi*. They are the types from which all the numberless buddhas emanate. Some consider the primordial Buddha, from whose meditation the *dhyani* are projected, to be Sŏkkamoni, others Virocharm.

The image of Sŏkkamoni, while retaining resemblance to the Indian prince, derives much of its universal appeal and inexhaustible serenity from the skillful blending of races which is manifest in many Korean representations. Buddha's representations must have an aspect of universality if for no other reason than that every facet of his being expressed Buddhahood: the undifferentiated primordial. The compassion of Buddha is like a circumference-less circle: every manifestation is the center, every center a personal aspect.

SHAMANISM

Clanging cymbals and the steady thump of an hour-glass drum draw women and children to the gateway of a Korean house. They know from the flood of sound in the alleyway that shamans are doing a *kut*, and a kut is high entertainment. The gods appear throughout the night in the person of the costumed shaman. The ancestors arrive and the family cries for the dead. The *kut* unfolds with music, dances, and song. When the gods speak, the women of the house, their neighbors, and friends talk back. Their is not a passive, fatalistic faith. If household gods

Other gods reside atop storage jars filled with pepper and soy pastes. Minor deities hover in every room.

Divination

When the household gods are satisfied, then the household is at peace under their rule. When the gods become angry, they drop their guard and malevolent forces attack the household from within and without. The dead move among the living and their touch brings sickness. Ghosts, wood imps, and

denounce the spread of wine and offering food, the women wax indignant. "So make us rich, then we'll give you more," they exhort.

Korean women look to the shaman as a ritual expert, prime officiant in the woman's ritual realm. While men give wine, rice, and delicacies to the family's ancestors, women honor the household gods. The housewife sets a cup of water on the lid of an earthen storage jar beside a burning candle. She leaves a plate of rice cakes and a cup of wine under the main roof beam of the house to demarcate the presence of deities hidden within the structure of the house itself.

Enthroned in an earthen jar by the back wall, the House Site Official reigns over everyone and everything within the walls.

baleful humors pour through the walls and strike the family.

If the druggist's powders and the doctor's treatment don't cure a lingering illness, when husband squanders wealth on a mistress, when thieves break into the house, when parents quarrel with children and husband quarrels with wife, the housewife suspects a supernatural malaise under her roof. She takes her anxieties to the shaman's house and asks for a divination.

Women also go to the shaman "to see the year's luck." The shaman divines for each member of the woman's family, including her married sons, daughters-in-law, and grandchildren.

The shaman uses simple divination tools.

She sits behind a low tray, fingering grains of rice and old brass coins. Shaking a brass-bell rattle in her own ear, she addresses her personal gods, giving the names and ages of her clients family and importuning her supernatural guides for correct visions. The shaman casts handfuls of coins and rice, and their random configurations suggest her clients' troubles.

With the woman's confirmation, more questions, and more visions, she develops a picture of the household situation and the supernatural forces behind it.

an even temper. She urges prudence in business ventures.

The shaman's therapy is family therapy. Housewives and shamans consider affliction symptomatic of a deeper malaise within the body of the house. Individual healing occurs while the shaman repairs the whole family's ruptured relationship with its household gods. When things have gone too far away, when the shaman divines that "the ancestors are hungry and the gods want to play," the family sponsors a *kut*.

Troublesome ghosts prolonging an illness can be exorcised with a pelting of millet grain. Angry gods are molified with treats and tribute. Sons with short-life fates can be "sold" to the Seven Stars, dedicated in the shaman's shrine to the deities who protect children.

The shaman mingles practical advice with ritual lore. Not hostile to medical science, she sends sick clients back to the doctor and recommendss home remedies. She tells young wives to keep their husbands' affections with

Left, a modern Chin-do mudang burns an offering to a restless and ancient Shaman spirit; right, the "flying" Chin-do *mudang* lures spirits.

The Shaman Kut: Ancient "Household Therapy"

During the *kut*, shaman and housewife invite the gods and ancestors to feast and play. The shamans put on their costumes and speak for the gods.

Greedy supernatural officials gorge themselves with wine and meat, make bawdy jokes, and demand more and more money from the housewife. The housewife shouts that she has spent all her money, and the Official lifts her skirt, revealing the bulging pocket on her pantaloons. The housewife knows her part. Teasingly, she draws out another bill of the shaman's prearranged fee.

Ghosts and baleful humors fear the Spirit

Warrior's broadword. A sick or chronically unlucky family member sits on the edge of the porch. To a steady crash of cymbals, she Spirit Warrior exorcises malevolent forces with a flash of the knife and a pelting of millet.

A *kut* winds on throughout the night. By the morning of the second day, the action moves back outside the house. The House Site Official plays in the courtyard, casting libations of wine all around the wall. The shamans bring their drum outside the main gate. They do a final exorcism and cast ghosts and noxious influences into the fields away from the house.

"Lewd Women" and "Charlatans"

Part ritual specialist, part performer, part folk therapist, the shaman has been a part of Korean life for centuries. Chronicles of ancient dynasties record shaman ceremonies held for the prosperity of ancient Korean kingdoms at least as far back as the 6th Century. Scholars suggest the Korean shaman's affinity with the Tungusic shamans of northern Asia.

But whatever the ancient source of Korean shamanism, shaman rituals have been colored and shaped by centuries of Korean history. When Koreans accepted Confucianism from China, the shamans fell into disfavor, denounced as "lewd women" and "charlatants." But even the most zealous reformers failed to expunge the shamans from the women's quarters of respectable house. Queens and court ladies summoned shamans to the palace itself. Sometimes shamans were implicated in succession struggles, accused of practicing "witchcraft" to further the interests of a particular faction.

In a more benign role, shamans appointed by the local magistrate offered *kut* to local tutelary gods for the prosperity and fortune of the entire community. The Tano *kut* at Kangnŭng in the spring is the most elaborate community rite surviving into the present.

In time of drought, shamans would offer *kut* to the rain dragon by a well or river. In one rain dragon *kut*, held near Seoul some 20 years ago, an overly-ambitious dragon sent a mid-July hailstorm before the shamans had finished chanting.

Catching a Kut

Your Korean hosts may deny the existence of shamans in present-day Korea. Shamanism, you may be told, died out long ago or, at best, exists only in the deep country.

Don't be discouraged. The telltale cocophony of drum and cymbals resounds from many an urban alleyway.

Cosmopolitan Koreans have an understandably ambivalent attitude toward shamans. They are embarrassed because shamanism represents a primitive past, or "superstitions" which are out of place in a rapidly developing nation. Korean intellectuals, however, recognize in shamanism a uniquely Korean religious, literary, and artisitic expression. Some even conceed the shaman's power as an indigenous healer.

The easiest way to a *kut* is with luck. In the back alleyways of any Korean city, follow the sound of drumming to a crowded doorway and remember to remove your shoes when the spectators gesture you inside the house.

Hike up to the Kuksadang, a public shrine in the hills above Seoul's Sajik Park. Shamans rent the shrine when clients are unable or unwilling to hold *kut* in their own homes. On a good day at the Kuksadang, three simultaneous *kut* unfold in different corners of the old wooden shrine. A stone Buddha stands just up the hill from the shrine. Women pray here to conceive sons and make special requests for their families.

Sometimes universities and folklore associations sponsor public performances of *kut*. Intended as an entertaining and educational display of Korea's cultural heritage, these performances preserve something of their original religious flavor. Inspired women from the audience make offerings and receive divinations much as they would at any village *kut*. See the entertainment sections of the two English-language newspapers for news of performances.

Shamans revel throughout an entire week at the Tano *kut* at Kangnung on the east coast. On the first night, townsmen and shamans in procession conduct a branch from the tutelary god's tree down into the town. Shamans raise the sacred branch amid a festive tent city of farmers' bands, folk operas, carnival acts, and hawkers of all manner of sublime and ridiculous wares.

In Seoul, shamans also celebrate Tano day, here with a day-long *kut* to the Dragon King of the Han River at a shrine on the bank. Tano is the fifth day of the fifth lunar month, usually early June by the solar calendar. Again, check the English-language newspapers for information on both the Kangnung festival and the dragon *kut* in Seoul.

Right, a neo-shaman scarecrow.

KOREAN ART

For insights into a nation's character, look at its art, particularly its architecture. For example, in the three principle East Asian countries—China, Korea and Japan—the buildings eaves have curved upwards for centuries. A subtle difference, however, exists in the manner of these upturns.

China's traditional architecture is vertical in feeling, elevated on high stone platforms above ground, with somewhat pinched in edges to the roof; her roofliness reflect a nation out to conquer or control nature. Even China's delicate porcelains express a determined struggle for perfection, an ethos of man-over-nature.

In contrast, Korean roofliness form soft curves which float ever so gently heavenward, flowing with nature's rhythms. And Korean ceramics appear less perfected, warmer and more approachable, so that the viewer touches the potter's hand in spirit.

Noticeable and striking patterns, meanwhile, seem to be a major characteristic of Japanese art. Japanese rooflines, even when turning upwards, appear more diagonal, their shallower curves making them more earthbound than those in China or Korea, Japanese ceramicists came to greatly admire the warm naturalness of Korean pieces, but in designing their own tea ware they developed a "contrived" effect. Some Japanese intentionally made pieces "as though careless."

The Aesthetics of Central Heating

How people choose to live in and design their houses also reveals their character. In the past, Korean architecture was designed to comfort the body and, even more, to lift the human spirit. The Korean peninsula experiences four distinct seasons, winter being sharp and long. Therefore, an efficient form of heating was a crucial element in local architecture. Even during the Stone Age, a sophisticated under-floor heating plan had been invented by Koreans. With the emergence of a historical period, this *ondol* system of central heating was further developed; it was used in every Korean dwelling until recently when some modern apartments discarded or used it for only one or two rooms (Japan made no such concession to the human body, although her winters are as cold). The *ondol* involves running a warm flue from the kitchen under the floors to each area at the far end of the house, thus using the kitchen's cooking heat to warm sitting and sleeping areas. More recently, this *ondol* system employs pressed briquettes of coal; it has been so economical that even as recently as the winter of 1979, an entire small Korean house could be warmed at night for about thirty-six cents!

Korea's long tradition of having warm winter floors prolonged the people's sitting there rather than on chairs. Koreans did not follow the Chinese mode when the latter began to use stiff-backed chairs and high tables about the 10th Century. In adopting such furniture, the Chinese lost a bit of humility. The Koreans remained closer to nature, to the earth. They chose to dine at low tables and to sleep on thin mattresses, and though they also designed beautiful chairs, these were usually reserved for formal occasions.

Paper Walls and Sharkskin Chests

In winter the Korean peninsula is hit by arctic winds blowing off nearby Siberia. These chilling winds leave Korea's northern ports icebound much of the year, but ironically, these winds are repelled by a thin material—paper—that keeps homes here warm and cozy.

The Chinese are credited with developing paper about two thousand years ago, but it was the Koreans who excelled in its manufacture; both Chinese and Japanese calligraphers prized Korean handmade paper because of its durability and special properties for absorbing ink.

Even as a building material, ivory-colored Korean paper is very useful. It is made by pressing the bark of a special mulberry shrub and when it is finally pressed traditional Korean homes are lined with it. This paper forms a wallpaper-insulation that covers the ceiling and walls and protects against winter's chill and summer's heat. Instead of being decorated with patterns, as in Japan, these paper surfaces are uniformly plain. The Korean aesthetic is not afraid of undecorated space. However, hinged, folding screens with cheerful designs are used for decor at important corners or along major walls. There is not the "emptiness" of a Japanese house. Having few closets, the Koreans use a variety of chests.

Within the Korean traditional-style house one passes from room to room through a series of paper-partitioned walls which slide on both an upper and lower track to form doors at certain points. The major sliding panels are ornamented with meander wooden fretwork exposed on one side. Thus one can appreciate the interlacing woodwork against its paper background; yet when closed and seen from the reverse side, silhouettes caused by sunlight or lamplight create their own subtle magic. These woodwork designs cross over each other generally with rectangular corners that never seem harsh as they form squares, rectangles, crosses and the Buddhist "reverse swastika." Ideographs meaning "good fortune," "long life," or other such lucky symbols also enliven the fretwork.

The ceilings of traditional houses have huge wooden beams made of logs, often with the bark not stripped off. One thus feels directly related to nature. Doors and windows are closed and locked from the inside by simple iron hooks, which are understated elements in the total design. Often a veranda runs around the outer edge of the principal rooms, so that during the daytime one may venture outdoors and still be within the house. Windows are placed low enough that those who live there may step over the wall.

Due to five hundred years under Confucian propriety and ethics, Korean women were expected to stay home, rear the family, and seldom venture beyond the confines of the house. The women's quarters, or *anbang*, was reserved for their use. Its privacy was not to be violated; no male except the husband could enter, since modesty ruled. The sexes usually ate separately.

This inner room was full of beautiful linen chests and wardrobes for clothing. Their outer surfaces were decorated; in richer homes they were embellished with mother-of-pearl inlay. Various woods were used in the furniture so that the beauty lay in the wood grains. Some of the better chests used three, four or even five different woods, although others were lacquered red or black and inlaid with sharkskin, as well as with silver or copper. The craftsman sometimes combined many of these materials, creating a picture such as a dragon with a body of inlaid sharkskin, surrounded by clouds of mother-of-pearl. Hinges play a conspicuous part in the decoration of these chests. This metal work was fabricated from bronze, made into the shape of lucky animals, birds and ideograms, all suggesting happiness, wealth, or longevity at the same time that they served as handles or hinges.

On the other side of the *maru* (the wooden-floored central section of the house) stood the master's room, the *sarang-bang*, which women were not permitted to enter. The furnishings here had more variety, such as writing desks and bookshelves for study, since the gentry or *yangban* class was expected to study the Confucian Classics. Male visitors were entertained here with music and wine.

An especially painstaking technique for furniture involved an effect created by shaving thin sheets of ox horn, painting them brightly on their undersides (in reverse design), and then gluing them to the surface. This underneath painting gave a suble effect that did not wear off.

Walls are among the most distinctive features of Korean architecture—from the farmer's house to the palaces of royalty. They serve for protection and demarcation but also add a subtle beauty through the geometry of their patterned brick and mortar. This color juxtaposition of bricks of different hues plays a part in the feeling of intimacy, even though it is a wall. Korean walls never seem "heavy" and forbidding as those of China nor yet so fragile and temporary looking as those in Japan.

Oftentimes one sees adobe put together with bits of broken tile or stones fitted to form patterns. Sometimes the country folk made fences of brushwood, or straw-roofed their stone or adobe fences. The stone fences were often erected without mortar as the farmer created rice paddies farther and farther up the mountainside in this land formed of granite.

Celadon: 'Sky Blue After Rain'

In homes of the wealthy today a few pieces of Korean 12th or 13th Century celadons repose on shelves, along with white porcelains of the more recent Yi dynasty. Almost every museum in the Western world has a few treasured pieces of Korean celadon, too. The outer silhouette of a Koryŏ-period celadon teapot or a Buddhist ritual vessel for holy water (*kundika*) may resemble a melon, a pumpkin or some other growing form, with a handle twisted into a simulated vine or a spout suggesting bamboo.

Korean celadon pieces for use by nobility were shaped into ducks, tortoises, geese, and even lion-dogs. One surviving wine pot was formed in the shape of a serving maid, and a tripod incense burner was placed on three tiny feet in the shape of long-eared bunnies.

No matter which of nature's shapes is suggested, the Korean potter created beautiful elongated curves, curvaceous lines which soar with controlled energy. These unknown craftsmen decorated their porcelains with a pale, gray-green celadon glaze which sometimes became "kingfisher," a bluish-green considered "a secret color." More than sixty shades can be distinguished by the attuned eye, but the most highly admired are "sky blue after rain," and "sea water washed by rain and wind."

Around 1150 A.D. Koreans began using inlay techniques in their porcelain production. The potter took a bamboo knife and cut designs in the leather-hard piece, then filled the recesses with an extremely thick, white slip of diluted clay. When the excess was wiped off and the piece was covered with celadon glaze and fired in kiln, creamy white pictures appeared where

tious and spontaneous. A glaze made partly from pine needle ashes was decorated with stamped designs of chrysanthemums, key frets and other abstractions. Sixteenth-Century Japanese tea masters came to value certain unself-conscious Korean peasant rice bowls as the most ideal tea bowl for their "refined poverty aesthetic." Today the best pieces have been bought by or taken by Japanese to their homeland.

Meanwhile, white porcelains were developed for upper-class use. Upon large jars, artisans painted sparsely, creating simple designs with iron-impregnated copper or malachite containing copper oxide, or, with cobalt, "Mohammedan blue." Unlike Ming dynasty blue and white ware potters, the Korean craftsman never went to the same

the slip had been pressed into the concavities. Again these designs speak of Korean closeness to nature: two or three winged cranes flying in white pattern over a sea of celadon green, or weeping willow trees with a pair of Mandarin ducks floating in water. If the knife entirely penetrated the clay surface, a reticulated design resulted so that delicate shades of the celadon glaze filled the openwork.

A new type of ceramics came to be favored with the suppression of Buddhism in 1392 A.D. This Yi-dynasty ware forsook the delicate and intricate to produce the unpreten-

Yi dynasty painting of a kisaeng house.

excess of the treating his pot's surface as though it were an easel for painting. Rather, he limited his decorations to hints of nature—such as a single, blossoming spray, a pair of fish, a dragon, or curving leaves with grapes. The underglaze painting with iron is casual rather than pretentious and so suggests an earthy Korean spirit.

Today Korean traditional homes of the upperclass tend to exhibit not only Koryŏ-period celadons and Yi dynasty white wares but also ancient 5th and 6th Century Silla dynasty gray stoneware and even earlier Kaya pieces. For many centuries in early times the Koreans preferred their own stoneware to the glazed ceramics of China. Korean ceramics has since been considered functional rather than a major art.

Yet its very simplicity and unpretentiousness has increased its appeal to outsiders.

The Apollos and Dianas of Asia

When Buddhism swept out of India and all over Central and Eastern Asia, the artists of each of a dozen countries responded by creating cave sculptures, free-standing images of Buddhas, and temples. They represented the human body thinly disguised as a deity with certain "sacred marks" such as long earlobes, a depression between the eyes and a pronounced "protruberance of wisdom" on top of the head. Figures of the Buddhist pantheon were anthropomorphic, following India's example. The features and repose of Buddhas in each Asian country differed although the basic conography

Buddhist wave and converted to it later. Countless numbers of Koreans went to Japan over a period of some 150 years to assist in erecting Buddhist temples, sculpting "Golden images" in wood and in bronze, and painting religious icons.

Buddhism dominated art in China for roughly a thousand years but it became a minor force after 1368 A.D. Korea also was influenced in art by Buddhism until the Yi government suppressed it in 1392 A.D. In Japan Buddhism ceased to be a meaningful force around 1600 A.D. when temples there became mere census indicators for the shoguns and produced little original art. Japanese Zen ideals had by this time been absorbed into the culture through the tea ceremony, gardens, ink painting, flower arrangement

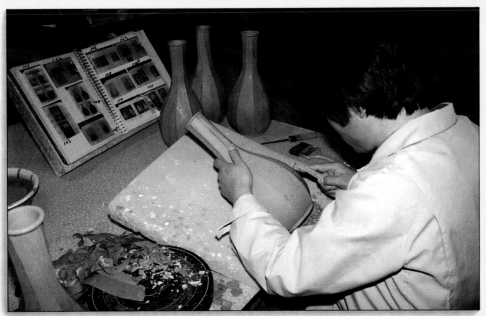

is the same.

Some art history books concentrate on tracing an "International Buddhist Style" in sculpture, but it is like grouping together all early Christian and medieval Christs and madonnas into a "Pan-European International Style." In Asia, as well as in Europe, each country developed its own particular marks of charm, revealing both national proclivities and also the inherent qualities within the various materials most frequently used in each region.

Korean Buddhist art was no more a subsidiary to China than French medieval art was to Italy, or British art to France. The story of early Japanese art stands as an exception since she lay at the remote end of this

and the martial arts.

In creating Buddha statues the Chinese carved solemn images out of sandstone and limestone, while Koreans used granite from their mountains and the Japanese favored wood, plentiful there. China's sculptured deities were at first basically reflective of her preoccupation with calligraphy, so her images appear linear and fairly two dimensional. Later, by 600 A.D., Chinese Buddhist figures gradually became more naturalistic, three dimensional and plastically modeled. By the 8th Century they had become excessively fat-faced, even jowled.

Korea's earliest bronze statuettes appear relatively flat and linear, also inspired by the calligraphic line; but soon her natural genius in metallurgy and her skilled stone chisellers initiated their own directions. By the 7th Century, Korean Buddhist art attained a peak of spiritual expression.

According to most art critics, China's apex of Buddhist sculptural expression lies in the stone images of the T'ien-lung-shan caves. Yet even at that spot there is evidence that the Chinese artisan had become so naturalistic and earthy that the aura of spirituality had lessened. As for Korea's development, two artistic peaks are the remarkable meditating Maitreya (in Korean, *Miruk*) figures in the Seoul National Museum, and the Sŏkkuram cave-grotto at Kyŏngju which date as late as the middle 8th Century. They have not lost their religious thrust. The cave-grotto has numerous relief carvings of deities sculpted on rectangular blocks which express the apogee of the Buddhist tradition in relief. In addition Sŏkkuram contains a giant central image which represents, actualized in a single piece of free-standing sculpture, the quintessence of Buddhism's spiritual momentum in the Far East!

The above evaluation does not preclude Japan's exquisite Asuka period (552–645 A.D.) of Buddhist art (her own peak). Yet much of the Asuka art work should be attributed to Korea since it was created by Koreans and then exported, or else made in Japan by Korean immigrant artists. Japan's purely native Buddhist sculpture became important only after 700 A.D. It adopted the fat-faced, sensual archetypes of T'ang China, which go so far towards realistic detail and voluptuousness that worldly overtones mask their spirituality.

How can one explain that the smallest of these three countries managed to attain the most sublime beauty? Were the Koreans more religious by nature? Can it be related or inspired by the actual anatomy of its people? Did their northern blood from the steppes of Siberia mix with Asiatic racial genes in such a way as to produce a race that is more classic in appearance? The Koreans seem taller and handsomer, in general, than the other Asian people. Absent are the flatter noses with a low bridge—or none—and the flared nostrils of some of the neighboring peoples. The Buddhas of Korea display gracefully arched eyebrows on either side of long, straightly chiselled noses, with a high bridge.

Sculptors and painters are naturally influenced by the people around them when they create their ideal. Ancient Greece's marble

Apollo statues reflected the Greek profile. In addition, the Greek columnar style (Ionic, Doric and Corinthian) of its temples was taken across the waters and copied by Roman architects, who also copied the Apollos and Dianas of Greece. In like manner, Korea's classical Buddha images and her stately, cloud-touching pagoda lines were eagerly copied and absorbed by the Japanese.

Heavenly Bells, Dolmens, Dancing Spirits

No one disputes that Korean artisans created the most intricate, the most melodious and most beautiful temple bells that the world was ever to hear or see. The oldest dated one was cast in 725 A.D. and now hangs at Sangwŏn-sa

in the Odae-san National Park area. The most famous is the "divine bell," or the Emille Bell (cast in 771 A.D.), now kept in a special pavilion at the right of the entrance to the Kyŏngju National Museum. It is said that the sonorous notes of this huge (3.78-metre-high) bell could be heard 40 miles away on a clear day. The sound chamber at the top took the form of a dragon, but the most spectacular decoration consisted of two pairs of Buddhist angels or devas, holding censers of incense and floating on lotus pods amidst wisps of vegetation and gossamer-thin garments which swirled heavenward and took the place of actual wings. These bells played a major role in ritual and worship. They should be regarded as major works of bronze sculpture as inspired by

Left, handicrafts are a great attraction for shoppers; right, names painted with birds and animals are an old art form.

Buddhism at its peak.

The Korean peninsula is dotted with Buddhist figures carved in rocks in the mountains. Korea excels in granite sculptural work. Perhaps due to the fact that their terrain is 70 percent mountainous, Koreans developed a special love for stone and a skill in using it both as building material and for sculptural pieces. Huge dolmens of early times speak of the strength and dexterity of unknown Neolithic inhabitants on the peninsula.

By the 4th Century A.D., Korean architects were erecting tombs half the size of the Egyptian pyramids. They used dressed granite blocks so perfectly engineered that they survive today as well as the frescoes on their walls.

In these Korean tombs one can view genre scenes on the walls and decorative symbols

of communication with these "spirits," largely through dance, and might go into trance. They could appease the angry spirits and send good fortune to these who made food offerings and other donations.

Silla's Shaman Kings

Even as late as the early 6th Century, when the rest of the Korean peninsula had adopted Buddhism as a state religion, the southeastern and relatively remote region of Silla was still ruled by Shaman kings. The people's belief in spirits, coupled with the custom of cairn-type tomb burial in which Shaman royalty went to their graves in full religious regalia, made the Silla capital, Kyŏngju, Asia's single most spectacular archeological site. Hundreds of tombs are yet to be explored in this city

on the ceilings and understand the old beliefs about death. Ancient musicians and dancing girls in frescoes are strikingly reminiscent of modern shaman dances. Considering that it is tomb art, these frescoes are extremely lively and cheerful, suggesting a flow of spirits. Perhaps this "flow of spirits" derives from the faster beat and blood through Korean veins! It shows in many of their art forms. This "faster blood" can be traced to the time of their migrations across the whole of north Asia when their culture was based on a belief in countless "spirits." Each mountain, river, tree, the sun and moon, the constellations, all had "spirit"—as did dead ancestors. Any of them might become angry if neglected. Shaman priests (*mudang*) possessed special skills

which already has become a veritable "outdoor museum" of the 5th and 6th centuries.

Breath-taking crowns designed for monarchial use were buried in Kyŏngju's mounded graves. It is not just the precious materials used, although jade is much worshipped in the Orient, but the intricate fabrication of these crowns. So far 10 slightly different "gold crowns of Silla" have been brought to light. Alongside the crowns, other royal possessions have been discovered, such as golden girdles, ornate belts, elaborate earrings, silver and gold goblets, necklaces, bracelets, finger rings and ceramics.

Of the golden crowns discovered so far, among the most intriguing was one unearthed in 1973 at the excavation of Tomb #155 in the heart of Kyŏngju city. When viewing it one first sees its outer circlet of hammered, beaten gold with saw-tooth or wave designs representing the nether world. (This lower region was associated with water.) An inner golden cap fits the head. Fifty-eight tiger claws carved of jade were suspended from the crown. In the shaman religion, the tiger is associated principally with three things: a strong power to destroy evil forces, human fertility and male virility. These curved pieces carved from jade formed a major part of the symbolism when these crowns were worn. They were suspended loosely with thin, twisted gold wires, and several hundred tiny golden spangles, suggesting golden raindrops, were affixed onto the crown with the same type of thin gold wires. If the ruler, who symbolized the power of the sun as well as

behind all this magnificence lies hidden in the three unusual upright pieces attached to each of the major crowns. These are some seventeen inches high and shaped in three forms: deer antlers, stylized trees, and pairs of curved wings.

Since shamanism is considered a superstition by today's government, native archeologists have been rather timid about discussing the shamanistic symbolism in these relics. However, clues indicating shamanistic influences in the design of the crown abound. Among the Tungus people from whom the Koreans descended, for example, climbing a tree is a shaman initiation rite; a three-branched tree represented the "three spirits" of shamanism—the heavenly world, which holds the "spirits" of sun, moon and constellations; the earthly world of "spirits,"

other forms of nature's energy, moved his head ever so slightly, he created a dazzling sight and vibrating sounds, unforgettably impressive upon his audience. Pendants—thick ropes of golden leaf-shaped droplets—hung on each side of the crown. Some golden crowns were more than two feet high. This profusely rich burial of objects proclaims the divine power of the old Silla rulers and their right to the wealth of the country and expertise of her jewellers.

The key to understanding the meaning

such as mountains, rivers, and trees; and the human world with ancestral "spirits."

The curving wing pieces suggest the shaman's power to levitate or to fly. The golden fabricated stag antlers of these crowns substituted for Siberian reindeer, whose fleetness the shaman-king acquired by wearing their horns. On the Tungus plains of Central Asia, shaman used to wear reindeer horns, fabricated from available iron, in the headdress. The Silla people were rich enough to create these talismen out of pure gold.

The Magical Flying Horse Tomb

After Tomb #155 had been excavated in 1973, archeologists and museum men ex-

Left, temple judges determine final afterlife judgements; right, the swastika door ornament graces a temple at Andong.

amined over 10,000 ancient pieces; most of them went to the Kyŏngju National Museum. The tomb was restored to its original shape with one exception—half of it was supported by a steel framework so that visitors could enter the area. A glass wall was erected across the mid-section so that tourists could enter the tomb and look at the exact position in which the crown, sword, girdle, pottery and many other objects were buried.

Also when Tomb #155 was excavated, at the head of the tomb where the shaman-ruler was buried, a "treasure box" was discovered; on this spot an actual royal horse had been offered in sacrifice. This recalls the traditional importance of horseriding to these people, former nomads of northwest Asia. Elaborate horse burials were not unknown in Siberia.

curving tongue suggests enormous exertion.

Horsemen were depicted on other flaps, and on another is a phoenix, symbol of immortality in ancient China, with outstretched feathers of yellow and vermillion. In tribute to the vivacity of this ancient painting, Tomb #155 was renamed the "Heavenly Tomb."

It might be noted that Silla's worship of white horses and their association with divine royalty passed over to Japan, which kept its shaman ways through Sintoism. As recently as pre-war times, Emperor Hirohito owned a white horse which was considered sacred until the end of World War II when it was surrendered to General MacArthur.

Protected by mountains rich in metals, such as silver and gold, artisans of old Silla

A special horse belonging to the shaman-king was believed to be a flying horse. This creature could levitate in the air just as a powerful shaman could. When the horse was killed, his saddle guards made of laminated birch back, sewn together with deer leather trimmings, were buried in the grave along with other horse trappings and treasures. Six of these saddle flaps have been found and they are as amazing as the golden crowns. The outer edges of the flaps have bands of floral patterns in red blue, green and white. Centered on one of these birch bark saddle flaps is a painting which shows a magical flying horse at full gallop—a "heavenly horse" as it were. His mane streams out behind, his hoofs are winged, and his long,

became extraordinarily skilled in metallurgy. Thus its shaman-kings were able to maintain and retain their ancient animistic religion against the encroachments of Buddhism until 527 A.D. After that shaman-type symbolism disappeared from Korean art objects (it did manage to survive in folk art though) and Buddhism was taken up by the court.

Japan has uncovered a few, small, simple crowns of bronze, but none of gold. The crowns found in Japan probably belonged to Puyŏ nobility who conquered the Paekche kingdom, the Kaya region (Pusan), and passed over to the Japanese islands where they became its ruling house or line of "sacred emporers" from 369–505 A.D. The crowns most comparable to those of old Silla legacy have been unearthed in the southern U.S.S.R. and date back to the 1st Century A.D. These Kyŏngju burial objects bear silent witness to an ancient people who believed in spirits, in tigers protecting against evil, and in various types of shaman magic, before and after they crossed the world's vastest continent. When they settled amidst the high mountains and sparkling streams of Silla, they clung to the religion of their remote forefathers, until the Buddhist wave of influence became too strong for even them to resist.

Koryŏ Paintings: Breathtaking Transparency

Almost as remarkable as uncovering the rich treasures of golden crowns from Korea's 5th and 6th Century and rediscovering her 12th and 13th Century pale green celadon wares has been the unveiling (in 1978–79) of 93 Koryŏ period paintings—Buddhist icons of unsurpassed beauty. It was thought that such art had vanished. Sad to say, though, all these beautiful Korean art works are now owned by Japanese. The same slender, refined curves of the best celadon pieces are seen in these Buddhist deities. Tucked away in various temples and shrines, these rarely-seen paintings on silk were largely labeled "Chinese painting" but the paintings reflect Northern Sung works in style, when Buddhism's influence was deep. Korean artists carried the lines of gold and the brilliant areas of clothing (scarlet, malachite green and sapphire blue) into further refinement and grace as well as complexity.

This fine, delicate and intricate work in Koryŏ Buddhist icons disappeared when the Yi government suppressed Buddhism in 1392 and encouraged a Confucian attitude. This "attitude" recognized only "the three excellencies"—poetry, calligraphy and ink painting—as created by the amateur scholar-artist. Having been educated in "nobility" by his constant reading of Confucian-approved classics, he could also use his hand, trained in calligraphy, to create landscapes in his leisure. These were not to be actual scenes, but rather "landscapes of his noble mind," and so they became rather abstract ink play.

Yi Genre Glimpses

During the Yi dynasty (1392–1910) an official "Painting Bureau" did exist, sup-ported by the court for its own purposes. Professional painters were hired to do portraiture. By the 18th Century Korean artists had begun to paint genre scenes which revealed insights into the mores of common folk doing ordinary things. Today these genre glimpses are more appreciated than the scholars' ink play.

An entirely different approach to art is revealed in Yi dynasty folk paintings. Charmingly naive and unpretentious, they reflect the actual life, customs and beliefs of the Korean people. Today they are still relegated to special museums, such as Emille Museum at Songni-san, because the national museums are perpetuated by a Confucian-type bureaucracy. Yet collectors, both native and Western, have "discovered" them, and the

value of such works is escalating. Yi folk paintings appear mundane and combine the symbolism of Shamanism, Taoism and Buddhism, but they transcend class lines and their domestic use. Even Confucian-influenced court art was colored by symbolism, such as "The Four noble Gentlemen" themes or "The Three Friends of Winter."

Due to a great respect for calligraphy among the scholarly class, auspicious ideographs were used for decorative themes in painting folding screens for the home. Important anniversaries were celebrated by the creation of new folding screens with motifs of longevity or good omen. Weddings also stimulated art activity; designs emphasized conjugal happiness with Mandarin ducks

Left, a meticulous lattice maker of Cha-in town south of Taegu peers through handwrought snowflakes; right, Koryŏ origins dot Korea's countryside.

swimming in pairs, or a "Hundred Babies Screen," since Yi-dynasty marriage was pre-arranged and for the main purpose of progeny. Fertility symbols were legion. Among the most commonly used flora and fauna were those which represented happiness, longevity and positive energy.

Korean folk art with its blue dragons, white tigers and magical fungi is based on symbolism which developed and evolved over a long period of time and came to be understood by all the people. Even today, a basic understanding of this complex system is essential to appreciate this lively art. A few

The Zodiac, Yang and Um, And the Fungus of Immortality

In the mists of China's remote antiquity, symbolic directions arose as part of a cosmology derived either from Taoism or an even more ancient shamanistic system of concepts. Among the most important were the correlatives of heaven and earth, *yang* and *yin*, male and female, along with five directions (north, south, east, west and center), five colors (black, red, white, blue and yellow), and five material elements (water, fire, metal, wood and earth).

Such ideas, which originated in prehistoric times, gained increased popularity during the Han dynasty (200 B.C.–200 A.D.), which gave rise to a number of Taoist-inclined emperors searching for the elixir of immortality. Cosmological symbols passed into Korean tradition and have remained ingrained there ever since.

During the peak of Buddhist influence, cosmological symbolism played a minor role in Korean art. The lotus, the official religious flower, and other such Buddhist symbols dominated art. However, with the suppression of Buddhism in 1392 A.D., Taoism, Buddhism and shamanism had become homogenized so that they were hardly separable in popular thought. For example, it is difficult to determine the exact origin of the 12 zodiacal images used in art. They usually relate to time and astrologers still use these animals to foretell suitability in marriage. The zodiac also was associated with *yang* and *yin* (in Korean, *yang* and *ŭm*). It read, in clockwise order: rat, ox, tiger, rabbit, dragon, snake, horse, sheep, monkey, chicken, dog and wild boar (or pig). Furthermore, the Korean astrological animals represented the 12 points of the compass.

Thus folk painting created for the home was based on the effects of such symbolism as accepted through centuries of use. Folk paintings, furniture, linens, clothes, all accessories, even hairpins, are decorated with it. All things, including outside walls, are full of the five elements, the 10 symbols of longevity, the four directional animals, the 12 zodiacal animals and propitious ideographs; all have become art motifs for folk painting and other minor arts. Flowers and birds are not represented accidentally or casually selected, but reflect an associated meaning. Even the educated put some measure of faith in these emblems, somewhat convinced that such symbols can repel evil and attract good fortune.

Even Confucian-influenced artists occasionally turned to folk painting themes. In approaching any of these works today, the viewer should be familiar with their basic symbolic meanings or associations in order to participate in a greater appreciation of them.

The major symbols used and their meanings are as follows:

Four Sacred Animals of Good Luck: Turtle, dragon, unicorn, and phoenix.

Ten Symbols of Longevity: Deer, crane, turtle, rocks, clouds, sun, water, bamboo, pine, and the fungus of immortality (*pullocho*).

Auspicious Ideograms: *bok* (good fortune), *su* (longevity), *yŏng* (peace), and *kang* (health).

Fertility Symbols: Pomegranate, jumping carp, 100 babies, and "Buddha's hand citron."

Special Guardians: Tiger (front gate or front door), dragon (gate or roof), *haet'ae* (fire or kitchen), rooster (front door), and dog (stroage door).

Four Noble Gentlemen: Orchid, chrysanthemum, bambon, and plum.

Three Friends of Winter: Pine, plum, and bamboo.

Individual Associations: Peach (longevity), pomegranate (wealth), orchid (scholar, cultural refinement), lotus (Buddhist truth, purity), bat (happiness), butterfly (romance), bamboo (durability), poeny (noble gentleman, wealth), and plum (wisdom of age, hardiness or independence, beauty, loftiness).

This list could be extended considerably. No one sat down and wrote a formal list; it was simply a part of Korean tradition, familiar to everyone from the itinerent painter to the "drunken master," or a member of the court's Bureau of Painting.

Right, "Kwanseŭm Posal with Willow Branch" was painted with mineral colors on silk by Sogubang, a 14th Century Koryŏ artist.

MUSIC & DANCE

Walking down one of the winding back alleys of Korea's cities, you may hear emanating from the window of a local tavern the sounds of hearty, and perhaps slightly inebriated, voices singing to the clickety-clack of chopsticks being beaten against the edge of a table. The singing will probably be punctuated by boisterous cries of "Chotha!" and "Ŏlssiguna! (variously translated as everything from "Bravo!" to "Right on!").

More often than not, nowadays, the song will be a modern one written in a style imitative of the contemporary Western popular idiom, or an older one reminiscent of the Japanese songs of twenty or thirty years ago, called *ppongtchak norae* here.

A hiking trip to a popular mountain spot will treat you to more of the same with the added element of dance. Korean picnickers, especially older ones, often bring along such traditional Korean percussion instruments as the *changgu*, an hourglass-shaped drum, and the *kkwaenggwari*, a small, ear-shattering gong, to use on their way back down the mountain when they stop to eat, drink, and be merry—being merry in Korea inevitably means singing and dancing.

All of this is just a small indication of the important place music and dance play in the cultural lives of Koreans. It goes to show that for the traditional Korean, the enjoyment of these art forms is in the participation and not in merely watching the polished-up, choreographed versions so commonly seen on stage.

Shouting calls of encouragement and rising briefly to move to the rhythm of the music have, perhaps for the worse, been banned from modern auditoriums such as the National Theater. On more than one occasion, the innocent country fellow who attends one of these performances in Seoul has been shushed or asked to leave if he persists in his delighted grunts and cheers. Get yourself to a performance outside in a tent for a true taste of the flavor of an old-time show.

Music and dance are by far the most highly developed of the performing arts in Korea, including, of course, the modern Western introductions, which have a great appeal to Koreans of the younger generations. There

are no traditional dramatic forms except those that appear as forms of dance. Acrobatics, juggling, and other circus-type entertainments exist but in a very limited and unevolved variety. The puppet plays, of which the only one widely known is the *Kkoktu Gaksi Norŭm*, are lively and interesting; but the puppets are crudely made—rustic, at best—and the techniques of manipulation are primitive.

Music and dance, by contrast, exist in a great variety and are of all levels of sophistication—from the simplest improvisations of

country grannies on an outing to the most subtle, intricate movements of skilled professional folk dancers. And they are of all types—from the ethereal Confucian ceremonial music to the raucous thumps of a farmers' band. They are a source of unending delight and joyful surprise to the foreigner who comes to them with open ears and eyes.

Hŭng and Mŏt

Korean dancers move with a total lack of emphasis on what Westerners call "technique." There is a complete absence of movements like those of ballet that require years of vigorous physical training. For the Korean those years are spent teaching the body to

Seoul nightlife is varied as it is multi-colored. Left, a *Hwagwan-mu* (Flower Crown) dancer whirls; right, a jazz celebrity.

express outwardly the inner mood of the dance he wishes to perform.

This brings us to two concepts that are never left out of any discussion of Korean dance. One is a state of mind called *hŭng*. It is *joie de vivre;* it is how you feel when the spirit moves you and the "feeling" in "once more with feeling." It is essential to all dance, not just that of Korea, but it is fairly easy to come by. The other is an elusive spiritual quality called *mŏt*. As applied to a person's dress or the appearance of an object, to have *mŏt* is simply to be very good looking. But when used about a person's behavior, personality, way of speaking, or more important here, his or her way of dancing, the term defies direct translation. It is charm, grace, that certain something—even a bit of

from above by an invisible thread which is attached to the upper back. This creates the straight-backed posture peculiar to Korean dance. The chest almost appears concave.

Virtually all movement is curvilinear, and angular articulation of the body parts is somehow made to appear curved as well. The cut of the traditional Korean costume worn for dancing helps produce this effect of joint-lessness. The sole exception to this is the foot which is turned sharply upwards; stepping and turning are done mostly on the heel.

In many women's dances the foot is rarely seen at all, being hidden beneath the floor-length Korean skirt. In certain dances the invisibility of the foot gives the dancer the appearance of floating smoothly from place

sexuality—all rolled into one. Without mŏt, even the most perfectly executed dance is but a pretty piece of choreography.

The more tangible aspects of Korean dance movement are described in terms of the way the dancer feels he is moving and of the effect he wishes to create, rather than of the actual physical movements he executes.

The dancer uses the body as a fluid unit without isolating parts. The upper part of the torso is the nucleus from which most movement originates. The arms usually float out at the sides as extensions of the upper chest, while the legs extend downwards to *relate* the torso to the ground, not to support the body weight. The body is supported as though

to place on an air cushion.

Korean dance does not use posturing or intricate hand motions to tell a story, as is so prevalently done in other parts of the Orient and in Oceania. The hand is merely an extension of the arm, with the fingers held in a natural position. Korean dance in itself never tells a story; it strives only to communicate its mood. Whatever stories emerge are told verbally or through acting that is supplemental to the dance, as in the masked dance dramas. True posturing is a no-no: A Korean dancer never moves into or out of a position—he moves through it. Even when the dancer appears to halt for a moment, he is never static; his whole body "breathes" in a slightly undulating movement.

Korean Sound:
Subtle Microtones, Startling Vibratos

While it is quite easy to learn to enjoy almost any kind of dance with a few exposures, it is another matter entirely to learn to appreciate the music of a culture different from one's own. Korean music poses a number of formidable problems here.

Most of the music uses a five-note scale rather than the more familiar seven notes. Different arrangements of the scale, called modes, are available, however, to enrich tonal resources. Except for the octave, the intervals between pitches are not the same as we are used to hearing.

No system of harmony is used, but this lack is more than made up for by melodic produce a rich rhythmic counterpoint.

Korean instruments are primitive compared to the multi-valved, steel-stringed, complex-action Western instruments; but they are exactly suited to their task. They are traditionally divided up into classes according to the material of which they are made: skin, silk, bamboo, metal, earth, stone, gourd, and wood. Representative of the skin instruments is the *changgu*, the hourglass-shaped drum mentioned earlier, which is seen everywhere Korean music is performed. The *Kayagŭm* is the most commonly heard of the silk category, so classified because the strings are of silk. It is a versatile zither having 12 courses, which are plucked with the fingers. Among the bamboo instruments we have the *p'iri* and the *taegŭm*. The *p'iri* has a double-reed

ornamentation including unusual attacks and decays, subtle microtones, starling vibratos, unexpected changes of the timbre of the instruments when changing registers, and highly complex rhythms.

The rhythm especially is to be noticed. In Korean indigenous music each rhythmic phrase contains twelve or nine beats, or some other multiple of three. Because twelve can be divided up so many different ways, instruments and voices simultaneously stressing different portions of the twelve-beat phrase

Left, female dancers perform in a confucian ancestral ritual; right, in a Korean classical setting, this *changgu* (hourglass drum) musician marks time.

mouthpiece like the oboe, and its sound reminds one of that instrument, though the *p'iri* is much shriller. The sound of the *taegŭm* might be said to be *the* sound of Korea—the wanderer's flute heard in the woods on a misty morning. In the metal category we have the bells that hang in their frame at the back of the full Korean orchestra balanced by the stone chimes on the other side.

There are more than 12 different genres of Korean music, though the repertory of all but the folk song is somewhat limited. Dates and places of performances of Korean music and dance cannot be predicted but are very frequent. Korean lunar holidays are a good time to look for outside performances that capture some of the atmosphere of the old Korea. These outside shows include farmers' music and dance, folk singing, and various kinds of folk dance such as masked dance drama. For other performances watch the schedules of large theaters and university auditoriums.

The Solemnity and Hilarity of Ancient Court Dances

Just as Korean dance as a whole can be divided into two main types, court and folk, so can court dance itself be put into two classes: *ilmu* and *chŏngjae*.

Ilmu is by far the smaller of the two classes, comprising only the dances done at the Sunggyungwan Confucian Ceremony and the Chongmyo Royal Ancestral Shrine.

ing the Yi Dynasty there were dozens of *chŏngjae* dances, fewer than a score can be reconstructed with any confidence and only about half a dozen have come down to use in an unbroken line.

Hwagwan-mu, the Flower-Crown Dance, is by far the most commonly seen of the court dances. It is used to begin almost every performance of Korean dance. The name derives from the tiny sparkling crown perched on each dancer's head. As in all court dance, the dancers wear sleeve extensions, called *hansam*, over the hands. The sleeves were originally just long enough to cover the hands but gradually became longer and longer as it was realized that the swirling motions added color and excitement to the otherwise slow, refined movements.

The dance, performed in rigid lines, involves very little movement from place to place and consists primarily of circular arm movements and bows to the cardinal points. The dance is in two sections, recognizable by the dancers' change in attire and symbolized by the objects they carry: For the civilian portion of the dance, each carries a feathered stick in his right hand and a flute in his left; in the military portion, the right hand holds an axe and the left, a shield.

The court dances you will see done on stage belong to the *chŏngjae* class. *Chŏngjae*, meaning "display of talent," were performed as entertainment for the king and his court; commoners who had no access to the inner court never saw these dances. Although dur-

Other court dances commonly done are *Ch'ŏyong-mu*, *Mugo*, *Ch'unaeng-mu*, and *P'ogurak*.

Ch'ŏyong-mu is one of the oldest extant Korean dances, having come down to us from the Silla period. The dance celebrates the life of Ch'ŏyong, a man who came to live in Silla from a distant land.

Mugo is done by eight dancers around a large horizontal drum. Four of the dancers have drumsticks hidden in their *hansam*, and the other four carry flowers. The climax of the dance is the beating of the drum.

Ch'unaeng-mu is the Dance of the Spring Nightingale. The dance is done by a solo performer entirely within the area of a long reed mat and is characterized by extremely slow, delicate movements.

P'ogurak must have added a big chunk of hilarity to the solemn atmosphere of the court. In the middle of the stage stands a high wooden screen with a hole at the top. Each dancer has two balls which she attempts to throw through the hole while dancing. If she manages to make at least one "basket," she is awarded a flower. The dancer who fails, gets a healthy swatch of black ink across her face.

Masked Dancers Laugh at Themselves And Sting With Satire

No one knows exactly where the masked dance drama originated, but they must have come from a single source because the story of the drama is everywhere the same. It is a

the Yangju Pyŏl Sandae Nori. One of the two the Bongsan is a bit more widely known— the Bongsan Players have even made a very successful tour of the United States and received rave reviews everywhere they went. The Bongsan dancing style is vigorous with lots of leaps and squats and broad body movements. The masks are humorously grotesque, though less so than in the past.

The Yangju dance style is more subtle and elegant, but less broad in its humor. The masks, too, are subdued by comparison.

Farmers, Dance: Shamanist Acrobatics and Bobs

Farmers' Dance is both the oldest and newest form of Korean music and dance.

series of satirical vignettes portraying the foibles and misadventures of a group of apostate Buddhist monks, a lecherous old gentleman with one-too-many concubines, a stupid nobleman and his smart servant, a traveling merchant, and a charlatan shaman; even a lion gets into the act. Masked dance drama was a way for the commoners to release their frustrations about their treatment by the upper classes and the clergy, as well as a way to learn to laugh at themselves.

In Seoul you're most likely to get a chance to see either the Bongsan Masked Dance or

Left, mask dancers poke fun with his bizarre presence and words; right, a royally robed flutist.

Chinese records of the 5th Century refer to the Korean country people's playing percussion and dancing at the same time as a part of their agricultural ritual. It is the newest in the sense that it is constantly being added to through the improvisations of the expert players.

There are two major types of Farmers' Dance: *Chwado-kut* and *Udu-kut*. *Chwado-kut* is faster paced and the dancing is more acrobatic.

Udo-kut is somewhat slower and the rhythms can therefore be more intricate and contrapuntal. Nowadays the two styles are often mixed: *Udo* music with *chwado* dancing.

Besides being a great form of entertainment, Farmers' music and dance are still considered by many to be efficacious shamanistic tools. They are performed to purify the village well, protect houses from thieves and fire, pray to the mountain spirit for his blessing, ensure a bumper crop, etc.

P'ansori Storytelling:

P'ansori is the art of the dramatic song. Developed out of the folk-singing style of the Southwest, p'ansori is done solo to the accompaniment of a barrel drum. The singer's voice must be extremely versatile: He sings all the roles and recites the explanatory narrative between songs, as well. It must be durable, too, for one complete p'ansori can last for up to six hours.

Of the original twelve p'ansori stories, only five are still performed. They are Ch'unbyang-ga, the Cinderella story of a country kisaeng's daughter and her prince charming from Seoul; Hŭngbo-ga, the story of two brothers, one rich and evil and the other poor but good; Sugung-ga, a charmingly funny story of the King of the Sea, who has fallen ill with a strange disease that requires a rabbit's liver as a cure, and of how the rabbit saves his own life; Simch'ŏng-ga, the story of a devoted daughter who offers her life so that her blind father's eyesight may be restored; and Chŏkpyŏk-ka, the adventures of a Chinese general.

P'ansori performances are given frequently on Saturday afternoons in the Small Audito-rium of the National Theater on Namsan. The Society for the Preservation of P'ansori sponsors other performances done in various theaters and auditoriums around town. Watch for announcements in the English-language newspapers. Some singers you'll want to be sure to hear are Human National Treasures Mr. Park Dong-Jin and Ms. Kim So-Hui and the brilliant young Mr. Cho Sang-Hyeon.

To get the fullest enjoyment out of the performance, it is wise to read an English translation of the story first.

Sŭngmu and Salp'uri

Of all the Korean folk dances, the two that carry the expression of mŏt to its pinnacle are Sŭngmu, the Priest's Dance, and Salp'uri, a dance of spiritual cleansing.

Sŭngmu is done in a hooded robe with floor-length sleeves that make the dancer appear somehow larger than life. A single drum stands in its frame at the back of the stage. There are various opinions as to what the drum represents: Some say it is the ecstasy of enlightenment; others relate it to the temptation of worldly pleasure. The dancer's own interpretation affects the mood he tries to convey through the dance.

The whole first section of the dance shows the priest vacillating between giving in to the call of the drum and ignoring it. Tension builds as he is alternately drawn to the drum and repelled from it. Finally, unable to resist, he draws his drumsticks out of the long sleeves and plays a breathtaking solo on the drum. When the rhythms are played well, the audience actually gets rushes in the chest and throat at climactic points. The speed builds until the drummer gives up in exhaustion. He leaves the stage with a dreamy, faraway look on his face and only the drum is left. Performances by the best specialist in this dance are known to leave audiences in tears.

Through the Salp'uri the dancer strives to free her spirit from trouble and anguish. A long white scarf her only prop, the dancer carries herself and the audience through a series of emotions from sad quietude to invigorating joy in the space of five minutes. When done without true emotion, this dance is nothing but a sequence of rote movements with a scarf. With mŏt, however, it is the epitome of Korean dance, enough in itself to convince you that this is a field truly worth exploring.

Left, the young zither musician performed at the turn-of-the-century; right, p´ansori singer swining "scat-style" at a Space Center recital.

HAN'GŬL, KOREA'S ALPHABET

The indigenous writing system Koreans currently use is called *han'gŭl,* which means "the Great Writing." The orthographical design of *han'gŭl* was completed in the 25th year (1443) of King Sejong, the fourth king of the Yi dynasty. He is the king best remembered by Koreans for his contributions in all areas of the Korean people's life—culture, economy, politics, society, religion, and national defense.

Sejong had commissioned the phonological researches, of which *han'gŭl* was a direct result, to the members of his famous academy,

Chip-hyŏn-jŏn (College of Assembled Worthies). The College, which previously had existed in name only, became a highly organized research institution beginning in 1420. The king took the keenest interest in all the activities of the College. It was staffed by young men of promise and ability.

The Deep-Rooted Tree

To test the new writing system, the king ordered his subjects to write the voluminous *Yong-bi-ŏch'ŏn-ga* (Songs of Flying Dragons) in *han'gŭl.* The *Songs* is a eulogy cycle in 125 cantos comprising 248 poems, composed to celebrate the founding of the Yi dynasty and praise the achievements of Sejong's predeces-

sors. As an elaborate product of linguists and literary elites, it is not only the first experimental use of *han'gŭl*—i.e., the first work of literature in which the actual language is accurately indicated—but an important historical statement of the policies of the new dynasty and a manifesto of Confucian concepts as applied to the mandate and function of Korean rulers. Comprising heroic tales, foundation myths, folk beliefs, and prophecies, it also marks the birth of a national vernacular literature. The second canto of the *Songs* is cited below as an illustration, along with an English translation by Peter H. Lee:

(Pulhwi Kiphŭn namgan)
The tree that strikes deep root

(paramae ani mwil ssae)
Is firm amidst the winds.

(kot tyokho)
Its flowers are good,

(yŏrŭm hanani)
Its fruit abundant.

(Saemi kiphŭn mŭrŭn)
The stream whose source is deep

(kamarae ani kŭch'ŭl ssae)
Gushes forth even in a drought.

(naehi irŏ)
It forms a river

(pararae kanani)
And gains the sea.

King Sejong promulgated *han'gŭl* to the public in the name of *Hun-min-chŏng-ŭm* (The Correct Sounds for the Instruction of the People) on October 9, 1446. The Korean people observe this day as a national holiday under the name of *Han'gŭl* Day. The king stated his reasons for inventing *han'gŭl* in the preface of *the Correct Sounds,* as follows:

"Being distinct from Chinese, the Korean language is not confluent with Chinese characters. Hence, those having something to put into words are unable to express their feelings. To overcome such distressing circumstances, I have designed twenty-eight letters that everyone may learn with ease and use with convenience for his daily life."

Before *han'gŭl,* Koreans had no writing system of their own except Chinese script which represented classical Chinese, a language not related to Korean either genetically or typologically. Korean belongs to the Altaic language family, consisting mainly of Turkic, Mongolian, and Manchu-Tungus languages. Chinese, on the other hand, belongs to the Sino-Tibetan family, together with Tibetan, Burmese, and Thai. Korean and Chinese are completely different from each other, not only in sound patterns, such as vowels, consonants, syllable structure, and tones, but in word formation and sentence structure. For this reason, Chinese script was inadequate to represent the sounds and structure of Korean. Koreans employed the script to express thoughts and information according to the

To solve this predicament, scholars made a limited use of Chinese characters for pronunciation and meaning. These systems, called *Idu* (Clerk Readings), were used during the era of Korea's three ancient kingdoms—*Silla, Paekche,* and *Koguryŏ*—and also later during the Koryŏ and early Yi dynasties. They were used to record vernacular songs, poems and proper names by means of Chinese characters borrowed in their Chinese meaning but read as the corresponding Korean word, or through characters borrowed in their classical Chinese pronunciation. *Idu* systems which

sounds and structure of classical Chinese, and not according to those of Korean. Moreover, Chinese script is an ideographic writing originally created from pictures of objects. Each concept is, therefore, associated with one character and is represented by one to thirty-two strokes. There are approximately 50,000 different characters. The Korean people couldn't understand the meaning of texts written in such characters, especially their allusions and metaphors. Yet, the ruling class of Korea devoted its lifetime to the study of classical Chinese, because it was the official medium of communications. Children of the ruling class started learning Chinese at about age five. However, most common people remained illiterate all their lives.

consist only of Chinese characters were entirely inadequate for communication. Moreover, they were difficult to learn. Therefore *han'gŭl* was created—a phonetic writing completely divorced from Chinese script.

In the Shape of Speech

Han'gŭl is one of the most remarkable writing systems ever devised. It is an alphabet which follows a rigorous phonological analysis of Korean speech patterns. King Sejong

King Sejong (left, as he appears on the grounds of Seoul's Tŏksu Palace) was the man who founded the *han'gŭl* system. His *han'gŭl* proclamation in Chinese print (above) is a linguistic classic.

and his assistants studied the rich Chinese linguistic tradition, such as the concepts of consonants (but not vowels), syllables, and tones, as well as their underlying philosophical background. Yet, the features of *han'gŭl* are designed to represent the Korean language; they are written in a unique kind of script never seen before.

The consonant letters were designed to depict the shapes of the speech organs. The symbol ㄱ, representing the sound *k*, depicts the shape of the root of the tongue blocking the throat; ㄴ *n*, the shape of the tongue touching the gum-ridge; ㅁ *m*, the shape of the lips; ㅅ *s*, the shape of an incisor; and ㅇ (zero or silent consonant), the shape of the throat. Other consonants were made by adding strokes to the above basic symbols. For example, ㅋ *k'* is pronounced using the same oral position (soft palate) as ㄱ *k*, but it has an added stroke because its articulation is more 'severe' or aspirated than that of ㄱ *k*. The sounds represented by ㄴ *n*, ㄷ t, ㅌ *t'*, and ㄹ *r/l* are all pronounced using the same oral place of articulation (the gum-ridge area), but compared with ㄴ *n*, ㄷ *t* an added stroke, symbolizing the blockage of the passage leading to the nasal cavity; whereas ㅌ *t'* has one more stroke by virtue of its aspiration or puff of air, and ㄹ *r/l* by virtue of its sound quality of flap or trill. In the same way, ㅂ *p*, ㅍ *p'*, and ㅁ *m* are all lip sounds, but the first two have some added strokes in view of their respective manners of articulation. Notice also the ingenuity displayed in devising the fricative sounds △ *z*, ㅈ *ch*, and ㅊ *ch'* in a way parallel to ㅅ *s*, and the throat sounds ㅇ *ng*, ㆆ (glottal catch), and ㅎ *h* which were modelled after ㅇ (zero consonant).

Believing that human speech sounds are based on Chinese cosmological principles, the king and his assistants related the speech organs to the Five Agents—water, wood, fire, metal and soil. The throat is water because it is deep and moist; the molar is wood because it is uneven and extended; the tongue is fire because it is pointed and moving; the incisor is metal because it is hard and cutting; and the lips are soil because they are squarish and yet joined. Just as water and fire are regarded as primary in that water is the source of life and fire is the operation that perfects things, so were the throat and the tongue sounds regarded as primary in that the throat is the articulator and the tongue the differentiator of speech sounds.

For vowels and semivowels, three basic letters and their combinations were devised: The

three basic ones are ·, ㅡ, and ㅣ which were viewed as representing the three cardinal vowels. For · (a sound somewhat similar to *aw* in *law*), "the tongue retracts and its sound is deep; the roundness of its shape is a depiction of Heaven." For ㅡ *ŭ*, "the tongue retracts a little, and its sound is neither deep nor shallow; the flatness of its shape is a depiction of Earth." For ㅣ *i*, "the tongue does not retract, and its sound is shallow; the uprightness

of its shape is a depiction of Man." Thus, the basic vowel symbols are based on the trinity of Heaven, Earth, and Man, whereas all the other vowels and semivowels are represented simply through the interactions of these three symbols, as illustrated below:

ㅏ *a*, ㅑ *ya*, ㅓ *ŏ*, ㅕ *yŏ*, ㅗ *o*, ㅛ *yo*, ㅜ *u*, ㅠ *yu*, ㅐ *ae*, ㅔ *e*, ㅒ *yae*, ㅖ *ye*, ㅘ *wa*, ㅝ *wŏ*, ㅙ *wae*, ㅞ *we*, etc.

In vowels like ㅏ, ㅑ, ㅗ, and ㅛ, the round (Heaven) is located above and on the outside, hence they are called Yang sounds. In vowels like ㅓ, ㅕ, ㅜ, and ㅠ, the round is located below and on the inside, hence they are called

264

Yin sounds. Yang and Yin sounds are relevant to such sound alternations as vowel harmony in Korean.

One of the most important characteristics of Middle Korean (i.e. 15th Century Korean) is that it was a tonal language. There were three kinds of tones: low, high, and low-high. These are marked by side-dots on the left side of each letter: low by a zero, high by one dot, and low high by two dots.

The 'Vulgar Script'

The road through which *han'gŭl* has evolved has not always been smooth. There was vehement opposition to King Sejong's promulgation of *han'gŭl* to the public. Ch'oe Malli, then Associate Academician (the highest purely academic rank in the College of Assembled Worthies) and his followers presented an anti-*han'gŭl* memorial to the Throne in 1444, which read (Gari Ledyard's translation) as follows:

"... Our Court, since the times of our Progenitor and Ancestors, has with utmost sincerity served the Great (China). We have honored Chinese institutions solely. But now, at this time of identical culture and identical cart-tracks, we create the Vulgar Script *(han'gŭl)*. We observe and attend this with alarm ... If these graphs should flow into China, and if people there should adversely criticize them, how could we be without shame, considering our service toward the Great and affection for China. ... Only types like the Mongolians, Tanguts, Jurčen, Japanese, and Tibetans have their own graphs. But these are matters of the barbarians, ... To now separately make the Vulgar Script is to discard China and identify ourselves with the barbarians. This is what is called 'throwing away the fragrance of storax and choosing the bullet of the praying mantis.' ..."

This memorial had little effect on Sejong's determination. After the death of Sejong, the opposition of the literary men to *han'gŭl* continued on into the reigns of Munjong (1450–1452), Tanjong (1452–1455), and Sejo (1455–1468). Both Munjong and Tanjong appear to have been rather lukewarm about the new script, but Sejo shared his father's (Sejong's) wish to propagate it along with Buddhism. Then, during the Japanese occupation of Korea, the use of *han'gŭl* was suppressed and the Korean people were forced to use Japanese as the only communicative means. Nevertheless, *han'gŭl* has been preserved and refined by scholars devoted to freedom and growth of the nation.

When Korea was liberated from Japan in 1945, *Han'gŭl* Day was established as a national holiday. The Korean people love *han'gŭl* and are proud of it. First, *han'gŭl* marks the reawakening of Korean national consciousness, its independence from China, and its sense of national solidarity. Second, it has democratized all walks of Korean life. Third, *han'gŭl* is an indigenous and original invention of Koreans. Finally, it is one of the most scientific writing systems in the world; it is the embodiment of enormous knowledge, and has served as a driving force towards the nation's prosperity.

Sejong declared that he created the writing system for the convenience of the people. "Talented persons will learn *han'gŭl* in a single morning, and even foolish persons will understand it in ten days," he said. Thanks to *han'gŭl* more than 90 percent of Korea's people are literate.

(Persons who would like to learn more about *han'gŭl* and its use should see the language guide and index-glossary in the Guide in Brief section.)

Spicy. Fiery. Earthy. Cool. Korean food is diverse and provocative. Its bold and subtle tastes, textures and aromas are sure to elicit comments, sighs, and even tears at every meal.

Most foreigners associate pungent garlic and hot chili pepper with Korean cuisine. It is true that garlic-eating has been heartily appreciated by Koreans since the race's first breath, but little is it known—even in Korea—that the chili pepper did not even exist in this country until the 16th Century when it was introduced to Korea by Portu-

of Korea's most important annual social events is *kimjang*, or autumn *kimch'i* making. At *kimjang* time, women gather in groups throughout the country to cut, wash, and salt veritable hills of cabbage and white radish. The prepared *kimch'i* is stored in large, thick earthenware crocks and then buried in the backyard to keep it from fermenting during the winter months. Thoughout the dark and cold winter, these red peppered, garlicked and pickled vegetables are a good source of much-needed Vitamin C.

During other eating seasons, a variety of

guese traders.

However these two ingredients reached Korean plates and palates, they are now used in many dishes—most liberally and notoriously in *kimch'i*. For the newcomer, learning to eat this mouth-watering dish is the first step to becoming a connoisseur of Korean food.

Kimch'i Culture

Kimch'i is *the* dish that has made Korean food famous. Next to rice (*pap*), it is the most important component in any Korean meal. It is not known when or how *kimch'i* originated, but like curry in India it's in Korea to stay. So institutionalized is *kimch'i* that one

vegetables such as chives, pumpkin and eggplant are used to make more exotic types of *kimch'i*. The summer heat makes it necessary to prepare a fresh batch almost daily, often in a cool, light brine. Raw seafood, such as fish, crab and oysters are kimchied too, and indeed, in Korea, a woman's culinary prowess often is determined first and foremost by how good her *kimch'i* tastes.

Exotic Herbs

Not all Korean food ingredients are quite so passionate as the garlic and chili pepper. In actuality, the earliest Korean dishes consist of understated ingredients. To Koreans, almost every plant and animal in their diet has an herbal or medicinal quality and certain dishes are purposely eaten to warm or cool the head and body.

Wild aster, royal fern bracken, marsh plant, day lily, aralia shoots, and broad bellfowers are just a few of the wild and exotic plants included in the typical Korean's diet. Others, such as mugwort, shepherd's purse, and sowthistle, also are seasonally picked and eaten.

More common table vegetables—such as black sesame leaves, spinach, lettuce, and mung and soy beans—are typically grow in

broth boiled from dried anchovies, and vegetable soups rendered from dried spinach, sliced radish or dried seaweed (*miyŏk-guk*). The latter is said to be beneficial to lactating mothers.

A seafood dish of some kind is usually included with various "side dishes" which are called *panch'an*. This may be a dried, salted and charbroiled fish or a hearty and spicy hot seafood soup called *mae-un-t'ang*. A good *mae-un-t'ang* usually includes a good portion of firm, white fish, vegetables, soybean curd

the backyard, but others are found only in the wild. All are collectively called *namul* when they are individually parboiled, then lightly seasoned with sesame oil, garlic, soy sauce, and ground and toasted sesame seeds.

Another vital part of the Korean meal is soup (*guk*), which is said to be one of Korea's earliest culinary techniques. Soup will always be found at a proper table setting. Especially popular is *twoenjang-guk*, a fermented soybean paste soup with shortnecked clams stirred into its broth. Also popular are a light

Left, dinner for two; right, cabbage and turnip vendors sell their crops during annual autumn *kimjang*.

(*tubu*), red pepper powder, and an optional poached egg.

Beefeaters' Choices: Pulgogi and Kalbi

Probably the most popular Korean entré ordered or automatically served to westerners is *pulgogi* (barbecued beef). Most beefeaters—whether Texans or Koreans— are unanimous in their appreciation of this dish which is essentially strips of red beef marinated and then grilled over a charcoal brazier. Another popular meat dish is tender and marbled *kalbi* short ribs which are marinated and barbecued like *pulgogi*.

To Koreans, however, rice—not meat—is

considered to be the main dish of the meal. In fact, one of the most common street greetings, "Pam mŏgŏss-ŏ-yo?" literally means "Have you eaten rice?"

When Koreans sit down to a traditional meal, they relax on a clean lacquered paper floor. The meal comes to them on a low table. Usually the food is served in a collection of small metal bowls which are neatly arranged. The utensils used are a pair of chopsticks and a flat soup spoon.

Westerners may be surprised to find that Koreans often will eat an entire bowl of rice and maybe have an extra helping even though tastier side dishes remain unfinished. Don't let this preference for rice bother you; if you run out of a particular item, the lady of the house will bring more. When you've had

liquor they pour from a battered aluminum teapot.

Welcome to *kul-jip*, or "cave-house," one of Seoul's most unusual drinking spots. A bomb shelter during the Korean War three decades ago, today it is operated as a winehouse by several aging ladies. The quality of the potent rice *makkŏlli* is excellent, so *kul-jip* never lacks for customers.

There are only a few other bombshelter winehouses in Seoul but there are many places to drink—probably more per capita than in most other countries. Within a few minutes' walk of *kul-jip* are a beer hall with draft and bottled beer, a market wine shop serving several alcoholic beverages, and a roadside drinking cart, where passersby can duck in for a quick snort on their way home.

enough to eat, place your chopsticks and soup spoon to the right of your bowl; don't leave them stuck in the rice or resting on any bowls.

A dish of sliced and chilled fruit is usually served as a dessert. Depending on the season, muskmelon, strawberries, apples, pears, and watermelon are among the fresh and sweet selections. At important celebrations, steamed rice cakes (*ttŏk*) are presented as tasty ritual food.

'Toasting The Spirits'

Deep within a cave beneath a hill in northern Seoul four men sit around a low round table, drinking small bowls of a milky white

Drinking is an important part of Korean culture. There are few proscriptions against alcohol here and many social reasons for imbibing, so most Korean men—and a growing number of women—drink.

Drinking with Koreans provides one of the easiest opportunities for a foreigner to penetrate Korean culture. This is partly because of the salience of drinking in the culture and partly because, like anywhere, alcohol removes inhibitions and speeds social and cultural interaction.

On Floating Cups and Kisaeng

History doesn't reveal when Koreans first discovered fermentation, but drinking was an important part of the culture even in Korea's early dynasties.

During the Silla dynasty, the king and his court relaxed at *P'o-Sŏk-jŏng* drinking bower outside Kyòngju. Here a spring bubbled up into an abalone-shaped stone channel. The drinkers set their cups afloat in the channel and competed to compose poems before the cups drifted all the way around.

Later Korean dynasties continued drinking. Probably the most popular surroundings were what today is known as the *kisaeng* party. *Kisaeng* were female entertainers who played musical instruments, sang, danced, composed poetry and practiced calligraphy to amuse the male aristocarcy at parties. They also poured drinks, served the men food, and flirted. According to tradition, high class *kisaeng* took lovers but weren't promiscuous. At one point in the Yi dynasty, says a historian, there were more than 20,000 *kisaeng*.

The most famous heroine in classicial Korean history was the *kisaeng* Non-gae, who lived in the late 15th Century when the Japanese invaded Korea. Forced to entertain a victorious Japanese general, Non-gae beguiled him into walking with her along the cliffs overlooking the Nam River. Embracing him, she lured him near the brink and forced him over the edge, sacrificing her own life to kill the hated enemy conquerer.

Today, few *kisaeng* can play classical instruments, compose poetry or write with a brush and ink. Instead, most *kisaeng* parties include a band with drums and electric guitar, and the *kisaeng* and their guests go-go dance around the table after eating. The main patrons are Korean businessmen who pay $100 per head to entertain customers, and Japanese tourists who pay even more in hopes of taking the girls back to their hotel for the night.

In Confucian Cups

Conservative Confucians would be distressed to find what has happened to drinking today. They would be particularly aghast to find college coeds and other supposedly respectable women drinking freely in public establishments.

But with a little attention, the Confucians would find that not all of the old practices

Left, a Korean businessman's lunch; right, local beer and spirits.

have vanished. There still are traditional weddings where the groom consumes rice wine and the celebration afterward also includes drinking. The guests may hang the groom upside down and beat him if the alcohol runs out—and old custom.

At memorial services for ancestor, filial Koreans still customarily set a bowl of wine among offerings on the altar. After the rites are completed, the living consume the wine, toasting the spirits and strengthening the bond with them.

Funerals and wakes also still involve drinking—to help the living forget their grief. Friends and relatives usually will drink, sing and gamble all night at the home of someone who has just died.

Never Drink Alone

The Confucians also might be surprised to find that although bowing while drinking has been largely forgotten, other elements of traditional etiquette still remain.

The cardinal rule is that one doesn't drink alone. Furthermore, a drinker doesn't pour his own glass, but humbly waits until his companion fills it for him. In this tradition, to serve one's self would be an act of arrogance and greed.

Generally, in a gesture of respect and friendship, one drinker will give his cup to the other, conveying it politely with both hands. His companion receives the cup with both hands and holds it thus while it is filled to the brim. He may then drink. After emptying the cup, he again uses both hands to return it to its owner. Then, grasping the wine vessel in both hands, he refills the cup for the owner, returning the favor.

In a group, several drinkers in succession may offer their cups to a single person, leaving an array of brimming cups before him. A person who has given up his cup can't drink until the recipient returns it or someone else gives him his. So whoever has received a cup has an obligation to empty it and pass it on without inordinate delay.

The custom of forcing drinks on each other hardly encourages moderation, which is probably why most drinkers in Korea go home rather tipsy. Drunkenness carries no social stigma. To the contrary, when most Koreans drink, they do so until they are drunk.

Fortunately, most Koreans still don't drive, which makes the habit less lethal. In keeping with the comaraderie that Korean drinking fosters, the members of a party who are least under the influence make an effort to insure that their companions get home alright. During the late hours of the night, the streets are filled with drinkers putting their inebriated friends into taxis or onto buses and telling the driver or conductor where they should disembark. Somehow, there is always somebody who stays sober enough to do this.

Makkŏlli: The Working Man's Brew

The most popular Korean brew has long been *makkŏlli*, a milky liquor that most rural households ferment at home from rice. Reputed to be highly nutritious, farmers found that a few cups during the long working day helped stave off hunger.

Makkŏlli was inexpensive in the cities, as well, making it the working man's drink. For many people, until the early 1970s, going drinking usually meant going to a *makkŏlli-jip*, an establishment that served *makkŏlli*.

Makkŏlli-jip vary in style and quality, but are generally comfortable unpretentious places where nobody can put on airs. The *makkŏlli* is dipped out of a huge tub or vat into cheap teapots or bottles, and any old bowl might serve as a cup.

The two most important factors about any *makkŏlli-jip* are (1) the quality of the *makkŏlli* and (2) the kinds of side dishes, *anju*, that it serves. All drinking in Korea involves eating.

The thing that go best with *makkŏlli* range from fresh oysters, peppery octopus, dried fish, squid or cuttlefish, to bean curd, soups, bean pancakes, scallion pancakes, or omelettes.

The other beverage with long popularity is *soju*, a cheap distilled liquor of around 25 percent alcoholic content, with a quality somewhere between gin and kerosene. Price and the high alcoholic content make it Korea's cheapest drink. While far from smooth, a bottle of *soju* goes down very well with certain foods, such as pigs' feet, barbecued pork, Korean sausage and other meat dishes.

Beer also has been popular in Korea for many years. However, beer has been more expensive than *makkŏlli* or *soju* making it somewhat more a rich man's drink, at least until recently.

But these days, Korean drinking tastes are gradually changing. Because South Korea's growing population began to eat more rice than the country could produce and because the economy was growing, people began buying more beer. Beer sales increased 48 percent in 1979 over 1978, while *makkŏlli* sales rose only 11 percent and *soju* sales gained 30 percent.

Higher Class Spirits

Western liquors like scotch and bourbon have always had very high import duties in Korea. But about 1975, the government authorized Korean distillers to import concentrate to produce their own whiskey.

The resulting Korean scotch, gin, vodka, rum and brandy are much cheaper than imported brands and sales of these liquors have increased markedly since then. As the *Dong-A Ilbo* newspaper remarked after reviewing the sales statistics for 1979, "A propensity to consume higher class liquors has appeared."

Where should the foreigner visiting Korea go drinking? To get a feeling for what remains of traditional Korea, the best place would be a *makkŏlli-jip*. Korea also has plenty of beer halls. Try the Myong-dong or Mugyo-doing districts in central Seoul or the area around Sin-ch'on Rotary in western Seoul.

If you are dining at Korean or Chinese restaurants, beer or traditional spirits may complement the meal. Restaurants usually don't serve *makkŏlli*, but they will have beer, *soju*, or chongjong, Korean *sake*.

If you are eating Western food, you might wish to try a Korean wine called Majuang. Most hotel restaurants stock it, as do grocery stores.

Right, food at a *hwangap*, or 60th birthday feast.

HANYAK, TRADITIONAL MEDICINE

According to Korean legend and history, a she-bear and a tigress who wished to be incarnated as human beings were once granted an herbal prescription by Hwan-ung, the heavenly king: Each was given a bunch of mugwort and 20 bulbs of garlic and told to retire from the sunlight for a hundred days. Only the she-bear carefully followed the king's advice, and emerged from her cave as a woman. She was then married by Hwan-ung and gave birth to Tan'gun Wanggŏm, the great ancestor of Chosŏn (Korea).

This tale illustrates the close bond Koreans

Silla doctor named Kim Pa-chin was sent to cure Japan's King Inkyo and was given a large reward for his medical favors.

Around the middle of the Three Kingdoms Period (57 B.C.–936 A.D.), Korea started to publish its own pharmacopoeia with original prescriptions which combined Korean and Chinese medical knowledge. The use of indigenous herbs came into prominence during the Koryŏ (936–1392) and Yi (1392–1910) dynasties. More than 150 medical manuals were published during the Yi dynasty, and one of the most valuable of these, the *Ŭi-*

have with nature and also their belief in the power of herbs. Mugwort and garlic have long been vital ingredients in the Korean diet and other basic herbs have for centuries been recognized as preventatives and curatives for human illnesses.

Chinese herbal medicine and acupuncture were officially introduced in 561 A.D. to the Koguryŏ court by a Han named Chih Tsung. Chih's knowledge dramatically expanded the possibilities in the field of Korean medicine. This knowledge was carried to the neighboring kingdoms of Paekche and Silla, and was assimilated with ancient Korean pharmacopoeia. Some knowledge of Chinese herbal medicine had been previously transmitted to Japan when as early as 414 A.D. a

bang Uch'wi, was stolen by a Japanese warlord Kato Kiyomasa, during one of the Hideyoshi invasions of the 1590s. This pharmaceutic manual is still retained in Japan as a national treasure.

Take Your Choice:
Hanyak or Yak-guk

In 1880 Western medicine was introduced by doctors from China and Japan. However, despite the pervasiveness of 20th Century medicine, *hanyak,* traditional Korean medicine, remains extremely popular. Western-style pharmacies *(yak-guk),* replete with men dressed in starched white gowns and waiting behind drug counters, can be found on just about any modern, commercial street in Korea. But *hanyak* shops are also everywhere—many of them distinguished by their fascinating window displays of snakes, enormous, human-shaped white ginseng roots pickling in belljars full of Korean wine, and a random collection of deer antlers, dried reptiles and insects. There are numerous *hanyak* shops in Seoul along Chong-no 5-ka and in Taegu on "Yak-chŏng Kol-mok," that city's famous "herb street." Raw herbs are also sold at most marketplaces. In addition, Korean-style pressure point massage, *chi ap,* and acupuncture, *ch'im,* and a variety of other traditional healing techniques are still practiced.

Some of the common ingredients used in prescriptions are iris root for feeble-mindedness, snakeberry leaves to help regulate the menstrual cycle, and chrysanthemum roots to cure headaches. Not all of the antidotes are vegetarian, though. Snake meat soup *(paem t'ang)* and snake wine *(paem sul)* are commonly prescribed potions—albino snake for longevity, yellow python for a cure-all, and viper for neuralgia and tuberculosis. Dog meat soup *(posin t'ang; posin ha-da* means to build up one's strength) is also a very popular body rejuvenator, especially when it's made from the meat of white and black dogs. Many small shops and cafes specialize in these reptile and canine soups, but westerners may find a more palatable tonic in an *insam ch'at chip,* a ginseng teahouse.

The cozy herb teahouse is usually identified by white, anthropomorphic ginseng roots painted on its door and by the pungent aroma of hot cinnamon and ginger tea. Inside the shop, belljars of foreign, dried herbs line the shelf.

More than just homemade ginseng tea is served. There are, to name a few delicious concoctions, aromatic ginger tea *(saeng kang ch'a)* made with boiled and strained ginger

root and raw sugar; *insam t'ang,* fresh white ginseng root blended with water and sugar; and porridges such as *chat chuk,* made of pine nuts, water, rice flour and salt or sugar to taste; and *kkae chuk,* toasted black sesame seeds, water, rice flour and salt or sugar. (Beware, however, of large heapings of sugar.) Herbs are steeped in earthenware pots (metal is said to deplete herbal potency) over a low-burning *yŏnt'an* (coal briquette) for at least an hour or two until an essence is thus extracted. Besides teas and porridges, fresh fruit juices and fruits, such as sliced persimmons,

Herb vendors display their medicinal wares in numerous colorful ways. At left is the window of a Seoul herb shop; and right are herb vats at Taegu.

strawberries and tangerines soaked in *soju* (25 to 50 percent proof drinking alcohol), also are served.

Panax Ginseng,
For Ills and Thrills

Among the herbs in Korea, *panax ginseng*, referred to as *insam* in Korean, is by far the most popular. As far back as the Third Millenium B.C. in China, herbal potions and poultices were used to maintain and restore the internal *ŭm-yang* (i.e. positive-negative,

seng" and exported to China during King Chŏngjo's reign (1776–1800).

Modern Korean ginseng cultivators have been able to raise superior grade ginseng. Ideal climatic conditions, especially between northern 36 to 38 degree latitudes where optimum mountain-forest simulated environment is maintained, have produced a cultivated root that is considered to be the international standard.

Extreme care is administered in nurturing the root. In the preparation of *yakt'o* (soil for herbs), only a moderately rich mulch of de-

acid-base, male-female) forces to proper balance by stimulating or repressing one side or the other. Ginseng, which originally grew wild along ravines and in the forests of Korea and Manchuria, was found to be bursting with *yang* energy. It became a vital ingredient used in medications prescribed in the first Chinese pharmacopoeia.

The exchange of medical knowledge with China encouraged trade in herbs. Ginseng flowed into China until the Koryŏ dynasty, when supplies began to diminish, and was exported during the Yi dynasty as a tribute to Chinese royalty. To boost the supply, ginseng cultivation was encouraged in the Kyŏngsang and then in the Chŏlla provinces. The herb was first processed into ultra-potent "red gin-

ciduous chestnut or oak leaves is used. Hand-thatched mats shade slopes of ginseng from direct sunlight. The main ginseng-growing areas are on Kanghwa Island, and in the Kimp'o, Puyŏ, and Kunsan districts. Once used, the land is not cultivated with ginseng again for 10 to 15 years.

The growth and maturation cycle of Korean ginseng takes from four to six years depending on the intended use of the root. In mid-May, the plant flowers. Seeds of the strongest, most mature, five-year-old plants are selected in mid-July and planted in late October. After harvest, the roots are washed, peeled, steamed, and dried. They are then produced in two grades—white *(paek)* and red *(hong)*. Approximately 60 percent of the best ginseng is selected for the red variety which is further processed to preserve the potency of its chemical components.

'Elixir of Life'

Although *panax ginseng* is also cultivated in China, Russia and north Korea, only the Republic of Korea exports it on a grand scale. While white ginseng is readily accessible, only about one percent of the red ginseng product is marketed domestically by the government Office of Monopoly (which also exclusively

from the North American *panax quinquefolius* variety) are glycocides, saccharides, fatty substances, volatile substances, inorganic elements, B-vitamins, enzymes, and alkaline substances. If consumed regularly in small doses, scientists claim the root will help stimulate the central nervous system. Larger doses, meanwhile, depress the nervous system by buffering out physical and chemical stress, and by promoting cell production which counteracts anemia and hypotension. Ginseng thus reportedly increases physical and mental efficiency, and enhances gastrointes-

controls the production of all ginseng-related commodities). As an indication of this herb's lucrative worth, the 1981 projected export market for Korean ginseng products was estimated to be U.S. $145 million. As of 1978, a box of 15 pieces of first quality white ginseng roots was selling in Korea for U.S. $32.30 and the same weight of top quality red ginseng (14 pieces) cost U.S. $121.

Modern, scientific analysis and testing of ginseng's mystic efficacy for the past 60 years has helped fan the herb's worldwide popularity. To the Western world, *panax ginseng* has been identified as a perennial radix plant of the *Araliaceae family*. Active components detected thus far in Korean, Chinese, and Russian ginsengs (which differ pharmaceutically

tinal motility and tone. It is also a common Western notion that ginseng vitalizes one's libido. Koreans, however, rely on more potent aphrodisiacs, such as powdered deer antlers and dog or snake soup. And perhaps to placate Western consumers who are wildly seeking an "elixir of life," ginseng comes in 20th Century pill form as well as in capsules, extracts, jellies, instant tea forms, soft drinks, body creams, jams, candies, chewing gums, and, would you believe, even in cigarets and shampoos?

Perhaps nothing is more symbolic of Korea than anthropomorphic ginseng roots preserved in a belljar (left); snake soup shops (above) are intriguing sidewalk purveyors of longevity potions.

KOREAN COSTUME

The contemporary Korean wardrobe, a very Western mode influenced during the 20th Century by scattered political and cultural events, is an odd assortment of imported styles—from prim military school uniforms reminiscent of the Japanese Occupation to *très chic* designer wares that are exact copies of fashions which debuted just last month in Paris or Rome. However, very comfortable and settled between these two modern extremes is the traditional Korean costume, the *hanbok*, a Mongol-influenced garment still proudly worn by young and old alike.

Before the introduction of Western garments in the latter days of the Yi dynasty, Korea followed fashion trends set by Chinese neighbors. Some 2,000 years ago, she adopted, for example, a costume typical of tribes in northern Manchuria. The earliest depiction of such a costume was found on a fresco painted in the Muyongch'ong (Dancers') Tomb in Manchuria. The clothes worn during that particular Koguryo dynasty period (500 to 650 A.D.) were loose-fitting, cross-breasted tunics with long sleeves extending past the hands. Baggy, bloused pants were bound at the ankles. Another costume in the same mural depicts an ankle length robe tied at the waist with a belt. Simple slip-on shoes were worn.

During the Silla and Koryŏ periods, T'ang China introduced elaborate silken mandarin garments to Korea, but they were worn only by Korean royalty and government officials as status symbols. It was also during this time that Korea's Buddhist monks began wearing ala T'ang China robes and adopted the T'ang custom of shaving the head as a sign of humility. The common Korean folk, however, continued to wear common Korean clothes.

Mongol Chic

Chinese clothing styles remained in vogue throughout Korea's history, but the biggest and most long-lasting fashion influence was made by the Mongols who conquered Korea and China in the 13th Century. During that time, the contemporary *hanbok*, with its short vests, baggy pants and puffy dresses began to evolve.

When Koryŏ became a vassal state of Mongolia during the Mongol Chinese Yüan dynasty, King Ch'ŏngyol, who as a tributary ruler had taken as his queen a princess from the court of Kublai Khan, began dressing in the Mongol fashion. Ch'ŏngyol ascended to the Korean throne in 1274, and by 1277, according to court records, every official in the Korean royal court—from the prime minister down to the lowliest petty functionary—had shaved off his hair except for a patch in the center of his head, and had adopted the costume of the Mongolian plains people

During the relatively short period that Korea was a Mongol vassal state (about a hundred years), three Korean kings after Ch'ŏngyol (Ch'ŏngson, Ch'ŏngsuk and Ch'ŏngmok) were born to Mongolian Korean

queens. Such politics were no doubt a persuasive factor in the setting of all kinds of social trends—including fashion preferences—in the Korean kingdom.

During this trendy period women began wearing their hair in plaits coiled on top of their heads. The skirt, or *ch'ima*, was shortened, and a waist-jacket, the *chŏgori*, was hiked above the waist and tied at the chest with a long, wide ribbon instead of a belt. Also the sleeves of the *chŏgori* were curved slightly.

The fine portrait (left) was taken at the Seoul YMCA in 1917 by a visiting photographer from Hawaii; (above) a bride and her doting relatives pose for a marital portrait.

These apparel modifications, especially in the Korean woman's costume, have remained *de rigueur* to the present day. Indeed, even the word *chŏgori*, which refers to either a man's or woman's traditional jacket, is a direct derivation of a Mongolian word.

Throughout these fashion-changing periods, the three preferred clothing fabrics were silk, cotton, and hemp. Silk, as aforementioned, was used nearly exclusively for court and bureaucratic wears. Cotton and hemp, however, were worn by all classes. According to some accounts, cotton too was an exclusive material until about the beginning of the Yi dynasty, because China held a firm monopoly on its cultivation and manufacture. Chinese officials refused to release cotton seeds for export, lest competitive fabric-makers would intrude on this lucrative industry. However, an early Korean ambassador to Peking cunningly obtained some cotton seeds, stashed them in his pen quill or pipe stem, smuggled them back to Korea, and thus was the cotton industry born in Korea. Or so the story notes.

'The White-Clad People'

However cotton reached Korea, it and hemp became Koreans' fabrics of common choice, and these utilitarian fabrics, usually in plain cotton white or hemp yellow were sewn into traditional Korean street attire. Because white was for centuries the primary color worn by Koreans, they became known—to themselves and to visiting outsiders—as "the white-clad people."

Korea's most unique fabric, however, is hemp, called *sambae* in Korean, which is coarse and yellowish in color, but extremely cool and comfortable during hot summer months. Hemp has traditionally been worn at times of mourning (perhaps because its unbleached, sombre color and coarse texture helps bring a mourner back in touch with nature), but it has long been popular for use in the construction of day-to-day street garments. Such gauzy clothes cut in a traditional and loose style breathe well during humid months, especially when worn with a bamboo vest and wristlets, which were designed to keep fabric off of a perspiring body.

Western clothes were introduced in the late 1800s, and again it was the trendsetting upper class which initiated a move to business suits and cocktail dresses. The first Korean to actually wear a Western suit, according to Korean fashion chronicles, was a Mr. Yun Ch'i-o, an aristocratic Korean who returned to Korea in 1899 after having studied abroad. Yun came

home in sartorial splendor ala Bond Street, and he reportedly even coerced his traditional wife into wearing Western dresses.

The Japanese attempted to suppress Korean nationalism in any way they could, and one way they did it was by forcing all students to cut off their traditional topknots, *sangt'u*, and by requiring that they wear military-style uniforms to school. These forced "customs" still prevail, even though the Japanese were removed from occupied Korea more than 30 years ago.

Since the Japanese were ousted from Korea after World War II, the biggest fashion influence has been an all-America blend of President John F. Kennedy and diplomatic corps pin stripes, G.I. and Peace Corps casual, and visiting industrial salary men. Pointed Italianate shoes, Gucci and Yves St. Laurent scarves and handbags, and permanently waved and bobbed hair are as common in Seoul as in Manhattan. It's not exactly Fifth Avenue or the Champs Elysèe, but in the locally swank Myŏngdong shopping area you'll see all types of modern Western gear being worn and voraciously purchased.

However, even in Myŏngdong you'll spot Koreans of all ages in occasional traditional wear—particularly on national holidays or when attending a social affair with distinctly Korean overtones. In other parts of town, and particularly in country towns, nearly all Korean *halmŏni* (grandmothers) and *haraboji* (grandfathers) wear the *ch'ima-chŏgori* and *paji-chŏgori* almost exclusively. Often a grandfather will wear a set of dangling, jewel-like amber buttons down his vest *(chokki)*, and everybody—men and women—sometimes don rubber shoes with traditionally upturned toes *(komusin)*.

Seldom will you see a distinguished Yi dynasty gentleman, or *yangban* Confucian complete with long beard, topknot and black horsehair hat *(kat)* in Seoul. But in old Confucian towns and villages, yes, you'll find grandfathers, sometimes by the dozens, who look as if they've just walked out of a late Yi dynasty genre painting and into your modern line of sight.

At the turn-of-the-century Seoul City women wore green military capes such as those at right. The capes long ago went out of urban fashion.

guide
in
brief

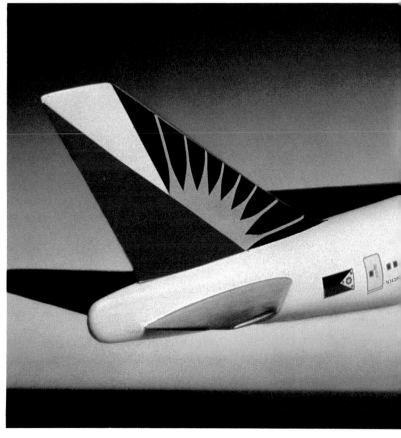

Philippine Airlines

OUT OF THE BLUE,
PHILIPPINE AIRLINES COMES SHINING THROUGH.

At **Philippine Airlines** we're flying with a new look, a new purpose and a new commitment to maintaining Asia's first airline as Asia's finest airline.

But through all the changes, one thing remains the same.

The natural warmth and charisma of the Philippines still shines on all our flights to

...ies in 21 countries around the world.

Some things you can change. And, happily,
...ne things you cannot.

1987 good
see Thaila

Majestic temples and magnificent elephants, glittering roofs and garlands of orchids, shining seas and shimmering silks, fascinating markets and fabulous silver, enchanting people and exotic cuisine…one could write a long book about the land they call Thailand (and many seasoned travellers have).

And never has there been a better year to see Thailand than 1987. For this is "Visit Thailand Year" in the Land of Smiles.

Among the kaleidoscope of festivities planned for 1987 you should try to catch some of these:

<u>Jan. 24-30. Don Chedi Memorial Fair</u> featuring historic and folk art exhibitions as well as traditional entertainment in Central Thailand.

<u>Feb. 13-15. Chiang Mai Flower Festival.</u> A million blooms, a thousand smiles. One of the unforgettable moments of your life.

<u>April 3-13. The Glory of Ayutthaya.</u> A spectacular son et lumiere, set in Ayutthaya, once the capital of Siam.

<u>April 13. Songkran Festival – The T Lunar New Year.</u> A nationwide water fest where you'll see the most extraordinary ritu Everything from "water-throwing" to the freeing of caged birds, from folk dancing beauty parades.

<u>May 9-10. Bun Bang Fai Festival.</u> "Ba indeed. Each May, in the northeast of Thaila villagers fire giant 20-metre rockets into the to ensure the monsoons come (and they alw do!). A fireworks show like no other you've seen.

<u>July 10-11. Candle Festival.</u> In the no east town of Ubon Ratchathani, beautiful embellished beeswax candles, some 25cm diameter and 2 metres high, are ceremonio paraded through the streets before being presented to temples.

<u>Sept. 23-Oct. 1. Vegetarian Festival. F</u> walking and vividly colourful parades in Phu

MNC&H/THA/4702J

reasons to
d this year.

brate the Vegetarian Festival of Thailand's
nese descendants.

Oct. 16. Royal Barge Procession. An
ada of brilliant colours, pageantry and rare
ndour not to be missed.

Nov. 5. Loy Krathong. Celebrated
on-wide, this is Thailand's loveliest festival
n, under the full moon, Thais from all walks
fe honour water spirits and wash away the
ious year's sins by floating away onto rivers
waterways small banana-leaf boats bearing a
ed candle, incense, a flower and a small coin.

The former capital of Sukhothai
ides a particularly picturesque setting for
festival.

Nov. 14-15. The Elephant Round-Up.
seen 100 elephants enact a mediaeval War
de? You will if you come to Surin in north-
Thailand for this extraordinary display of
igence, strength and gentleness.

Nov. 26-Dec. 4. River Kwai. Come to a

thrilling son et lumiere spectacle set around the
world-famous bridge.

Nov. 22. Bangkok Marathon. A major
sporting event commemorating His Majesty the
King's 60th Birthday Anniversary.

Dec. 15. Light and Sound Presentation. A
glittering occasion not to be missed at the Royal
Grand Palace and the Temple of the Emerald
Buddha.

These are only a small selection of the
truly stunning special events that mark 1987 as
Visit Thailand Year – events that also include a
Floral Float Contest in March and the Ploughing
Ceremony on May 8 which marks the beginning
of the official rice-planting season.

Make your holiday plans now. And make
sure you fly on Thailand's own
airline, Thai International.

Where the exotic sensations *Thai*
that are Thailand start from the moment you
step on board.

Don't leave home without them.

American Express ® International Inc. Travel Related Services.

GUIDE IN BRIEF

Traveling to Korea

By Air:

Kimp'o International Airport, 24 kilometers west of Seoul, receives more than 200 flights weekly from Japan, Taiwan, Hong Kong, the Philippines, Thailand, Singapore, and other world destinations. It is served from the United States by Korean Air Lines (Korea's national flag carrier), Japan Airlines, and Northwest Orient among others. Carriers routed through Seoul include Cathay Pacific, China Airlines. Malaysia Air Service and Singapore Airlines.

Seoul can often be added as a stopover on North-east Asia air tickets at no extra cost. It is less than 13 air hours from the U.S. West Coast, 2½ hours from Tokyo and 3½ hours from Hong Kong.

Flight connections from Tokyo, Fukuoka, and Osaka, Japan, may be made to Pusan at the southern tip of Korea, and to Cheju-do, the southernmost Korean island.

By Sea:

The overnight *Pukwan* ferry to Pusan disembarks from Shimonoseki, Japan, at 5 p.m. every day except Saturday. First and second class "western style" berths are available on this 952-passenger ferry. The adaptable traveler, however, may want to try the economy Japanese-style "suite"—a communal cabin with a mat-padded floor (blankets and straw pillows are provided). There are discount fares for round-trip passengers, students, and children under 12 years old.

The top deck of the *Pukwan* is a pleasant, breezy vantage point for a first hour sail before dusk, as the ferry chugs past islets that trail into the East Sea. At 6 p.m. the ship's *mogyok-t'ang* (Korean-style bathroom) opens until 8 p.m. and features a hot tub for passengers' leisure and soaking pleasure. Dinner fare is nothing special and is pricey. Travelers are advised to pack *kim-pap* (laver-wrapped rice and vegetable rolls), hard-boiled eggs, fresh fruit, juice and other snacks to tide themselves over to the next day. Japanese and Korean beer and spirits are served in a dark, shippy bar on the second deck.

The *Pukwan* pulls into the "Land of the Morning Calm" at 8.30 am.

Note: The outgoing *Kampu* ferry runs from Pusan to Shimonoseki at the same time the *Pakwan* ferry sets out. For more information, contact:

Tokyo Office: (03) 567-0971
Osaka Office: (06) 345-2245
Shimonoseki Office: (0832) 66-8211
Seoul Office: 752-9716
Pusan Office: 463-3161/8

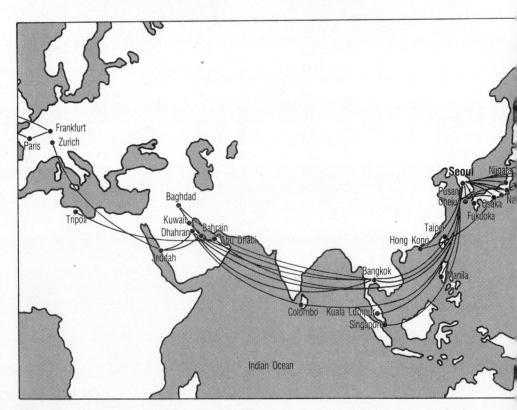

Travel Advisories

Immigration

Visitors to Korea must present a valid passport or travel document. Except for those whose itineries include cholera-infected areas, no certificate of vaccination is required. Tourists in transit with confirmed flight onward may stay in five days without visa. For longer stays visas are required of all except: citizens of Austria, Chile, Greece, Mexico, and Switzerland, who are permitted 90 days; citizens of Belgium, Denmark, Finland, Iceland, Italy, Lesotho, Luxembourg, the Netherlands, Norway, Spain, Surinam, Sweden, Turkey, the United Kingdom, and West Germany, 60 days; and citizens of France and Tunisia, 30 days.

On departure, there is a 1500 won airport tax.

Customs

Visitors may bring in 400 cigarettes, 50 cigars or 250 grams of pipe and 100 grams of powdered tobacco, two bottles of liquor and two ounces of perfume. Items needed for personal use (except certain exclusive goods such as vehicles, guns and musical instruments) may be brought into Korea duty free, but visitors must leave with these personal effects. Literature and items deemed "subversive" or "detrimental to public interest" are prohibited.

Korean antiques and cultural properties dating earlier than 1910 should be checked and appraised by the Cultural Property Presevation Bureau near the Capitol Building (tel: 725-3053) and a permit should be secured. For five or fewer antiques checking may be done at the Bureau's Kimp'o Airport office (tel: 66-0106). Even good imitations should be checked to prevent hassles at the airport. A limit of three kilograms of red ginseng with a sales receipt also may be taken out of the country.

Currency

Procuring won, Korean currency, outside Korea is virtually impossible. In country, however, there are foreign exchange counters at the airport, major tourist hotels (which charge a few won per exchanged bill or traveler's check), major banks (some with branches in large hotels) and a few major department stores (e.g. Midopa and Lotte) in Seoul. The most viable currencies to carry in Korea are Japanese yen and American dollars. Other foreign currencies are difficult to exchange. Remember to retain all exchange receipts for reconversion on departure. Up to $500 may be reconverted without a receipt. As of early 1986, the exchange rate per US dollar is w890.

Won comes in 1,000, 5,000, and 10,000 denomination notes and 1, 5, 10, 50, 100, and 500 won coins.

Bank drafts for large amounts are available.

Banking hours are 9:30 a.m. to 4:30 p.m. Monday through Friday, 9:30 a.m. to 1:30 p.m. Saturday.

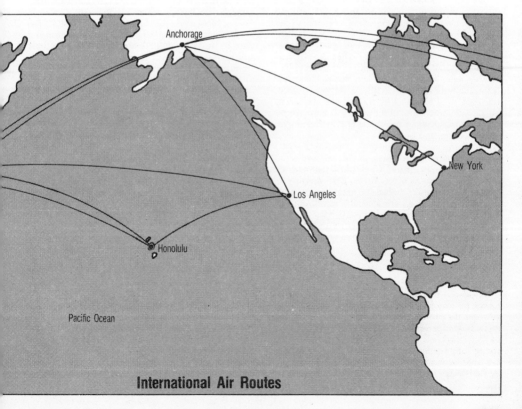

International Air Routes

Credit Cards

American Express Cards, BankAmericard-Visa, Master Charge, and Diners Club cards are popularly accepted in major hotels and restaurants.

Time Conversion

International time differences are staggered as follows:

Korea	12 noon today
Japan	12 noon today
Hawaii	5 p.m. yesterday
San Francisco	7 p.m. yesterday
New York	10 p.m. yesterday
London	3 a.m. today
Paris	4 a.m. today
Bonn	4 a.m. today
Bangkok	10 a.m. today

Climate

Korea's location in the mid-latitudes and East-Asian Monsoon Belt means four distinct seasons with varying moods. A spring thaw comes in mid-April and lasts little more than two months. Early spring northwesterly gusts bring swirls of golden dust from the Gobi Desert and a light rain. As summer approaches, humid southerlies vie for control and the spring drizzle becomes an occasional downpour by summer (June–October).

July and August are the hottest, most humid months, especially in the inland basin around Taegu; the temperature there climbs into the upper 20°C to lower 30°C. Autumn, by far the most splendid time to be in the country, comes in late October when the air currents shift back to the crisp northerlies. This climatic ideal intensifies by the end of November when the Siberian freeze whips down the peninsula for six months in a cycle of three consecutive cold days followed by four milder days. The northern inland region of the peninsula has a winter temperature mean of minus 20°C (Chungkangjin, north Korea, the peninsula's coldest spot, has a temperature mean in January of minus 20.8°C) while the southern provinces, in contrast, winter in less severe temperature (Cheju-do's temperature mean for January is 4°C). The coldest months are January and February when the temperature drops to minus 12° to 1.5°C. The favorable months in Korea are April (50°F or 10°C in Seoul), May (60°F or 16°C), June and September just before and after the summer rains (66°F or 19°C) and in October (54°F or 12°C).

What to Wear

Influenced by climate and occasion, clothing in Korea follows function rather than style. Business suits are the proper mode, even in the summer, for metropolitan business activities. Otherwise, dress is casual. Backless and mini-dresses and shorts, though appropriate for muggy weather, are not acceptable wear in public. An umbrella, sunglasses, and rainy day footwear are practical accessories to pack.

Medical Advice

Immunizations are administered at the International Clinic at Severance Hospital, which uses disposable needles, and at the Seoul Quarantine Office to the right of the USO compound in Kalwŏl-dong, Yongsan-ku.

Many kinds of medicines and health care goods—from bottled sweetened vitamin tonics to contraceptives—are available at local pharmacies. Many drugs are imported. Except for the sales of narcotics and barbiturates, there is little government control over these businesses, and drugs are sometimes diluted or mixed, repackaged, and then sold. Placèbos are not unheard of. Hospital pharmacies are more reliable drug outlets.

Dentists and optometrists are generally reliable and their work is reasonably priced.

Major hotels have house doctors. For medical attention elsewhere, check the directory in this book.

Transportation

The majority of people living in Seoul depend on public transportation. According to 1978 government statistics, 70 percent of the traffic was handled by approximately 5,000 city buses; 11 percent by subway; and 7 percent by 12,000 taxis. Since then, a special fleet of 1,000 "radio call" taxis has been added to the streets. Privately chauffeured cars, though heavily taxed, are common.

The subway is also heavily used and it is the most convenient form of public transportation for visitors. It covers 116.5 kilometers with four lines and hooks up with the Korean National Railroad. Trains run from 5 a.m. to midnight at three minute intervals during rush hours, and six minute intervals at other times.

Getting to Seoul from Kimp'o Airport

Three transportation alternatives to and from downtown Seoul are: taxi (about w4000), the airport bus (w500), and regular city buses (w130). Taxis are queued in front of the customs exit door, ready to whisk passengers off to any destination.

There are two airport buses which run every 20 minutes from 6:30 a.m. to 10:30 p.m. daily. Follow the signs at the airport to the stop in front of the terminal. Line 1 runs from Kimp'o to the Seoul Garden Hotel, the Koreana Hotel, Sheraton Walker-Hill and back. Line 2 runs from Kimp'o to the Palace Hotel, the Express Bus Terminal in Panpodong, the Riverside Hotel, Nam Seoul Hotel, the Korea Exhibition Center, the Olympic Sports Complex and back. Both bus trips cost w550 and take about one hour to Walker Hill and 45 minutes to the Sport Complex.

City bus #41 runs every five minutes from the airport to Midop'a Department Store in downtown Seoul. It costs w130 and pick-up point is at the bus terminal next to the airport parking lot. However, for the traveler with a lot of baggage, the city bus is not recommended.

City Buses

During less hectic commuting hours, getting around on the local city bus can be interesting, quick and cheap. The driver usually turns up his radio so all may listen to the local baseball game, a melodrama, or to the latest rock'n roll or classical hits. Confucian ethics generally prevail on board the bus: students offer their seats to mothers toting babies and to grandfolk, and out of mutual consideration, those seated relieve those standing of their schoolbooks and shopping bags. Smoking is prohibited.

Buses run frequently from 5 a.m. to around 11:30 p.m. daily. Tokens available at most stops cost w120. Fares paid in cash cost an extra 10 won, payable upon entrance.

In addition to the regular city buses, there are express buses, which follow similar routes but with fewer stops and for a somewhat higher fare (w350). These are designed for commuter use and generally make few stops downtown.

A word of caution: beware of pickpockets on the bus and at crowded bus stops.

Destinations are written on the side of the bus in han'gŭl and on street signs at the bus stops. Route maps for the entire system are virtually non-existent and change so frequently that it is impossible to keep track. The routes are mapped out on a panel inside the bus, but destinations are again written only in han'gŭl. The best way to get around the matter is to take the subway, and with directions from a hotel concierge or a business partner it is possible to brave the crowds. Two rules of thumb: when the bus comes, run to where it stops and leap on; at the other end, get to the exit before the bus stops and jump off just as fast.

Taxis

By far the most expedient public transport, taxis are everywhere—weaving in and out of city traffic and darting along rural roads. Fare for regular cabs begins at w600 for the first two kilometers and w50 for each additional 300 metres. The meter also runs on time when movement is slower than 15 kilometers per hours. The special beige radio call taxis are more expensive: w1,000 for the first two kilometers and w100 for each additional 400 meters. (For call taxi service, check the directory in this book.)

Cabs may be hailed to curbside and shared with other passengers bound in the same direction. Each passenger pays only for the distance he travels (two or more travelings as one party pay as one passenger). This taxi-sharing system is called hapsong.

After midnight, passengers are expected to pay a 20 percent surcharge on taxi fares. The driver should have a chart available listing officially calculated surcharge totals.

Long-distance rides can be bargained for. Few drivers understand English, so try to have your destination written in han'gŭl before entering the cab.

U.S. military I.D. holders may also use Army-Air Force Exchange taxis, which charge slightly higher rates in dollars.

Kiamaster pick-up trucks transport bulky baggage and packages at metered and negotiated rates.

Car Rentals

Thus far there is only one car rental service in business—Korea Rent-a-Car, affiliated with the American Hertz Rent-a-Car Service operation. They have four Seoul offices: one at Kimp'o Airport, one in the Chosun Hotel, one in the Lotte Hotel, and the main office in Hannamdong. There is also an international reservation line (tel: 02-752-1851). Check the directory in this book for telephone listings.

Inter-City Buses

Eight expressways cut across the farmlands and mountains of Korea: the Kyungjin (Seoul—Inchon); Yongdong (Seoul—Kangnung); Tonghae (Kangnung—Pohang); Kuma (Taegu—Masan); Kyongbu (Seoul—Pusan); Namhae (Masan—Kwangju); Honam (Kwangju—Taejon); and the '88 Olympic (Taegu—Kwangju) Expressways.

There are three kinds of inter-city buses: kosok (highway express bus—the speediest, and therefore the most dangerous), chikhaeng (first class local and direct route), and wanheang (roundabout with frequent stops). Because of the high rate of inter-city bus accidents, trains are strongly recommended. It is advised to buy bus tickets in advance for a reserved seat. Listed below are eight main bus stations in Seoul and their more popular destinations (check Seoul map for locations):

1. **Kangnam Kosok Bus Terminal**
   Located across the Han River in Banpo-dong; provides the only express bus service to cities out of Seoul. (tel: 591-3402; 598-4151)
2. **Tongbu Bus Terminal**
   In Majang-dong; several meters away from city bus #41 stop; service to Ch'unch'on, Sorak, Sokch'o, Yangyang, Yongmun-sa, Kangnung, Yoju, Chungju, Kwangju, Wonju, Andong. (tel: 966-6760)
3. **Nambu Bus Terminal**
   In south Yongsan along the main road; service to Kanghwa-do, Kosam, Taech'on Beach, Puyo, Kongju, Chonju, Songni-san, Ch'ongju, Taejon. (tel: 798-3355)
4. **Sinchon Bus Terminal**
   Service to Kanghwa-do: 6 a.m. to 8 p.m.; trip takes 1 hour 15 minutes. (tel: 324-0611)
5. **Miari Bus Terminal**
   Service to Soyo-san (north of Uijongbu, and Tongduch'on) for mountain climbing. (tel: 980-7638)
6. **Ch'onho-dong Bus Terminal**
   Located southeast of Seoul city limits; service to Namhan-sansong Fortress in southern Seoul, Kwangju. (tel: 478-1563)
7. **Yok Chon Terminal**
   Across the street from Seoul Train Station, to the left of the Daewoo building; service to Suwon, Inch'on, P'yongt'aek. (tel: 755-0988)
8. **Seoul Sobu Bus Terminal**
   In Pulang-dong (northern Sodaemun-gu); ser-

vice to Haengju-sansong, Uijongbu. (tel: 388-5103)

Guided Bus Tours

Seoul city tours and excursions outside the capital are conducted by numerous commercial tour guide agencies. Agencies with English and Japanese speaking guides are listed in the directory section of this book.

Two organizations which plan tours particularly for resident foreigners and welcome outsiders are:

The Royal Asiatic Society (RAS)
Christian Building, 6th floor
Chong-no 5-ka
Tel: 763-9483
The USO (United States Service Organization)
104 Kalwŏl-dong, Yongsan-ku
Tel: 792-3028

KTB Tours

The Korea Tourist Bureau offers tours to Panmunjŏm, the Folk Village, Kyongju and Pusan, Kyongju, and around Seoul by day or night. Reservation counters can be found at the Hotel Lotte (tel: 778-0150), the Chosun Hotel (tel: 755-0207), the Hyatt (tel: 798-0681), the Shilla (tel: 295-3731), Hotel Koreana (tel: 724-2930), the Hilton (tel: 754-7380), the Ambassador (tel: 269-5675), and Sheraton Walker-Hill (tel: 444-3865).

The main office number in Kangnamgu is (tel: 5855--1191).

Tours to Panmunjŏm must be reserved 48 hours in advance with full name, nationality and passport number. The trip, including lunch and a "briefing," takes eight hours and kids under 10 years of age are not admitted. Travelers must wear good clothes and pointing at the DMZ or speaking with north Korean officers at the DMZ is strictly forbidden. Buses leave Monday through Friday from the Lotte Hotel, but guests registered at the Chosun can be picked up there as well.

Subway

Korea's subway system, which opened in August 1974, runs from Seoul Railway Station to six major destinations: Chongnyang-ni Train Station and Songbuk district to the north, and, connected with electrical tracks, to Inch'on (39 kilometers west), Suwon (41.5 kilometers south), Chamsil and Kuro. Trains come every five minutes. Smoking is prohibited in the cars. Following are points of interest within walking distance of each subway stop within the city walls:

1. **Seoul Train Station**
2. **City Hall (T'aepyŏng-no)**
   City Hall
   Tŏksu Palace
   British Embassy
   Major hotels, banks, department stores

Route Map of Subway

LEGEND
LINE 1
LINE 2
LINE 3 ('85.6)
LINE 4 ('85.6)
K.N.R.

Seoul Tourist Information Center
3. **Chonggak (Chong-no)**
Posin-gak (city bell tower)
Bookstores (with foreign-language sections)
Korean National Tourism Corporation
Ch'ogye-sa (Buddhist Temple)
Communications Memorial Center
Seoul Immigration Office
Kyŏngbok Palace, National Museum, Folk
Museum
Embassies of U.S.A., Japan, Canada
Sejong Cultural Center
Yi Sun-sin statue at Kwanghwa-mun Intersection
4. **Chong-no 3-ka**
Pagoda Park and shopping arcade
Chongmyo (Royal Confucian Shrine)
Insa-dong (Mary's Alley antique shops, art galleries, etc.)
5. **Chong-no 5-ka**
East Gate marketplace
Herb shops
6. **Tongdae-mun**
Big East Gate
Seoul Baseball Stadium

Trains

The introduction of the locomotive to Korea was not without political motives. Several foreign powers, including Russia, Japan, France, and the United States, bid hard for the contract, which was awarded to an American, James R. Morse. Soon after initiating construction with standard 1.435 meter gauge rails, Morse, beset with financial difficulties, was forced to pass the project on to the Japanese. The Korean government directed Japan to complete the line in the standard gauge system Morse used rather than import narrow gauge rails in from Japan. The first railroad, which linked Seoul to Inch'ŏn, was opened in September 1899. Other major lines were laid by the Japanese, including lines originating in Mokp'o, Masan, and Pusan to Seoul and to Sinuiju in North Korea, which linked with the Trans-Siberian Railway. At one time, a serious traveler could train from Pusan to Paris. The railroad suffered considerable damage during various wars, but since 1953 the railway system in South Korea has been steadily modernized over the years to accommodate tourists comfortably.

Today, five kinds of train services are available. Their classifications in order of increasing speed, comfort and punctuality are: *wanhaeng* (stops at each station along the way), *pot'ong kuphaeng* (ordinary express with berths, stops frequently and runs at night), *tukkup* (limited express, reserved seats available, occasionally with diner car), *udung* (air-conditioned), and *Saemaul Ho* (luxury, air-conditioned superexpress with diner car. It is wisest to purchase tickets in advance, especially during the summer vacation months. Round-trip tickets are not sold.

Domestic Flights

Korean Air Lines conducts the only domestic air travel service. There are daily flights from Seoul to Cheju-do (56 minutes), Pusan (40 minutes), Taegu (40 minutes), Yosu (70 minutes), Kwangju (50 minutes), Sokch'o (50 minutes), Chinju (70 minutes), and Ulsan (50 minutes). Tickets are available at major hotels and tourist and travel agencies. Security at the airport is tight; passengers and baggage are checked and umbrellas, cameras, knives, and certain other articles are withheld during the flight. Tourist passports are neccessary.

Domestic Ferries

Numerous ferries and fishing boats make regular connections between the coasts and the outlying islands. The schedules change frequently and boats will cancel trips at any time if the weather gets bad. Travel arrangements should be made with travel agents and time should be allowed for last minute changes if you travel during the monsoon season.

Several routes on the south coast in the Hallyŏ Waterway may be traveled either by ferry or by hydrofoil. Although the hydrofoil is faster, it is small and cramped. If time allows, the ferry is by far the more pleasant mode of transportation and it allows the passengers to take in some scenery. There's not much of a view from the hydrofoil and those prone to seasickness should definitely avoid it.

Accommodation

Six kinds of accommodation are open to the visiting foreigner:

Hotels

For all the comforts, conveniences, and privacy of home, nothing beats western-style hotels—which range in standard and price.

Yogwan

Korean guest might request: *pori ch'a* (barley tea), *Yo* and *ibul* (mattress and blanket, respectively), *pegae* (pillow), ondol (heated floor), and inexpensive home-cooked Korean meals. Some inns prepare a communal hot bath. Prices range from w5000 on up for single occupancy.

Yoinsuk

The *yoinsuk*, another type of Korean inn, offers lodging in a private compound and isn't as consistently clean, convenient, nor as appealing as the *yogwan*. But the room rates are usually lower. Accommodation is native all the way.

Hasuk Chip

The *hasuk chip* (boarding house) has its place among students, working bachelors, and itinerants. Rooms are rented by the month, usually to long-term residents. Rent includes very simple home-cooked meals.

Setbang

For the working foreigner, the *setbang*, a rented room in a local home is yet another option. Except for the fact that he happens to share the same roof with others, the tenant is generally on his own.

Youth Hostels

A chain of youth hostels has been established in many of the provinces, and such facilities are open to international members. Menbership is open at any of their branches. Some of the hostels, such as the Seoul Bando Youth Hostel and the Puyŏ Youth Hostel, are a combination hostel-hotel, with communal rooms as well as plush, private rooms and suites. For a list of youth hostels in Korea, refer to the hotel directory which follows.

Communications

Mail

The first modern post office was opened in 1884 in Seoul on An'guk Street to the right of the Chogyesa Buddhist temple. It was burned during a political riot soon after opening, but was reconstructed into a Communications Memorial Center in 1969. Old telegram sheets designed in 1904, a map showing the layout of telephone subscribers in Inch'ŏn in 1900, offical seals, records, and documents and other relics are displayed. Also, a collection of stamps—from the first T'aekuk design stamp in 1884 to the 1978 dedication of the Sejong Cultural Center—presents the commemoration of some key historical events in the country. Commemorative stamps sold there, at regular post offices and in *up'yo* (stamp) shops around town. The memorial is open business hours weekdays and until noon on Saturday.

The contemporary central post office, however, is located on Chungmu Street across from the Chinese Embassy a block east of Shinsegye Department Store. Two other post office branches are located near the corner of T'aep'yŏng-no and Chong-no and on Yulkok Street between the U.S. Embassy Housing Compound and the An'guk Immigration Office. General post office hours are 9 a.m. to 6 p.m. Monday to Saturday.

Aerograms are w350. A 10-gram airmail letter to the USA is w440, to France or Germany w470, and to Hong Kong or Japan w370. Postcard rates are w350 to the USA. w380 to France or Germany, and w280 to Hong kong or Japan. (Postal rates listed were good as of December 1985.)

Letter to the U.S.and Europe take 9 to 14 days, and vice-versa, as all mail is subject to government inspection.

Public Telephone
Intra-City Calls

Red, orange, and green public pay phones take two w20 coins per intra-city call. The call automatically disconnects after three minutes. Inter-city and overseas calls cannot be placed from these phones.

Inter-City Calls

Large rectangular public telephones are used for inter-city calls. To place a direct dial inter-city call, use the following prefixes before the desired phone number:

Anyang	0343	Kyŏgju	0561
Cheju City	0641	Masan	1551
Ch'olwŏn	0353	Mokp'o	0631
Chonju	0652	P'ohang	1562
Ch'ŏngju	0441	Pusan	051
Ch'unch'on	0361	Seoul	02
Inch'on	032	Sŏgwip'o	0642
Iri	0653	Songnam	0342
Kanghwa-Si	0349	Suwŏn	1331
Kangnŭng	0391	Taegu	053
Kumi	0546	Taejon	0452
Kuri	0346	Uijŏngbu	0351
Kwangju	062	Ulsan	0552

Telegrams

The Korean Int'l Telecommunications Office at 21, 1-ga Chungmuro Chung-gu handles telegram messages over the telephone (tel: 115). To make sure the message is conveyed correctly, write it out at the office. There are two types of telegrams: Urgent, which takes about six hours to reach its destination, Ordinary (ORD), 12 hours, and Lettergram (LT), about 24 hours.There is also a special telegram service for the press.

Office hours are 9 a.m. to 5 p.m. Monday to friday, 9 a.m. to 1 p.m. Saturday.

Overseas Calls

Overseas calls can be dialed direct from major hotels by dialing the international access code (001) plus a country code and the number. To call from private lines, you must dial the operator and calls are placed immediately. To book a call from Seoul to the USA, France, Germany, Canada, Australia, Hong Kong, Italy, the Philippines, Singapore, Spain or Taiwan, call 1035. For Japan, Saudi Arabia and other countries call 1037. Information and complaints are given and taken at 1030. From Pusan, dial 117 for all countries.

The Press

There are twelve national newspapers including two English newspapers. All national dailies print 46 pages a week while most of the provincial papers publish 24 to 36 pages. The two English-language papers,*The Korean Herald and The Korean Times*, use international wire services and are available at news-stands and bookstores except on Mondays, during the New Years holiday (January 1st to the 3rd), and on special national holidays. The pacific edition of *Stars and Stripes*, a U.S. military newspaper, is sold at U.S. military installations and areas nearby, and to subscribers in Seoul. *The Asian Wall Street Journal* and *The Far Eastern Economic Re-*

view are also circulated locally. All publications must undergo government censorship.

Periodicals

Weeklies, semi-weeklies, bi-weekies, monthlies and bi-monthlies flood the bookstores. The popular English language periodicals are *Korea Journal* by UNESCO and *Business Korea*, monthly and weekly newsmagazines respectively. *Time* and *Newsweek* are prominently displayed in bookstores. (Other foreign publications are available at diplomatic mission libraries.) Among the distinguished local periodicals with a readership of over 30,000 are *Madang, Chung Kyung Munhwa*, and *Shin Dong-a*. A cultural magazine, *Korea Quarterly*, published in English is available in major bookstores and through subscriptions (call the Royal Asiatic Society: 763-9483).

Radio

In the winter of 1980, Korean radio broadcasting was consolidated into three broadcasting stations: Korean Broadcasting Systems (KBS), a government-owned station; Munhwa Broadcasting Company, owned by a semi-government foundation; and the Christian Broadcasting System, which was established by religious sponsors in 1945. U.S. Armed Forces Korea Network (AFKN) offers English programs with news on the hour, 24 hours a day, to its military community.

Television

Television broadcasting in Korea began in 1956 with a privately-owned, commercial station which burned down three years later. On December 31, 1961, the government established its own network, the Korea Broadcasting Service (KBS-TV). Presently, there are two major Korean networks: KBS-TV, and MBC-TV (Munhwa Broadcasting Company). A third network, AFKN-TV (American Forces Korean Network), caters essentially to the U.S. military community and to others peripherally. Broadcasting hours vary from station to station (shorter on weekdays, longer on weekends). Daily program schedules are listed in the English-language papers. Monthly subscription fees are charged to help defray program expenses. Therefore, registration of television sets is required. In 1977, government records showed a rate of 1.8 television sets per household. TVs are not limited to houeholds, however, and are commonly found turned on in local cafes and shops.

Museums, Cultural Centers

Korea's cultural history is vividly displayed in numerous museums (municipal and national) and cultural centers. Drama theaters and libraries present more contemporary perspectives. Listed below are the larger public and private museums and cultural centers. For a more definitive list, refer to the cultural map in the Korean Art feature section.

Museums

1. **National Museum and National Folk Museum**
   Located on the grounds of Kyŏngbok Palace, the National Museum houses excavated and national treasures. The National Folk Museum just west of the National Museum renders articles and settings of traditional folk life. The museum buildings are replicas of three architectural national treasures: Palsang-jŏn (the five-story pagoda at Popju-sa), Hwaom-sa and Kŭmsan-sa.

2. **National Museum of Modern Art**
   A permanent collection of Korean modern art and special shows during the year are held in this museum at Tŏksu Palace.

3. **Onyang Folk Museum**
   The largest and finest collection of Korean folk art is exhibited in Onyang, a pleasant country town southwest of Seoul. It is especially rich in crafts, but is limited in folk painting.

4. **Puyo and Kongju Museums**
   Museum collections include archeological finds made in the vicinites of these two ancient Paekche (18 B.C.—660 A.D.) capitals. At the Kongju Museum, treasures from King Muryong's tomb, excavated in 1971, are exhibited. The tomb itself is a few miles away and is open to the public.

5. **Kwangju Museum**
   This two-story museum in Chŏllapuk-do was recently built specially to house Yuan Dynasty bounty salvaged from a sunken 600-year-old Chinese ship discovered in west coast waters in 1976. Cholla-do treasures are displayed on the second floor.

6. **Kyŏngju Museum**
   Opened in 1975 on the site of an ancient Silla building, the Kyŏngju Museum is located on the outskirts of Kyŏngju town. Silla dynasty articles, including the famous Emille Bell, the largest Buddhist temple bell in Korea (cast in 771 A.D.), are on display. There is also a folk museum in the center of town.

7. **Ancient Tombs (Tumuli) Park, Kyŏngju**
   This cluster of 21 tombs built before the unification of Silla lies on the eastrn fringe of the city. Excavation from 1973 to 1975 led to the discovery of King Mich'u's tomb (reign: 262–285 A.D.) and the tomb with the mysterious "Flying Horse" painted on a saddle. Some of the original relics and some replicas (many originals are in the National Museum) are exhibited in glass cases for public viewing.

8. **The Korean Folk Village**
   In Suwŏn, south of Seoul, a complete traditional Korean village has been recreated for visitors to wander through and observe the folk customs and lifestyle being re-enacted. Food and drink are prepared and sold at profitable prices.

9. Emileh Museum

The world's largest collection of Korean folk painting is newly housed in Songni-san, near Popju Temple. The Emileh Museum is privately owned by Zo Zayong, author of several art and cultural books about Korea.

10. Sejong University Museum

Located in eastern Seoul near Children's Park, this museum is one of six folk museums in Korea. Over 3,000 articles, especially of traditional dress, ornaments, furniture, and art paintings are on display.

Cultural Centers

1. Sejong Cultural Center

Opened in 1978 near Kwanghwa-mun, the Sejong Cultural Center holds foreign and Korean classical and contemporary concerts and dramatic plays. (tel: 722-2721/8)

2. Korea House

Situated on the slopes of Namsan off Toegye-ro. Korea House stages free folk dance performances at 3 p.m. on Saturdays and Sundays. Art displays decorate the rooms and Korea-related books are sold in their bookshop. A Korean restaurant overlooks an oriental garden. (tel: 266-9101)

3. National Theater and Classical Music Institute

Just past Tower Hotel on the slopes of Namsan is the school where many of the nation's finest classical musicians of different genres, including Royal Court musicians, practice and teach their art. Performances are given in the concert hall. Check the entertainment section of newspapers for engagements. (tel: 253-1153)

4. Drama Center

The Drama center is off Namsan Street in Yechang-dong. Everything from P'ansori to Shakespeare is performed. Check newspapers for current performances. (tel: 778-0261)

5. Open Music Hall

Periodic Korean and western concerts are given here on the western slopes of Namsan near the Central National Library.

6. Space Center

Housed in an architectural artpiece near the Secret Garden of Ch'angdŏk Palace, the Space Center stages a variety of shows from classical *kayakŭm* (Korean zither) solos to Dixieland jazz to drama. The Center also publishes a cultural magazine called *Space*. (tel: 763-0771/3. ext. 23)

7. Center Culturèl Français

Across the street to the right side of Kyŏngbok Palace just past the Hyundai Modern Art Gallery and Andre Kim's boutique is the Center Culturèl Fançais, a French Embassy cultural contribution to Seoul. In this multi-media oasis, one can browse through a modern art gallery, sit and view French cultural videotapes and, for a token w100, watch a classic French film (subtitled in English) in a small theater downstairs. The CCF is open from 12.00 p.m. to 6.00 p.m. daily. A variety of films are shown from noon to 6 p.m., except Sundays.

Libraries, Reading Centers

Literature

Reading material in English or European languages are difficult to locate in Seoul but there are several places where titles can be regularly found. The major hotels have bookstores which carry periodicals although they are usually late in coming and are extremely expensive. For the lastest issues (also at high prices), the most reliable bookstore is in the basement of the Kyobo Building which is near the American Embassy on Taepyong-ro 2-ga.

Used books and magazines can be found in Myong-dong just across from the Chinese Embassy. There are several small shops here which are overflowing with books and old magazines which are sold for much less than their original cost. You can also trade in your own used paperbacks or bargain for lower prices, particularly if you purchase several books at a time.

On the outskirts of It'aewŏn, about halfway toward the third tunnel through Namsan, there is another foreign bookstore which both buys and sells. The titles here are limited, however, especially adventure stories and war novels. The owner also drives a rather hard bargain.

1. Royal Asiatic Society (RAS) (tel: 763-9483)

The RAS is the Korean chapter of an international British association. Its office is in the Christian Center Building (136-46 Yunji-dong, Chongno-ku) near Chong-no 5-ka. There you'll find, most books written locally in English about Korea and a complete collection of their magazine, Transactions, which contains Korea-related articles that have been written by lecturing members since 1900. Visitors are welcome to sign up for tours conducted by the RAS and by an affiliate, the Korea Art Club.

2. Korean Research Center (tel: 723-4533)

The Korean Red Cross is located at Pyong-dong, Chongno-ku, near Sodae-mun Rotary. The Center publishes cultural research articles in Korea with some translations in English but also provides a quiet library of old and recent Korea-related books written by foreign explorers, diplomats, and expatriates. Some current periodicals written in other languages are available. The Center is open weekdays from 9 a.m. to 5 p.m.

3. United States Information Service (USIS) (tel: 732-2601)

USIS offers an art gallery and library for public viewing and study. It is located across the street from the Lotte Hotel on Ŭlchi-ro. Passport identification is needed to enter the library. Art gallery hours are 8:30 a.m. to 5 p.m. weekdays and library hours are 9:30 a.m. to 6 p.m. weekdays.

4. UNESCO Library

Back issues of the *Korea Journal* and *The Courier*, Korean cultural magazines, are avail-

able, the latter in English, French, and Spanish. The library is also stocked with other reference publications.
5. **Ewha, Sogang, Yonsei,** and other universities also invite foreigners to use their library facilities.

Performing Arts, Other Media

Cinemas

Giant painted billboards of *kungfu* duels, infernal disasters, love, and despair draw thousands of people to Korea's commercial theaters. Foreign films, including an occasional American film, also are screened, usually with Korean subtitles. Films undergo government censorship and sometimes are edited if too long to allow impressarios to squeeze in a maximum number of showings. During cold months, hot water pipes heated on the floor provide some warmth in the theater. Check the entertainment section of *The Korea Times* or *The Korea Herald* for current engagements.

Modern Drama Theaters in Seoul

Cecil Theater
3-2, Chung-dong
Chung-ku
Tel: 723-5773

Drama Center
8-19 Yejang
Chung-ku
Tel: 778-0261

Elcanto Art Theater
51 1-ga, Myong-dong
Chung-gu
Tel: 776-8035

Minye Studio
56-1 Daehyun-dong
Söpdaemun-ku
Tel: 762-7522

Munyae Theater
1-130 Tongsung-dong
Chongno-gu
Tel: 274-1151

Silhom Theater
114, Unni-dong
Chongno-ku
Tel: 765-4481

Space Theater
219 Wonsŏ-dong
Chongno-ku
Tel: 763-0771/3

Photography

Opportunities for photography in Korea abound but it is important that the visitor respects the privacy of his hosts. Koreans do not like ceremonies to be photographed and older Koreans don't like photos at all. Ask before you shoot.

A 24-shot roll of Kodachrome costs about w1800 and processing of the same about w2500. Hotel photo shops are far more expensive. Black and white film is very difficult to find in Korea. Also, you must specify the kind of processing you desire for all film—if you don't say Kodak, they'll use a local processing company which may be of lesser quality.

Korean Language Institutes

Korean language courses are offered at a few insitutes in two to three-month terms. Student visas can be arranged. Among prominent schools are:

1. **Language Teaching Research Center**
   (tel: 723-4641)
   16-17 T'aep'yong-no 1-ka
   Chong-dong, Chong-no ku
2. **Yonsei University** (tel: 392-6405)
   Korean Language Institute
   Taek 134
   Sinch'on-dong, Sodaemun-ku
3. **Ewha Womans University** (tel: 392-6405)
4. **Yongsan Education Center** (tel: 7904-3194, 7904-6708)
   (University of Maryland Program)

Local Customs, Lifestyle

The National Flag

The Korean flag, *t'aekuk ki*, was adopted as the national flag in August, 1882, not long after the "Hermit Kingdom" opened its front and back doors to foreign aggressive powers. Appropriately, the flag symbolizes the oriental *yin-yang* (in Korean, *üm-yang*) philosophy of the balance and harmony in nature of opposite forces and elements which are in perpetual motion. The colors of the flag are red, black, and blue against white. The red and blue circle in the center of the flag symbolizes the dualism of the universe. The upper red paisley represents *yang* nature: positive, masculine, active, constructive, light, heat, dignity, etc.; complemented by the lower blue paisley, *ŭm* nature: negative, feminine, passive, destructive, dark, cold, hope, etc. The black trigrams in each corner are also of Chinese origin (from the Tao Te Ch'ing). They basically symbolize the four seasons and cardinal directions. In clockwise starting with the upper left corner, the three solid bars (*K'un*) represent heaven, spring, east and benevolence; the upper right bars (*Kam*): moon, winter, north, and wisdom; lower right bars (*K'on*): earth, summer, west, and righteousness; and lower left bars (*I*): sun, autumn, south, and etiquette.

National Anthem

"Aeguk Ka" ("Love of Country"), the Korean national anthem, was written during the Japanese occupation (composer unknown) and set to music later by Ahn Eak Tai. The national anthem is played throughout the Republic every workday evening over the radio in Korean government offices and in main thoroughfares as the flag is lowered. Proper public protocol—silence and standing at attention—is requested.

Civil Defense Alert Drills

Held usually on the 15th of each month around 2 p.m., the 15-minute civil defense alert drill brings city traffic to a grinding halt. Everyone takes cover in buildings or underground arcades, temporarily abandoning their vehicles. Every few months, a 15-minute blackout drill is held around 9 p.m. Advance notice is given in the local media.

Tipping

This western custom is expected only in businesses which cater primarily to westerners. A 10 to 15 percent service charge is automatically added to major hotel room and restaurant tabs (read the bill to make sure before tipping). Airport baggage porters are tipped generously at the exit door according to a set standard. Taxi drivers do not expect a tip unless they perform extra service. They may not return the change if it is small unless it is requested. Bellhops usually receive around w150 tip per bag.

Water

Potable water is available in hotels. In establishments for locals, *bori ch'a* (roasted barley boiled in water), distinguished by its light brown color, is served instead. Another popular water substitute is *sungnyung*, tea boiled from browned rice from the bottom of a rice pot. It is also quite safe to drink water which spring from certain mountain sites at temples in the countryside. Unboiled tap water is never advised for drinking. Bottled water can be purchased for use in private residences from Diamond Water. The company will deliver the water, which costs about w500 per liter, to your doorstep on a regular basis. (Tel: 324-3907/8)

Electricity

The 100 volt current is sufficient and safe for 110 volt electrical devices. It is slowly being converted to 220 volt power.

Lost and Found

To recover lost possessions, including those left in taxis, contact the nearest police box or ask the hotel front desk clerk to help you do so. Call the Seoul police Lost and Found Center at 755-4400. For articles forgotten in taxis or trains, call the Korean Broadcasting system (tel: 780-3311) or on the railroad (tel: 755-7108). On the subway call 744-2400 or 633-0063.

Korean Names

Korean surnames, most of which are but one syllable, are easy to learn as they are to forget. The problem is that many Koreans share the same romanized surname (although some of the Chinese characters may be written differently). Referring to someone by his surname can only become confusing and futile after meeting many Koreans. To compound the problem, Korean wives retain their maiden names (but they usually will make allowances for foreigners who mistakenly call them by their husband's name). Thus, it is ideal to learn the entire Korean name.

Korean surnames were dervied from the Chinese during the early Three Kingdom Period. The most common surnames in order of the most numerous are Kim, Yi (Lee I, Rhee), and Pak (Park), followed by Choi, Chung, and Cho. Throughout the ages, surnames have dicated one's social position, a tradition still honored only in reclusive villages. Whether *yangban* (aristocrat) or *pyŏngmin* (commoner), however, one's name was recorded in a family tree book, *chokbo*, which traced one's lineage back to the origin of the clan. The *chokbo* is a kind of heirloom still updated and passed on these days.

Given names are usually two syllables and of Chinese origin. Either the first or second character is predetermined and is related to the "theory of the five elements." It is given to all family members of the same generation. The other character is freely selected.

Name Seals (Tojang)

Seals, engraved by professional artisans, are as important as personal signatures, especially on legal documents. It, too, was originally a borrowed custom from China, initially a status symbol, used by royalty. During the three Kingdoms period (57 B.C.—918 A.D.), a dethroned king had to symbolically transfer power by handing over his imperial seals.

Seals today are more popular than ever as they are used by goverment offices, companies, and organizations, and for personal flourishes on stationery. The seals are carved of ivory, stone, marble, plastic, wood, smokey topaz, jade, and other materials. the ink is made of a sticky scarlet vegetable dye which is permanent.

Defining Korean Land Boundaries

Land is defined from province to the block and street. In the city, land is boundered by *si*, city; *iku*, ward; and *dong*, precinct. In rural areas, the land divisions are: *do*, province; *si*, city or large town; *up*, town; *kun*, district; *myŏn*, township; and *ri*, residential area. Other commonly used Korean road words are *no*, *ro* or *lo* for road or street and *ka* for block.

Dining Out

Types of Eating Establishments:

Pul Koki Jip (Barbecue Meat Restaurant)

Beef (*so-koki*) and pork (*toechi-koki*) and short ribs (*kal bi*) are marinated in soy sauce, sesame oil, garlic, green onions, and toasted sesame seeds, then char-broiled.

Saengson Hoe Jip (Raw Fish Restaurant)

Fresh raw fish is served sliced with a soy sauce (*kan-chang*) or red pepper sauce (*cho-chang*). Other kinds of fish dishes such as *maeun t'ang* (hot pepper soup of fish, soybean curd, egg, and vegetables) are served.

Samgyae T'ang Jip (Ginseng Chicken Dish Restaurant)

Chicken stuffed with rice, white ginseng, and dried oriental dates are steamed and served hot. Deep-fried chicken and other chicken dishes are also served.

Mandoo Jip (Dumplings Restaurant)

Meat, vegetables, and sometimes soybean curd are stuffed into a dumpling and steamed, fried or boiled in a broth. Chinese-style cookie pastries baked in the restaurant fill the display window.

Poonsik Jip (Noodles Restaurant)

Noodle dishes are the specialty but so are easily prepared rice dishes. Some of the popular dishes are *Momil kooksoo*, buckwheat noodles served with a sweet radish sauce; *Naengmyŏn*, cold potato flour or buckwheat flour noodles topped with sliced meat, vegetables, a boiled egg, and a pepper relish sauce and ice; *K'ong kooksoo*, wheat noodles in fresh soymilk; *Odaeng kooksoo*, wheat noodles topped with oriental fishcake in a broth; *Ramyŏn*, instant noodles in instant broth; *Udong*, long, wide wheat noodles with onions, fried soybean curd, red pepper powder, and egg; *Pipim-pap*, rice topped with parboiled fern bracken, bluebell root, soysprouts, spinach, and a sunny-side-up egg, accompanied with a bowl of broth; and *Chap Chae*, rice vermicelli stir-fried with vegetables and meat slices.

Paekpan Jip (Steamed Rice Restaurant)

A bowl of rice is served with a variety of *kimch'i*, *namul* (parboiled vegetables), fish, and soup (usually made of soybean paste—the basic Korean meal. Other simple dishes, such as *naengmyŏn* and *pipim-pap* are often on the menu. In the evening, the *paekpan jip* switches into a *makkolli jip* (see Drinking section).

Posin T'ang Jip

Posin-hada means to build up one's strength. *Posin t'ang* is dog meat soup, a delicacy to the people.

Other popular Korean dishes include:
Sinsullo: chopped vegetables, meat, quail egg, fish balls, and gingko nuts in a brazier.
Sollong t'ang: rice in a beef and bone stew.
Pindaettŏk: the Korean bean flour and egg pancake, filled with different combinations of vegetables and meat.
Chinese Shantung restaurants are as popular as Korean restaurants. They are designated by a red or green door plaque draped with a red strip of cloth. Homemade wheat noodles with various sauces make for a slurpy meal, *Tchajangmyon* is a popular order: pork, seafood, and vegetable tidbits stir-fried in a sweet-sour black bean sauce, and topped with a boiled egg. Larger Chinese restaurants have a more varied menu that includes delicacies such as sweet-sour fried fish and meat.

Japanese restaurants complete with *sushi* (laver-covered rice rolls), *sashimi* (raw fish), and *tempura* (deep-fried batter-covered fish and vegetables) bars are scattered all over Seoul, and are even more common in the southern port of Pusan.

Drinking Establishments

There are at least five kinds of *sul jip* (liquor house).

Makkolli Jip

The common bar or pub is usually a small, simple cafe which serves a variety of refined rice wines and beer. *Anju* (hors d'oevres) are served at an additional cost in most places. The cheapest liquor is *soju* (sweet potato wine). *Makkolli* (rice wine), however, is the most popular people's drink and is poured from a teapot or unique clear plastic *makkolli* bottle. Other expensive grades of booze such as *popchu* (popular in Kyongju) and *ch'ungchong* (the drink of Ch'onju) are also available in some Seoul pubs.

Beer Halls

Crown and OB (Oriental Brewery) *maekchu* are the only beers brewed locally. They come either bottled *(pyong)* or draft *(saeng)*. Because of a high tax on beer, beer halls are more expensive drinking joints than *makkolli jip. Anju,* too, are comparably pricier but are nevertheless customarily ordered.

Cabarets

Often located in narrow alleyways in Mugyo-dong and Myong-dong in Seoul, cabarets are easy to notice because of the loud band music, neon signs and/or bow-tied doormen attempting to lure in passers-by. Dance hostesses inside do their part and expect a tip of at least w5000 for their efforts. Highballs and beer are served. Patronize these *jip* with caution or with a good Korean friend. Closing time is usually 11 p.m.

Salons

Salons are exclusive cabarets in a tidier setting (which customers pay for).

Nightclubs and Discos

Major western-style hotels have their own nite-clubs and discotheques. Drinks are taxed high in hotels. In Seoul there are a few disco-nightclubs in Myŏng-dong and It'aewŏn. Some are taxed high; e.g. a w3000 bottle of beer is cheap. It'aewon discos cater mostly to GIs from the nearby US 8th Army Compound. Blues, jazz and rock music are spun.

Roadside Carts

Roadside canopied carts lit in the evening with kerosene tapers serve *soju* along with *anju* specialties that vary from steaming mussels and broiled clams to fried chicken and pork. Prices are reasonable, starting at w100 for a bowl of mussels, and the environment is cozy—warm and convivial. Some carts are set up at lunchtime, but most begin business at nightfall.

Casinos

Blackjack, anyone? There are casinos in five hotels where one can gamble at roulette, poker, bacarat, craps, dice, *tai-sai* and other games of chance. Casino business hours differ from hotel to hotel. These gaming parlors are located at the following places:

Sheraton Walker Hill (Seoul)
Kwangchang-dong
Tel: 444-5261

Olympos (Inch'ŏn)
Hang-dong
Tel: (032) 72-0181

Haeundae (Pusan)
Tongnae-ke
Tel: (072) 72-1461/7

Kolon (Kyŏngju)
64 Ma-dong
Tel: (0561) 2-9001

Cheju KAL (Cheju-do)
Ido 1-ka-dong
Tel: (0641) 7-618

Cheju Hyatt
Sogwipo
Tel: (0642) 32-2046

Tearooms (Tabang)

Tabang (or *tasil*) is one of the most common signs in any Korean town. Koreans go to the *tabang* for everything but tea (in fact, the tea is free) or coffee. It is where businessmen strike deals, where students practice English with "native speakers," where friends gather to gossip, joke, and listen to music, and where lovers tryst. It is also where the honk, grind and smoke of the city is rivaled—but nobody complains. A cup of thin coffee is but a token to hours of socializing. The *tabang* has become a vital institution in contemporary Korean culture; a meeting hall outside the home and office for young and old, male and female. And with eight million souls in the capital alone, there is always room for one more tearoom to open above, below, or next to all the others.

Unlike teahouses or coffeeshops elsewhere, the Korean *tabang* provides a personal delivery service: a girl dressed in a uniform will deliver a hot cup of coffee in a scarf-wrapped thermos bottle to customers who call in orders and clearly indicate their whereabouts.

Other Pleasures

Businessmen visiting Korea, like readers of economic journals around the world, know that Koreans are reputed to be among the most diligent workers on earth, logging endless hours to keep production at a peak, and to ensure the perpetual prosperity of the country's export-oriented economy.

Foreign residents too, both old-time and new, generally concur with characterization, but also know that the "Land of the Morning Calm" harbors some of the world's most hearty and enthusiastic drinkers, who are often loath to abandon their watering holes before dawn.

These two stereotypes do seem to complement each other, since a people who work hard might naturally be expected to play hard as well, but there is yet a third side to the modern-day Korean—a passive but pleasing contrast to the other two, which is somewhat less well know to the outside world.

Timeless Delights

During the Yi Dynasty, a proper Confucian gentleman might have found calm and contentment in an after-dinner ritual with his pipe, filling its small brass bowl with Korean tobacco, and drawing slowly through the long bamboo stem to cool the soothing smoke. His descendants today can seek diversion in a variety of establishments offering all manner of indulgences and female companionship. These range from beer halls where the waitress might share a drink and squeeze one's hand, to secret salons where the whiskey flows freely and the customer's every wish is his hostess-cum-partner's command.

Somewhere between those ancient and modern extremes on the spectrum of hedonistic delights, there lie a number of common pleasures available, in startlingly similar forms, to contemporary Koreans ranging from day laborers to tycoons.

When a Korean has been working or playing (or both) with perhaps more zeal than wisdom, he is likely to seek refuge and relief through one of the few such simple pleasures which remain amid the excesses and inconstancies of urban-industrialization. Depending on his whim, he might well choose a bathhouse or a barber shop, both of which abound in every urban setting, as well as in most sizable rural communities.

A haircut is ever so much more than just cutting hair in a Korean barber shop (ibalso). One can easily spend an hour, and perhaps two, in laid-back languor as a crew of young ladies and gentlemen attend to nails, whiskers, face, ears, muscles, aches and—not to forget—hair.

The actual clipping is mere prologue, a ritual of 10 minutes or so more aptly termed a "trim," lest the customer be tempted to wait too long before his next visit. A manicure is usually begun just about the time one's stockinged feet get comfortably settled on a cushion placed over the sink, and it inevitably lasts much longer than the haircut.

As soon as the barber has dispensed with his pro forma exercise, he disappears, and the chair is tilted into a full reclining position for more leisurely informalities. The sequence is not strictly prescribed, but those interested in a shave generally get one quite soon after the haircut. Young ladies traditionally perform this service, which is not always limited to the conventional heavier growths of whiskers; upper cheeks, noses, foreheads and even selected parts of the ear are all fair game for a well-trained and unrestrained Korean razor maid.

The next step is often a face massage (massaji in Korean, after the Japanese rendering of the English). This can, with luck, encompass the scalp as well, along with those chronically understimulated muscles and vessels around the base of the skull. Between soothing applications of a hot towel, the young lady in charge might apply a plastic-like facial pack, peeled off later like congealed glue, or perhaps just a simple layer of cold cream. In either case, as the face is absorbing allied benefits, the lady will produce an ear spoon, preferably made of bamboo, and carefully begin to excavate hidden reserves of wax—unless the client recalls the old doctor's dictum that only one's elbows are to enter one's ears. When the delicate digging is done, each ear is given an unnerving twirl with a tool resembling a doll house duster—a tympana-tickling sensation comparable to hearing kittens' claws on a blackboard.

Kneading Is a Joint Effort

By this point, someone has no doubt already begun a body massage (anma in Korean, from two Chinese characters roughly meaning "rub" and "rub"). This can coincide with other services, and can involve a number of people who come, go, and reappear, according to the needs of other customers. It is not uncommon to have three or four girls and fellows at work in a single curtained cubicle, each kneading a separate extremity. One of them is usually a young man equally well versed in Oriental finger pressure therapy and the orthopedic limitations of the human anatomy—although he occasionally loses his feel for the fine line between stimulation and pain.

Even as a joint effort, a body massage can last half an hour or longer. Ordinarily, it concludes with an extraordinary ritual. First one's wrists, then palms, and then fingers are firmly massaged. Next the young lady gives each finger a sharp, snapping tug, perhaps to realign the knuckles. Finally, she interlocks her fingers with the client's, bends his hand backward, and, while gently running her thumbnails across the taut palm, blows on it ever so softly, telegraphing tingling signals up well past the elbow.

After all this, it's time for a nap, presuming the customer has time. (If he doesn't, he should have postponed his visit until another day.) A towel placed over his eyes softens any harsh visual stimuli, and he is left to dreams and fantasies.

Later on, someone eventually has to mention the code word "shampoo," and the customer knows his respite is nearly over. Not only is the barber chair about to be raised abruptly to the upright position, but also that foot-supporting cushion will be removed from the sink. Within seconds, said groggy gent is roused from his delightful daydreams—not just sitting up, but bent over a basin, head soaked and soapy.

The end comes quickly. A brief towel fluffing is followed by the barber's final touch--the "turai" (dry) with a comb and hand-held blower—as the client receives a ritual offering: a cigarette and a shot of a sweet yogurt drink. Then it's time to button up, straighten up, settle the tab (US$5 to $10) and bid a fond, but hardly final, farewell to tonsorial therapy.

The Mogyokt'ang

Just as a visit to the barber shop involves more than a simple haircut, so a call at the bathhouse offers much more than a mere turn in the tub. For the seeker of a slightly more active treatment for weary bones, the bathhouse (mogyokt'ang) presents a moderate alternative to the passive pleasures of the barber's chair.

At the baths, one is free to set one's own schedule, regimen, timing and style. That last choice offers perhaps the widest variety of options, and the images conjured up by the behavior of an ordinary bathhouse's clientele might run the gamut—from scolded puppies to walruses in rut.

There is quite a range of bathhouse types, as well, but all offer the same basic accoutrements, focusing around the same essential enjoyment of a steamy, soothing soak. As visitors to Japan learn from their guidebooks—or perhaps from an embarrassed or offended Japanese—the proper form is to bathe before entering the communal tub, and in Korea, too, soap and dirt should be kept out of the bathwater.

One begins by soaping up, shampooing and rinsing down, either by dipping a basin at the edge of the main tub, or under a shower, if there is one. Next should come a leisurely soak in the central tub, where muscles can relax and pores dilate. Then, back on the curb-like lip ringing the tub, it's time to commence some serious scrubbing, again using a basin.

Westerners seems to cling to the illogical conviction that towels should be kept dry, although they only perform their rightful function by getting wet. In the *mogyokt'ang*, a handtowel is just the right size, doubling both as an ample washcloth and as a fig leaf substitute, for modesty's sake, as one moves around. Small red washcloths are available, too—very abrasive, but very popular for doing away with dead and dying skin and stubborn city grit. And for the patron who doesn't savor the strain of a vigorous scrub, attendants are usually on hand to rub, rub, rub with cloths until the customer's skin approaches the hue of that raspy red fabric.

A scrubbing session is by far the most apropos opportunity for a shave. Steam, suds and sweat combine to create the fleeting impression that there is no blade in the razor—an innocent illusion swiftly given the lie if one later slaps on a little aftershave.

All that accounts for the literal *"mogyok"* (bathing) in *mogyokt'ang,* but one is no more restricted to a mere bath in a bathhouse than to only a haircut in a barber shop. Time and the facilities at hand are the only limits, and none but the improvident take towel in hand with less than an hour or two to kill.

Nearly every ordinary bathhouse *(taejungt'ang,* or "masses' bath") offers, in addition to the central tub and showers, an extra-hot tub, a cold tank and, in many cases, a sauna dock as well. These present many alternatives to the basic cycle of bathe, soak, bathe.

The properly heated hot tank greets the bather with a sharp, tingling sensation that is easily mistaken for pain, but which gradually mellows into simply stimulating heat. (If the tank is overheated, on the other hand, it turns out to be real pain.) The sauna is often so hot that it hurts to inhale quickly, and persons with abnormal blood pressure or heat sensitivity are advised to exercise appropriate caution.

Alternate visits to the sauna and hot tub, interspersed with breathtaking plunges into the cold tank, can give the pores a healthy workout. A few such rounds, however, can leave one a bit lightheaded, not a little enervated, and frankly ready for a short nap. A well-planned bathhouse will have a corner, or perhaps even a mezzanine, where those with the time can stretch out and doze off.

The last step in the bathing area is usually a final rinse under the shower—hot or cold, or both. But that is hardly the end. There is more to enjoy out in the dressing room. After all that time in the baths, most patrons seem to feel it a bit abrupt simply to dress and leave. Smokers smoke; thinkers sit and think; trimmers trim (a nail clipper is usually available); and browsers read ads on the walls for products such as soap, ginseng nectar, and "Happiness"—a mysterious compound touted as an aid to a happy married life. Some people, of course, simply dry themselves at considerable leisure, perhaps in front of a fan, but better yet while grabbing one last catnap. (That soggy handtowel, once wrung out, turns out to be quite up to the task.)

Gentlemen can get the same finishing touch they would in a barber shop—a blow dry—while on the ladies' side, bathers can relax one last time under a hair dryer. Eventually, though, every-one has to leave. Korean bathhouses, incidentally, close around 8 p.m., hours earlier than the counterpart *ofuro* in Japan, but they open hours earlier as well, about 5 or 6 a.m.

On Pampering One's Pores

The man with a little extra cash, and a yearning for a little extra luxury, is likely to patronize a so-called *"saunat'ang,"* essentially a plusher version of the *taejungt'ang.* For perhaps five times the ordinary bathing fee, the customer can spend all day, if he likes, soaking, sweating, napping, snacking or even negotiating business deals over coffee, clad only in a towel or short gown.

One of the oldest and most popular such establishments in Seoul is in the Shin Shin Hotel, a modest brick complex in the alley beside the Bank of Korea's head office (across a broad intersection from the Shinsegye Department Store). The *saunat'ang* in the Shin Shin's main building provides each guest with his own private section of warm, Korean *ondol* floor to nap on, complete with pillow and sheets, dressing gown, adjacent mini-closet and a menu listing every type of refreshment. There is also a spacious lounge with well-padded easy chairs, a television set and a lunch counter.

Those who make it to the Shin Shin's bathing area check their gowns with the young attendants on the way in, and grab fresh towels from a handy pile. Numbered signs mark a seven-step circuit for the uninitiated, beginning with a dip in the main tub or pool (the *ont'ang*). A small statue of an elephant helps establish the tropical mood.

Next are the two sauna docks—hot and hotter. One can perspire surrounded by the warm tones of golden-grained wood, gazing at quotations on the wall such as "Patience is the skill of having hope."

From the sauna, of course, one could proceed only to the cold tank *(naengt'ang),* which is appropriately adorned with a statue of a polar bear. A helpful sign notes that there is no further benefit to be gained from remaining in the 18°C water after one has rinsed off all that sweat.

The fourth stop is the hot tub *(yŏlt'ang),* kept at 48°C, which should loosen up the pores again. The *yŏlt'ang* leaves one well prepared for the next stop, the vigorous rubbing away of grit and grime and

Join the dots before you leave and save 50%* when you get there.

● Banda Aceh

Medan ●   Batu Besar (Batam)   Manado ●

Pekanbaru ●   ● Pontianak   Balikpapan   Biak ●
          ● Jambi   Sorong ●
Padang ●   ● Palu   Jayapura ●
        Pangkal Pinang   ● Pelangkaraya   Ambon ●
Palembang ●   ● Banjarmasin
Bengkulu ●   Tanjung Pandan   Tembagapura ●
Bandar Lampung ●   ● Kendari
                JAKARTA   ● Ujungpandang
                  ● Semarang
        Bandung ● Solo ● ● Surabaya
Yogyakarta ●   ● ● Mataram   Dili ●   Merauke ●
              DENPASAR
                    Kupang ●

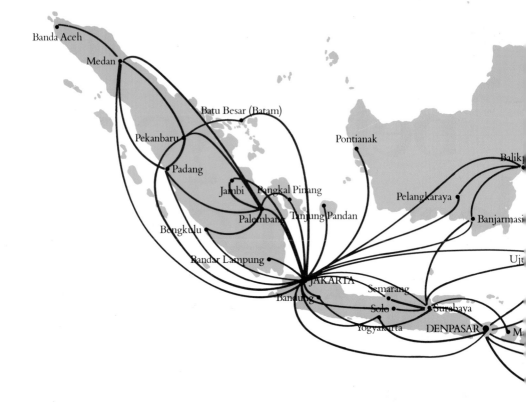

Now you can fly throughout Indonesia for around half the price that Indonesians pay.

With the Garuda Indonesia 'Visit Indonesia Airpass'.

All you have to do is nominate the Indonesian cities you wish to visit, and purchase your ticket before you get there.

Once your ticket is written, you can't change your route, but you can change the dates, and the times, of your travel.

5 Places, 10 Nights.	
Normal cost	US$571.20.
Airpass cost	US$300.00.
You Save	US$271.00.
10 Places, 20 Nights.	
Normal cost	US$1,147.30.
Airpass cost	US$ 400.00.
You Save	US$ 747.30.

The more cities you visit, the more money you save, sometimes a little less than 50 percent, and

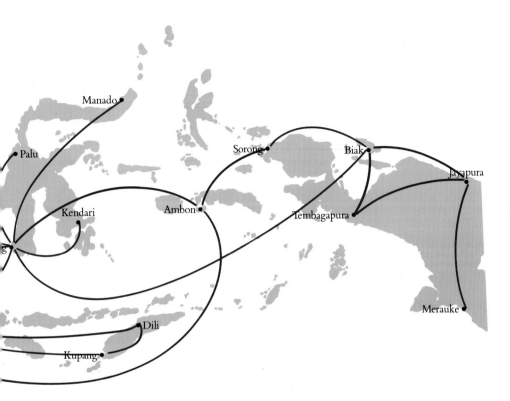

sometimes considerably more.

The discounts are even more dramatic for children.

Your Airpass is activated on the day of your first domestic flight, and you must complete all flights within the duration of the ticket.

However, you're free to spend as much time as you like in your starting or finishing location.

Airpass is only available in Australasia, Japan, Europe, North America and Taiwan.

Contact your nearest travel agent or Garuda Indonesia for more information.

At these prices, you'd be mad to travel any other way.

Garuda Indonesia

0130 BW 250

0113 H36

0136 BW 67

HK 214

0130 LI 10

0103 DJH 007

HK 317

0117 BW 273

0103 DJH 480

HK 236

0126 DJH 1042

2326 AE 270

Reproduced here are images from our vast collection
of photography, by some of the finest photographers.
All manner of subjects and themes are covered and are
available for a variety of uses. Call or write for a
selection that suits your needs.

Apa Photo Agency
23 Emerald Hill Road   Singapore 0923
Tel: 737-2525   Telex: APAVIL RS 33621   Fax: 861-6438

Insight Guides

"Bringing colour to the dreary world of guide books"

Popular Photography – Feb 1987

(hopefully) dead skin by one of a squad of young men.

By this point, one might well feel a bit groggy, in which case Stop No. 6 comes just in the nick of time. It's called *rireksyon* in Korean, a slight muddling of "relaxation," and that's exactly what it entails. At a row of massage tables, more young fellows administer 20- or 30-minute rubdowns, using either cold cream or mentholatum.

The last stop, once again, is the shower, for a final soap and rinse. Stepping out of the bathing area, one promptly receives another fresh (and *dry*) towel and, moments later, the same, carefully cared for dressing gown. The remainder of one's time can be spent eating, drinking, reading or watching TV. One can also request the services of a blind masseur, should a few kinks or wrinkles have survived the bathing process. And of course one can simply sleep, for a good session in any sort of *mogyokt'ang* can turn even the most tense or torpid physique into a tingling and squeaky-clean bundle of bait for the sandman.

Nearly every Korean *saunat'ang* offers comforts and accommodations like those at the Shin Shin, with the little extras (rubdown, scrubbing, etc.) costing, naturally, a little extra. Another establishment in downtown Seoul boasts a cold tank reputedly filled with mineral water piped directly from nearby Namsan (South Mountain), and one might also find such conveniences as a five-minute hourglass in the sauna dock, or a urinal right in the bathing area (to spare customers the indignity of having to relieve themselves over the drains).

Actually, the clientele in the plusher *saunat'ang* facilities seem more interested in loafing and laying about than in bathing per se, since they probably can afford to bathe in hot running water at home. Thus they embody the core spirit of Korea's modern pleasure principle, as pursued by those fortunate enough to have the means.

Egalitarian Cleanliness

To observe the spirit of Korean humanity at large, however, foreign visitors ought to bathe at least once in an ordinary *taejungt'ang*, where everyone can be seen doing his own thing. Europeans sometimes attract a few stares, but they should most certainly feel free to return the compliment.

There are many styles to observe. While one unassuming soul sits modestly facing a wall, another may appear to be drilling for the national splash-and-thrash platoon, exalting in generating frothy waves accompanied by ecstatic grunts and harrumphs to the assembled. Many bathers concentrate on modified calisthenics, such as "push-ups" against the edge of the main tub, or deep knee bends in the cold tank. Some simply fashion a pillow from an overturned basin and a towel, and sack out on the tiled floor.

All in all, the public bathhouse is perhaps the most egalitarian of the institutions to be found amid the considerable Confucian influence in contemporary Korea, stripping customers of all trappings of wealth or power (except perhaps a prodigious stomach), and offering each an identical opportunity to play any role he or she pleases. And that equality does extend generally to the sexes, for while they are strictly segregated in the public facilities, the two remain equal in terms of opportunities for indulgent enjoyment. (The *saunat'ang* remains an exception, sharing with most of Korea's pleasure-oriented enterprises an almost exclusive focus on the male.)

There are a host of other comforts related to the *mogyokt'ang*, or at least appealing to the same more or less wholesome hedonism that keeps bathhouses and barber shops in business. At a large *mogyokt'ang*, for example, one might find a private bathing room upstairs (called a *tokt'ang*) suitable for a couple or a family; and a fellow who happens to be alone can often even arrange for a young lady to come in and scrub his back—a service which incidentally is taken for granted at any place calling itself a "steambath."

Another facility, the *anma sisulso*, specializes in the services of blind masseurs and masseuses. Those services can often be obtained more conveniently— and more cheaply—by phoning to summon the masseur/masseuse to one's lodging or home. Downtown hotels and yŏgwans should be able to offer such arrangements, and some apartment complexes in Seoul have round-the-clock, on-call massage service, even during the strict midnight-to-4 a.m. curfew.

This common symbol identifies *mogyokt'ang* (public bath houses) throughout Korea.

Shopping

Korea's unique arts and crafts and the towns which traditionally produce the best of particular products are:

1. Bamboo craft—Tamyang
2. Hemp cloth—Hansan, Andong
3. Lacquerware—Wŏnju
4. Oriental paper—Chonju
5. Pottery—Ich'ŏn
6. Porcelain—Ansŏng
7. Rushcraft—Kanghwa City
8. Silk—Ch'unch'on, Kanghwa City
9. Brassware—Ansŏng, Taegu

Popular merchandise and where to shop for them in Seoul include:

1. Brassware—It'aewŏn
2. Antiques—Ahyŏn-dong, Insa-dong Chungang Sijang (Central market). It'aewŏn
3. Boutique goods—Myong-dong, Idae-ap
4. Calligraphy paint brushes—Insa-dong, Kyŏnji-dong
5. Silk Brocade—Tongdae-mun Sijang (2nd

floor), Chong-no 2-ka, Myŏng-dong (K'o Silk Shop)
6. Oriental paper—Insa-dong, Kyŏnji-dong
7. Korean Costumes—Tongdae-mun Sijang, and most other marketplaces
8. Topaz, "smokey topaz," amethyst, jade—underground arcades
9. Sweatsuits and athletic shoes and gear—It'aewŏn, Namdae-mun Sijang (across the Tokyu Hotel)
10. Korean cushions and blankets—Insa-dong, marketplaces
11. Custom-tailored men's suits—hotels, Myŏng-dong
12. Name seals (custom-made name seals in stylistic characters carved of hard wood, stone, etc.)—along the busy streets
13. Korean herbal medicine—Chong-no 5-ka, Chong-no 6-ka

One needn't even go outside of Seoul to find these things. Huge marketplaces and alleys unfold bounteous displays that exhaust most shoppers. Department stores help narrow down the choices somewhat. Major Seoul shopping areas outside central city hotels are:

Lotte	Namdaemun 2-ga	771-25
Shinsegye	Chungmuro 1-ga	752-1234
Midopa	Namdaemun 2-ga	754-2222
Saerona	Namchang-dong	778-8171
New Core	Panpodong	532-3300
Youngdong	Nonhyundong	541-1190

Underground Arcades

Specialty shops can be found in underground shopping malls. Don't let the price tags intimidate you from bargaining. The larger more centrally located arcades are:
1. Namdaemun Arcade
2. Myŏng-dong Arcade
3. Sogong Arcade
4. Hangram Arcade
5. Ulchi-ro Arcade
6. Lotte Center 1st Avenue Arcade
7. Arcade Bando-Chosun

Marketplaces

Seoul marketplaces run on for blocks. Anyone who has anything to sell is out there—from the button merchant to the antique dealer to the rice cake *ajumoni*, and including *chige* (A-frame), bicycle, and Kiamaster delivery men. Plus haggling shoppers. The distinguishing feature of Korean markets, however, is that shops with the same goods tend to group together—even set up the same way. Merchants say they are not hurt by competition caused by the close proximity; instead, the area becomes known for specializing in, say, second-hand books, sinks or antiques. Most things can be found at all of the markets.

Sports

Volleyball, soccer, basketball, tennis, table tennis, baseball, swimming, shooting, wrestling, gymnastics, and track and field are some of the western sports that have been integrated with Korean sports and are enthusiastically supported. Korea first participated in the World Olympic Games in 1946 in London. These days, athletes train at an indoor 18-acre camp at T'aenŭng on the eastern outskirts of Seoul. Sports facilities at T'aenŭng include an indoor swimming pool, shooting range, and gymnasiums for wrestling, boxing and weightlifting. All kinds of sports events take place at the Olympic Sports Complex in Chamsil which was built for the 1988 Seoul Olympics. The stadium here has a seating capacity of 100,000 and there are facilities for a wide range of games.

Other sports which draw wide attention and participation by visitors are:

Martial Arts

T'aekwŏn-do, literally the way of combat kicking and punching is a martial art exercise that has been developing in Korea for more than 2000 years. It focuses the combined strengths of body, mind, and spirit in devastating fist and foot blows. This empty had-fighting technique was originally learned from China during the T'ang dynasty and has been developed since the Three Kingdoms Period (post 650 AD) into the form in which it is practiced today.

The National T'aekwŏn-do Association has a membership of 80 nations. In Korea, students train at some 1100 centers. the World T'aekwŏn-do Federation (tel: 566-2505) is headquartered at Kukki-won, the main t'aekwon-do practice gymnasium in the southern outskirts of Seoul. Regular exhibitions are staged there for tourists.

Yusul ("soft art"), another martial art, was introduced from China to the Korea Royal court in 1150, but declined in popularity by the 17th Century. It was a characteristically passive defense which consisted of throwing, choking or blocking an aggressor, *Yusul* was taught to the Japanese, who called it *judo* and was later reintroduced to Korea during the Japanese Occupation when it was restyled and called *yudo*. It is now a compulsory martial art for Korean policemen. There are many national *yudo* centers, including a *yudo* college in Seoul.

Ssirum, Korean wrestling was introduced by the Mongol invaders during the Koryŏ Period. Once a form of self-defense, *ssirum* today is a simple folk sport for students and villagers. Contestants hold each other around the back and wrap a cloth strip around their opponent's thigh and try to throw each other down using leg, hand, and body maneuvers. *Ssirum* matches are held during Tano and Ch'usok (spring and autumn festivals, respectively). Western wrestling is taking a firm hold on Koreans, since their enthusiasm was fueled by a major victory in the 1976 Montreal Olympics (in the featherweight freestyle event).

Korean Archery

Once a means of hunting, a weapon of war, and a prerequisite for Yi dynasty military leaders, Korean archery is perpetuated these days as a recreation. Contests are held at various traditional sites annually by the Korean Archery Association. One of these ancient sites, the Pavilion of the Yellow Cranes, is located above Sajik Park in Seoul (see Soul of Seoul map).

Hiking and Mountaineering

Hiking and mountaineering are popular pastimes for young and old. Hills and mountains cover nearly 70 per cent of the peninsula, but none of them exceed 2800 meters in altitude.

Hunting

Hunting on Cheju Island and other particular areas is allowed in the fall to those with a proper license. Hunting equipment, rifles, and dogs are rented. Game animals include the male ring-necked pheasant, quail, turtledove, wild boar, hare, and rive and roe deer.

Fishing

Fishing is a leisure activity enjoyed along rivers, lakes, reservoirs and along the sea coasts. Fishing gear is sold at sporting goods shops everywhere.

Skiing

Introduced to Korea in the 1920s by a missionary, skiing is now being promoted at the Yongp'yong (Dragon Valley) Ski Resort in the Sŏrak Mountains. Snow machines have helped extend the ski season two months longer from December to March. Ski lifts and hotel accommodations are available.

Golf

There are 16 golf courses operated on a membership basis but guests are welcome. Most of the courses are just outside of Seoul. All of them are 18-holed. Korea is on the ninth leg of the annual Asian Circuit with a $30,000 prize.

Horse Racing

Korea's only horse-racing track is in the southeast part of Seoul across the Sŏngsu Street Bridge. Referred to as Happy Park, this race track is run by the Korean Equestrian Association, which is affiliated the Ministry of Agriculture and Fisheries. Races are held three days a week, Friday, Saturday and Sunday. The horses are imported mainly from Japan and the United States and none are privately owned.

Traditional Games

Nearly 70 per cent of the folk games in Korea are said to have been created and played during the winter. Traditional games and recreation which are still the delight of Koreans include:

Ch'anggi

Ch'anggi is the Korean version of chess which was introduced from Mesopotamia through China. Men can be seen crouched over engrossing games on sidewalks, in shops, and in parks. Sixteen pieces are given per player: one general, two chariots, two cannon, two horses, two elephants, two palace guards, and five soldiers, which are represented by Chinese characters written on checkers. The object of the game is to checkmate the general.

Paduk

Paduk (called *go* in Japan) is a contest of wits between two players to occupy more territory (houses) on a board divided by 19 vertical and horizontal lines. Black and white button-like stones are used as markers. Once the game of only high officials during the Koguryo and Paekche days, *paduk* increased in public popularity after 1945. In fact, paduk halls have been established in almost every town, and national tournaments in the spring and autumn are held by the Professional Paduk Association in Seoul.

Hwat'u

Korean playing cards are called *hwat'u*. A pack consists of 48 matchbook-sized hard cards, representing the 12 months of the year. January is symbolized by a pine tree; February, a plum tree; March, cherry; April, bush clover; May, orchids; June, peony; July, iris; August, the moon; September, chrysanthemum; October, maple; November, paulownia; and December by rainfall. A bit of gambling spices the game. These flower cards are also used for fortune-telling, and in Japan are called *hanafuda* cards.

Yut

Yut is a form of backgammon that is sometimes seen played on the ground by young men. Four 10-inch sticks used as dice are tossed in the air, and the player moves his pawns according to the number of backs or faces that turn up on the sticks. The first player who gets all four of his pawns to a goal wins.

Kite-Flying

Perhaps kite-flying was originally used in 1380 by a Koryŏ general in his conquest of Cheju Island, but is has seen a series of uses since then. Not too long ago, it was a pastime of children during the winter months. Children traditionally flew their kites on the 15th of January (by the lunar calendar) and strung names of evil sprits and diseases onto the kites in hopes of ridding themselves of all evil. Kite-flying contests are held annually. One is held in Seoul by *The Korea Times* newspaper, usually in January or February according to the lunar calendar. The participants aren't all children either. Kite strings are reinforced with ceramic filings to sharpen them for combat against other kites. Most are constructed of bamboo and paper and are judged in various divisions.

Swinging and Jumping-Seesaw

The simple pleasures of swinging and jumping-seesaw are traditionally celebrated by women these days on Tano. Young girls stand on swings which are suspended by 20-foot lengths of rope, and gleefully pump their way skyward. The jumping-seesaw also draws giggles as girls on either end of a solid length of wood, set on a large bag stuffed with rice straw, spring each other into the air. Some say these recreations were designed to allow the aristocratic Korean women of old to see up and over their compound walls, as they were not permitted to step outside their premises during the day.

Annual Holidays

January 1, New Year's Day

The first three days of January are recognized by the government as the beginning of a new year. Most Koreans, however, celebrate the new year according to the lunar calendar by exchanging greetings, worshipping at family ancestral shrines and eating rice cake soup.

March 1, Samiljol (Independence Day)

Observance of the March 1, 1919 independence movement against colonial Japanese rule which features an annual reading of the Korean Proclamation of Independence at Pagoda Park in Seoul.

April 5th; Arbor Day

Attention is given to Korea's reforestation program.

Han sik-il (Cold Food Day) (Mid-April)

On the 105th day of the lunar calendar, Koreans visit their ancestors' graves with offerings of fruit, rice cakes, meat, wine and other dishes. Traditionally fires were not lit on this day for reasons long since forgotten.

Buddha's Birthday (Mid-May)

This "Feast of the Lanterns" day is celebrated on the 8th day of the 4th lunar month in honor of the birth of Buddha. Buddha's Birthday was designated a national holiday in 1975. It is colorfully commemorated with temple rituals and parades throughout predominantly Buddhist Korea.

May 5, Children's Day

This successor to a former "Boy's Day" was also proclaimed a national holiday in 1975 to honor Korea's youth and to focus attention on the importance of the family institution in Korea. On this day children are dolled up, usually in traditional clothes, and taken on holiday excursions to parks and children's centers.

Tano (Early June)

This summer festival day on the 5th day of the 5th lunar month is one of Korea's most important celebrations. On this day new summer food is offered at family ancestral shrines in traditional homes. It has traditionally been a day when girls dressed in *hanbok* dresses gather in parks and compete in stand-up swinging matches; thus the name "Swing Day."

June 6, Memorial Day

On this solemn holiday the nation remembers and honors war dead. Memorial services are conducted throughout the nation, but perhaps the biggest tribute takes place at the National Cemetery at Seoul.

June 15, Farmers' Day

A day to honor the nation's agricultural workers. Farmers' Day is a day of feasting and celebrating with ancient "farmers'" folk music and dance.

July 17, Constitution Day

A legal national holiday to commemorate the proclamation of the Constitution of the Republic of Korea on July 17, 1948. Patriotic gatherings are held in town squares and other such public places throughout the country.

August 15, Liberation Day

A national holiday commemorating Japanese acceptance of Allied surrender terms in 1945 and thereby releasing Korea from some thirty-six years of Japanese colonial domination. This day also marks the formal proclamation of the Republic of Korea in 1948. This is a day of speeches, parades and other such activities by Korean patriots.

Ch'usok (september or October)

Ch'usok—which occurs on the 15th day of the 8th lunar month—is the Korean counterpart to America's Thanksgiving. On this day people visit family tombs and make proper food offerings to their ancestors. Traditional Korean costumes color every street in a festive and classical way.

October 1, Armed Forces Day

Colorful military parades, honor guard ceremonies, and other such martial activities honor Korea's defense forces. A major gathering of military personnel and citizens usually takes place at the reviewing plaza at Yoido Island in the Han River region of southwest Seoul.

October 3, National Foundation Day

Also called Tan'gun Day, this national holiday recalls the day in mythical times when Tan'gun, the legendary son of a bear-woman, was born and became Korea's first human king. Tan'gun's reign is said to have begun in 2333 B.C. and continued until 1122 B.C.

October 9, Han'gŭl Day

Han'gŭl Day joyfully and respectfully recalls the anniversary of the promulgation by King Sejong of *han'gŭl*, Korea's indigenous alphabet. Sejong commissioned the creation of this unique writing and phonetic writing form in the mid-15th Century (see the feature essay on this subject in this book).

December 25, Christmas Day

Because of a large Christian community, Christmas is observed as a national holiday in Korea in about the same way it is observed in most Occidental countries.

Survival Korean

Korean *han'gŭl* is romanized in two ways: by the Ministry of Education system and by the McCune-Reischauer system, an internationally recognized romanization scheme. Both romanizations are used in literature, maps, and signs, which can confuse those unacquainted with the language. Thus, learning the Korean alphabet, which is simple, would prove most beneficial, especially for the lone traveler.

Provided below are commonly used questions and statements romanized according to the McCune-Reischauer system. No matter what village, town or city in Korea you visit, you should be able to survive with the following common questions and statements. At least this simple lesson will lead you to a taxi, bus or train station, and then to food, shelter and a hot bath.

Numeral System

The following is a list of basic numbers and their Korean pronunciation:

1 *Il*		50	*O-sip*
2 *Ee*		60	*Yuk-sip*
3 *Sam*		70	*Ch'il-sip*
4 *Sa*		80	*P'al-sip*
5 *O*		90	*Ku-sip*
6 *Yuk*		100	*Paek*
7 *Ch'il*		200	*Ee-paek*
8 *P'al*		300	*Sam-paek*
9 *Ku*		567	*O-paek yuk-sip ch'il*
10 *Sip*		1,000	*Ch'on*
11 *Sip-il*		2,000	*Ee-ch'on*
20 *Ee-sip*		4,075	*Sa-ch'on ch'il-sip o*
30 *Sam-sip*		10,000	*Man*
40 *Sa-sip*		13,900	*Man Sam-ch'on ku-baek*

the airport	*konghwang*
the subway	*chi-hach'ŏl*
the taxi	*taeksi*
Seoul train station	*Seoul yok*
express bus terminal	*Kosok t'ominal*
the ticket office	*p'yo p'a-nun kos-i*
entrance	*ipku*
exit	*ch'ulku*
the public bathhouse or private bathroom	*mogyok t'ang*
the restroom	*hwajang-sil*
the restaurant	*sik-tang,umsik-chom*
the tea or coffee house	*tabang*
the bank	*unhaeng*
the hotel	*hotel*
a good Korean inn	*cho-un yogwan*
the post office	*uch'e-guk*
the police box	*kyongch'al-so*
the embassy	*tasea-kwan*
the International Telecommunication Office	*Kukche-Chŏnsin-chonhwakuk*
the dry cleaners	*saet'ak-so*
the public telephone	*kongchung-chonhwa*
the department store	*paekhwa-jom*
the duty free shop	*myonse-p'um-jom*
the marketplace	*sijang*
the souvenir shop	*t'osang-p'um-jom*

How many kilometers is it from here?
Yogi-so myot kilo im-nikka?

How long does it take to go there?
Olmana kollimnikka?

It takes _____.
_____. *kollimnida.*

30 minutes	*samsip-pun*
1 hour	*han si-gan*

Please call a taxi for me.
Taeksi jom pullo ju-seyo.

Just a moment, please.
Cham-kkan man kitari-seyo.

Please go straight.
Ttok paro ka-seyo.

Please stop here.
Sewo ju-seyo.

What is this place called?
Yogi-nun odi imnikka?

Hello (to get the attention of a waiter, sales clerk, etc.)
Yobo-seyo.

I will have coffee (or) please give me some coffee.
K'op'i-rul chu-seyo.

May I have more beer?
Maekchu to ju-seyo.

May I have the bill?
Kaesanso-rul chu-seyo.

Do you have _____?
_____ iss-umnikka?
amethyst   chasujong
(see index-glossary for other items)

Please show me another one.
Tarun kos-ul poyo ju-seyo.

How much does it cost; what is the price?
Olma imnikka?

Can you give me a discount?
Tisukauntu rul hal-su iss-umnikka?

It's too expensive.
Nomu pissamnida.

Thank you.
Kamsa-hamnida.

I will buy this.
Ee Kos-ul sa kess-umnida.

Good-bye (said to somebody *not* also departing).
Annyŏng-hi ke-seyo.

Good-bye (said to somebody who is also departing).
Annyŏng-hi ka-seyo.

Can you speak English?
Yong-o Halsu-iss-umnikka?

Do you understand me?
Ee hae ha-seyo?

Please bring me some _____.
_____ chom katta ju-seyo.
beer   maekchu
cold drinking water   naeng su
hot water (for bathing)   ttugo-un mul
barley tea   pori ch'a
Korean food   Han chong sik

Good morning. Good afternoon. Good evening.
Annyŏng ha-simnikka.

Excuse me.
Sille-hamnida.

I am sorry.
Mian-hamnida.

You are welcome.
Ch'onman-eyo.

Yes.
Ne.

No.
Anio.

(Something, someone is) good.
Cho ssumnida.

(Something, someone is) bad.
Nappumnida.

Good Telephone Connections

Emergency

Police	112
Fire	119
Ambulance	119

Courtesies

Time of Day	116
Weather Information	725-0365
Information	114
International Calls	1035, 1037
International Call Information	234-5151
Domestic Telegram Information	115
International Telegram Information	115
Operator (to check on overseas calls already placed)	1030
Seoul Post Offices	
Central	752-0007
Kwanghwa-mun	732-0007
International	777-0020
Seoul Immigration Office	776-8858
39-1 Seosomundong Chung-gu	
Kimp'o Customs Office	636-7070
Kimp'o Airport Information	662-2182
Lost and Found Center, Seoul	755-4400

US Military Community

To call the following locales from off-base, dial the prefixes below and then the desired number:

Yongsan	7904
RGH Housing Area	7904-2929
American Embassy and Housing Compound II	732-2601
Golf Compound	7904-4340
8th Army Library	7904-7382

Airlines

Air France	752-1027
Air India	778-0064
Alitalia Airlines	779-1676/8
American Airlines	775-3314
British Airways	777-6871/5
British Caledonian Airways	777-8131
Canadian Pacific Airways	753-8271/5
Cathay Pacific Airways	779-0321
China Airlines	755-1523
Continental Airlines	778-0394
Delta Airlines	753-3202
Eastern Airlines	777-9786/8

Japan Airlines	757-1711
KLM Airlines	777-2495
Korean Airlines	751-7114
Lufthansa German Airlines	777-9655
Northwest Airlines	777-9786
Pan American World Airways	777-2993
Quantas Airways	777-6872
Sabena Airlines	778-0394
Scandinavian Airlines System	751-5123
Singapore Airlines	755-1226
Swiss Air Transport	753-8271/5
Thai Airways International	779-2621
Trans World Airlines	777-4864
United Airlines	753-3202
Varig Brazilian Airlines	779-3877
Western Airlines	778-0394

Banks

Bank of Korea	777-8611
Bank of Seoul and Trust	771-60
Citibank	730-7141
Citizens National Bank	771-40
Choheung Bank •	733-2000
Commercial Bank	771-30
Export-Import Bank of Korea	753-8101
Hanil Bank	771-20
Korea Development Bank	771-65
Korea Exchange Bank	771-46
Korea First Bank	771-60
Bank of America	754-4445
Bank of Credit & Commerce Int'l Ltd.	752-6162
Bank of Tokyo	752-6325
Banque Nationale de Paris	753-2594
Chartered Bank	777-3190
Chase Manhatten Bank, N.A.	777-5781
Daichi Kangyo Bank	777-9781/5
First National Bank of Chicago	753-9690/2
Fuji Bank	755-1281
Mitsubishi Bank	777-9561/4
Marine Midland Bank	733-3501
Sanwa Bank	752-7321/2

Embassies

Foreign Diplomatic Missions in Korea

Argentina
It'aewŏn-dong, Yongsan-gu,
135-53
Tel: 793-4062

Australia
The Salvation Army Bldg., 58-2,

Sinmun-ro 1-ka
Tel: 720-6490/5

Austria
Samil Bldg., 25F. Kwanchul-dong
Tel: 722-7330, 6649

Bangladesh
10, Kwanchul-dong, Chungro-ku,
Samil Bldg., 13F.
Tel: 730-8872

Belgium
Dongbinggo-dong, 1-65
Tel: 730-4565

Bolivia
Namsan Village, Itaeweon-dong,
13-100.
Tel: 793-1301/5(Ext 576)

Brazil
New Korea Bldg., 301/6, 192-11,
Eulji-ro
Tel: 730-4769

Canada
Kolon Bldg., 10F. 45,
Mugyo-dong, Chung-ku
Tel: 776-4062/8

Chile
42-5, Itaewon-dong
Tel: 792-9519

China
Myeong-dong, Jung-gu, 83 2-ga,
Tel: 776-2721/5

Colombia
125, Namsan Foreign House
Itaewon-dong, Yongsan-ku
Tel: 793-1301 (Ext. 694)

Costa Rica
1-125, Sinmun-ro, 2-ka
Tel: 734-0494

Cominican Republic
A-212, Namsan Foreign Apt.
Itaewon-dong, Yongsan-ku
Tel: 792-1850

Denmark
701, Namsong Bldg., 260-199,
Itaewon-dong, Yongsan-ku
Tel: 792-4187/9

Ecuador
133-20, Itaewon-dong
Tel: 792-1287/1195

Finland
1-1, Kyobo Bldg., 604
Tel: 732-6223, 6737

France
30, Hap-dong, Seodaemun-ku
Tel: 362-5547/9

Gabon
Daeyong Bldg., 43-2, Nonhyun-
dong, Kangnam-ku
Tel: 562-9912/3

Germany
51-1, Namchang-dong, Chung-ku
Tel: 779-3271/3

Greece
12-1, Seosomun, Chung-ku
Tel: 752-9662

Guatemala
A-206, Namsan Village, Itaewon-
dong, Yongsan-ku
Tel: 793-1319

Holy See
2, Kungchong-dong, Chongro-ku
Tel: 720-4278

India
174, Pilun-dong, Chongro-ku
Tel: 793-2088/4142

Indonesia
1-884, Yoido-dong
Youngdeungpo-ku
Tel: 782-5116/8

Iran
726-126, Hannam-dong
Tel: 793-7751/3

Italy
1-169, 2-ka, Sinmun-ro
Tel: 720-4092

Japan
18-11, Chunghak-dong
Tel: 733-5626

Libya
Banpo-dong, Gangnam-gu, 305-1
Tel: 532-0329, 0306

Malaysia
4-1, Hannam-dong, Yongsan-ku
Tel: 792-9203

Mexico
142, Namsan Village,
It'aewŏn-dong
Tel: 795-0380/1

Netherlands
1-48, Dongbinggo-dong
Tel: 793-0651/2, 0545

New Zealand
105-2, Sagan-dong, Chongro-ku
Tel: 730-7794/5

Norway
124-12, It'aewŏn, Foreign
House 32
Tel: 792-6850/1

Pakistan
58-1, 1-ka, Sinmun-ro, Seoul
Tel: 313-0427

Panama
Unni-dong, 98-78
Tel: 765-0363

Peru
Namsan Village, It'aewŏn-dong.
House, 129
Tel: 792-3669, 2235

Philippines
559-510, Yeoksam-dong
Tel: 568-9434, 6141

Saudi-Arabia
1-112, 2-ka, Shinmun-ro
Tel: 735-9263/5

Spain
726-52, Hannam-dong
Tel: 730-4564

Sweden
108-2, Pyong-dong, Chongro-ku
Tel: 734-0846

Switzerland
Songweol-dong, Jongro-gu,
32-10.
Tel: 744-9511/4

Thailand
133, Namsan Village,
It'aewŏn-dong, Yongsan-ku,
Tel: 792-3098

Turkey
Hannam-dong, Yongsan-gu
Tel: 794-0255, 3778

United Kingdom
Chong-dong 4, Chung-ku
Tel: 735-7341/3

United States of America
82, Sejong-ro, Chongro-ku
Tel: 732-2601

Uruguay
Hannam-dong Yongsan-gu, 60-27
Tel: 795-0561

Hospitals

(Call 275-7066 for information)

Cheil Hospital   845-8111

Ewha Women's University Hospital	633-9111
Hanyang Hospital	293-1112
Korea University Hospital	762-5111/9
Kyonghoe Hospital	962-2411
National Medical Center	265-9131/49
Seoul Adventist Hospital	244-0191
Seoul Red Cross Hospital	723-4581
Seoul University Hospital	762-5171
St. Mary's Hospital	771-66
Severance Hospital	392-0161

Media

Korea Herald	777-5611
Korea Times	732-4161
Seoul Foreign Correspondents Club	734-3275

Noted Organizations

American Chamber of Commerce	753-6471
Japanese Chamber of Commerce	777-6930
Korea Amateur Sports Association	777-6081/5
Korea Red Cross	777-9301/4
Korea Trade Promotion Corporation	753-4180/9
Korean UNESCO	776-2661/3
Lions International	265-7454
Seoul JAYCEES	244-6015
Seoul Rotary Club	265-1095
YMCA	777-5725
YWCA	766-9706

Places of Worship

(All listings for English language services)

Christian Science Society
Miju Apartment House (behind Daehan Theatre)
62-16, Pil-dong 3, Chung-gu
Tel: 7904-3702
Services: Sunday 11 a.m.
Sunday school 9:30 a.m.
(1st Wednesday of every month 7:30 p.m.)

International Lutheran Church
Hannamdong on road to Pusan Expressway
Tel: 794-6274
Services: Sunday — 8:30 a.m. 10:45 a.m.
Sunday school 9:30 a.m.
(June to August service only 9 a.m.)

Seoul International Baptist Church
Yoido, next to Dong office
Tel: 324-2896
Services: Sunday 11 a.m. 5 p.m.
Sunday school 9:45 a.m.

The Memorial of the Catholic Joil du Sans Martyrs
96-1 Hapchong-dong, Mapo-ku
Tel: 322-2973
Services: daily mass 3 p.m.
Sunday school 11 a.m.

Jewish Services Center
Yongsan Base, Building T-3601
gate passes at Gate 10
Tel: 7904-4363
Services: Fridays 7:30 p.m.

Yoido Full Gospel Church (evangelical)
1-20 Yoido-dong, Yongdungpo
Tel: 782-9673, 782-4851/5
Services: Sunday 9:30 a.m.
Sunday 6:30 p.m. at Hotel Shilla

Transportation

Call Taxi	441-0150/9
Train Station Information	392-7811

Ferry Terminals

Pusan	(051) 463-3161 international
	(051) 44-0117 domestic
Cheju	(0641) 2-4225
Kunsan	(0654) 3-2936
Inchon	(032) 882-1714
Masan	(0551) 2-8301
Mokpo	(0631) 2-4226
Pohang	(0562) 2-0711
Yosu	(0662) 63-2441

Tourist Information

Korea National Tourism Corporation CPO Box 903, Seoul	757-5927
Korea Tourist Bureau, Ltd.	722-1191/6
Korea Tourist Association 70, Kyungun-dong Chongno-gu, Seoul	734-9939
Seoul Tourist Complaint Center	725-0101

Seoul Tourist Information Centers

City Hall	731-6337
Kimp'o Airport	662-9248

Seoul Railway Station	779-3643
Express Bus Terminal	598-4152
Chongno Center	734-0023
Kwanghwamun Center	734-0027
Myungdong Center	779-3645
Namdaemun Center	779-3644
Tongdaemun Center	272-0348

Tour Agencies

| Royal Asiatic Society | 763-9483 |
| United States Service Organization (USO) | 792-3028 |

International Tour Agencies

Aju Tourist Service	Seoul:	755-5845
	Pusan:	22-2222/4
East-West Travel Service		734-1612
Global Tours, Ltd.		323-0131
Hana Tours		725-0071
Hanjin Tours		777-0041/7
Hannam Sightseeing Co.		753-0601
International Air Travel Service		777-6545/9
ODCO Travel Service		762-8770
Korea Express Co.		753-1631
Korea Tourist Bureau		585-1191
Korea Travel International		777-31
Korea Travel Service		778-1941
Lotte Travel Service		273-4161
Orient Express Corp.		735-0641
Oriental Air Travel Service		753-9233
Sana Travel Service		778-3101
Samyong Travel Service		719-4814
Seoul Tourist Corp.		566-0211
Universal Travel Service		733-5341
Walker-Hill World Travel, Ltd.		776-9801
World Tours, Ltd.		313-3401
Y.S. Travel Agency, Ltd.		23-0311/4

Hotels

(*denotes deluxe hotel)

Seoul Deluxe:

Chosun Hotel	771-05
Hilton Hotel	753-7788
Hotel Lotte	771-10
Hotel Shilla	233-3131
Hyatt Regency Seoul	798-0061
Seoul Plaza Hotel	771-22
Sheraton Walker Hill Hotel	453-0121

Seoul First Class:

Ambassador Hotel	275-1101
Hotel Seoul Garden	713-9441/9
King Sejong Hotel	776-4011
Koreana Hotel	720-8611
New Seoul Hotel	735-9071/9
Pacific Hotel	777-7811/9
President Hotel	753-3131/9

Seoul Palace Hotel	532-0101
Seoul Royal Hotel	771-45
Seoulin Hotel	722-0181/8
Tower Hotel	253-9181/9
Yoido Tourist Hotel	782-0121/5

Seoul Second Class:

Astoria Hotel	267-7111/18
Bukak Park Hotel	734-7102/4
Central Hotel	265-4121/9
Empire Hotel	777-5511
Hamilton Hotel	794-0171
Metro Hotel	776-6781/8
New Kukje Hotel	732-0161/9
New Naija Hotel	723-9011/5
New Oriental Hotel	753-0701/6
Savoy Hotel	776-2641/50
Seoul Prince Hotel	752-7111/5
Seoul Rex Hotel	752-3191/4
Seoul Tourist Hotel	725-9001
Dehwa Tourist Hotel	265-9181/9

Seoul Third Class:

Academy House	993-6181/5
Eastern Hotel	764-4101
Hankang Tourist Hotel	447-0181/5
New Town Hotel	777-4251/8
Hotel New Yongsan	795-0052/8
Chonji Tourist Hotel	265-6131/3
YMCA Tourist Hotel	732-8291/8
Boolim Hotel	965-0020

Pusan: (prefix 051)

Arirang Hotel	463-5001
Ae-rin Hostel	27-222/7
Bando Hotel	44-0561
Crown Hotel	69-1241
Dong Yang Hotel	22-1205
Ferry Hotel	463-0881
Haeundae Glory Hotel	72-8181/5
Kukdong Hotel	72-0081
Kukje Hotel	642-1330
Moon Hwa Hotel	66-8001
Paradise Beach Hotel	72-1461
Phoenix Hotel	22-8061
Plaza Hotel	463-5011
Pusan Hotel	23-4301
Royal Hotel	23-1051
Shin Shin Hotel	88-0195
Sorabol Hotel	463-3511
Tai Yang Hotel	43-8801
Westin Chosun Beach Hotel*	72-7411
Tong Nae Hotel	53-1121
Tower Hotel	23-5151
UN Hotel	26-5181

Taegu: (prefix 053)

Daegu Soosung Hotel	763-7311
Dongsan Tourist Hotel	253-7711/6
Dong In Hotel	46-7211
Hanil Hotel	45-2301
New Yongsan Hotel	752-5551
Royal Hotel	23-9862
Tourist Center Hotel	45-0872

Inchon: (prefix 032)

International Seamen Hotel	883-9841
Olympos Hotel*	72-0801

Kyungi-do:

Anyang Hotel	(0343) 3-8111
Brown Hotel	(0331) 7-4141
Ichon Seolbong Hotel	2-5701/5
New Korea Hotel	(0343) 3-3841
Songtan Tourist Hotel	4-5101/5
Yulim Tourist Hotel	2101/4

Kangwon-do:

Chunchon Sejong Hotel	(0361) 2-2181
Hotel Nagsan Beach	7-7540/50
Junhwa Tourist Hotel	273-9341/6
Kukdong Hotel	(0391) 3-2277
New Sorak Hotel	(0392) 7-7131
Sorak Park Hotel	(0392) 7-7711
Soraksan Hotel	(0392) 7-7101
Soyang Hotel	(0361) 3-8285
Wonju Hotel	(0372) 42-1241

Chungchongpuk-do:

Cheongju Hotel	(0431) 3-0111
Cheongju Jeil Hotel	(0431) 4-2111
Sooanbo Hotel	(0441) 3-2311
Songnisan Hotel	(0433) 2091

Chungchongnamdo:

Daejon Tourist Hotel	23-0131/4
Dogo Hotel	2-6031
Jeil Tourist Hotel	2-6111/23
Joongang Tourist Hotel	253-8801/5
Mannyonjang Hotel	822-0061 (0418)
Onyang Hotel	(0418) 2-2141/7
Shiwon Tourist Hotel	822-8220/8
Yousung Tourist Hotel	822-0811/4

Chollapuk-do:

Jeonju Hotel	(0652) 75-2811
Kunsan Hotel	(0654) 3-4121
Naejangsan Tourist Hotel	4131-7
Victory Tourist Hotel	(2) 6161-3

Chollanam-do:

Gwangju Hotel	(062) 7-0671
Yeosu Hotel	(0662) 2-3131/5

Kyungsangpuk-do:

Bulkuksa Hotel	2-3821
Geumosan Tourist Hotel	52-3151/9
Kolon Hotel	(0561) 2-9001
Kyongju Chosun Hotel*	(0561) 2-9601
Kyongju Tokyu Hotel*	(0561) 2-9901
Sangdai Hotel	349-350
Paek Am Resort Hotel	5005-09
Po Mun Ho Hotel	3-4441
Pohang Beach	(0562) 3-1401

Kyngsangnam-do:

Bugok Hawaii Hotel	(0559) 4-6331
Bugok Royal Hotel	4-5817
Bugok Spa Hotel	4-5181/90
Changwon Tourist Hotel	83-5551/60
Chungmu Tourist Hotel	2-2091/5
Daewoo Okpo Tourist Hotel	4-3703/4
Diamond Hotel	(0552) 5-7171
Hotel Ocean	43-8991/5
Lotte Crystal Hotel	(0551) 2-1112
Taehwa Tourist Hotel	73-8191/8
Ulsan Hotel	(0522) 72-7146
Ulsan Grand Hotel	3-1101/9

Cheju-do:

Cheju Grand Hotel*	(0641) 7-2131
Cheju KAL Hotel*	(0641) 6151
Cheju Hyatt Hotel*	5-2001
Cheju New-Plaza Hotel	(0641) 7-6161
Cheju Royal Hotel	(0641) 7-4161
Free Port Hotel	(Seohai) 7-4111/40
Hotel Paradise Jeju	2-3111
Hotel Paradise Sogwipo	2-2161/7
Sogwipo Lions Hotel	2-4141/4

Youth Hostels

Seoul:

Academy Youth Hostel
San 76, Suyo-dong, Tobong-gu, Seoul
Tel: 993-6181

Bando Youth Hostel
679-3 Yoksam-dong, Kangnam-gu, Seoul
Tel: 567-3111

Pusan:

Ae-Rin Youth Hostel
41, 1-ga, Posu-dong, Chung-gu, Pusan
Tel: (051) 27-2222

Kangwando:

Naksan Youth Hostel
Chun jin-ri, Konbyun-myun
Yangyang-gun
Tel: (0396) 3416

Surak Youth Hostel
Tomun-dong, Sockcho, Kangwondo
Tel: (0392) 7-7540

Chungchongpukdo:

Hanal Youth Hostel
223, Onchunri, Sangmyo-myun
Chungwon-gun, Chungbuk
Tel: (0441) 3-3151

Chungchongnamdo:

Puyo Youth Hostel
105-1, Kukyo-ri, Puyo-up, Puyo-kun
Tel: (0463) 2-3101

Kyungsampukdo:

Kyongju Youth Hostel
105-1, Kujongdong, Kyongju
Tel: (0561) 2-9991

Suggested Readings

Adams, Edward B. *Korea Guide.* Seoul International Tourist Publishing Co., 1977.
_____. *Kyongju Guide: Cultural Spirit of Silla in Korea,* Samhwa Printing Co., 1979.
_____. *Palaces of Seoul: Yi Dynasty Palaces in Korea's Capital City.* Taewon Publishing Co., 1972.
_____. *Through Gates of Seoul: Trails and Tales of Yi Dynasty,* Vol. I and II. Saham-bo Publishing Corporation, 1971, 1972.
Bartz, Patricia M. *South Korea.* Clarendon Press, 1972.
Berger, Carl. *The Korea Knot: A Military-Political History.* Philadelphia: University of Pennsylvania Press, 1957.
Bishop, Isabella B. *Korea and Her Neighbors.* Yonsei University Press, 1970.
Brandt, Vincent S., *A Korean Village Between Farm and Sea,* Cambridge: Harvard, 1971.
Buck, Pearl S. *The Living Reed.* New York: John Day Co., 1963.
Bureau of Cultural Properties, ed. *The Arts of Ancient Korea.* Kwang Myong Publishing Co., 1974.
Carpenter, Frances. *Tales of a Korean Grandmother.* Seoul: Royal Asiatic Society, 1973.
Choe, Sang-su. *Annual Customs of Korea.* Korea Book Publishing Co., 1960.
Clark, Allen D. *An History of the Church in Korea.* The Christian Literature Society of Korea. 1971.
Clark, Allen D. and Clark, Donald N. *Seoul: Past and Present, A Guide to Yi T'aejo's Capital.* Seoul: Royal Asiatic Society, 1969.
Clark, Charles Allen. *Religions of Old Korea.* The Christian Literature Society of Korea, 1961.
Crane, Paul S. *Korean Patterns.* Seoul: Royal Asiatic Society, 1967.
Daniels, Michael J. *Through a Rain Spattered Window: Essays on Korea.* Taewon Publishing Co., 1973.
Deuchier, Martina. *Confucian Gentlemen and Barbarian Envoys.* Seoul: Royal Asiatic Society, 1977.
_____. *The Traditional Culture and Society of Korea: Art and Literature.* Honolulu: University of Hawaii Center for Korean Studies, 1975.
Lee, Sun-ju. *Korean Folk Medicine.* Publishing Center of Seoul National University, 1966.

MacMahon, Hugh. *The Scrutable Oriental.* Sejong Co., 1975.
Mattielli, Sandra. *Virtues in Conflict: Tradition and the Korean Woman Today.* Royal Asiatic Society, 1977.
Mattielli, Sandra; Rutt, Joan. *Lee Wade's Korean Cookbook.* Pomso Publishers, 1974.
McCann, David R. *An Anthology of Korean Literature.* Ithaca, New York: China-Japan Program, Cornell University, 1977.
McCann, David R.; Middleton, John; Shultz, Edward J., editors. *Studies on Korea in Transition.* University of Hawaii Center for Korean Studies, 1979.
McCune, E. *The Arts of Korea, An Illustrated History.* Charles E. Tuttle Co., Inc., 1962.
McCune, Shannon. *Korea: Land of Broken Calm.* Princeton: D. Van Nostrand Co., Inc., 1966.
_____. *Korea's Heritage: A Regional and Social Geography.* Charles E. Tuttle, Co., Inc. 1956.
Michener, James A. *The Bridges at Toko-ri.* New York: Fawcett Crest, 1953.
Middleton, Dorothy H.; Middleton, William D. *Some Korean Journeys.* Seoul: Royal Asiatic Society, 1975.
Moffett, Samuel H. *The Christians of Korea.* Friendship Press, 1962.
National Academy of Arts. *Survey of Korean Arts: Folk Arts.* Information Service Center, 1974.
Osgood, Cornelius. *The Koreans and their Culture.* Charles E. Tuttle, Co., Inc., 1954.
Phil, Marshall R., *Listening to Korea: A Korean Anthology.* New York: Praeger, 1973.
Rees, David. *Korea: The Limited War.* New York: St. Martin's Press, 1964.
Ridgeway, Matthew B. *The Korean War.* New York: Doubleday & Co., 1967.
Rutt, Richard, editor and translator. *The Bamboo Grove: An Introduction to Sijo.* Berkeley: University of California Press, 1971.

_____. *Korean Works and Days: Notes from the Diary of a Country Priest.* Taewon Publishing Co. 1973.
Sohn, Ho-min. *The Korean Language: Its Structure and Social Projection.* 1975.
Stewart, Ruth. *Under the Snow the Bamboo Shines.* 1973.
Wade, James. *Early Voyagers.* Hollym Corporation; Publishers, 1969.
_____. *One Man's Korea.* Hollym Corporation; Publishers, 1967.
Wickman, Michael, *Living in Korea,* Seoul: The American Chamber of Commerce in Korea, 1978.
Won, Pyong-o; Gore, M.E.J. *The Birds of Korea.* Charles E. Tuttle Co., Inc. 1971.
_____. *Rare and Endangered Species of Birds and Mammals in Korea.* Korea Association of Conservation of Nature, 1975.
Yi, Sun-sin; translated by Ha, Tae Hung. *Najung Ilgi: War Diary of Admiral Yi Sun Sin.* Yonsei University Press, 1977.
Zong, In-sob. *Folk Tales from Korea.* Hollym Corporation; Publishers, 1970.
Zozayong. *Korean Temple Paintings, Depicting the Life of Buddha.* Seoul: Royal Asiatic Society and Emillle Museum; 1975.

ON READING, SPEAKING HAN'GŬL

More than 500 years have passed since King Sejong and a group of Korean scholars devised the *han'gŭl* alphabet, but with only slight modifications this remarkable reading and writing system is still used much as it was during its 15th Century debut. Because this phonetic form is so easy to master, Korean is one of the world's most convenient communication forms.

Korean *han'gŭl* letters, however, have undergone considerable modifications due partly to changes in sound that have since taken place in Korean, and partly to research conducted by a great number of *han'gŭl* scholars. First, the two consonant letters △ z and ㆆ (glottal catch) have been abolished because the former sound disappeared from the Korean language and the latter turned out to be insignificant in differentiating the meanings of words. Second, the consonant letter ㆁ, formerly representing *ng*, is no longer in use. Instead, o takes on a dual function, assuming zero sound quality in the syllable initial position and *ng* quality in the syllable final position; e.g. as in 앙 *ang*. Third, the vowel sound of the basic letter · has since disappeared from the Korean language. Thus, the letter no longer functions as an independent sound symbol but is used only in combination with the other basic vowel letters to represent other vowel or semivowel sounds. Fourth, the letter · has been changed to a short horizontal stroke when combined with ㅣ and to a short vertical stroke when combined with — ; e.g. as in ㅏ instead of ㅏ, ㅗ instead of, ㅗ, etc. Finally, tones have disappeared from most dialects of Korean. Accordingly, tone markers have been abolished.

In the following, current *han'gŭl* letters are arranged in the order taught in school.

(1) Consonants

Basic sounds in McCune-Reischauer symbols		Sound equivalents in English
ㄱ	k	Similar to *k* in *kilometer*, but much less aspiration (puff of air).
ㄴ	n	Same as English *n*.
ㄷ	t	Similar to *tt* in *letter*.
ㄹ	l	Similar to *l* in *letter*, e.g., 'light' *l*.
	r	Similar to *r* in British English *very*, e.g., flap *r*.
ㅁ	m	Same as English *m*.
ㅂ	p	Similar to *p* in *position*, but without aspiration.
ㅅ	s	Similar to *s* in *school*, not to *s* in *sun*.
ㅇ	ng	Same as English *ng*.
	ZERO	Silent.
ㅈ	ch	Similar to *j* in *Japan* but voiceless.
ㅊ	ch'	Similar to *ch* in *chill*.
ㅋ	k'	Similar to *k* in *kill*.
ㅌ	t'	Similar to *t* in *till*.
ㅍ	p'	Similar to *p* in *pill*.
ㅎ	h	Similar to *h* in *hill*.

Twin Letters

ㄲ	kk	Similar to *c* in *school*.
ㄸ	tt	Similar to *t* in *stop*.
ㅃ	pp	Similar to *p* in *speak*.
ㅆ	ss	Similar to *s* in *sun*.
ㅉ	tch	Similar to *t-y* in *what you . . .*

(2) Vowels and Semivowels

ㅏ	a	Similar to *a* in *park*, but without the *r* color.
ㅑ	ya	Similar to *ya* in *yah*.
ㅓ	ŏ	Similar to *u* in *ugly*.
ㅕ	yŏ	Similar to *yo* in *canyon*.
ㅗ	o	Similar to *o* in *tow* or *toil*.
ㅛ	yo	Similar to *yo* in *yoke*, but without the *w* color, or *yo* in *York*, but without the *r* color.
ㅜ	u	Similar to *oo* in *boot*, but without length.
ㅠ	yu	Similar to *eu* in *euphony*, but without length.
ㅡ	ŭ	Similar to *u* in *put*, but without lip-rounding
ㅣ	i	Similar to *ea* in *beat*, but without length.
ㅐ	ae	Similar to the first vowel of *air* or *a* in *gang*.
ㅒ	yae	Similar to *ya* in *Yankee*.
ㅔ	e	Similar to *a* in *aid*.
ㅖ	ye	Similar to *ye* in *yet*.
ㅚ	oe	Similar to *oeu* in French *coeur* 'heart' but without length or to *wa* in *wait*.
ㅟ	wi	Similar to *wi* in *will*.
ㅢ	ŭi	Similar to *wi* in *will*, but without lip-rounding.
ㅘ	wa	Similar to *why*, but without the last vowel sound *i*.
ㅝ	wŏ	Similar to *wo* in *wonderful*.
ㅙ	wae	Similar to *we* in *wear*.
ㅞ	we	Similar to *wa* in *wait*.

In the preceding chart, only the basic sounds associated with the *han'gŭl* letters are given. While vowel sounds remain constant, consonant sounds are vulnerable to the influence of neighboring sounds and thus themselves undergo certain changes. Some major changes include the following.

(1) The flap *r* and trill *l* sounds are associated with ㄹ, *r* occurring between two vowels or at the beginning of a word and *l* occurring only at the end of a word or before a consonant, as in 라디오 *radio* 'radio', 나라 *nara* 'country' as compared with 달 *tal* 'moon', 결과 *kyolkwa* 'result', and 빨래 *ppallae* 'laundry'.

(2) ㄱ, ㄷ, ㅂ, and ㅈ, which are basically voiceless, pronounced without the vibration of the vocal cords, become voiced between voiced sounds, as shown in the second ㅂ in 바보 *papo* 'fool'.

(3) At the end of a word or before another consonant, ㅋ and ㄲ are pronounced like ㄱ; ㅅ, ㅈ, ㅊ, and ㅌ like ㄷ; and ㅍ like ㅂ. Thus, for instance, we pronounce ᄉ 'sicle', ᄂ 'daytime', ᄎ 'face', ᄇ 'a piece', and ᄇ 'happened' all in the same way as ᄂ nat 'a grain' at the word-final or pre-consonantal position. This is because Korean consonants are pronounced without release in these positions.

(4) All consonants other than nasal and l sounds become nasal sounds when they occur before a nasal consonant, while retaining their oral place of articulation. Thus, for instance, 앞문 'front door' is pronounced as ammun, not aphmun.

(5) When ㄹ l and ㄴ n co-occur, n assimilates to l resulting in ll, as in 신라 silla 'Silla dynasty' and 칠년 ch'illyŏn 'seven years'.

(6) When ㄹ l is preceded by a consonant other than ㄴ n, it is pronounced as n, as in 박람회 pangnamhoe 'exhibit and 압록강 amnokkang 'the Yalu River'. Notice here that ㄱ k in the first example changes to ng and ㅂ p in the second example changes to m due to the following nasal n sound, as stated in (4) above.

(7) When a syllable ends in double consonants, one of them becomes silent at the end of a word or before another consonant, as in 값 kap 'price' and 앉는다 annunda 'to be sitting' compared to 값은 kap-sun 'as for price' and 앉아라 anja 'Sit!' The consonant which gets silent is the one which is relatively 'weak': in general, fricative sounds (ㅅ, etc.) are weaker than stop (ㄱ, ㅂ, etc.) or lateral (ㄹ) sounds, which, in turn, are weaker than nasal sounds. This phenomenon is ascribed to the fact that Korean does not allow more than one consonant at the beginning or end of a word and no more than two in the medial position.

As has been illustrated, han'gŭl letters are arranged in syllable blocks. For instance, the word han'gŭl has two syllables and is written as 한글, consisting of ㅎ h + ㅏ ŭ + ㄴ n and 글 consisting of ㄱ k + ㅡ ŭ + ㄹ l. The word Sŏul 'Seoul' is again composed of two syllables as 서울. Notice that when a syllable begins with a vowel as in ul of Sŏul, we use the zero consonant ㅇ as in 울. The rules of binding letters into syllables are as follows:

(1) A written syllable is composed of three positions; i.e., initial, medial, and final, to be filled in that order. The initial position is filled by a consonant letter including the zero consonant ㅇ, as ㅅ s in 서 sŏ and ㅇ (zero) in 울 ul. The medial position is filled by a vowel or a semivowel + vowel sequence, as ㅓ ŏ in 서 sŏ and ㅘ wa in 콰 kwak. The final position is either filled with a consonant letter or a sequence of two consonant letters, or left blank, as in 물 mul, 닭 tak, and 서 sŏ.

The arrangements of the three positions in the syllable block are shown below. The basic principle is to make it as square as possible. The numerals 1, 2 and 3 are used to indicate the initial, medial, and final position, respectively.

a. A vowel letter or a semivowel + vowel letter which has its longer stroke standing upright has the initial consonant at its left side. Examples: 가 ka, 꺼 kkŏ, 떼 tte, 예 ye.

b. A vowel letter or a semivowel + vowel letter which has its longer stroke lying horizontally has the initial consonant on top. Examples: 고 ko, 느 nŭ, 요 yo, 슈 syu.

c. When a semivowel + vowel letter has both a vertical and horizontal longer stroke, it has the initial consonant on the left of the vertical and on top of the horizontal stroke. Examples: 쥐 chwi, 꽈 kkwa, 쇄 swae.

If needed, the final or closing consonant letter or a sequence of two consonants is written below the blocks a, b, and c as shown in d, e, and f, respectively.

d. Examples: 땀 ttam, 삯 sak.
e. Examples: 줄 chul, 굼 kum.
f. Examples: 휠 hwŏl, 빠 pwat.

Notice that the shapes of the han'gŭl letters are altered slightly depending on the positions they occur at. This is a result of an effort to arrange different numbers of letters within equal-sized squares.

A list of common facilities and other regularly used terms and social phrases is included in the Guide In Brief section to assist you during travels throughout Korea. If you're having trouble communicating a destination, simply point to the han'gŭl version and nearly any Korean will obligingly assist and send or speed you on your way.

For further assistance with words, purchase a more detailed language guide or English-Korean, Korean-English dictionary and/or phrase book at any local stationery or book store.

Han'gŭl
Sounds and Symbols

Symbol	Sound	Symbol	Sound	Symbol	Sound	Symbol	Sound
	Vowels				Consonants		
ㅏ	a	ㅕ	yŏ	ㄱ	k	ㅌ	t'
ㅓ	ŏ	ㅛ	yo	ㄴ	n	ㅍ	p'
ㅗ	o	ㅠ	yu	ㄷ	t	ㅎ	h
ㅜ	u	ㅒ	yae	ㄹ	r,l		Double Consonants
						ㄲ	kk
ㅡ	ŭ	ㅖ	ye	ㅁ	m	ㄸ	tt
ㅣ	i	ㅢ	ŭi	ㅂ	p	ㅃ	pp
ㅐ	ae	ㅘ	wa	ㅅ	s	ㅆ	ss
ㅔ	e	ㅙ	wae	ㅇ	ng zero	ㅉ	tch
ㅚ	oe	ㅝ	wŏ	ㅈ	ch		
ㅟ	wi	ㅞ	we		Aspirated Consonants		
				ㅊ	ch'		
ㅑ	ya			ㅋ	k'		

310

Continued from page V

Also important to the graphics of the book were the drawings of Jim F. Goater, a roving British artist who is fond of Korea and its art; and antique Korean maps from the collection of Melvin P. McGovern of Honolulu. Special thanks also to Hubert D. Vos of Greenwhich, Connecticut, who gave Apa permission to reproduce 19th Century Korean paintings by his grandfathers, the celebrated Dutch artist Hubert Vos.

A very warm *komapsumnida* is also due Dr. and Mrs. Samuel Moffett who allowed us to photocopy and publish several late 19th Century photographs from their family archive. These Moffett Collection photos are among the earliest taken in Korea and are an important photographic record of the country's first contact years with the West. Other institutions and persons who contributed to *Korea* in one or many ways were the Royal Asiatic Society; Korea Branch; the University of Hawaii Center for Korean Studies, UNESCO; the U.S. Peace Corps; the Korean Overseas Information Service (KOIS) of the Ministry of Culture and Information; the Korean National Tourism Corporation (KNTC), Singapore office; the Seoul Tourist Information Center; the Korean Art Club; *The Korea Times; The Korea Herald; Korea Quarterly; Ppuri Kip'un Namu;* the Seoul Correspondents Club Orient Press; the Baptist Mission of Korea; the Seoul Correspondents Club, Orient Press; the Baptist Mission of Korea; the Soul Foreigners Counseling Service; the United States Information Service; the U.S. Army; the International Crane Foundation; *Silver Kris;* Korean Airlines; the Space Center; Pacific Media; *Chosun* Magazine; Cornie; Choy; Hahn Changgi; Carl F. Miller; Roe Hun-ho; Shin Changho; Frederic Dustin; Margaret Cho; Paul Ensor; Peter Bartholonew; Chan Jae Lee; Jim and Roberta Troestler; the late Alexander Rankin; Jheung Woo-yong; Chung Keum-hwa; Kang Joom-hyuk; Cho Chung-Kwan; Shin In-sup; Bae Su-ja; Jim and Martha Lopez; Kang Chang-hyo; Hong Son-hi; Choi Dal-yong; Tom Chapman; Homer Williams; Don Severson; John Anderson; Ronn Ronck; Sanford Zalburg; Bob Mattielli; and many others.

To all, *taetan-hi kamsahamnida.*

—Apa Productions

Art / Photo Credits

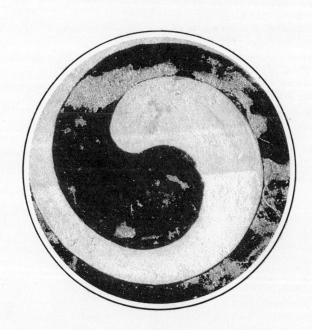